Officially endorsed by the
American Fighter Aces Association

Companion book to the television series
Hunters in the Sky-Fighter Aces of WWII

Produced by Anthony Potter Productions

Executive Producer-Anthony Ross Potter

Created by Herbert Molloy Mason, Jr.
          Howard D. Gutin
          Anthony Ross Potter

HUNTERS IN THE SKY

FIGHTER ACES OF WWII

James R. Whelan

Introduction by Raymond F. Toliver

REGNERY GATEWAY
Washington, D.C.

LIBRARY OF CONGRESS
CATALOGING-IN-PUBLICATION DATA

Whelan, James R. (James Robert), 1933-
    Hunters in the sky : fighter aces of
WWII / James R. Whelan : introduction by Raymond F. Toliver.
       p.   cm.
    "Companion book to the television
series, Hunters in the sky."
    Includes index.
    ISBN 0-89526-526-5
    1. World War, 1939–1945—
Aerial operations. 2. Fighter pilots—
interviews. I. Title.
D785.W43 1991
940.54'49—dc20   91-30747
                      CIP

Published in the United States by
Regnery Gateway
1130 17th Street, NW
Washington, DC 20036

Distributed to the trade by
National Book Network
4720-A Boston Way
Lanham, MD 20706

Designed by Christine Swirnoff

1991 printing

Printed on acid free paper

Manufactured in the
United States of America

ACKNOWLEDGMENTS

This book is the result of the collaboration of many people. It is the end product of two years of interviews with leading fighter aces of World War II. The television series was produced in collaboration with, and has been officially and exclusively endorsed by, the American Fighter Aces Association. It was developed by Anthony Ross Potter and Herbert Molloy Mason, Jr., with the assistance of Howard Gutin.

The interviews, which formed the basis for the series, were conducted primarily by Howard C. Gutin, Frank J. DeMeo, a senior producer at Anthony Potter Productions, former NBC News Correspondent Jack Reynolds, and German journalist/producer Gustav Froder.

The executive producer, Anthony Ross Potter, wishes to thank consultants Christopher Shores and Ray Toliver, without whose cheerful and continuing assistance this project could not have been completed. In addition, Yuri Koshkin was invaluable in the Soviet Union, as was archivist Elly Beintema in Great Britain. Of course, the entire project would not have been possible without the support of William Lee Hanley, Jr.

Further thanks must go to Terry DeMeo and Gerald O'Reilly, of Anthony Potter Productions, for their conscientious efforts in gathering photographs for the book, and coordinating activities with the publisher.

In the Soviet Union, Sovtelexport and Gostelradio were extremely helpful in supporting this project.

At Regnery Gateway Press, Patricia B. Bozell deserves kudos for editing the book under extremely difficult deadline pressures, as does Ernest Blazar for assisting with photograph selection, and Jennifer Reist for her untiring management of the project. Designer Christine Swirnoff and the production team of Harriet and Linda Ripinsky deserve particular thanks for turning the raw material of words and photographs into a polished book.

It may seem obvious, and yet I could not let it go unsaid: There would have been no project, there would have been no book, had it not been for the heroic deeds of the gallant men who people the pages of this book. In the process of attempting to bring a sense of their exploits to you, the reader, I not only came to feel that I knew these men of so many diverse and different backgrounds, but felt profoundly privileged that I could come to know them.

Closer to home, I am indebted to Maximiliano and Alejandra Blasquez for enduring with me so many late nights of printing, copying, collating—and, I confess, a bit of cussin', too. But it is to their mother—my beloved wife, Guadalupe—that I owe the greatest debt. Every day and every night of the five months of the *via dolorsa* that the writing of this book became, Guadalupe was there, patient, caring, and uncomplaining, helping with research, giving valued advice, copying computer files, dispatching express packets, and, above all, insulating me against the internal demons of doubt and frustration and such external intrusions as telephones, bills, and junk mail.

It is to her that I lovingly dedicate this book.

JAMES R. WHELAN
Arlington, Va., July 1991

"A top World War II ace once said that fighter pilots fall into two broad categories: those who go out to kill and those who, secretly, desperately, know they are going to get killed—the hunters and the hunted."

—GENERAL NATHAN F. TWINING, USAF

CONTENTS

INTRODUCTION

What Is An Ace?

To become an ace a fighter must have extraordinary eyesight, strength, and agility, a huntsman's eye, coolness in a pinch, calculated recklessness, a full measure of courage—and occasional luck!

—General Jimmy Doolittle

The clashing dynamism of the medieval joust was reborn in this century in the form of aerial combat. Ground and naval warfare still exacted earthbound heroics of its warriors. But in the clean and open struggle for the sky, man flew against man in skilled combat.

This kind of fighting was easy to comprehend and even easier to glorify against the inhuman tapestry of the war on the ground and sea. The result was the emergence of the fighter ace as this century's most glamorous warrior.

A new heraldry blossomed in wildly colored and patterned airplanes, often decorated with mascot designs of the pilot's own design and the name of the girl of his heart's desire.

The kind of war these airmen fought bore little relationship to the mass effects of modern armies and navies. Their individualistic type of fighting was an echo of the past before the juggernaut of technology intruded upon the settlement of disputes. Many of the characteristics and much of the spirit of a game were present in aerial combat in WWI and have continued in attenuated form down to the present day.

As a consequence, the men who flew fighter planes, regardless of the uniform they wore, are joined by a common bond of almost mystical quality. Among the thousands so joined there is an inner and elite brotherhood—the fighter aces.

Just as the fighter pilots rose above the impersonal nature of modern warfare, so have the fighter aces risen above their fellow fighter pilots. The factors that make a fighter ace are so variable, so elusive of analysis, and so far beyond the reach of the ordinary fighter pilot that the United States has been able to produce only some 1,400 fighter aces in this century—702 of whom are still alive.

HUNTERS IN THE SKY

In the nearly twenty years of warfare involving America since 1917, over 60,000 fighter pilots have taken to the air for Uncle Sam. Less than 3 percent of these men became aces.

Wartime publicity, novels, and motion pictures have etched an archetypal fighter ace as a devil-may-care girl-chaser, a hard-drinking glamorous hedonist who flies, fights, and loves on a prodigious scale. Despite these exertions, he is always first into the air as the Dawn Patrol goes bucketing up to challenge the hated Red Baron.

If this fictional fighter ace ever existed in the world of reality, few authentic aces ever knew him. There have always been aces who were drinking men, and plenty of playboys and ladies' men—that is part of the ace image—but these frivolous aspects of behavior invariably concealed sterner qualities. Without these qualities, few could survive in aerial combat, let alone become aces.

The real fighter ace is likely to be a man of above average intelligence and education, but even this is not universal. There are many men short on academic quality whose character, will power, and natural ability enabled them to win through to the coveted title of "ace." Drive, persistence, and fighting spirit could and did make up for educational deficiencies.

The ace is more than likely to be a direct and plain-spoken man, often forceful of manner. The overwhelming majority of aces are individualists. This might be expected, for no other individual fighting man in any era, dependent in the end entirely on his own abilities, has wielded the deadly powers conferred on a pilot by a fighter plane.

America's aces include many professional aviators, men who made aerial combat and the preparation for it their life's work. Most aces have nevertheless come from other occupations, or even directly from school and college in wartime. All shared a common attraction to the magnificent adventure of flying. War brought this adventure within the reach of many who otherwise would never have known its magic.

Combat flying developed in many men personal capacities and skills that would otherwise have lain dormant. Skill, dash, courage, and judgment have always been required to an exceptional degree—all qualities drawn from the individual's inner resources. These qualities cannot actually be taught.

These inner resources in aerial combat meet and mingle with such uncontrollable external factors as luck and opportunity. Interwoven with these in turn, and exerting a decisive influence on the success of the individual pilot has been that special plexus of powers and skills that make a man a good shot.

Contrary to popular idea, shooting ability and not flying ability has always been the fighter pilot's most important asset and the asset most likely to make him a fighter ace. Air-to-air shooting ability with machine guns, cannons, and rockets is a highly esoteric skill. Those blessed with the native ability to shoot at a moving target from a moving platform, the movement of both being three dimensional, were almost certain to become aces—even if they were not exceptional flyers.

The ham-fisted rough pilot often reacted unpredictably when bounced. His salvation lay in his sheer crudity as an airman. He might wrench his aircraft into turns which an experienced pilot would never have attempted out of elegant concern and sophisticated knowledge of and for the airplane, or plunge himself into a negative G maneuver that would throw off a pursuing enemy.

Whether he was rough or smooth, however, the fighter pilot who would shoot was likely to become an ace if given, as many were not, adequate opportunity.

Summarily, in the making of an ace there is the scientifically indefinable force conveyed by the word *drive*. The overwhelming majority of aces, and virtually all top aces, were those who strongly desired combat and would fight to get into combat.

Studies by the USAF have revealed that aces had been strong and aggressive competitors since boyhood. They were limit-testers, rule-benders, risk-takers, and precedent-breakers all their lives. These qualities made them excel in the grimmest contest of all—aerial combat.

The aces' value in terms of their contribution to victory is out of proportion to their numbers. Though less than 3 percent of all fighter pilots to take the air for Uncle Sam, the aces have accounted for some 40 percent of all enemy aircraft downed by fighters.

The arcane blending of shooting and flying ability, intuition and eyesight, physical coordination and endurance, instinct and technology, luck and opportunity—all welded together by the drive and eagerness for combat—will probably always elude precise scientific analysis.

What is certain is that the medieval knight never needed to bring such formidable powers to the joust. Nor required such a host of dedicated seconds and supporters to make the aerial joust possible and record its outcome for posterity.

RAYMOND F. TOLIVER
Former Historian, American Fighter Aces Association

1 KNIGHTS OF THE SKY

Fighter pilot.

The words have long had a special ring, evoking visions of flamboyant men born to play out their deadly dramas beyond the reach of mortal men. Hear Cecil Lewis—who reported for combat in France in 1915 shortly before his 18th birthday—tell of the mystique of it:

"To belong to the Royal Flying Corps was to be singled out among the rest of the khaki-class world by reason of the striking double-breasted tunic, the cap set over one ear, and the wings—but more than this by the glamour surrounding the birdmen. Flying was something of a miracle, and we who practiced it were thought very brave, very daring, very gallant. We belonged to a world apart."

It *was* a world apart, a world closer in the mind's inventive eye to Camelot and the chivalrous struggles of plumed and noble knights than to the beastly carnage and grotesquerie of wars waged far below, where mere men were doomed to fight and die in the mud and the muck. The kind of war, in a word, which led Winston Churchill to growl: "War was once cruel and magnificent; now it is cruel and squalid."

The ace-of-aces, Erich "Bubi" Hartmann, fought in 800 dogfights in the course of flying 1,425 Eastern front missions in World War II, and he did what no man before him had ever done and no man after him is ever likely to do—he shot down 352 enemy planes. Now, he expresses the horror most fighter pilots feel witnessing the other kind of war up close. Shot down over Russian lines, then escaping back to the front lines, the 21-year-old German pilot watched in horror as 500 to 700 Russian soldiers—most of them drunk—lurched up a hill. "Our sergeant said to his men, 'Wait until they are a hundred meters in front of us.' And everybody goes in the hole and he looks and then he says, 'Fire at will.' It was awful for me the first time to see how a lot of people got mowed down." Then, reflectively:

"When you fly into the sky, you really don't understand what's going on on the ground, what people are doing. You're really free from it all. That is what's most fascinating about it."

Johannes "Macki" Steinhoff, with 176 air victories, adds his own impressions: "You don't hear the shooting. You don't see any blood. Shooting in a plane is a relatively clean affair."

To the surprise of many, the magic, the mystique—if not the strict reality—of young Cecil Lewis's other kind of combat lived on into the next world war, and beyond. In part, perhaps, because chivalry *was* so much a part of it, in the beginning at least, and on many fronts right down to the end. German pilots in World War II were under orders never to shoot an enemy flyer forced to bail out or to land.

Adolf Galland, who not only led Germany's fighter pilots in World War II but personally scored 104 air victories, will tell you that "if you talk about the cavaliers of the air, it's due to the fact that beginning in World War I, they were an elite group. They were recruited from the best sections of the armed forces, from the cavalry. So they brought with them an air of superiority. A healthy air of superiority. And they had a certain code of honor. They honored bravery, even on the opponent's side."

Gunther Rall, 275 kills, believes that "treating the fighter pilot as a hero goes back to World War I . . . where man fought one-on-one in a duel-like situation. Each is threatened equally and the better man wins. But when the fighter pilot sees the results of his deeds, when he sees the remains of his adversary, his broken machine, he doesn't think of heroism."

Desmond Frederick Burt Sheen, Australian, seven and one-third kills, is more succinct: "They had a job to do, which was shoot us down, and we had a job to do, to shoot them down. And that's the way it goes . . . it was a gentlemanly war, we were all gentlemen."

Even when chivalry failed—and it did, increasingly, even during World War I and more widely during World War II—a strong man confessed that "my heart ached with grief" after violating that higher code of honor. Afterwards, that Japanese ace, Takeo Tanimizu, vowed he would never again fire upon a parachuting pilot, but would instead seek to rescue the fallen enemy—and he did.

The Pulitzer Prize-winning poet W.H. Auden observed at the height of World War I: "The closest modern equivalent to the Homeric hero is the ace fighter pilot." Years later, one of Britain's top World War II aces, James Edgar "Johnny" Johnson, recalled: "I became a fighter pilot because when I was a young man it was the golden age of flying . . . People in the air force flew their nice stubby open biplanes, gaily painted, open cockpits, rather like the people flew in the first war. And it was just a very beautiful type of flying. And the other thing was that I was always fascinated by the stories of the legendary flyers."

The first name to roll off his lips was, indeed, a legend: Richtofen, the fabled Red Baron. Movie buffs remember Manfred von Richtofen as the quintessence of a swashbuckling modern aerial knight astride his spirited chargers. And spirited they were, each in its own time the scourge of the skies: the Albatross D.III, a sleek (for the times) biplane armed with twin 7.92 Spandau machine guns; later the faster Fokker DR1 triplane. Whatever the planes, they were unmistakably the Red Baron's, rakishly painted solid red with white-bordered black crosses. Before he was shot down himself on April 21, 1918, von Richtofen bagged 80 Allied aircraft, making him Germany's (and, arguably, the war's) top fighter ace; and his *Jagdeschwader* (Fighter Wing) #1 would bring down 930 allied aircraft in just 16 frenetic months.

Sir Hugh "Cocky" Dundas, 11 kills, sums it up: "Flying was more fun than marching."

The fighter plane came of age in World War I, a war in which the old jousted with the new in the smoke of awful battles. But the old ways died hard, and except for a few inevitable (and inevitably ignored) visionaries, the new ways were little understood. At the outset of the war, British officers were ordered to sharpen their swords as they prepared for combat. At the end of the war, the horse was still in higher esteem than horsepower. The Royal Air Force, which began the war with 63 aircraft, ended it as the world's largest: 22,171 planes, 27,333 officers, and 263,837 men.

In Germany at war's end, the largest army in the world, learning in stupefaction of the November surrender, ignored orders and commanders, marched east in disgust, and simply demobilized themselves. In the navy, there was mutiny. Only the *Luftstreitkrafte*, the Imperial Air Service, remained intact. Bitterness at the sudden surrender was perhaps greatest among these pilots, for they felt they had not been defeated.

It has all happened so fast—from the Sopwiths to the space ships—that it is hard to imagine how long aviation has been around. Although man's first recorded attempt to fly dates to 400 B.C., another 18 centuries would go by before Leonardo da Vinci and a handful of others ushered in an era of systematic, scientific design. Still another three centuries passed before the first manned flight took place: on November 21, 1783, Pilatre de Rozier and François Laurent, the marquis d'Arlandes, soared 3,000 feet in their balloon over a Paris crowd which included Louis XVI and Marie Antoinette. Eleven years later, a company of French revolutionaries became the world's first military aviators, using a balloon on April 2, 1794, to reconnoiter troop movements at Maubeuge, near the Belgian border. On another continent, observation balloons used during the American Civil War piqued the interest of the great Prussian inventor Ferdinand, graf von Zeppelin, who went up in a Union army balloon during the war. By 1900, he had built a rigid airship, the

Top German ace Erich Hartmann, 352 kills, 800 dogfights, 1,425 missions, said fighter pilots are "really free" from war's devastation, such as on the battlefield below.

LZ 1, 420-feet long, nearly double the length of the standard Boeing 747.

The dramatic breakthrough took place at Kitty Hawk, on North Carolina's Outer Banks, at 10:35 A.M. on December 17, 1903, when Orville Wright flew a contraption—Flyer I, a 200-pound machine powered by a 12-horsepower gasoline engine—into a 20-22 mph wind, covering 120 feet in 12 heart-stopping seconds. By the following year, Wilbur Wright was piloting a much-improved model 24 miles in 38 minutes.

Two years later, the U.S. War Department spurned the Wright brothers' offer to build a military aircraft. Across the Atlantic, the British War Office was rejecting a number of similar proposals. In France, meantime, in 1908, an army captain named Dorand built the first aircraft designed specifically for military use, but it never got off the ground. Another plane that did get off the ground that year made history—and transformed the flying machine from an eccentric curiosity into the centerpiece of man's inventive imagination and energies. On July 25, 1908, Louis Bleriot became the first to cross the English Channel in a heavier-than-air machine, traversing the 30 miles in 76 minutes.

Back in the United States, the army reversed field and placed an order with the Wright brothers for an aircraft capable of carrying two persons at a speed of at least 40 mph for a distance of 125 miles. After a false start, the Wright brothers delivered "Airplane No.1, Heavier-than-air Division, United States aerial fleet," in the spring of 1909. But between 1908 and 1913, the United States earmarked a mere $430,000 for its "aerial fleet." During that same period, France and Germany each invested about $22 million in military aviation, the Russians about $12 million, and even Belgium about $2 million.

The British, like the Americans, were moving more slowly. On October 16, 1908, "Army Aeroplane No.1," a bamboo contraption, flew 1,390 feet in a trial flight. The event caused the British high command to conclude that the

Japanese ace Takeo Tanimizu, with a Nambu pistol tucked in his belt, later in the war swore off firing on Allied airmen who had bailed out of their crippled machines.

Royal Engineers' Balloon Service had "squandered" £2,500. Funds for such "aeroplaning" were promptly cut off for another two years. In 1911, matching a development a year earlier in Germany, British Maj. Robert Brooke-Popham of the air battalion, Royal Engineers, outfitted his French-built Nieuport two-seater with a machine gun, only to be promptly ordered to remove it.

Major Brooke-Popham was not the only pioneer to be rebuffed. In the United States, Col. Isaac Newton Lewis demonstrated a low-recoil machine gun mounted on a Wright Model B biplane in trials at College Park, Maryland, June 2, 1912. When the U.S. Army Ordnance Department refused a request for ten more guns, Lewis took his invention to Europe where, in January 1913, he formed a company named Armes Automatiques Lewis, at Liege, Belgium, to manufacture what would become a warfare standard—the Lewis gun.

A number of military aviation firsts were recorded over northern Africa by Italian pilots in 1908 during Italy's war with Turkey. On October 22, Capt. Carlo Piazza flew his Bleriot XI on a reconnaissance of Turkish positions, the first operational flight undertaken by a military aircraft. That same day, on another reconnaissance flight, a Captain Moizo's Nieuport was hit by enemy groundfire, another first. On November 1, a Lieutenant Gavotti flew the first bombing sortie ever in a flying machine. Reaching Turkish positions near Tripoli, he plucked four 4.5-pound bombs from a leather bag, placed the bombs on his knees, fitted them with detonators he had in his pocket, and lobbed them over the side of his craft onto the Turkish positions below.

With such experience, it is not surprising that an Italian emerged as one of the first visionaries of air war. As early as 1909, Lt. Col. (later Brig. Gen.) Giulio Douhet predicted that future wars would be fought in the air. Douhet's persistence earned him a year in jail in 1916 as a troublemaker, anticipating by nine years the court-martial of U.S. Col. (later Gen.) William "Billy" Mitchell, who led a tireless fight for air power. (Like Douhet and Mitchell, Capt. Bertram Dickson, the first British military officer to fly, believed that fighters would rule the skies.)

Aviation's role in war was far from evident as World War I erupted. It was mainly the flyers themselves, through their own inventiveness, who made the airplane an impressive instrument of war. Consigned to observation work at war's outset, the planes were usually unarmed; the British were under orders to ram a Zeppelin should it be sighted. But soon, heavier-than-air machines began bombing raids, including a particularly destructive one on October 8, 1914, in which two British, single-seat Sopwith Tabloids, carrying a few 20-pound bombs, hit the railway station at Cologne and airship sheds at Dusseldorf.

By 1917, twin-engined German Gotha biplanes—the "pusher" type with the engines behind the pilot—were hitting London regularly in formation flights. In 1918, they were joined by four-engined giants known as the *Riesenflugzeug*, or R-planes. Measuring 72 feet 6 inches, these metal giants had a 138-foot 5 ½-inch wing span, a crew of seven, and carried a bomb load of up to 4,000 pounds. These German planes were inspired by earlier giants built by the Russian genius Igor Sikorsky.

In 1913, the Russians built the first successful four-engined aircraft, the *Russky Vityaz*, followed still later by the *Ilya Mourometz* bombers, that carried out about 400 raids on German targets, losing only one plane.

No mention of World War I bombers would be complete, of course, without including Italy's three-engine Caproni, thought to be among the finest then flying.

As noted, these were not the first aerial bombing missions; indeed, the first recorded was launched in 1849 by the Austrians, who floated small, hot-air balloons carrying 30-pound bombs fitted with time fuses over Venice. The bombs caused little damage and few casualties.

It took the early wartime pilots a while to get the hang even of observation flying. On the first reconnaissance mission from the Royal Flying Corp's (RFC) new headquarters at Maubeuge, Captains Joubert de la Ferte and Mappleback got lost, and on the round-trip via Tournai and Cambrai they had to ask directions. As a result, it took them eight hours to fly the 145 kilometers (95 miles). But they learned quickly: air reconnaissance on September 3, 1914, alerted the French to German weaknesses in their advance to the River Marne; had the Germans not been stopped there, the war might have ended with a German victory in a matter of weeks.

No fighter planes as such existed when the war started. Planes at best were fragile structures wobbling uncertainly at low altitudes. But by war's end, fighter pilot aces were dueling at 15,000 feet, blazing away with twin synchronized machine guns at speeds of 125 mph or higher. But all that was yet to come.

As encounters with enemy planes increased, minds struggled to provide flyers with greater firepower than the pistols, rifles, and carbines they carried. Not only were the Lewis and other machine guns too heavy for the flimsy craft, but firing them through the maze of struts, control and support wires—not to mention the propellers—proved too difficult for most pilots. Suggestions were not long in coming. Among some proposals was the use of a blunderbuss and steel darts. Among still others, one seemingly bizarre idea was actually used (at least once) by the Russian ace, Staff Capt. Alexander A. Kazakov: trailing a small bomb affixed to a three-pronged grappling hook beneath a fast scout airplane, then detonating it electronically from the cockpit when contact was made with the enemy craft.

Yet another example of raw determination was displayed by Lieutenant Harvey-Kelly of 2 Squadron in the RFC's first "kill" of the war on August 25, 1914. Piloting one of three planes, Harvey-Kelly forced down a German two-seater. Setting his own ship down nearby, he lit out on foot with his observer after the frightened Germans, who had disappeared into the woods. Returning, he set fire to the German plane.

The French aviator Roland Garros, the first "ace" of the war, made the machine gun a permanent part of an airplane's arsenal. A prewar aviator who had won races on both sides of the Atlantic, Garros joined up when war started and by early 1915 was the first to mount a machine gun on the front of his Morane-Saulnier monoplane single-seater. The gun was rigged with an interrupter to fire through the twin blades of the propeller, which he attempted to protect against damage by affixing steel deflectors. So armed, Garros scored his first kill on April 1, 1915, his fifth (and last) sixteen days later. On April 19, he was forced down behind German lines, captured, and, after three years in a prison camp, escaped only to be shot down a month before war's end. The Germans studied his innovation carefully, but were uncharacteristically slow to imitate it.

British pilots, meanwhile, brought their own blend of ingenuity and bravery to aerial combat. Capt. Lanoe George Hawker rigged a single-shot hunting

gun and then a Lewis gun to the port side of the fuselage, just under the cockpit. Because the Lewis gun was set to fire at an angle and thereby miss the propeller blades, and because the gunsight was attached at an awkward angle, Hawker was forced to fly his plane crabwise. That did not prevent him from becoming Britain's first successful air fighter and the first to be awarded Britain's highest medal for air combat. On November 23, 1915, he fell beneath the guns of another ace: the Red Baron.

Still other British pilots grappled with machine guns mounted on the top wing of their Martinsyde Scout biplane. To reach and reload the drum-fed gun, pilots had to stand while flying the plane with the control stick wedged between their knees. Even the first British planes specifically designed as fighters—the FB5 Vickers "Gunbus" and FE2 series, put in service in 1915 and 1916—required dangerous contortions for firing. The FE2d, a "pusher"-type aircraft (engine behind), for example, required the observer to stand on his seat, in a bucking airplane, in order to fire backwards over the top wing, where most attacks came from. To make matters worse, parachutes did not come into widespread use until late in the war.

Guns were not the only vexation. Even the fighter pilot's famous scarf, so much a part of his panache, entered his wardrobe out of necessity. Pilots were forced to swivel their heads continually in order to keep a sharp lookout for

Elliot White Springs, walking away from his Sopwith Camel aircraft near Doullens, France, during the summer of 1918.

the enemy. And so, to avert chafing their necks, soft silk scarves were adopted by the flyers.

The fighter plane finally came into its own through the inventiveness of a young Dutch designer who turned to the Germans after both the British and French had spurned him. His name, destined to reverberate through the annals of fighter plane history: Anthony H.G. Fokker. Fokker solved the problem almost as soon as he stated it: how to shoot between propeller blades.

Within three days, Fokker had the solution. Essentially, it involved designing an engine-driven system of cams and push-rods so that, in effect, the propeller—not the pilot—fired the gun, and once during each revolution. A lightened Parabellum machine gun was installed on Eindecker monoplanes beginning in June 1915, and although only 86 Eindeckers reached the Western front by the end of the year, the period became known as "The Fokker Scourge." On January 14, 1916, faced with the enemy's unprecedented mastery of the skies, the RFC ordered an escort of at least three fighters in close formation for its reconnaissance planes.

One of the most remarkable things about the first days of military aviation is how fast and furiously change came. At the outbreak of the war, the RFC had 63 aircraft arrayed in five squadrons, the Germans had 246, the French 138. By the end of 1914, the French had surged to the lead with 801, the Germans had 575, and the British 133. At mid-1916, Germany had 4,856, France 4,990, Britain 1,741. From the very beginning, they were a mixed bag: BE2s, Bleriot monoplanes, Farman biplanes, Albatroses, the Tabloids. Over the course of the war, France built 67,982 aircraft, Britain 55,093, Germany 47,637, and Italy about 20,000; the United States, which flew none of its own planes during its 19 months in the war, built 15,000 British, French, and Italian planes.

As the war progressed, not only the numbers but the types of airplanes multiplied wildly on both sides, each new model improving on its rapidly discarded predecessor. Among those introduced as the war ground into its third year were: Germany's Albatros Scouts, with their twin Spandau ma-

A Niueport tears into the sky from a grass field during the war to end all wars.

chine guns; the French Nieuport 17, a fast (110 mph), highly maneuverable biplane, the airplane that ended the Fokker Eindecker mastery of the skies; and the British DH2 and FE2b, the latter two "pusher"-type planes with a nose-mounted machine gun.

Still later, in 1917, came two Allied planes, the match of anything German. The first was the SPAD XIII: armed with two synchronized Vickers guns and powered by 220-horsepower Hispano-Suiza engine, it flew faster (139 mph) than any other and could climb higher (22,000 feet) than most. So popular was it that 8,472 were built and flown by every Allied nation except Russia. Then came the celebrated British Sopwith Camel. Also armed with twin Vickers guns, the Camel, though skittish with novice pilots, was capable of an unequalled maneuverability and responsiveness. Another formidable late-comer, in April 1917, was the Bristol Fighter, used first (unsuccessfully) in defensive roles, later (very successfully) as an offensive fighter.

But beyond machines, it was a war in which the flyers themselves made the dramatic difference. At first they were the loners, men such as Germany's Max Immelman and Oswald Boelcke and Britain's Albert Ball, only 19 when he scored his first kill, only 22 when he disappeared on a lone patrol. By then, he had 47 kills. But by mid-1916, fighter pilots were learning to fly and fight together.

Perhaps no one was more instrumental in bringing this new sophistication to air warfare than the one-time loner, Oswald Boelcke. Though only 25, he not only was the creative and moving force behind the organization of Germany's first fighter *Jagdstaffeln* ("hunting flights"), but his extensive writing on tactics, organization, and aircraft included a celebrated set of seven rules for fighter pilots. Issued to all German pilots in World War I, the *Dicta Boelcke*—as the rules were called—made so much sense they were given to Luftwaffe pilots in World War II. Although Rule 7 stressed the need for Jasta teamwork, Boelcke continued at times to fly as a loner himself. His score stood at 40 when he was killed in 1916, ironically, in a collision with one of his own men while practicing teamwork.

Others added their names and inventions to the rapidly evolving aerial warfare. One was "the Immelman turn," for the German ace Max Immelman, a widely imitated maneuver for attacking from above and behind. Another was the Lufbery Circle, used by American flyers of both world wars. Using this tactic when attacked, bombers or reconnaissance planes flying in formation would circle in such a way as to have each plane cover the tail of the plane in front. The maneuver was named for the French-born American pilot Raoul Lufbery of the immortal Lafayette Escadrille.

By war's end, the now-consolidated Royal Air Force (RAF) was launching Combined Offensive Patrols of as many as four, 18-plane squadrons. The fighter plane was now firmly established as part of a larger war-fighting machine.

No nation emerged from World War I more gutted than Germany. Under the Treaty of Versailles, not only was war-weakened Germany compelled to pay staggering reparations after losing all of its overseas colonies and huge chunks of territory, but the country was stripped of its air force and forbidden the construction of powered aircraft of any type. The ban on construction of nonmilitary aircraft was lifted four years later.

By then, the secret rebuilding of the German air force was already well underway. Beginning in 1920, General Hans von Seeckt, chief of the German general staff, held a series of secret meetings with Leon Trotsky, commissar of war of the Soviet Union. The Bolshevik Revolution had decimated Russia's officer corps; Germany had officers but nowhere to train. By 1922, far from the eyes of a prying world, some 400 German air war experts and technicians were operating a joint, Soviet/German air training school at Lipetsk. The arrangement lasted until 1933 with the rise to power in Germany of the ardent anticommunist, Adolf Hitler. But, by then, both sides had extracted full advantage from the clandestine arrangement: the Soviets had learned from the world's master military aviation experts; the Germans had the nucleus of the new Luftwaffe.

The Soviet dictator, Josef Stalin, was an early believer in air power, and in 1933, insisted that 100,000 trained pilots be ready at all times. As for the Germans, their planes emerged mainly from the genuis of such designers as Willi Messerschmitt, Kurt Tank, Ernst Heinkel, and Claude Dornier. The civilian aircraft they designed were built with an eye to ready conversion to military use. In exchange for granting the Lufthansa a monopoly, the government retained a one-third interest in the civilian airline. This enabled von Seeckt to install trusted men in key positions.

Adolf Galland, enrolled in a parallel training program at age 20, explains: "In those so-called 'camouflaged' days, at first we practiced only the fighter pilot aspect of military aviation, because if we had started with bombing training, we would have been stopped. So this is how I decided to become a fighter pilot."

Germany resorted to another ruse to continue training its airmen during the years of restriction: Hitler's fellow fascist Benito Mussolini, in power in Italy, agreed to allow advanced training with his *Regia Aeronautica*.

Finally, in March 1935, the Versaille Treaty was swept aside and Germany embarked on a furious campaign to build its military might with air power at its center. From 1934 until 1939, German factories turned out 15,927 combat aircraft and 13,889 trainers. Former World War I ace Hermann Goering, who established the Luftwaffe as a separate service equal to the army and navy, recruited many of his former cronies to key places in the new Luftwaffe. That, plus 13 years of secret training, enabled him to unveil a full-blown air force virtually overnight.

Blooded as fighter pilots in World War I like those of no other nation, German veterans returned in throngs to aerial combat in World War II. Their exploits, unique in World War I, would be equally unmatched in the new war rising from the ashes of the old.

To say that is not to diminish the heroism nor the derring-do of the pilots of the many other nations who flew and fought in the two wars. Rather, in both wars, German flyers were so badly outnumbered and outgunned that they were forced to fight longer and harder. German fighter pilots flew a thousand sorties or more—until they were dead or maimed; American pilots flew 80 or 100, British pilots rarely more. Inevitably, the Germans shot down more of their enemies than did the pilots of other countries. Furthermore, the Germans, unlike the Allies, did not use the term "ace." For the Allies, an ace was a pilot who shot down five enemy aircraft in air combat. For the Germans, an *Experten* earned that coveted title only through continuous performance.

As noted, Germany's top ace, Erich "Bubi" Hartmann, "The Black Devil of the Ukraine," downed 352 enemy planes, the equivalent of 15 Allied squadrons—a mark unlikely ever to be equalled. But Hartmann was not the

Between the wars Adolf Galland readied his skills for the future German air force in covert training under the aegis of the German airline monopoly Lufthanse. He later became the youngest commanding general of the Third Reich's fighter command.

only German pilot to register more than 300 kills: Gerhard Barkhorn, shot down twice during the Battle of Britain, went on to down 301 planes. In addition, the Luftwaffe boasted 13 pilots who scored between 200 and 300 victories, 92 who had between 100 and 200, and about 360 who scored between 40 and 100. (Although the above tallies apply only to the war in Europe, for purposes of comparison, Japan's top ace of World War II, navy Lt. Tetsuzo Iwamoto, had 94 kills; the top American ace in the Pacific, Maj. Richard I. Bong, 40).

The guns of August were still echoing when British fighter pilots were back in action, this time in the skies over Russia, attempting to help the White forces stem the Red tide of revolution. Arriving in Russia in the spring of 1919 as "volunteers," the men of RAF Squadron 47, commanded by the Canadian ace Ray Collishaw, suffered few losses while inflicting heavy damage before withdrawing at year's end.

But in terms of tactics and aircraft, Russia was really a postscript to World War I. The preludes to World War II—Manchuria (1931), Ethiopia (1935), Spain (1936), and Finland (1939)—were yet to come.

* * *

In the years following the Great War, military aviation was largely quiescent. The large glut of leftover airplanes, the wave of pacifism, and the Great Depression stilled the ambitions of most military planners. Improvements in aircraft, and there were many, came about largely as the result of international civilian competitions, such as the one that spurred Charles A. Lindbergh to make his historic first solo crossing of the Atlantic, May 20-21, 1927.

Yet one element of military aviation, which gathered significant momentum during World War I, continued in the decade following. As early as 1910, Eugene Ely, a civilian pilot, took off in a Curtiss biplane from a platform erected on the bow of the cruiser USS *Birmingham*. By 1922, the United States put its first carrier—the converted collier USS *Langley*—into operation. That same year, Japan did the same with its first carrier, the *Honsho*.

Japan also paced the United States and Britain in the development of naval dive-bombing tactics. On October 22, 1926, in their first fleet demonstration, Curtiss F6C-2 Hawks of the U.S. navy's Squadron VF-2 made almost vertical simulated dive attacks from 12,000 feet on the heavy ships of the Pacific fleet as they left San Pedro, a feat that greatly impressed the Imperial Japanese Naval Air Service. (The Japanese were also influenced by a British training mission in 1921-1923.) Those attacks fully vindicated Billy Mitchell, who had attempted to demonstrate the vulnerability to air power of traditional large naval vessels. During the late 1920s, aircraft carriers—among them the USS *Saratoga* and the USS *Lexington*—emerged as the distinctive ships of World War II. By the early 1930s, most of their essential features were in place, including arrester hooks to halt planes landing on the deck and folding wings to move planes below decks, which greatly increased the ships' capacity.

No nation moved more aggressively to develop its carrier force and naval aviation arm than Japan. Central to its success was a plane which knew no peer during the first two years of the Pacific war, the Mitsubishi A6M, known to the Allies as the "Zero."

Spain was among the more ideologically entangled preludes to World War II. To this day, "the Spanish Civil War" conjures up images of idealistic visionaries waging heroic battle against hordes of fascist barbarians. The truth is otherwise, although it is true that fascists—German and Italian—played vital roles in the war. But the propaganda and the temper of the times that fueled that image helped explain why so many Americans went into World War II with a special hatred in their hearts towards Germany—long before the heinous crimes of Hitler's "Final Solution" were known to the world.

Walker M. "Bud" Mahurin—who went on to fly and fight in three theaters in two wars—was enrolled in a flying school in Chickashay, Oklahoma, when Pearl Harbor was attacked. Years later, he would remember "a lot of things that were emerging in our Pathe newsreels and in the press and so forth about Hitler and Mussolini, and the bad things they were doing . . . And so we hated Hitler and we hated Mussolini and we hated what the Germans were doing and what the Italians were doing."

Spain also presaged the magnitude and mechanized horror of the coming holocaust in which air power would play the crucial role, although for the most part, the fighter pilot managed to soar above the image of the inhumanity and cruelty.

The civil war in Spain was only a few weeks old when on July 31, 1936, a small contingent of Luftwaffe "volunteers" was given a fiery send-off by the

Cadet Tetsuzo Iwamoto, seated on the ground, went on to become the empire's top-scoring ace with 94 kills.

new Gen. Erhard Milch. They were shortly (and disastrously) in action against what was then the world's most formidable fighter plane, the Soviet I-16. The Mosca (Fly) to its Republican friends, the Rata (Rat) to its Nationalist enemies, it was the first low-wing, single-seat fighter with retractable landing gear to see service with any air force, and it quickly gained undisputed superiority over Spanish skies.

Faced with disaster, Hitler early in 1937 dispatched a full-fledged German expeditionary force, known as the Condor Legion, to Spain. With it went Germany's premier fighter plane: the Messerschmitt Me.109. Arguably the most successful fighter plane ever built, it was also the most extensively produced fighter plane in history: 35,000 between 1935 and 1945. (From the

The design of the Laird-Turner was indicative of early, metal interwar aircraft. It was clearly outdone by Willi Messerschmitt's preproduction Me.109 model as early as 1934.

time it was first unveiled by designer Willi Messerschmitt in 1934, this adaptable plane's power was increased from 610 to 2,000 horsepower, its top speed ratcheted up from 292 to 452 mph, its gross weight increased from 4,850 to 7,438 pounds, and its armament up from three rifle-caliber machine guns to two 15 mm and one 30 mm cannon. Rate of climb was increased from 2,700 to 4,850 feet per minute, and the ceiling from 29,500 to 41,400 feet.)

The first 109B2s quickly gained air superiority over Spain. They were later replaced by 48 109Cs. The Legion's *Jagdgruppe* 88 (Fighter Group 88), constantly recycled so as to provide training opportunities for the largest number, racked up 314 victories before war's end early in 1939. Though outnumbered in Spain, tactics as well as equipment played an important role in the Luftwaffe's success.

Werner Mölders, leading one of the four squadrons, developed a new tactic to replace the three-plane V formation favored by virtually every air force in the world. In its place, he introduced the *Rotte*, two airplanes flying about 600 feet apart, one pilot primarily attacking, his wingman covering his tail. Next, two *Rotten* combined to form a *Schwarm*—once again, one *Rotte* leading the attack, the other flying cover. It gave Mölders 14 kills, making him the top German ace in Spain. And it worked well enough to give the Luftwaffe a decisive tactical advantage over other air forces going into World War II.

Adolf Galland, at 30 Germany's youngest general and commander of the Fighter Arm, flew 300 missions in Spain. He comments: "This open, four-finger flight formation gave every pilot the possibility to see the air space and [gave] tactical superiority vis-à-vis the French and the English which we used to our advantage."

The development of two-man formations brought a new and lasting concept to aerial warfare: the wingman. Typically, the leader would attack while the wingman covered him. On few subjects do fighter pilots wax more emphatic. Andrew R. Mackenzie, who rose to flight commander while flying with the Royal Canadian Air Force in Europe, tells of an experience he had: "As you know, in the fighter world, you fly in pairs, Number Two looks after Number One. Well, the Luftwaffe boys were quite gallant and very well disciplined. So well disciplined that I was lining up my aircraft to shoot down this Number Two and was only about 50 feet away from him. Instead of breaking off and leaving his Number One to be shot down, he preferred to die. He was looking right at me when I shot him. But he was covering his Number One, where he should have been."

Herbert Ihlefeld, 130 victories, winner of the Knight's Cross with Swords, raises the relationship to the level of character. "Above all else," he says, the fighter pilot "has to possess an exemplary character, he has to act loyally. Although he is flying alone, he helps his wingman and his comrades. They all fight together, particularly in crisis situations."

Heinz Marquardt, who scored 121 victories, reinforces MacKenzie's story. The most important thing he learned, he explains, "was that it was preferable to let an opponent get away and to help a wingman who was in trouble than to go after your opponent." Like many great aces, Marquardt's proudest boast was that he never lost a wingman.

Although the Italians deployed two innovative airplanes to do combat in Spain—the all-metal GR 50 fighter and the SM 79 bomber—both were eclipsed by still another aviation development of the war: the Ju.87 dive-bomber, the notorious "Stuka." Although these two-seater dive-bombers saw only limited combat in Spain, they came to symbolize the new terror of warfare: a plane screaming (and scream they did) straight down at a helpless target.

The war in Europe, so long in coming, finally exploded at 4:45 A.M. on September 1, 1939, when 62 German divisions—including six armored and ten mechanized—swept into Poland across a 1,750-mile arc. Against them, the Poles deployed some 40 divisions, including a few old tanks and 12 brigades of horse cavalry.

Overwhelmed by the German blitzkrieg on the ground, the Polish air force fought tenaciously against the Luftwaffe, thanks mainly to the skill and courage of its pilots. Waclaw S. Krol was one of those pilots, flying an antiquated PZL P-11c in 121 Squadron. Built in 1931, the P-11 was a high, gull-winged, open cockpit plane, slow (254 mph top speed), but well armed: two 20 mm cannons and two machine guns.

The Germans committed 1,581 of their total force of 3,652 front-line fighters, bombers, and dive-bombers to the conquest of Poland. Against them, the Poles had only about 300 planes; but the Poles had taken the precaution of scattering their planes to secret air bases so that when the Luftwaffe struck not a single squadron remained at its prewar base. During the four weeks of the brief war, the Poles managed to bring down 285 German planes and damaged an equal number sufficiently to render them unserviceable. At least 126 of those kills were in air-to-air combat against the vastly superior German planes. In some instances, the Poles did it with pure guts: in an air battle over Warsaw, 2nd Lt. Leopold Pamula shot down an He.111 and Ju.87 transport and then, when he ran out of ammunition, rammed an Me.109 before parachuting to safety. Other pilots discovered that they could unnerve the Germans if they dove head-on into formations. The P-11s alone were credited with 120 kills against 114 losses. Krol was credited with two and-a-half kills, plus one probable.

Poland's top ace, Stanislaw F. Skalski, who shot down six and-a-half planes with the 142 "Wild Duck" Squadron, scored his first kill on the opening day of the war, a Heinkel 125 reconnaissance plane. Skalski followed him down, landing in the same field where the German had flipped over

Few Americans realized that war was imminent in 1940. Even fewer could foresee what kind of conflict lay ahead for the nation. And none could have pictured himself among these navy pilots rushing to their aircraft aboard the USS *Hornet* somewhere in the China Sea, February 1945.

Inset:
Pilots of the USS *Lexington* during a mission briefing for a December 4, 1943, strike against Kwajalein. Feigned boredom masked anxiety.

attempting a forced landing. Skalski landed upright: "I was young, stupid, but lucky." One German was wounded; Skalski gave him first aid. The other had escaped into nearby bushes. Skalski approached, holding a silver cigarette case—his only weapon. The German came over, hands up. "I gave him a cigarette. He gave me his Mauser [pistol]."

Skalski explains that in Poland, if you were aggressive, they made you a fighter pilot; if "steady, quiet," a bomber pilot. A fighter pilot, he adds, acts first and thinks later. (The American ace, Michael Russo, tries to put that in perspective: "You had to be young and foolish—not too stable or mature—or you wouldn't take the chances you did. Not bright enough to realize you could die.")

Poland was out of the war; Krol, Skalski, and tens of thousands of other Poles were not. Indeed, Poland would field the greatest number of soldiers, airmen, and sailors battling the Wehrmacht down to war's end of any Allied power after the U.S. and Britain.

Across the ocean, most Americans believed it was only a matter of time before they were drawn into the conflagration, but for the moment they were busily shaking off the Depression blues. Thanks to an upsurge in war-impelled industrial activity, joblessness was declining sharply. Long lines formed to see the Hollywood sensation, *Gone with the Wind*, while Hildegarde's "Deep Purple" topped the record charts. The New York Yankees blitzed the Cincinnati Redlegs in four straight games in the World Series to win their fourth straight series. And along with the euphoria, sadness. The dying Lou Gehrig moved the entire nation when, in his farewell in Yankee Stadium, he described himself as "the luckiest man alive."

The following year, as the war in Europe heated up, Franklin Roosevelt was elected to an unprecedented third term with a pledge to keep America out of the war while supporting those nations that upheld the Four Freedoms with all measures "short of war." The Neutrality Act was amended to permit "cash and carry" sales to the belligerents and, still later, a deal transferring 50 moth-balled destroyers to the hard-pressed British in exchange for 99-year leases on a number of bases. The first peacetime draft was enacted.

Still, as 1940 ended, an Elmo Roper survey showed that 67.4 percent of Americans wanted no part of the war.

On the day the war broke out in Europe, Brig. Gen. George C. Marshall was sworn in as new chief of staff of the United States army. It was one of the most effective military measures isolationist America would take. Marshall took command of an army with 227,000 soldiers but with equipment for only 75,000. A few months after taking charge, he reported to Roosevelt on the antiquated state of American armed forces.

Roosevelt not only believed that the United States would enter the war but was convinced that air power would win it. Early in 1938, he sent his trusted aide Harry Hopkins to the Pacific coast to survey how quickly aircraft factories could convert to the production of warplanes. Hopkins' 1938 statement that the United States needed 8,000 airplanes distressed nearly everyone, including generals and admirals. A significant exception was air corps Gen. Henry H. "Hap" Arnold. Arnold estimated at the time that Germany had up to 8,000 bombers and fighters whereas America had 1,650 pilots, a few hundred obsolete planes, and 13 B-17s on order. Even the new P-40 planes were dated; like the late-model 1918 planes, their machine guns were synchronized to fire through the propellers.

When the order to build was given following the German blitzkrieg of May 1940, production mounted slowly towards Roosevelt's proclaimed aim of a 50,000-plane army/navy air arm. In 1939, U.S. military air production was 2,141 planes; the last year of the war, the U.S. produced 47,714 planes.

Official Washington wasn't alone in believing war was inevitable. Scores of young Americans refused to wait. Reade Franklin Tilley of Clearwater, Florida, was one of them; he joined the RAF early in the war. With that jocular flippancy Americans so often use to disguise deeper feelings, Tilley tells us: "I planned to be a racing car driver, but that didn't turn out too well, so I started looking around for something else important to do. There were a few wars going on and I finally decided to pick this one."

"The heavens were the grandstands and only the gods were spectators. The stake was the world, the forfeit was the player's place at the table, and the game had no recess. It was the most dangerous of all sports and the most fascinating. It got in the blood like wine. It aged men forty years in forty days. It ruined nervous systems in an hour."

The speaker is Elliott White Springs, Princeton bon vivant who shot down 13 Germans over the Western front in World War I. The words, for a fighter pilot, are timeless. Hear him go on:

"No words can describe the thrill of hiding in the clouds, waiting for human prey. The game is sighted, then a dive of 5,000 feet, 30 seconds of diabolic evolutions, the pressure of triggers, and the adversary hurtling downward in a living hell.

"The first time it happened to me, I was sick for three days. The last time it happened, five months later, I did not even look down to see the end. I was busy fixing my glove.

"It was a fast game. No man could last six months at it and remain normal. The average life of a pilot at the front was 48 hours, and to many it seemed an age."

Years later, a top American ace in the Pacific Theater, Col. John W. Mitchell (16 kills, Navy Cross, DSC, DFC with four Oak Leaf clusters, Air Medal), updates those sentiments: "There's nothing greater than combat in an aircraft with another aircraft. That's the epitome. Nothing else can touch it. Anybody who hasn't been there, they've missed a great part of life."

There it is—the excitement of it all, the sense of mortality on a stage reserved for the immortals. That was part of it, surely; but there was more, much more—the motivations, the fears, the ideals of those who would join battle over the scourged skies of a world at war.

Now, as that war closed in on the world, it is time to meet a few of the men—and women—who wrote aviation history. They speak first of motivation.

* Kenneth "Ken" A. Walsh, lieutenant colonel, a marine, a Medal of Honor winner, 21 kills: "When I was about twelve years old, I made up my mind that someday I would like to be a pilot. We used to sketch fighter air battles of World War I aces. That's where the enthusiasm began."

* Sadamu Komachi, warrant officer, 18 kills: "We were imbued with a strong spirit of sacrifice and devotion. We were teenagers, strongly attracted to the sky. The China Incident [July 7, 1937] had started, and when I had to fight, I wanted to fight bravely."

* Johannes "Macki" Steinhoff, general, awarded Germany's highest decoration, 176 kills: "Heroism was the leading theme. My generation was educated that to be a soldier was the greatest honor in a man's life."

* Ivan A. Lakeyev, stocky grandson of a czarist peasant, blooded in Spain, awarded the Hero of the Soviet Union medal, 13 victories: "I was devoted to upholding the security of our Motherland."

They speak of the qualities that make a fighter pilot—that keep him alive.

* Sergei Dolgushin, who fought the Luftwaffe from the opening battles in Russia, 24 kills: "He must have a love of hunting, a great desire to be the top, top dog."

* George Chandler, American, who shot down five enemy planes: "A fighter pilot—the very best of them are unusually quick. I mean quick in reflexes, quick in their analysis."

* Sir Harry Broadhurst, Spitfire pilot with 12 kills: "I mean, I had fast motor cars and fast motor bikes, and when I wasn't crashing airplanes, I was crashing motor bikes. It's all part of the game."

* General Steinhoff again: "The fighter pilot must be an individualist, not a member of mass society. He has a touch of the playboy, too. And he must be able to withstand shocks. I was shot down seven times."

* Jack Ilfrey, Texan, who got eight: "The hunters are the ones who go out and kill. Maybe one out of ten good fighter pilots will be one of the hunters."

* Friedrich Oblesser, who shot down 127 planes, sums up: "The fascination of flight can't be expressed with words. But it really lies beyond the capabilities of human endeavor. Once you've experienced it, you'll never be able to forget it."

2 DEFENDING THE REALM

It took the German blitzkrieg only four months to complete the conquest of France and the Low Countries. The last transports from Dunkirk were being loaded when Winston Churchill rose in the House of Commons and told his embattled countrymen—and the world— that the British were far from defeated:

> We shall fight on to the end, we shall fight in France, we shall fight in the seas and oceans, we shall fight with growing confidence and growing strength in the air, we shall defend our island, whatever the cost may be, we shall fight on the beaches, we shall fight on the landing grounds, we shall fight in the fields and in the streets, we shall fight in the hills; we shall never surrender . . .

Hurricane fighter aircraft formed the backbone of the Royal Air Force until the Spitfire was produced in larger numbers. Both aircraft were later outclassed by entirely new aircraft such as the Typhoon.

On June 4, 1940, 338,226 British and French soldiers were plucked from the beaches of Dunkirk, saved by the most improbable armada ever assembled. The fleet included cruisers and destroyers, small sailboats and Dutch *skoots* manned by civilian volunteers. Under heavy pounding from the Luftwaffe, 243 of the 861 vessels were sunk. But they managed to rescue roughly seven times the number of fighting men the British high command had estimated could be saved. Bad weather played a part in deterring the Luftwaffe, but in large measure, the vaunted German air arm was foiled by the outnumbered men of the Royal Air Force (RAF). Taking to the air tirelessly in Hurricanes and their new Spitfires, the RAF pilots challenged the Luftwaffe successfully for the first time. The worst, for both, was yet to come.

Like many other RAF pilots, Dunkirk was Colin Falkland Gray's initiation into the rites of aerial combat. Gray already had about a hundred hours' training on Spitfires, "and that," he advises, "is about what one needed to give you a chance of survival." A native of Christchurch, New Zealand, Gray joined the RAF in 1938, sitting out the "phony war" during the winter and spring of 1939-1940 while honing his skills. "We'd all been looking forward to getting into action," he relates, "because our friends were all fighting over France. But Dunkirk was a long way to go: if we stayed an hour on patrol, it took you two hours to get there and back, and that was a long way in a Spitfire which was designed for not much more than 60 minutes' flying. And whereas at Dunkirk we were on the offensive, if you got hit, you had a fair chance of coming down in the water or in foreign territory."

Gray learned that lesson fast. "I got hit by an enemy aircraft quite early on at Dunkirk. We'd been escorting a squadron of Swordfish, old single-engine biplanes. And they went across to bomb Granville [on the Cherbourg peninsula] and only did about 90 knots, so it was a pretty slow journey. They did their dive-bombing and came back home.

"But the squadron commander decided that we'd carry on with our patrol since we were over on the other side anyway. Just after we'd started our patrol, we came across a whole gaggle of aircraft. Somebody said, 'Bandits!' I thought, 'Well, they're wrong, they look like a lot of Blenheims being escorted by Hurricanes.' Although, if I'd only thought, at that time there wouldn't be many Blenheims across the other side, or Hurricanes. In fact, they were [Messerschmitt] 109s and either Heinkels—I don't remember now—or Dorniers or Ju.88s. As we turned in to attack them, we got set upon from behind by 109s. My leader, who was a sergeant pilot, called, '109s behind!' So we had to turn and have a scrap with them.

"I managed to get on the tail of one of them and give him a good burst, and I was surprised to see him pull up and bail out. While I was watching him do this, there was a hell of a clatter, like somebody running a stick along a corrugated iron fence. And I realized I was being shot at, and this gave me a lot of fright!

"Fortunately for me, one of the cannon shells hit the port wing and jammed the ailerons in the up position so that the aircraft flicked over into a dive. I couldn't have devised a better escape maneuver! So I never saw him again, but I did have a bit of trouble getting the stick back because it had been jammed into one corner with this action. When I set off for home, I pretty smartly pressed the emergency boost lever, which gave double-takeoff power. But I noticed that my air speed wasn't moving and, as I was climbing, it should have dropped. Suddenly, I realized that this cannon shell had knocked the pitot head off my wing. And, of course, that meant I had no air speed indicator. So I checked around and found that I didn't have any air pressure, either. And that meant I couldn't fire my guns and I couldn't lower my flaps. There was no hydraulic pressure, and that meant the undercarriage wouldn't come down, either. Quite a traumatic experience!

"When I got back to Hornchurch, the controller suggested I should bail out, but I didn't think much of that. It seemed a long way to go, and a pity to throw away a good aircraft. But the undercarriage came down all right—we had an emergency carbon dioxide bottle—and it came down. I still had no flaps and no air speed indicator, so I made a bit of a mess of landing the first time around—I was going too fast. But I managed to get down all right on the second try."

For Gray, a near miss. For the unlucky pilot of a German Me.109, a hit— the first of 27 enemy planes Gray would send down in flames.

By contrast with the inexperience of the British, most of the Luftwaffe pilots in action over Dunkirk already had extensive combat experience, training, or both. Like Gray, Walter Hoffmann had training—but had never tasted combat. When he joined the Luftwaffe in 1936, he had already flown everything from such vintage "flying kites" as the Stieglitz and Kadett—single-engine, tandem-wing aircraft—to twin- and three-engined fighters and fighter bombers. Now, at the controls of a Messerschmitt 110—a twin-engine heavy fighter mounting two 20 mm cannon and five machine guns—Hoffmann met a formation of RAF Spitfires and Hurricanes covering the Dunkirk exodus. He shot down one of each. And that, he recalls, despite two strikes against him: "The English were excellent pilots. And the Spitfire was a wonderful aircraft—far superior to the 110. I was only able to shoot down the Spitfire because the 110 was so massively armored and had superior firepower, very concentrated."

Another German pilot flying a 110 was lucky to get out alive. And Hans-Joachim Jabs (50 air victories) was already battle-tested by the time he got there: Poland, Norway, France. He reports: "We were flying as destroyers. We saw and experienced personally how good, fast, and how excellently the Hurricanes and Spitfires flew. We experienced the difference between the French and English pilots. Still, despite the fact the Me.110 was too slow to fight against the fighter pilots of the RAF, we were of the opinion, at least at the beginning, that we could hold our own. Then we saw that they were faster, very skillful, well organized, and flew very well in formation, so that the first considerable losses among the destroyers took place above Dunkirk. We realized that the losses we suffered over Dunkirk would occur on a much larger scale over England if we had to provide escort for the bomber formations—much worse. Our destroyer was *greatly* inferior to the British, at least to the Spitfire." He was dead right, of course, about what lay ahead for the Luftwaffe.

Still another Luftwaffe pilot at Dunkirk—Fritz Losigkeit (68 victories)—had combat experience going back to Spain. "That's where we fought the first really tough air battles—Dunkirk. We always preferred to take on a Hurricane, because we felt they were somewhat slower than the 109, whereas the Spitfire was very stable in the curves and was able to quite easily assume a better position, bank long before you could react and fire." As with Jabs, he learned an important lesson there: "The English had a very large group of very excellent pilots."

Dunkirk signalled the death rattle of freedom in Western Europe. Poland was the beginning of that end. Despite its antiquated equipment, the Polish air force had fought stubbornly against the superior Luftwaffe forces, downing 285 planes, 109 of which were bombers. But bravery alone could not halt the juggernaut, and by September 28, 1939, the Warsaw garrison capitulated. With the Russians now attacking from the east, the last fragments of the Polish defense were smashed by October 5.

Although Britain and France had promptly declared war on Germany, they took virtually no action. The ensuing lull between October 1939 and May 1940—interrupted by the German seizure of Denmark and the invasion of Norway on April 9—became known as the "phony war." To the German public, the interlude was *Sitzkrieg* (the sit-down war); to the French, *drôle de guerre* (the odd war).

But if it was a phony war on the ground, there was nothing phony about the war on the seas—and in the air. Men from the far-flung corners of the vast British Empire were among the first to rally to Britain's side. Some had flocked to the RAF even earlier, in search of adventure, or of a love of flying. Patric Geraint Jameson, like Colin Gray, hailed from New Zealand, and like Gray, had signed on with the RAF before the war. Ironically, as it turned out, he had decided to go for a career in the navy if the RAF wouldn't take him. In the spring of 1940, he was in action over Norway—way up beyond the Arctic Circle, north of Narvik—and soon far more involved with the navy than he could have ever imagined. Jameson tells his story:

"We took part in the battle of Narvik when it was recaptured by the British and Poles and the French, and the Norwegians, of course. Fighter operations there were a little easier than in, say, England or France because we were out of range of the Messerschmitt 109s. The Messerschmitt 110s, the twin-engine fighters, could get there, but not the single-engine ones. So it made it very simple. We only had the 110s and the bombers to contend with, and they were fairly easy."

A Hurricane pilot, he scored his first kills on May 28, sharing with two other pilots the destruction of two Dornier 26 Flying Boats on the water in a fjord. "We spotted these enormous great flying boats sitting on the water, with cliffs all around—a long, narrow fjord. So we had to attack down between these two cliffs. It was quite exciting really, like an aerobatic display. We did several attacks, and they burnt and sank."

The next morning, Jameson intercepted a Heinkel 111, the heavily armed (six machine guns) bomber carrying a crew of five. "It was hard to see a camouflaged aircraft against the ground, so I climbed up underneath this lad. He didn't see me, so I got to within about 90 yards of him and let him have it.

"I must have got the rear gunner because there was no return fire at all. Oil came all over my windscreen on that first attack, so it was difficult to see for a little while, but soon it cleared. So I went in to do another attack on him, and he jettisoned his bombs. Then an engine started to burn, then he was all on fire. Didn't see anybody get out except at the very last minute—one fellow got out just before it crashed."

The German invasion of the Low Countries on May 10 forced the evacuation of the 25,000-man Franco-Polish-British Expeditionary Force from Narvik early in June, only ten days after having finally subdued the greatly outnumbered Austrian Alpine troops and sailors holding that important port city and vital railhead. Says Jameson: "The poor old Royal Navy didn't have enough ships to support us way up in the north of Norway. Although we were winning the battle up there with just one squadron of Hurricanes and one of Gladiators we were ordered to get out.

"Then came the question of what we were going to do with our Hurricanes

For the German pilots with combat experience from the civil war in Spain, the formidable British pilots offered surprising flying ability and strong resistance.

Patric Jameson landed an RAF Hurricane on the aircraft carrier HMS *Glorious* without the use of tail hook or arresting device. The *Glorious* was shortly shelled and sunk by the *Scharnhorst* and *Gneisenau*.

because, before we left England, we lent three of them to a combined team of the Royal Air Force and the Royal Navy to see if it was possible to land on carriers without hooks on them. At the end, they said it wasn't. It was possible to take off, but not to land.

''But my boss, Kenneth Cross—who finished up as air chief marshal— went out and had a chat with the captain of the *Glorious* who promised to get full steam up and go as fast as he could so that we could have a shot at landing on her. I was asked to volunteer to lead the first ones out since I had carried out some trials at the little runway at Bardu Fjord. For taking off purposes, I had fitted a three-bladed metal propeller to the plane—much heavier than the little two-bladed wooden prop that they used normally. But we had to find some way of jamming on our brakes without tipping up on the nose, so I found that a 14-pound sandbag, right in the very tail, was about right. So I went out to try it with two other lads. One of them, just as we were approaching the carrier, had engine trouble.

''Now, the navy had very strict rules that you mustn't land unless you get the signal to land. The radio was pretty useless, talking between the aircraft and the ship. And this chap had to get down somewhere. We were about 120 miles out at sea, in the Arctic—the only place he could get down was the ship. So down he went and landed all right. That was a relief! So then I went down next and got on, and so did the next chap. So I sent a signal to my boss that it was all right and gave him some instructions on how to do it because I had very nearly landed on the quarterdeck, coming in very, very slowly, right on the stall with lots of engine. Of course, if you come down too low, you get in a down draft, and it pushes you down onto the deck below, which nearly happened to me.

"But fortunately, the dear old Rolls Royce Merlin, when I opened it up flat out, it just dragged me up over the round at the stern of the flight deck, and I only used about a quarter of the deck to land on. Which was excellent. Then we got the CO, and the rest of the lads came out, ten of us all together, safely."

And that is how RAF pilot Jameson happened to be aboard the ancient British aircraft carrier HMS *Glorious* when, the next night, the two German battle cruisers, *Scharnhorst* and *Gneisenau*, "came along, unannounced." "And," Jameson continues, "one got on each quarter of the ship." The first salvo missed the *Glorious*, Jameson reports, "by about ten yards. The next one set on fire the five Swordfish which were on the deck loaded up with antisubmarine bombs. And the next ones nearly all hit. The first salvos also set our Hurricanes, which were in the top hangar, on fire, and that's where the torpedoes were kept for the torpedo bombers. So they couldn't launch a torpedo attack on the battle cruisers.

"It was a terrific din as the shells came in. We could see the red flame coming out of the guns. It seemed to take about three minutes for the shells to arrive, but they did. And the clatter when they hit! If you've heard a firecracker going off in a four-gallon kerosene tin, it gives you some idea, on a very teeny-weeny scale. It was a tremendous noise.

"And then they got a direct hit on the bridge which killed the captain and most of the senior officers. A commander took over, and we got the order to abandon ship. And then that was canceled. I was getting cold, so I tried to get down to my cabin to get my greatcoat, but all the watertight doors were closed, and I only got down one deck.

"After a while, I came up again onto the quarterdeck, and everybody had gone. They'd got the order to abandon ship, and there was hardly anyone home anymore, except one little chap. He was from Newcastle-on-Tyne, and we had a little chat, and he decided to go over, and I said, 'Well, watch where you're going and aim for the nearest raft,' which he did.

"But unfortunately, the ship was carrying a wooden raft alongside at the end of a long rope, and he jumped in front of this raft, and there was an awful clunk as it hit him on the head. So I took my flying boots off. I had my ordinary uniform on, but had left my life jacket on the tail of my airplane, so that was all burned up. So I had to jump over without one.

"I was a fairly good swimmer and made sure I jumped behind the raft and not in front of it. But the ship had a tremendous list by this time. The starboard side of the carrier was just about in the water. I daren't go down there in case she rolled over on me. And I was afraid to jump over on the other side because the propellers were still spinning—she was still doing about 12 knots. Anyway, I had to jump over there because there was nowhere else to go.

"I took a beeline on a Calais float, about a mile away, and swam to that. And there's my boss sitting on it, I was very pleased to see. I asked permission to come aboard, and he said, 'Of course, get on.' We had 29 on that raft, which made it very heavily laden because it was only meant for about 15 or something like that. The first one died of exposure after four and-a-half hours. He was a little plump chap, a young fellow; you'd have thought he would have lasted for a long time. Unfortunately, he'd taken all his clothes off, except his singlet and his underpants. So the chill factor got him.''

For men such as Jameson, there was nothing phony about this war at all. For three days, the small band of survivors bobbed on the frozen sea, their numbers thinning almost by the hour. By the time they were picked up, only seven were alive, and two of those men were soon dead. Jameson's legs were so badly frostbitten that the nerves had died. ''When they started to come to life, it was terrible. As a fighter pilot, it just made me keener to have a go at the Germans again.''

Action in the air on the Western front followed by a few days the invasion of Poland. Both sides gingerly avoided attacking civilian targets, concentrating during the ''phony war'' on naval targets. One year before the outbreak of war, the British Fighter Command, organized in July 1936, consisted of 573 obsolete biplanes and only 93 modern monoplanes. The Hawker Hurricane, although an outstanding single-seater fighter plane, lacked gun heating to allow it to operate above 15,000 feet, and the first Spitfire 1 fighter planes weren't delivered until 1938.

By the time war broke out, 27 of Fighter Command's 37 squadrons were equipped with either Spitfires or Hurricanes. Air Chief Marshal Sir Hugh Dowding now demanded 53 minimum squadrons for the command. Fortunately, the ''phony war'' gave the British aircraft industry the breathing space it needed to put more muscle on the RAF.

In 1939, as in 1914, the RAF promptly deployed aircraft to France, but this time the best of the planes, the Supermarine Spitfires, were kept at home. First to arrive in France were ten squadrons outfitted with Fairey Battles, a large, low-wing, single-engine bomber with a crew of three. (A Battle shot down the first German plane of the war, on September 20, 1939.) They were quickly joined by two squadrons of pointy-nosed Bristol Blenheims, a twin-engined craft and the first British plane in action in World War II.

Roland Prosper Beamont, who ended the war as a wing commander with both the Distinguished Service Order and Distinguished Flying Cross, recalls just how green the first RAF arrivals were. Nearly five months went by before he saw his first combat.

It was a day in March, and he was flying at 20,000 feet on patrol between Dover and Calais, when he saw an airplane above him. ''There were two of us, and I climbed up after it. As I got fairly close to it, I recognized it as a Heinkel 111. My Hurricane proved faster than my colleague and I was out ahead of him. And then I noticed there were sort of funny things flying by the cockpit . . . I was totally green and didn't really know what was happening. But I realized eventually that it was the rear gunner of this Heinkel shooting at rather long range at me, and the sparks were tracer bullets going by. And so I thought, 'Well, that's all right, he's in range, perhaps I can shoot him.' And then, all of a sudden, everything started to go purple and black and I just lost contact with the situation. I came to in an inverted dive, going very fast just above the cloud sheet. I'd lost contact with this enemy airplane and was able to roll out level just before going into the clouds, a good thing because the bottom of the cloud was pretty well on the deck. I found out later I had oxygen starvation and, in the hurry to scramble for this particular operation, I'd failed to plug my oxygen pipe into the socket in the cockpit. A pretty unsatisfactory first combat.''

Green, perhaps; unresourceful, never! Walter ''Count'' Krupinski, one of the most colorful (and successful—197 victories) of the Luftwaffe's aces, describes his first combat mission. Flying in the same squadron with Gerhard Barkhorn—who would rank as the Luftwaffe's number two ace with 301 victories—Krupinski recalls the alert: a Bristol Blenheim reconnaissance aircraft was heading out from France, back across the Channel to Britain.

"We took off immediately just as he was out to sea and we shot all our ammunition on that bird, but he got home safe. Every time when we were in shooting position, he turned—very hard. We two 'top guns' of the Luftwaffe couldn't hit him at all!"

France's *Armée de l'Air*—founded in 1933 but not a substantive reality until 1936—went into the war with 1,200 modern planes, including 826 fighters, plus 1,500 aircraft which dated back to the early 1930s. By the invasion, on May 10, 1940, the number of front-line aircraft had been increased to 1,501, including 784 fighters. Many of the latecomers—Curtiss P-40 Warhawks—had been acquired in the U.S. following the "cash-and-carry" exception to the neutrality laws. The best of the French fighters—the new Dewoitine D 520, a fast aircraft armed with four machine guns and a 20 mm cannon—were too few and too late to affect the outcome. The backbone of the French defenses, the Bloch MB 151s and MB 152s, and the Morane-Saulnier M.S. 406, were clearly outclassed by the Me.109Es.

Two top German aces discuss the French. Hans Jabs: "The French were very talented pilots. But they had inferior aircraft. Personally, I believe the French were as well trained as the English." Fritz Losigkeit (68 victories): "A poor comparison. The French were so demoralized that there was little fighting spirit or discipline. It was very seldom that a French pilot engaged, and when he did, he'd turn back almost at once. They rarely fought, although we tried to challenge them. Naturally, there were pilots who did—for example, I lost a first lieutenant in a battle over southern Paris."

The Belgians were able to add only 11 Hurricanes, 27 Italian Fiat CR 42 biplanes, 15 Gloster Gladiators—the RAF's last biplane—and a handful of Fairey Battles. The Dutch, who had stayed out of World War I and wanted nothing to do with World War II, had 125 planes in all.

Opposing the Allied air forces were 3,634 front-line aircraft of which 1,562 were bombers and 1,016 fighter planes, including 860 operational Messerschmitts.

During the autumn and winter months of the phony war, both sides concentrated on bombing raids. Such fighter plane duels as occurred came about in random meetings of stray aircraft. Increasingly heavy losses suffered by the RAF's unescorted Wellington bombers—12 of 24 shot down over Wilhelmshaven on December 18, 1939—finally convinced the RAF to halt daylight bombing raids altogether, a decision they stubbornly adhered to.

German bombers suffered, too. The first attack on the UK was staged by a force of Ju.88 bombers on October 16, 1939, against shipping anchored near Forth Bridge, Scotland. One of the leading attackers was shot down by Flight Lt. G. Pinkerton piloting a Spitfire—the first kill over Britain since World War I. A few months later (February 22, 1940) yet another episode evoked the picturesque tradition of World War I. Flying Officer G.V. Proudman, flying a Spitfire Mk.IIB, which was one of the first equipped with a 20 mm cannon, blasted large chunks off a disabled bomber. His commanding officer and squadron leader A. D. Farquhar followed the bomber down as it made a crash landing on the Scottish coast so as to prevent the Germans from setting fire to their plane. But Farquhar had the bad luck to set down on soft ground and

German ace Hans Joachim Jabs did not have a particularly high opinion of the fighting spirit or ability of French pilots.

flipped over. He had to be rescued by the German crew—but not before they set fire to their plane.

Training and tactics in the RAF did not evolve as rapidly as improvements in the aircraft themselves. Mainly, those tactics reflected a conviction that the fighter plane's principal mission was to interdict massed formations of bombers and an underestimation of the resilience of fighter pilots, such as their ability to retain control of their planes while maneuvering at high speeds.

Another RAF tactic—flying in three-plane V formations, a tactic discarded by the Germans in Spain—proved a death-trap for some in the early days of the war.

Adolf Galland, soon to lead Germany's entire Fighter Arm, comments: "From our first encounter with Western opponents, they flew in close formations—right up to and including the Battle of Britain. We took advantage of the disadvantages of the English tactics."

The RAF, in time, changed its tactics—for two reasons. The first was its disastrous losses during the Battle of France. The second was an extraordinary man: the aforementioned Air Chief Marshal Sir Hugh "Stuffy" Dowding, commander of Fighter Command from 1936 through 1940. Sir Harry Broadhurst, who would one day rise to air chief marshal rank himself, explains: "You have to remember, all the basic training had been defense against bombers . . . the commander-in-chief was wise enough to foresee that we were going to have fighters as well as bombers to fight against."

Sir Harry, who had already won dispatches for his flying exploits in 1931 in India, had seen for himself from the first days of the war just how dangerous a situation the RAF faced. He had volunteered for service in France "and had only been there about 24 hours and I wished I had never volunteered to go near the place. We were completely outnumbered. Bombed the morning I arrived. I hid under the wing of my airplane as protection. There was nowhere else to hide. I got to the wing I was taking over, it was Hurricanes. There were no squadron commanders fit to fly, and my predecessor had left with a nervous breakdown. Completely outnumbered, hordes of 109s and dive-bombers and so on. We were attacked all night as well as by day. . . . " Sir Harry got his first kill, an He.lll bomber, on November 29, 1939. By the time he headed back to England in the summer of 1940, he was commanding two wings, but they had by then been shot up so badly they only had the strength of one original wing.

On the evening of May 9, 1940, the Germans struck lightning blows from the air and on the ground. The phony war was over.

At 2:30 A.M. on the morning of May 10, 64 German soldiers crossed the border of neutral Holland to launch the invasion. Two hours later, airborne units began landing in Belgium. To the south, the main force—the 44 divisions of General Von Rundstedt's Army Group A, including seven panzer divisions—drove deep into the Ardennes, a feat the French military had thought impossible for tanks.

The air attack began at break of day (May 10) with coordinated strikes on allied air fields at Lyon, Nancy, Metz, Dijon, and Romilly. Scores of planes were destroyed on the ground, and in many instances, French pilots returning to their bases discovered in dismay that the airfields had already fallen to the rapid German advance. More than 150 Morane-Saulniers were trashed by ground crews to keep them from falling into German hands.

German ace Adolf Galland recalls his first encounter with the RAF, over Arnhem. "I thought they were Belgians, because our information was so miserable we didn't even know that the English had ten squadrons on the mainland already." Galland, who ended the war with 104 public kills (and many more he didn't bother to count because, as a general officer, he wasn't supposed to be flying combat), scored his first combat victory that day (May 12). Flying with Lt. Gustav Rodel, he attacked eight Hurricanes and shot down two. Later that day, he shot down another Hurricane in a five-plane flight.

Junkers Ju. 88s such as this one conducted the first German air raid over a British city—the first step in a reciprocal campaign that would eventually lead to unprecedented, devastating Allied aerial attacks on almost every major German city.

Allied aircraft losses mounted steadily, peaking on May 14, 1940. That day—which the Germans named *Tag der Jagdflieger* (the day of the Fighter Pilot)—the Luftwaffe launched 814 fighter sorties, shooting down 90 planes, among them 40 of the 71 Fairey Battles in action.

Not everything went the way of the Germans, however. The first time a Spitfire and a Messerschmitt 109 met, the Spitfire prevailed. It happened on May 23, 1940, when two Spitfires, assigned to escort a two-seat trainer on a rescue mission to France, were attacked by a handful of Me.109s. The Spitfire pilots, Alan Deere and Johnny Allen, took them on and scored at least one kill while damaging one other.

By the end of May, the entire British Expeditionary Force and much of the cream of the French were fleeing the beaches of Dunkirk. The Dutch, who had not fought a war since 1830, put up surprisingly stiff resistance. But the Dutch will was broken on May 13 when the Luftwaffe—in an air raid triggered by a mistaken reading of a ground signal—bombed the center of Rotterdam, killing 814 civilians. The high command surrendered the next day. The Belgians, who had balked at cooperating with the British and French for fear of compromising their neutrality, fought stubbornly once war came. But the 700,000-man Belgian army survived only 17 days of blitzkrieg, capitulating at midnight on May 27.

A rapidly disintegrating French army continued to fight for another three

May 23, 1940, marked the first meeting of a Messerschmitt.109 and a Supermarine Spitfire in combat—a meeting in which the Spit prevailed.

weeks. On June 3 and 4, Parisians got their first acrid taste of war when German bombers dropped an estimated 1,000 bombs on the city. The end was not long in coming. On June 17, the aged World War I hero, Marshal Henri Philippe Petain, heading the Vichy government, announced the surrender on the radio. In those three weeks before the end, another 220,000 Allied troops were rescued by British ships from France's northwestern ports—Cherbourg, Saint-Malo, Brest, and Saint-Nazaire. In those three weeks, the Germans took one million prisoners. Under the harsh terms of the armistice, two million French soldiers went into German captivity.

Britain was now alone.

On July 16, Hitler gave his generals until mid-August to prepare a landing operation against England. It was code-named Operation SEALION. On July 19, in the last of his great Reichstag speeches, Hitler offered England peace. Three days later, the British turned him down cold.

The die was now cast; the Luftwaffe was assigned the role of softening up the enemy for the attack. It had a week to do the job, after which the Führer would decide whether to go ahead with the jerry-built invasion plan. Unlike most of his commanders, Hermann Goering was almost buoyant about his new responsibilities.

But Goering had not reckoned with the RAF.

Some Luftwaffe pilots went into the new war cockily, jauntily. Herbert Ihlefeld, born in Pinnow, Pomerania, on June 1, 1914, had already seen action in Spain, where he scored seven victories. Now a lieutenant commanding JG.77's 1st Group, Ihlefeld had his mechanic paint a large ship on the nose of his Me.109, with Churchill, smoking a fat cigar, towing it. "We as pilots," he remembers, "were entirely convinced at that time that we could defeat the English air force."

Others, viewing the coming struggle from a higher perch, weren't so sure. Adolf Galland, already a colonel at 29, says flatout: "England should not have been attacked at all. The Luftwaffe should not have been exposed to the Battle of Britain."

Johannes "Macki" Steinhoff, ultimately a full general, then a group commander like Ihlefeld, considers the battle in more cosmic terms: "The Battle of Britain differed from other battles, from other campaigns of World War II, in that it was basically a struggle between two air forces. No ground troops were involved. The navy was not involved. It was fought by young people who were actually identical. They were brought up the same way. They had the same concepts. They were sportsmanlike, intelligent. And both of us, the English and the Germans, were people who were almost identical. The tragic aspect of this was we tried to kill each other."

Dietrich Hrabak (125 kills) learned, as would so many other Luftwaffe aces, that what they faced now bore little resemblance to what they had known before. In Hrabak's case, he had already seen action in Poland and France. He describes the new arena of combat: "There was a new quality in the kind of combat compared to what I had experienced before . . . The difference was primarily that other kinds of aircraft were being flown there, and my first contacts with the Spitfire were very unpleasant for me." The first time Hrabak faced Spitfires, he lost two wingmen. The next time, he attacked "what I thought was the last plane in the string and had a good position behind him, but he wasn't the last one, he was the second to last—so I was shot down again."

The German aces soon discovered that they were up against more than just tough new aircraft. Fritz Losigkeit, who flew with and against pilots from Spain, France, England, America, Japan, and assorted other countries, describes the British pilots as "excellent. We realized that very quickly due to the quick reactions of the English pilots. They knew when to engage and when to turn back. That became particularly evident in the period before the Battle of Britain, because we always tried to lure them away from England, and they simply never came."

Pilots were (and would remain) the RAF's big problem as the Battle of Britain approached. The Germans had 10,000 trained pilots in 1939; Fighter Command had 1,450. But with each week, Fighter Command was able to add 50 more pilots to its anemic ranks.

Though inferior in numbers—and, at that point, tactics and training—the RAF possessed important offsets, not the least of which was that it fought to defend its homeland. German aces discovered very quickly the maelstrom into which they had plunged.

Hans-Joachim Jabs: "At Dunkirk, we fought against the British for the first time. Then, in August, when we began the attack against England, which we flew to from the French coast of the English Channel and from Guernsey, we experienced for the first time the real fighting power of the English. They utilized the full power of their fighter squadrons, which we felt very, very quickly. They had the same kind of personalities that we did, but their Spitfires and Hurricanes were better aircraft than our Me.110s."

Besides operating close to its own bases, Fighter Command enjoyed yet another advantage: a control and warning system. Its ground Observer Corps and, above all, the 50 "Chain Home" radar warning stations lined the coast from the Orkney Islands north of Scotland to Land's End in Cornwall.

The Luftwaffe would operate at one other major disadvantage: its premier aircraft, the Me.109, was frequently forced to fight at the limits of its 410-mile operational range. As a practical matter, that typically meant an Me.109 had only 20 minutes for combat over England, and the German pilots never knew where the defending aircaft would be until they were hit. Heading home over the English Channel, these pilots, lacking the fuel to fight, could only dive home to safety in France or the Low Countries. (On September 9, for example, 18 Messerschmitts crashed along the French coast, some in the water, when they ran out of fuel.) By contrast, the RAF pilots, with their sophisticated warning system, could wait until minutes before the battle began to take to the air, then hone in directly on the preidentified incoming raiders, frequently chasing the defanged 109s all the way back to France. Furthermore, a German plane downed over Britain meant the Luftwaffe lost a pilot as well as a plane; more often than not, the British lost only the plane.

The war in the skies would ultimately prove decisive. But none could know it in that tense summer of 1940. At the time, it appeared inevitable that the war would be fought finally on the ground. Once again, as Armageddon neared, factories were the first .LS1/line of defense for the woefully weak British forces.

Some of the complacency of the phony war lingered on even after the fall of France—but only briefly. Wing Comdr. Roland Beamont: ''When we came back to the UK, we were coming back to what appeared to be a peacetime England. Nobody back in this country had any idea of what was going on across the Channel. The day I flew back, I remember looking down at village greens across Sussex and seeing games of cricket going on, as if nothing had ever happened.'' (But Beamont knew, and he imparted not only an urgency, but skills as well to his pilots. The Australian Desmond Sheen, who served with him, reports that ''at Maidstone, I think the outstanding man was Rollie Beamont, who had a fantastic reputation.'')

Alone now, the complacency of Britons gave way to anxiety. Shop windows were taped to limit bomb-blast shattering. Blackouts were strictly enforced. Gas masks were carried everywhere. In increasing numbers, men signed up for the Territorial Army, young women for the Land Army so as to free farmers for military service.

The Battle of Britain really began even before Hitler launched Operation SEALION. On July 10, in the first phase, German bomber formations of 20 to 30 planes began pounding cities along the south coast as well as any convoys they sighted. Alan Geoffrey Page, brand new to 56 Squadron at Manston, remembers that day well: ''There were six of us, six Hurricanes, and we were advised that there were about 90 aircraft approaching—20 of them bombers going for a convoy in the Channel, and the remaining 70 fighter escorts. Three in our formation were assigned to go down and attack the 20 bombers, and the other three of us to go up and attack the 70 enemy fighters. Well, being young and stupid, it didn't really worry me too much because I was too busy getting the airplane organized for combat: putting the guns on the fire position, seeing that the gun camera was working, setting the engine for maximum power, and so forth. So suddenly we saw them, this mass of ants with wings coming towards us: Messerschmitt 110s—a twin-engine fighter, not very good for daylight fighting—and the Messerschmitt 109—a deadly opponent.

''So our leader took us just above the Messerschmitt 110s which, strangely enough, formed themselves into a defensive ring. So, when they went into this defensive circle, I dived into it. We'd lost formation, the three of us, by then. And I distinctly remember clearing my eyes, firing my guns, and diving through the middle of it and coming out the other side. At that point, the dangerous 109 fighters came down from above. And this was all just a mess of German Iron Crosses and not knowing what you were doing. I'll tell you something which is quite extraordinary, and I'm sure that other fighter pilots will vouch for this: you're in the middle of a big fight and then it's as if the Almighty took a cloth and wiped the slate completely clean, and there's nothing else in the sky. You're all alone.

"But on this first occasion, I saw one other fighter, a German 109, circling in the distance. So I turned towards him, and we did a head-on attack. I could see little lights twinkling on his wings—he was firing at me!—and I'm sure he could see the same. I think we passed within six feet of each other, neither giving way at all. And 17 years later, someone came to interview me and they threw a German magazine on the table and said, 'Have you seen that?' And it showed a photograph of this German fighter pilot standing beside his burned-

Three members of the 242nd Squadron: (left-to-right) Flight Officer Willy McKnight, the legendary Douglas Badar who lost both legs in a prewar training "prang," and Flight Lt. Eric Ball.

out Messerschmitt and the caption underneath was—whatever his name was, Daul, I think—who had a head-on attack against a pilot of Ag-Page-56 Squadron. So 17 years later, I got another confirmed victory. But that was my first combat and I remember it well." Page scored his first "official" kill three days later, and ultimately got 15.

Gunther Rall, the world's third-scoring ace (275 victories), flew one of those "deadly" Me.109s. But much of its sting had been neutralized by the role assigned to it. Rall voices the complaint of many Luftwaffe fighter pilots as he describes those initial encounters with the "mighty Royal Air Force" over the English Channel: "We had to escort the Ju.87 Stuka dive-bombers— a slow-flying aircraft, heavily loaded. And you know, there's a mentality among bomber pilots; they would always want the fighters very close to them. So we had to stick with them under orders from higher command. In some cases, I had to lower my flaps to stay with the Ju.87s—and that made us an extremely beautiful target for the Spitfires on top of us. We lost a lot of pilots that way." In fact, of 36 pilots in his 8th Group of the legendary JG.52, 32 were lost in the early stages of the Battle of Britain.

Fritz Losigkeit is even more emphatic: "The duty as an escort pilot protecting the bomber formations is both terrifying and awful. My Me.109 was much too fast for the bomber formations. One couldn't engage the enemy at low altitude when you spotted him underneath because you can't fly too far away from the formation. You have to stay close, otherwise the enemy can move in and you can't return in time to protect the formation. So one has to curve around the formation, either up in front or behind, or above or below, and the commanders of the bombers wanted you to fly parallel with them, as close as you could.

"We couldn't do that and still provide adequate protection because the attacker moves in very fast, typically in a high speed dive, releases his air mines or torpedoes, and then pulls out at low altitude and flies off.

"For that very short period of time, you had to have a very good position to be able to defend at all. They flew unbelievably fast. When I'm in a bank trying to return to the formation, he's already attacked the formation. That means those couple of escorts, usually a pair, would have to split up to defend against the swarms of attackers, and one of the escorts would have to remain close to the bombers. Otherwise, you don't have any protection."

Rall adds an oblique reference to Luftwaffe Commander Herman Goering's slurs against his own pilots—slurs which galled—blaming them for the failure to bomb Britain into submission: "It wasn't a question of cowardice of the young pilots. Inexperience was one reason for those quite unacceptable losses. But wrong tactics was another reason."

Dietrich Hrabak—who ended the war as a major general—seconds Rall: "My mission during the Battle of Britain was, firstly, attack fighter, which meant I had the freedom to hunt in the area south of London due to our range limitations, and to try to engage any enemy aircraft which were about to enter combat. The English strategy was to send out aircraft only when our bombers were in range, which meant that we were then used as bomber escorts. These escort missions were very unpopular, because we had to fly at the same altitude and speed as the bomber formations, which meant that we could not utilize the tactical superiority of our fighter aircraft: the speed, the climbing capability, and the maneuverability. As a result, we suffered great losses at the hands of the English."

The Germans lost 296 planes in July and August in this phase of the attack;

Bimmel Mertens, crew chief and comrade in arms, stands next to Erich Hartmann who is sitting in the cockpit of his Me.109 fighter. Luftwaffe pilots were tactically excellent but hamstrung by ineffective strategic leadership.

the British 148 fighters—also four destroyers and 18 merchant ships. By July 25, all coastal convoys had been stopped; on July 28, the Dover destroyer force had been withdrawn, and the following day the use of destroyers in the Channel by day was prohibited. But here, as in the Battle of France, the iron nerves and determination of Air Chief Marshal Hugh Dowding, chief of Fighter Command, made a crucial difference. Now, as then, he refused to allow his main force fighters to be drawn into the battle, frustrating the Luftwaffe's main objective.

One of the fiercest fights of that first phase of the Battle of Britain took place on July 28 and included a dogfight between two of the top and most colorful aces of the European theater: South African Adolph Gysbert "Sailor" Malan and Werner Mölders. Malan saw his first action over Dunkirk, shooting down five German aircraft. He ultimately ran his score up to 35, the highest- scoring pilot in the RAF until 1944. An innovative tactician, Flight Lieutenant Malan was among the first to break his squadron out of the V-formation (or "vics") and meet the Germans in pairs; his *Ten Rules of Air Fighting*, published in 1942, was distributed to all RAF pilots. As for Mölders, as a measure of the man's grit, he had continuously to fight against air sickness in order to fly combat. The top Condor Legion ace in Spain (14 kills) and Germany's foremost fighter pilot combat tactician, Mölders was the first German fighter pilot to reach 20 kills. He already had 39 kills when selected to take command of JG.51's 120 planes. The very next day, July 28, in a battle involving over 300 German fighters and approximately the same number from the RAF, Mölders' plane was shot up by Malan. Although the plane was badly damaged and he himself wounded in the knee, Mölders managed to limp across the Channel and make a belly landing near Calais. (The following year, Mölders became the first in the Luftwaffe to shoot down 100 planes, the first of the German armed forces to receive the Knight's Cross with Diamonds, and the youngest *Oberst* [group captain, or colonel] in the Luftwaffe. With 115 kills to his credit, he had just been promoted to the newly created post of General of the Fighter Pilots when, in September 1941, he was killed in a bad weather crash. He was 28 years old.)

Two of Malan's men salute their leader: Robert Lawrence Spurdle, from Wanganui, New Zealand, "He was the cohesive force in the whole squadron"; and Desmond Frederick Burt Sheen, out of Canberra, Australia, "One of the finest fighter pilots the world has ever known."

The next phase of Operation EAGLE was a fiasco from the start. The goal was the destruction of the RAF. To that end, the Germans assembled two primary air armadas grouped in *Luftflotten* (air fleets). Across the Channel, Fighter Command was organized in four groups. Although it had occurred to Fighter Command early on to move its fighter planes deeper inland so as to force German bombers to fly without fighter cover, this was not done. The reason: the bases were more than mere airfields; they were integral parts of the elaborate command/control structure. The RAF would have to stand and fight where it was.

Delayed six days by bad weather, *Adler Tag* (Eagle Day) was finally set for dawn of Tuesday, August 13, the day Fighter Command was to be destroyed. But the day broke with heavy overcast and fog on most airfields and thick cloud cover over the Channel. Orders were given to delay the attack until the afternoon—but arrived too late to reach some units. A handful of bombers reached Eastchurch airfield at the mouth of the Thames but, having lost their fighter cover in the confusion and bad weather, they were easy prey for Hurricanes. The Luftwaffe lost 34 planes that day, the RAF only 13. And Day Two wasn't much better: because of poor coordination, the 250 attacking planes were mauled by 14 squadrons of Hurricanes and Spitfires.

Dietrich Hrabak flew some of these missions. The new experiences did nothing to temper his earlier misgivings: "Without question, at least for myself, our most serious contenders were the English. I first experienced the enemy superiority over the Channel during the Battle of Britain. Their aircraft, the Spitfire and the Hurricane, were an equal match for our Me.109, and the pilots were, in my opinion, much superior to the pilots we engaged over Poland and over France."

Thursday, August 15, 1940, the fighting reached a crescendo. The Luftwaffe launched 1,800 sorties in seven raids from all three air fleets. All seven raids were met—with punishing results. The Germans lost 75 bombers, twin-engined fighters, and a few Me.109s; British losses were 34 planes. Air Fleet 5 was also knocked out of the Battle of Britain that day. Because the Germans were hitting the south so hard, they supposed that the north would be largely undefended. Wrong: Approaching Tyneside, a force of 100 Air Fleet 5 bombers and their 34 Me.110 fighter escorts were set upon by seven squadrons of Hurricanes and Spitfires.

Both sides continued to make mistakes in tactics, as well as in choices of weapons. "Sailor" Malan was not alone in breaking away from the rigid "vic" formations; Wing Comdr. Roland Prosper recalls: "Changes didn't come from command. We evolved tactics to suit the battle by seeing how the Germans went about it. Once we adopted the German 'finger-four' formation, then it became very much more satisfactory."

On the German side, fighter pilots were hamstrung by orders to fly close to the slow bombers. General Galland describes it as a case of "crippling the missions by high command orders . . . I had the biggest fights with Goering, telling him that a German fighter pilot, even if he is at least equal to the British Spitfire and Hurricane pilots, can only be effective when he has their speed, not the low speed of the bombers. A fighter pilot should be aggressive and offensive all the time."

Peter M. Brothers, an ace with 15 kills, remembers that RAF pilots "took a lot of advantage" of the plight of the German fighter pilots." As the Battle of Britain wore on, the German fighter pilots increasingly resorted to *freir jadg* (free chase) tactics.

But although the Luftwaffe took heavy losses—595 planes—during the first two phases of the battle, it nevertheless managed to grind away at Fighter Command. With 372 planes lost in the first two phases, RAF reserves were down to 230 aircraft. And only 63 of the 154 pilots killed, missing, or severely wounded had been replaced; those still flying were beginning to feel the fatigue and tension of being forced to scramble again and again.

The next phase—attacks on aircraft production and inland fighter bases—began on August 24, following a five day weather-enforced lull. Over the next two weeks, the Germans sent over 1,000 planes a day; in all of August,

Hawker Hurricanes, such as I.R. Gleed's here, inflicted heavy damage on the Luftwaffe at the outset of the Battle of Britain, forcing German pilots to reconsider the difficulty of destroying the RAF.

the Luftwaffe flew 4,779 sorties against Britain. The attacks concentrated on 11 Group's seven key sector stations: Biggin Hill, Debden, Hornchurch, Kenley, Northolt, North Weald, and Tangmere. Sited on the airfields themselves, and poorly protected against bombs, the sector stations—each of which controlled three fighter squadrons—suffered heavy damage. The worst was reserved for Biggin Hill, the key station defending London.

Examples of heroism abounded as those late August attacks intensifed. Entire squadrons, such as 56 Squadron, were virtually wiped out, the pilots dead, wounded, or burned-out. The strain on the Germans was equally harsh. Perhaps worse, in that, unlike the RAF, they were never given a moment's respite but thrown back again and again into battle, no matter their exhaustion.

Johannes Steinhoff—one of Germany's top aces with 176 air victories—remembers well those savage days. ''The Battle of Britain was for me the toughest part of the war. '' He returns to his earlier theme: ''Looking back now, it was ridiculous that young people of two nations, being completely alike, were trying to kill each other. The whole battle was a fair duel, a fair fight between knights. And the old-fashioned dogfights still took place—turning around in circles for two to five minutes.''

The RAF lost 466 fighters in that phase, but what was worse, another 103 pilots were killed, with 128 seriously wounded. German losses were lighter: 214 fighters, 138 bombers.

Werner Mölders and his aide Hartmann Grasser reviewing the tactics of a recent air battle that resulted in a kill for Grasser. Cooperation between flight leaders and wingmen was considered crucial in maintaining an edge against enemy flyers.

Had the attacks continued, the British Fighter Command could never have survived. But Hitler ordered the attacks shifted to London itself. It was one of the greatest blunders of the war. The blitz, as it came to be known, began on September 7 and continued for 57 consecutive nights, not ending altogether until May 16, 1941.

It began with a navigational error. On the night of August 23, a dozen German bombers missed their aircraft factory and oil tank targets on the outskirts of London. Instead, they dropped bombs on the center of the city, destroying some homes and killing some citizens. The next night, the RAF retaliated, sending 81 bombers to Berlin. Only about 29 of the bombers threaded their way through the dense cloud cover and found their targets. Damage was negligible, but the effect on German morale was tremendous—it was the first time that bombs had ever fallen on Berlin. And not a single British plane was downed.

Those first ten days of September were remembered by all who lived them as days of blue skies, brilliant sun—and gut-wrenching anxiety. At night people huddled together in shelters, listening to their world literally crumbling overhead. The mornings were filled with the sounds of attacking airplanes and the screams of defending RAF fighter planes; the skies were splashed with trails of smoke and dotted with the puff balls of parachutes descending.

One of those parachutes over Kent on September 5 belonged to Desmond Sheen, who had to fight to get free from his plummeting Spitfire after being ''bounced'' from behind. He finally freed his feet, which had been wedged in the cockpit: ''I bailed out at about 12,000 feet,'' he recalls, ''and I had a grandstand view of the whole of the battle, because there were bombs falling in London, or near London, near the dock area. Others over Dover. And there were dogfights overhead—an Me.109 went down in flames quite close to me.'' He came down in a field at the edge of Maidstone Wood, landing ''light as a feather.'' Struggling out of the 'chute, ''an army chap came up and waved his revolver at me—I had my Australian air force uniform on, which was dark blue. Anyway, we established good relations. A good party.'' He also reported seeing a policeman on a bicycle followed by spectators. ''The policeman's first action,'' he reported, ''was to produce a flask, the second to express surprise that I had waited so long before getting out of the aircraft.''

Barry Sutton wasn't quite so lucky when he was shot down. Badly burned hands prevented him from hanging onto the parachute shroud lines, so he dangled helplessly until ''finally I began to see the trees and telegraph wires coming up very closely, and a road, and then people running. The people running turned out to be women, and I actually landed in the middle of the street in a village near Canterbury, and these old dames came running out, I am not absolutely certain, but I think with rolling pins in their hands—they were very hostile looking and quite certain I was a German.''

David Cox—David George Samuel Richardson Cox—thought it was curtains when he was forced to bail out over Kent in September of 1940. ''One had heard stories about some of the German pilots shooting our chaps down when they were coming down in a parachute. I'd been shot down by four Me.109s, and they circled me. I thought, 'Ooh, you know, this is it!' But nothing happened.'' (Did he put much stock in the parachute-shooting stories? ''Personally,'' he says, ''I think there may have been the odd occasion, the odd hothead.'') Colin Gray recalls circling the crash of a 109 he had shot down and watching as three men approached the pilot climbing out of the wreckage. Taking off his parachute, the German jumped on it. Gray says he "assumed he was an 'ace' whose vanity was hurt."

That phase of the war was lost, but the battle raged on. The Luftwaffe flew a total of 7,260 sorties during September. At mid-September, they employed a new and damaging form of attack: delayed action bombs, which had to be dug out, at great risk, while entire areas around remained cordoned off. On one night in September, German planes flew 1,500 sorties, dropping 2,200 tons of bombs.

The Luftwaffe paid a heavy price for those bombs: from the onset of the blitz through the end of the month, the Luftwaffe lost 380 planes; the RAF lost 178. The July-through-October toll was 1,773 aircraft—over half the Luftwaffe's total strength. The RAF lost 915 fighters and 414 of its 2,500 fighter pilots, including 44 from Allied nations, mainly Poland. (Though only 5 percent of the total of RAF fighter pilots, Poles accounted for 15 percent of the Luftwaffe planes shot down.)

Duncan Smith—who had to overcome his mother, malaria, and his own rambunctiousness to win his RAF wings—remembers well his first combat victory during that dramatic autumn of 1940. "It's rather like your first love affair," he avers. "I don't think you could forget anything about it, really." Actually, the very first time he nearly downed a plane it turned out to be one of his own. It happened as he was finishing Spitfire training at Harden. With neither radio nor oxygen and not much experience (around six-seven hours in Spitfires to that point), he took the fighter up to 40,000 feet—which was about 4,000 feet higher than the plane was supposed to go. Not surprisingly, "I suddenly found myself tearing down towards the earth with all bells ringing . . . completely iced up . . . I couldn't see anything." Coming in to land, "there was a bloody great tail section immediately ahead of me; I'd never seen it because it had come motoring in from miles away, very low, straight into the airfield to land." The "bloody great tail" belonged to an Avro Anson light transport plane "come to collect ferry pilots, or dump some, or something or other." Trying to pull out, Smith "went straight through his tail. There was a great sort of sizzling noise and I spun in. I don't remember anything until I came to in the ambulance. The old Anson, being a lady that she was, she just went skating on and landed on her tummy. Everybody was all right, though, except for one wrecked Spitfire, one badly damaged Anson, and a not-too-happy young pilot officer."

Somehow, Smith managed to persuade his superiors that he really ought to fly this "number one airplane, not just in the RAF, but in the world. I mean it saw the Messerschmitt 109 off and it saw the Italian Macchis off. It saw everybody off." Which is how he happened to be at 611 Squadron in the Midlands where, "except at night, not an awful lot of German activity went on other than the occasional 'recky' [reconnaissance plane] and the occasional Heinkel or Dornier raiding the shipping lanes on the east coast of England and on up to Scotland.

"It was on one of those days," Smith relates, "and we were at readiness when we were called to scramble. We went off just off Boston, in Yorkshire, and lo and behold, we intercepted a Dornier 17. I did three attacks and I think I hit the engine and the fuselage area, and then we had to break away because we ran out of ammunition." Down below, Observer Corps spotters watched as the bomber plunged to the sea about two miles off the Norfolk coast—the first of 19 victories Smith would score.

Smith adds: "I got the rear gunner and I can see him now go slumping over his gun. I was terribly pleased with that until later on in the evening, and I thought, you know, what a four-letter chap I really was because he hadn't a hope. Anyway, we got the airplane, and that was our job, really—wasn't it?"

As the bombing switched from daylight to night raids, the British struggled desperately to upgrade their night-fighter capability. Going into the Battle of Britain, they had only the obsolete Bristol Blenheim Mk.lF twin-engine aircraft. Experiments with airborne interception (AI) equipment led to the introduction late in the battle of a twin-engine aircraft expressly designed for night fighting: the Bristol Beaufighter (Mk.IV-AI), armed with four 20 mm cannon and six machine guns.

The bombing went on: 9,911 sorties in October, including a new weapon—incendiary bombs. A total of 70,000 were dropped in the first fire-bomb raid on October 15, forcing Londoners to take to the roofs rather than to the basements so as to form a gigantic fire-watching network. But Britons learned to live with the danger.

The raids tapered off, picked up again, and finally halted. Hitler had his eye on a bigger target: Russia. But before it ended, the blitz took the lives of 40,000 British civilians, wounding another 50,000. Over 100,000 homes were destroyed.

The blitz claimed two other casualties: Churchill inexplicably fired Air Chief Marshal Dowding, and Group 11's Vice-Marshal Keith Park—viewed by many as the real brains behind the RAF's winning air war against the Luftwaffe.

The twin engine and seemingly pencil thin Dornier 217 was used in light bombing and reconnaissance roles.

* * *

Looking back on the decision to switch the attack from the RAF itself to London, General Galland avers that "London saved England." Then, analytically: "If you ask where the mistakes were that caused the loss of the Battle of Britain, you have to cast a wider net and ask yourself: was the Luftwaffe suited or built and armed for such a purpose? Were the airplanes suited, were the tactics suited? And then you come up against all sorts of hurdles and you realize that the Luftwaffe was never meant to fight Britain."

"Macki" Steinhoff expresses a similar view: "It was lost from the beginning." This man, who went on to wear four stars as the leader of Germany's postwar air force, ticks off the handicaps faced by German pilots: tactical but no strategic concepts; fighters that could reach only one-tenth of Britain's territory; no "drop" fuel tanks to extend range; amateurish leadership that kept changing the main targets. "The Battle of Britain is seen by many, correctly, as a turning point in the war. I concur with this view because the mastery of the sky was lost by the Germans at that point."

Winston Churchill summed it up in an immortal phrase before the House of Commons: "Never in the field of human conflict was so much owed by so many to so few." The Few were the 2,500 fighter pilots of the RAF.

3 RED STAR RISING

Fedor Archipenko with medals.

Fedor F. Archipenko was eight years old when he decided to be a pilot. An R-5 biplane had crash-landed in the Byelorussian village next to Bobruisk, where he lived. His grandfather harnessed the horse and the two set out for the scene of the wreck, five kilometers away. That day, he saw a pilot for the first time ever, and then and there his dream of becoming a flyer was born.

It was a day to remember.

Below:
Three German soldiers wave to an Me.109 as it heads off to do battle.

Mikhail Komelkov with medals.

There would come another day to remember—Sunday, June 22, 1941.

At approximately 3 A.M., 6,000 big guns opened fire with a mighty roar. In fast order, 80 infantry divisions, 18 panzer divisions, and 12 motorized divisions blitzed across the Soviet border from the Baltic to the Black Sea. Backed by 2,400 tanks and 2,700 Luftwaffe planes, they were the vanguard of a 3.4-million man army, the mightiest military juggernaut the world had ever seen: Operation BARBAROSSA. Before it was over, more than 20 million men, women, and children would be dead.

"That day I will remember for my entire life, I will remember to the end of my life," said Fedor Archipenko. Newly commissioned as a junior lieutenant in the Red air force, Archipenko was the operations duty officer of the 17th Fighter Aviation Regiment in the city of Kovel, in western Ukraine. He recalls: "Beginning at 4:25 in the morning, around 50 German planes bombed our field, coming back four times. Only myself and the duty pilot, my squadron leader, Ibragimov, and the guards, the security forces, were there. Because it was Sunday, the rest had been allowed to go home on leave.

"The air field was small, two by three kilometers. You can imagine the kinds of horrors that took place at the air field. Then, by afternoon, the pilots and ground crews started arriving. Many of them, their hair had turned white. And some of them had even begun to stutter from fear after experiencing that kind of bombing.

"Around three o'clock that afternoon, the first day of the war, I was able to make one reconnaissance flight, from Brest to the region of Lvov along our border. I could see the entire area on our side was—if one could put it that way—on fire. Everything, the towns, the villages, the settlements, everything was burning.

"That was how my first day of war with fascist Germany ended."

The experience of Archipenko—who would go on to become a colonel and an ace with 30 kills—was far from unique. All along the front, the 66 Soviet frontline air bases were hit, their neatly parked planes blasted to bits. Pilots had to take turns flying the remaining planes. Mikhail Komelkov, only 19 when the shooting started, was among them, stationed with the 122nd Fighter Pilot Regiment near Grodno.

"At 3:40 in the morning, 19 Messerschmitt 109s hit our field. An hour and a half later, they came back again for a repeat attack. Of the 76 IL-16 fighter planes, only ten remained."

So stunning, so total, so fierce, was the attack that, by the end of that first day, 1,800 Red air force planes had been destroyed—1,500 of them on the ground. The Germans lost 32 planes. Surprise had been total.

And yet, there is no reason why it should have been.

On the night of August 23-24, 1939, in Moscow, the foreign ministers of Germany and the Soviet Union signed one of the most cynical treaties in the annals of man—a Pact of Nonaggression, which allowed them to swallow up Poland, Latvia, Lithuania, Estonia, the Bessarabia region of Romania, and to regard Finland as part of the Soviet "sphere of influence."

When Adolf Galland first learned of the plan to attack Russia, he was "shocked, completely shocked by the idea that this would be the opening of a second front." Galland had time to adjust psychologically, because he heard it from Goering around Christmas 1940. Many Luftwaffe pilots did not. Walter Krupinski remembers:

"As we left Ostende [on the English Channel, in Belgium], we crossed Germany in two or three stages, finally reaching a field in East Prussia, my old homeland. We thought we would fly all the way through Russia to engage the British somewhere in Persia [Iran]. That's basically what the young pilot at that time in the war knew and believed. Our propaganda had said up to that time that we had a first-class pact with the Soviet Union, and as a result of that, we received a lot of important raw materials. To that moment when we landed in East Prussia, we had absolutely no idea that this meant that we were going to attack the Soviet Union."

Within a week, the Luftwaffe destroyed more than 4,000 Russian warplanes. The "relatively small numbers of I-16 fighters that rose to defend their bases were swatted like flies by the experienced Luftwaffe pilots in their superb Bf.109s." Walter Krupinski, a swashbuckling fellow his cronies called "Graf Punski," or "Count Punski" (one of Germany's top aces with 197 kills), recalls: "After approximately 14 days of combat, we didn't see any Russian aircraft whatsoever. Not for a long time."

Yet the Russian air force was far from finished, though it was well into 1942 before it could recover from the first punishing blows. Russia went to war with the largest (though far from most modern) air force in the world—12,000 planes. Between August and October 1941, 80 percent of Russia's factories were moved deep inside the country, beyond the reach of Germany's short-range bombers. The Luftwaffe soon regretted its fateful decision in 1936 not to build a long-range, four-engine bomber. In 1942, Soviet factories, secure beyond the Ural Mountains, rolled out 10,000 planes, which, moreover, were more the equal of their German attackers. Still more planes came from across the seas.

But at the beginning, the Russians had to make do with what they had, and most of what they had was no match for the battle-hardened Luftwaffe and its fleet of modern fighters. Col. Fedor F. Archipenko, who went on to score 30 kills in 102 dog-fights, remembers: "Our planes were old and slower than both the fighters and bombers we were up against. That's why we had such heavy losses that first year of the war—that and the fact that so many planes

Me.109s provide cover for a formation of four Ju.87D Stuka dive-bombers.

This prewar Polikarpov 1-16, shown being assembled on an airfield, was no match for German aircraft.

Sergei Dolgushin in uniform.

were shot up at air fields along the border." Said Krupinski of the antiquated Russian fighter planes, mainly Polikarpov I-154 biplanes and Polikarpov-16s, the stubby, slow, and weakly armed "Ratas" (Rats) of Spanish Civil War vintage: "We called them rat-a-tats."

Lakyev recalls another problem cited by many Russian pilots: poor radios, or none at all. Lakyev said the idea of installing radios in fighter planes was one cribbed from the Japanese in Manchuria when Russian pilots noticed that their adversaries had "some way" of communicating with each other in the air. Finding a "kind of a box with a radio receiver" in a downed Japanese plane, he said, the Russians "took it, studied it, and they made one just like it."

Sergei Dolgushin was assigned to one of the "rat-a-tats" at a base only 17 kilometers (12 miles) from the border when the attack began. "At three o'clock, the alarm went off," he recalled. "We all ran towards our airplanes. At 4:20, when the Messerschmitts appeared over the air field, I had to take off. While I was taking off, during that first dogfight, I was hit 16 times."

Looking back on those early days, the German ace Johannes Steinhoff comments: "We had no idea what the Russian air force would look like, and they arrived in masses . . . flying airplanes that were completely obsolete— old biplanes, old Martim bombers, with a maximum operating altitude of about 3,000 feet and very slow. So shooting them down was peanuts, absolutely peanuts. But the other side of the coin is that they were insanely brave."

So "insanely brave," indeed, that many among them, their ammunition exhausted, simply rammed German bombers. Soviet ace Fedor Archipenko relates one incident later in the war. He had just blasted one Ju.87 out of the sky when, out of ammunition, he found himself closing on another. "I decided to ram the plane. I was approaching from behind, to ram it with my propeller, when it made a turn and opened the bomb bay. The bombs started falling, and I barely got away without having the bombs fall on me and blow me up. That is a mistake I didn't make again."

Erich Hartmann—the ace of aces—talks of another problem plaguing the Russians in the early days of the war. "The Russians were never allowed to make decisions on their own. They attacked only when they had the order to attack. The Russians came with 30 to 40 planes; the leading plane would give

the orders over the radio—number such-and-such, attack number such-and-such. We could always make our own decisions.'' Walter Krupinski amplifies: ''The Russians were extremely good bomber pilots. They would fly wing on wing, very closely packed, providing us with a large target which we could strafe from side to side. But they would maintain formation, nonetheless, carrying their rockets and bombs to the target. They were very brave, but I would say, even today, that the Soviet pilots were simply not flexible enough.'' Johannes Steinhoff agrees: ''In the first day of the war with Russia, I saw bombing units down to their last plane. And the last bomber kept on flying until he was shot down. They were not very flexible, but they were very brave.''

By the end of November, German tanks were only 18 miles from the center of Moscow. By year's end, 3.5 million prisoners had been taken, another million Russians killed or wounded. But by then, the Germans were facing a new and deadly enemy, the one that vanquished Napoleon's Grand Army of 1812: the Russian winter—and a winter of historic proportions it would prove.

Fighter pilot Friedrich Oblesser remembers well ''the time I came to the combat unit itself [and] the temperature was 40 degrees below zero, the wind blowing, snow more than a meter high [39 inches]. At that time, I was flying ground attack missions, and I can't remember one mission when at least one of the guns didn't jam. The problem was that we were not then prepared to keep our guns—certain moving parts of the aircraft itself—working with the oil we used. To start the engines was already a problem, a nightmare. Later, we used wax instead of oil to lubricate the guns and the moving parts.''

Reflecting on it, he adds: ''Today's pilots couldn't possibly imagine the conditions under which we had to fly. The mud, the rocks—taking off and landing in deep snow. The snow was cleared only superficially, so the planes had to plow their way through deep snow when landing and taking off. It took great skill to take off. Going forward and backward and maneuvering the plane in the snow.'' Once in the air, things didn't get any better: ''At that time, the aircraft themselves weren't heated. It was as cold in the cockpit as it was outside. The engine had to be running half an hour or so before it was comfortable in the cockpit.'' Dietrich Hrabak remembers ''sitting and freezing and hoping that the enemy was coming, because your heart beat faster then and you got somewhat warmer.'' Ace Gunther Rall cites another problem:

Erich Hartmann sits in the cockpit of his Me.109. Ursel, his wife's name, is painted inside a heart on the side of his aircraft.

Werner Mölders explains a point in the application of tactical air power to General, later Field Marshall, Heinz Guderian in Russia.

"The men weren't prepared for a winter campaign. They didn't even have the right kind of gloves."

German fighter pilots, accustomed to superior housing, learned to adjust to primitive living conditions during the Russian campaigns. Heinz Marquardt explains: "We lived in tents, officers and [pilot] sergeants together. There were no showers in Russia. Cigarettes, small talk and waiting—that was about it."

Winter did bring one respite. "During the summer, we flew an average of six sorties a day on the Eastern front," said Friedrich Oblesser. "Each sortie lasted around an hour and fifteen minutes. In the winter, because there was so much less daylight, we flew only three. So much flying, with the other tasks we had to perform, meant you were always very tired and wanted to sleep every chance you got. Looking back, I would say that lack of sleep was the hardest part of all."

As for the Russians, no matter how accustomed they were to harsh weather, winter gnawed at them too—particularly the epochally severe winter of 1941-1942. Arkady Kovachevich puts it in focus. "By 1939 or 1940, we had stopped using skis on the planes. That meant we had to clear the snow covering the air fields. Second, we had to keep the engines constantly warm, and that meant turning them over every 20 to 30 minutes or so. Pilots worked through the night with the ground crews. Then there was the problem of where to live. Since we were living in the field, that usually meant digging into the earth and making dugouts, and then figure out how to heat the dugouts."

On December 6, the Russians launched their first great counteroffensive across a 1,000-mile front against the exhausted and winter-paralyzed Wehrmacht. The Germans were forced back as much as 200 miles; it was the first time since German troops goose-stepped into the Rhineland in 1936 that Nazi Germany had tasted defeat. In the air, the reinvigorated Russians formed elite Guards Regiments equipped with newer LaGG-3 fighters. The brainchild of the talented designer Semyon Alexseyevich Lavochkin, this single-seat monoplane went into service in 1941, mainly on the Finnish front. Although it would never live up to the interceptor role originally intended for it, the LaGG-3 proved versatile as ground support, bomber escort, and attack plane

Arkady Kovachevich, center, joins other Russian pilots around a campfire, fending off the bitter cold.

Dietrich Hrabek, in front of his airplane,
talking with his crew chief.

against the less dangerous of the German fighters. Russian pilots, noting
weaknesses which included a tendency to go into a spin following particularly tight turns, dubbed them "guaranteed varnished coffins."

Still, the Soviet pilots climbed into their cockpits and took to the skies,
vowing, "Fight to the last drop of blood and last breath—forward to victory!"
Ivan Lakyev explains: "I think patriotism is the main thing . . . During the
war, I saw people pick up and carry a truck. Word of honor. You'd say it was
impossible, but they did it. Each person had that strength, that force. Where
did we find the strength? In love for our motherland."

In those first months alone, four German *Jagdeschwadern* (108 to 192
fighter planes) accounted for more than 1,000 kills apiece, shooting down as
many as 114 planes in a single day. Dietrich Hrabak, already a seasoned air
warrior, tells of his first contact with Russians: flights of the ancient (1931),
huge (four-engines, crew of 6 to 10), slow (top speed, 134 mph) and low
(ceiling, 12,469 feet) Tupolev TB-3 bombers. They flew unescorted across the
Black Sea to bomb the Romanian oil fields at Constanta. "We were at an
abandoned air base and didn't have any radio, we didn't have anything. So I
put some planes up, and we were on cockpit alert when we got the call,
scrambled and hit them. We shot down around 51 bombers that first week."
But no matter how many were shot down, hundreds more took their place.
Friedrich Oblesser (ultimately, Lt. General Oblesser) remembers: "I think the
Russians were always the majority. There were always masses. [So] you had
to keep your eyes in the back, to the left, to the right, ahead and down and up
because they were everywhere."

Ask Gunther Rall. November 28, 1941, began with the cold—minus 40
degrees that day. Like Oblesser and so many of his Luftwaffe colleagues, Rall
and his people simply didn't know how to cope with those frigid tempera-
tures. "It was a hell of a job getting the engine running, especially in the
morning. We learned our lesson and later on we pumped fuel into the oil lines
right after our last mission to get the oil more fluid in the morning. On that
particular day, I had a fighter sweep about 2 P.M., when darkness was setting
in. It turned dark and I ran into Russian fighters. We were not very high. And
I hit one fighter [his 36th kill] . . . got blinded by the flames of that plane. And

Third-scoring German fighter ace
Gunther Rall.

right then another Russian fighter squeezed underneath me and shot off my engine, or shot my engine dead.''

When a German tank crew finally figured out how to extricate Rall from the cockpit of his downed plane, he was unconscious, bleeding from head wounds and, he learned later, with his back broken in three places. He came to in the back of a frozen and bouncing truck, in excruciating pain. The doctors took one look at him and said, ''Poor boy, forget flying!'' The doctors were wrong; he was back in a cockpit six months later and would go on to become the world's third-ranking ace with 275 kills.

In Russia, Luftwaffe fighter pilots were forced to learn new tactics. Over Britain, the battles had been fought at relatively high altitudes and high speeds, but the Russian pilots brought them closer to earth, slowed them down.

Heinz Marquardt, the flying sergeant who shot down 12 planes in a single day, remembers being forced to fly below clouds as low as 100 to 300 meters (330 to 1,000 feet) from the ground. Dietrich Hrabak, who had already seen action over Poland, France, Britain, the Balkans, and Greece, explains: ''The battles with the British took place at the maximum altitude of the Me.109. In Russia, it was completely different. We never fought above 4,000 meters [13,200 feet], usually without oxygen, and usually at much lower altitudes because the Russians attacked with their Sturmoviks and flew at altitudes under 1,000 meters [3,300 feet], or they flew with bomber formations at a maximum altitude of 3,000 meters [10,000 feet].'' Other German aces reported treetop combat at speeds as low as 100 to 280 miles per hour. Not a few of those fighter planes crashed into trees during such low-level dogfights, among them, top ace (204 kills) Lt. Anton Hafner, killed in low-level combat with a Soviet fighter when his Me.109-G Gustav hit a tree.

German aces called the Sturmovik ''the cement bomber.'' Officially designated the Il-2, it first reached Soviet units in April 1941. The entire front section, from engine support to cockpit, was a single armored shell, and the entire fuselage was protected with 4 to 13 mm-thick steel plating and 5 mm-thick duraluminum. The result was to make this flying tank practically invulnerable to light weapons. Two 20 mm cannons, two machine guns, and 600-kilogram bomb load also made it a formidable weapon.

But even ''cement bombers'' have Achille's heels. The Sturmovik's was discovered by the man his friends called ''Bubi,'' by the Russians ''the Black Devil.'' That man was Erich Hartmann, the world's top-scoring fighter pilot with a stupefying 352 victories.

Hartmann, born April 19, 1922, in Weissach, Wurtemberg, had been flying since he was 14. His mother, an aviation enthusiast, taught him first to fly a glider, and two years later, a powered airplane. He joined the army in 1940 and transferred to the Luftwaffe six months later. ''I was in the last grade,'' he said, ''and we were told that if we volunteered to go to the front, we wouldn't have to take our final exam. That was the main reason for volunteering.''

Despite his youthful air experience, young Hartmann's military career had a decidedly inauspicious beginning: he taxied a Stuka dive-bomber into a building, one of three planes he piled up during training. In October 1942, he was assigned to the crown jewel of the fighter squadrons, JG. 52, based at Soldatskaya in the Caucasus. He made a mess of his very first combat mission.

''I was flying with Sergeant [Edmund] Rossmann,'' Hartmann recalls, ''and was surprised when he called me on the radio to say he saw the enemy. I didn't see any enemy, so I flew behind Rossmann. He made a kill, and I made

Opposite page, clockwise from top left:

Ilyushin Il-2 in flight over the clouds.

Walter Krupinski, wearing Knight's Cross and leather jacket.

Tupelov Tu-2 in flight.

A field-stripped Erich Hartmann works on his Me.109.

Gratz, Gunther Rall, Wachowick stand in front of an Me.109.

a sharp turn—and lost him. Then I climbed another thousand meters in order to fly back. And then I saw a plane heading towards me and thought it was a Russian. But it was Rossmann. This time, Rossmann flew behind me.'' If that weren't enough, the young pilot made a crash landing, which earned a reprimand from the new wing commander, Dietrich Hrabak.

Hrabak impressed two rules on his pilots: ''Fly with your head—not with your muscles,'' and, ''If you return from a mission with a victory, but without your *Rottenflieger* [wingman], you have lost your battle.'' He assigned the wayward Hartmann to a man who, in 1,100 missions, had never lost a wingman, the legendary Walter Krupinski. Although only 18 months older than Hartmann, Krupinski already had 60-odd kills to his credit. He taught Hartmann to get so close to his prey before firing that a hit was guaranteed.

On November 5, 1942, the pupil got a chance to put the lessons to work. At noon, his four plane *schwarm* was airborne, intercepting 18 Sturmoviks escorted by 10 LaGG-3 fighter planes. As usual, the Soviet pilots were flying in tight formation. Heading for the nearest Sturmovik, Hartmann quickly closed to 300 feet, as he had been taught, then watched as his cannon shells bounced off the plane's heavy armor. Maneuvering his Me.109 below the Russian, he aimed for the plane's underslung oil cooler in the nose. The Sturmovik belched smoke, then exploded. Before he knew what had happened, debris from the shattered Sturmovik showered Hartmann's plane, setting his engine afire and forcing him to crash-land. Twice more, Hartmann would be forced down by debris from planes he fired upon at close range.

Hartmann gradually developed another useful tactic. ''I would attack only if I was 2,000 meters above them. Then I would come down with great speed and shoot them down. I would always tell my colleagues that when your windshield was filled with the enemy aircraft, that was the time to pull the trigger and shoot.'' Bubi Hartmann had something else going for him: ''Graf''

Lily Litvak smiles over one of the unlucky Luftwaffe flyers she downed.

Litvak poses.

Krupinski: "He was a very good shooter, even from long distances." Such a crack shot, in fact, that he sometimes scored a kill with a single cannon shot.

From mid-March until May of 1942, the two mighty armies hunkered down. The Russians had lost a million dead, with more than three million taken prisoner. German losses were 900,000. But the Germans held (and would, until the summer of 1944) the heartland of Russia, their dreams ending at Stalingrad.

But not only men were fighting and dying at Stalingrad. In the skies over the tormented city, a 22-year-old girl created a legend. Her name was Lily Litvak. Against great odds, this diminutive, dark-haired girl became a fighter pilot, shooting down an even dozen German bombers and fighters. They called her "Rose of Stalingrad." Killed in an aerial duel over the crumbling city, she was followed in death by her fighter pilot-fiance.

Then-Lt. (and later Lt. Gen.) Gunther Rall:

Q: "Were you aware that Russian women were flying as fighter pilots in combat?"

A: "Never. You know, this was a story we also heard during the war, but nobody, nobody ran into a woman pilot."

That's because they never "ran into" Lily Litvak—or Anna A. Timopheeva Egorova, senior lieutenant. When war broke out, Egorova was an instructor at an air club in Kalinin, 100 miles northwest of Moscow. By September 1941, she had overcome official resistance and was flying a plywood P-02 on reconnaissance missions (277, in all) on the Southern front, the only woman in her squadron. (The P-02, she explains, is "a very small plane . . . it could be shot down by any kind of weapon, really—practically by a rifle. And the only thing we had was a pistol.") By September, she was in assault aviation, but instead of the Sturmovik she expected, she got an Su-2 (a two-seater fighter-bomber plagued by problems). Jokes Egorova: "The motor was fueled by castor oil. The pilots said the air field smells of pancakes." During the next two years, she flew combat, winning the grudging respect of the men who flew

Erich Hartmann, wearing wreath and holding a glass, is surrounded by fellow pilots and ground crew.

with her. "It was hard. It was particularly hard to lead a group of men into combat. That was more difficult than flying the plane, controlling the formation, controlling the battle itself." She did it well enough to be awarded her country's highest decoration, Hero of the Soviet Union, added to her Order of the Red Banner.

On August 19, the 6th German Army—300,000-men strong—laid siege to Stalingrad, a siege destined to last for 60 days. On the night of the 23rd, the Luftwaffe pounded the city in an air raid comparable to the worst of the London blitz. By morning, smoke and flames rose a thousand feet into the air. As a strategic objective, the city was finished. But Hitler was as stubborn in insisting it be taken as Stalin was that it not fall.

During those 60 desperate days of siege, the Luftwaffe was given the job of supplying the trapped garrison with the 300 tons of supplies it needed daily to fight on. But the Luftwaffe had suffered heavy losses during the siege of Moscow and had diverted many of its transport planes to support the new German offensive in North Africa. On February 2, the Germans capitulated. Of the 100,000 Germans captured and marched to Siberia, only 5,000 ever saw their homeland again. In Germany, normal broadcasting was suspended for three days; in Moscow, the bells of the Kremlin were rung.

Johannes Steinhoff was there: "Stalingrad was a crime. A crime of bad leadership. How could they leave 320,000 soldiers to their fate? I flew back and forth into Stalingrad to protect those planes that were removing the survivors, the wounded, and the starving. Flying back once, over a stretch of 100 kilometers or so of no-man's land covered with fog I saw a plane carrying the wounded under attack by two Russian fighters. It was circling the Don [River], trying to get away. I had no more fuel and asked myself, 'Can I engage?' I knew if I did I would have to make a belly landing—so I did, shooing them away from the transport. It flew off, and ten minutes later, I landed on my belly."

A pair of P-39s in a power dive.

The fall of Stalingrad is etched on Dietrich Hrabak's memory. Like Steinhoff, Hrabak was among the German fighter pilots flying in and out of the shattered city. "I saw the German troops being surrounded, I saw German troops retreating before the Russians—something I had never seen before. I saw the encirclement worsen, and eventually, I saw them bombarded with rocket and artillery fire. Stalingrad is my most powerful memory of the Russian war." For Walter ["Count"] Krupinski, "It was when we realized this isn't working anymore—a bitter memory, very hard to deal with."

Sergei Dolgushin was there, too, at 21 already a squadron leader in the Red air force. He remembers the cold—especially hard on the ground crews ("they were the ones who had to heat the oil and water for the engine, get the plane ready")—and he remembers being outgunned. But he was never a leader without followers: "I never had to utter any lofty, loud, patriotic words. I simply said, 'Let's go,' and that was that. Everybody understood that they were fighting for their motherland."

"Graf" Krupinski remembers another element of it as though it were yesterday: "We were on patrol over the Kuban bridgehead [June 1942] when one of my pilots behind me called out—'Spitfire!'

"I was shocked. Everybody was shocked, because we were thinking, not only do they have Spitfires now, but they also have British pilots flying them. So all the pilots did just what we had done in England—looked around to see where he was coming at us from. But they were Russian pilots and they flew their Spitfires as badly as they had flown their other planes."

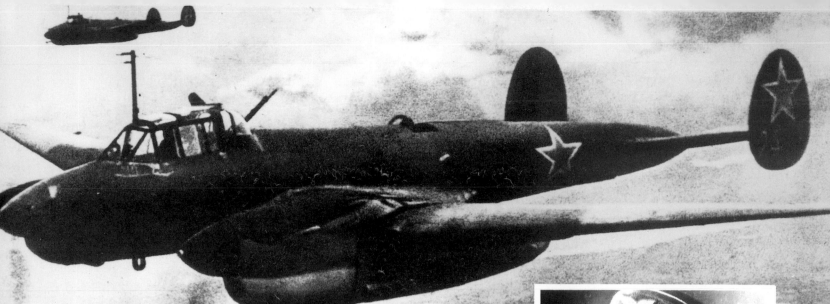

The Spitfires were the vanguard of a whole new dimension to the war: Lend-Lease, massive shipments of arms to the Soviet Union from its major allies, Britain and the United States. For many German fighter aces, the entry of the United States into the war meant the tide had decisively turned against them.

Erich Hartmann: "Stalingrad—that's when Lend-Lease came in. After Stalingrad, we saw American Airacobras [P-39s], Kingcobras [P-63s], and we saw Spitfires and Hurricanes from England, but no Russian planes. . . . this is what caused our downfall." Colonel Hartmann's bitter judgment was echoed by other Germans.

As for the Soviets, Arkady F. Kovachevich described his first encounter with Lend-Lease in the flesh: "I remember when the American representatives and pilots and the British forces came and saw the conditions in which we were working at the air fields, they were surprised and indignant. They said, 'How can you work in these conditions?' We were taking off from a freshly dug potato field!"

Johannes Steinhoff.

Above:
Pe-2 in flight.

The British hated the P-39D. After only a few days in the Battle of Britain, British pilots said squaring off against the Germans in an Airacobra was tantamount to suicide. The Russians loved them. To Mikhail Komelkov—Hero of the Soviet Union and one of its top fighter pilots with 32 kills—one press of the P-39's button, and it was curtains for the enemy: "the plane you were attacking," as he put it, "simply fell to pieces."

The Bell P-39D Airacobra packed a 37mm cannon and four heavy and two light machine guns. It was fitted with racks to carry a 500-lb bomb load, and made an ideal ground attack plane for the kind of war Russian airmen were fighting. It was also deadly when Russian pilots got close enough to open fire on their German opponents.

"This armament," said Mikhail Komelkov, "was really a sheath of fire." He was serving with the 25th Regiment in the southern Caucacus when the first Airacobras and American bomber planes began reaching them in December 1942. As welcome as they were, they came with a problem: "All the signs in the planes were in English, and most of us didn't speak English." Arkady Kovachevich clarifies: "But we learned to master it quickly, in 10 days, in fact." Komelkov called the Airacobras "outstanding." Kovachevich "would have wanted it to be even better. But, without going into the shortcomings, I would point out that the pilots very much liked how comfortable the cockpit was, all of the systems, including the weapons systems—highly reliable.''

The P-39s brought the Russian fighter pilots something else: their first reliable radios, including two transmitters and three receivers. What a difference they made! Fedor Archipenko explains: ''The radios in our planes at that time weren't very good. But with the Cobras, we could maintain communication with other pilots, with ground stations, and it didn't give you a headache because it was so easy to work with.'' Arkady Kovachevich amplifies: ''Without exaggeration, I can say that our pilots felt that their success, the success of their actions, to a significant extent was due to that excellent radio communication. They even said that we cut our losses by about half because of that.''

Mikhail Komelkov illustrates with a combat anecdote from the 1943 campaign in the southern Ukraine. It was north of Tokmak, near the Dnieper River, and his Airacobras were coordinating the ground attack. Advancing Red tanks bogged down again and again attempting to breach a 30-kilometer antitank trench the Russians themselves had dug in 1941. Diving low on a reconnaissance flight, Komelkov saw that the Germans had set up camouflaged fields of fire so that ''no matter how many tanks attacked, they ran into the barrels of those guns, and the tanks just kept burning. When I reported what I saw, the division commander said to me on the radio—there was a great radio on the Cobra!—'Go back again, make sure!' I went back, this time without my wingman, and reported again what I saw. As a result, our troops were able to move into fruit orchards, and that's how our troops managed to get through. And that's where they cut off Crimea for the enemy. They simply slammed the door there.'' (Behind that door, the German 17th Army was wiped out. More than 100,000 Germans and Romanians were killed, 30,000 captured.)

A P-39 in flight.

Rall, together with Field Marshall Wolfram Von Richtofen.

Colonel Komelkov offers another example of just how important a role the Airacobra would play in the crucial days ahead: "It was after the battle of Stalingrad, when there were battles raging in the Kuban—about 200 fighters concentrated on each side. It started on February 16, 1943, and that was when the Soviets made mincemeat of the best fascist air groups."

American and British planes were far from being the only secret of Soviet success. Russian designers and factories equipped their forces with not only great numbers of new aircraft, but greatly improved planes. The first of the important additions was the MiG-3, introduced in 1941. Unlike the Airacobra, which performed best at the lower altitudes the Soviets preferred, the MiG shone at over 16,000 feet. But relatively few were built, because by 1943 the Soviets had a far better fighter, the Yakolev Yak-3. Erich Hartmann and Gerhard Barkhorn rated the Yaks "the most troublesome and dangerous of Soviet fighters." Though lightly armed (one 20 mm cannon, two 12.7 mm machine guns), the Yak was fast (403 mph at 16,400 feet), and highly maneuverable.

German pilots noticed the difference. Friedrich Oblesser comments: "As the war in the East went on, the Russian pilots became more and more experienced in the fighting business, and the aircraft they had were absolutely first class . . . Our aircraft became heavier and heavier. The Russians went the opposite way, building aircraft sometimes better in climbing and in turning and maneuverability. The Russians really built aircraft then with excellent aerodynamic performance."

Amid the madness of it all, there were lighter moments. One time, Gunther Rall recalls, "We were stationed in a field near the Terek [River] in the Caucasus, and we were plagued by field mice. They entered the planes and gnawed on everything. The ground crews really hated those mice. Well, comes an alarm because a Russian reconnaissance plane is in the vicinity. I jumped into my plane, took off—and then noticed there was a hole in my instrument panel, an instrument was missing. I had climbed to an altitude of 6,000 or 7,000 meters [20-23,000 feet] when all of a sudden a mouse stuck its head out of that hole—probably suffering from a lack of oxygen at that point. It looked at me, and I looked at it, and I just had to laugh, it was so funny. Then it disappeared, and was never seen again."

Following his defeat at Stalingrad, the Red army went over to the offensive, inflicting heavy losses on the Wehrmacht. But the Russians both overextended—and underestimated—the man many believed was Hitler's most gifted general, Field Marshal Erich von Manstein. Counterattacking on February 3, 1943, Manstein soon recaptured the territory the Russians had gained, and the front stabilized. Now, the Kursk Salient became an irresistible target for a new German offensive.

At 2 A.M., July 5, the Russians, forewarned, launched an attack one hour before the Germans were to strike. The next ten days witnessed the greatest tank and aerial battles of the war. The Soviet attack caught the Luftwaffe flatfooted.

The view from the Soviet side: "At Kursk, we were fighting with everything we had. Our main assignment was to cover the battlefield, to protect our troops crossing rivers." The speaker, Vasily Kubarev, scored 10 of his 18 kills in the violent skies over Kursk, earning a Hero of the Soviet Union decoration.

At the climax of the battle on July 14, eight Yak-3 fighters attacked a

Hartmann in his Me.109 somewhere in Russia before he painted his wife's name on the aircraft.

Vasily Kubarev in uniform.

formation of 60 Junkers Ju.88 bombers and Messerschmitt escorts—without losing a single plane. Kubarev led six of them. ''We left that fight without letting them even bomb the target,'' he adds. That same day, another flight of 18 Yaks engaged 30 Messerschmitts, shooting down half of them while losing only one of their own.

The days of the reluctance of Russian pilots to attack—the days of German mastery of the skies—were over. Fedor Archipenko, an Airacobra pilot: ''Superiority was on the side of Soviet aviation now.''

A new sense of pride radiated from the Russian pilots. Gunther Rall remembers well: ''They painted their aircraft, some red, from the nacelle to the cockpit. They were very proud, self-confident, aggressive then. There had been a tremendous development from 1943 onwards, from an obsolete, poorly equipped, defensive air force to a highly skilled, well-equipped air force.'' Mimicking the Germans, Rall recalls, the Russians established *experten* (expert) units, ''one headed by Pokryshkin.'' Pokryshkin, Alexander Ivanovich, was Russia's second-scoring ace, with 59 kills, most of them in Cobras. Mikhail Komelkov flew with him in an Airacobra regiment and knew him to be ''a first-class pilot, superb, the best kind of pilot.''

An aircraft mechanic before becoming a pilot, Pokryshkin was 28 when the Germans invaded. His first victory in the sky was very nearly his last. He watched transfixed as the Me.109 he had shot down spun to the ground in flames. Like many other pilots with their first kill, he was so engrossed watching that he was very nearly flamed by a second Messerschmitt; he escaped by putting his MiG into a screaming dive, levelling out at ground level. That lapse aside, he brought a studious, methodical approach to air combat. Some of his ideas he adapted from *Mes Combats*, a book written by his hero, the French World War I pilot, René Fonck. Others came from a diary in which he made careful notes of what worked, what didn't.

Pokryshkin gradually weaned other Russian pilots to his ideas, key to which was his doctrine: ''Altitude, Speed, Maneuver, and Fire.'' Among tactics he developed was a snap-roll to reduce speed, causing his adversary to overshoot and get ahead of him. The essence of his approach was psychological: sudden, swift, violent attack maneuvers to unnerve the enemy pilot. Ultimately, he would become part of the elite Guards Regiment.

In five weeks of continuous, man- and machine-consuming carnage that summer, the *Ostheer* had been forced back 150 miles along a 650-mile front. The battle at Kursk was a disastrous failure for the Germans.

During the summer of 1943, the survival chances for German fighter pilots on the Eastern front plummeted—only 25 percent of them lived through their first four missions. Among those shot out of the sky that summer was the ace-of-aces, Erich Hartmann. While flying escort over the Donetz basin in southern Ukraine for a force of Stuka bombers, Hartmann's squadron was bounced by about 40 Russian fighters. ''Flying low, you don't hear it over the noise of the engine until too late—the *wak-wak-wak*.'' It was ground fire. Next: ''Smoke belching from my engine. I headed back for the west, thinking I could make it to our lines. Then, fire erupts from the engine, and I made a crash landing. I was climbing out of the cockpit when I saw a truck, but then I engine might explode, I slumped back into the cockpit. Then the Russians came—I didn't understand anything. Maybe because they thought I was wounded, they dumped me in the back of a truck without a guard.'' According to one account, four hours later a Stuka dived on the truck; the driver lurched into a ditch, the Russians ran for cover, and ''Bubi'' Hartmann

A ground crew member adjusts Hartmann's parachute straps somewhere in southern Russia, June 1944.

Alexander Pokryshkin in uniform.

Above left:
A twin-engined Me.110 with shark teeth artwork displayed.

ducked into a field of high sunflowers. Several hours and several adventures later, he was back in German-held territory.

The Russian fighter pilots were more than emboldened now; they were dauntless avenging angels. Arsenii V. Vorozheiken was a fighter pilot with the soul of a poet whose verses were forged in battle. At the beginning, he tells us, there was the ''child, a child who doesn't know what fear is and rushes into battle.'' That's how it was for him during the ''shadow war'' of 1938-1939 between the Russians and the Japanese in Manchuria. Vorozheiken was blooded at the battle of Khalkin-Gol, shooting down six Japanese planes in dogfights that, he said, involved 500-600 fighter planes in combat.

Vorozheikin comments: ''I started the war at the Khalkin-Gol without fear. I was like a child who doesn't know what fear is and rushes into battle. When I landed, I looked at the plane and I thought, well, I realize how dangerous it was to be fearless.'' The colonel adds an afterthought: ''When they say of someone that he is a fearless person, that's a lie. I think a fearless person is an abnormal person.''

During World War II, 46 German planes fell before his guns; quite remarkably, he was never shot down himself. He speaks of the summer of 1943 and the Battle of Kursk: ''The sun was already starting to set, but the order came and four of us took off. We flew towards the front line, but there was nobody there. Below, two tank armies were engaged in a great battle, but in the air, everything was quiet. We decided to fly into enemy territory, deep, so that we might find an enemy plane to shoot down. We are perhaps 15 kilometers behind the front lines and the sun is nearly gone from the horizon when I see a suspicious-looking cloud. The cloud turned out to be enemy Heinkel 111s, their best bombers, the ones which had so often bombed Moscow and Gorki, my home town. Here they are headed for some strategic objective, and there are only the four of us to stop them. Only a little light remained.

''The first attack was a failure, because more than a hundred guns—maybe even more than 200 cannon and machine guns—were firing at us. It was a rain of fire bristling at us. One of our planes was hit and had to leave the fight. The second attack failed as well. On the third, we ran out of ammunition. Our weapons were now useless in countering that armada. To that point, we had shot down four bombers, but the rest of them formed up even more tightly, like one black cloud of steel. Popular wisdom says there are three features of human character that are tested and tried in only three cases: Friendship, when you're in trouble; courage, when in battle; and wisdom, in rage. Rage was boiling up in us.

''I felt helplessness, hatred. I wanted to charge into that cliff. One weapon was left to us: ramming them, to finish off three more bombers. But experience told me that we would die without repelling the onslaught of the entire armada. We needed to ram them in a different way. All three of us had to

He-111 in flight.

Arsenii Vorozheikin with medals.

move in front of this armada, with our wings very close together and, like a shell, split that cliff of metal.

"The decision was taken, and when we turned, the enemy met us with a rapid fire, head-on attack. I aimed right for the lead plane, the flagship plane, intending to hit him from the top with the propeller. I waited for the strike, for the blow. There was none. I didn't understand. I heard nothing.

"I opened my eyes. Sky. Why sky? Where did that come from? Turning around, everything became clear. Those huge, enormous, colossal planes, those multi-ton bombers, had been unable to resist our offensive, our head-on attack. Like butterflies, they fluttered away through the skies, dumping the bombs on their own troops, then turning back.

"Afterwards, the three of us landed. My wingman was Demian Chernyshev, from Belgorod. When this battle took place, he was a young boy, 23 years old, with very, very dark, black hair. But after that mission, his temples had turned white.

"There's a saying that people fight with their nerves alone. Some of these folklore sayings you understand only when you yourself live through what they tell us. After that flight, we understood what it means 'to fight with your nerves alone.' In that battle, our nerves, our will to victory, turned out to be stronger than the steel of the fascists."

In the aftermath of Kursk, the Soviets pounded the Germans. They out-armed and outmanned them. In the air, the picture was the same: in 1942, Germany produced 15,409 planes, Russia 25,436; in 1943, the numbers were 24,807 and 35,000.

But it was in manpower that the tide had turned decisively; the Russians now enjoyed four to one superiority over Germany. By the following year, 20 million Soviet men and women were in uniform, the largest military force the world has ever known.

The brutality of the war was to turn uglier yet. Both sides feared the war's horror. Heinz Marquardt echoes other German pilots: "The worst fear was of being shot down over Russia. It was well known that pilots downed over Russia were shot upon capture."

The once-mighty Axis war machine was crumbling. German cities and factories were being pounded night and day. On September 8, 1943, Italy surrendered. German forces were ousted from Africa, were soon driven from Sicily, and in September, found themselves facing British and American troops on the European continent for the first time. The Luftwaffe and other units in Russia began to withdraw to the West. Defeat was in the air.

4 TIGERS OVER CHINA

There were never more than 70 of them fit to fight at any one time, and they only lasted for seven months, but during that time, this small band of brave men, by their dash and deviltry, their daring and their gallantry, guaranteed a place for themselves among the immortals of aviation. They were the Flying Tigers.

P-40 flight line.

Their sudden appearance over the China skies stunned the Japanese; their reckless stunts filled the American heart with pride; their cocky deeds captured the imagination of the world.

Their mission was to protect the rickety supply lifeline to a sprawling nation which had been battling raw and bloody aggression since 1937. Born in American-style ''secrecy''—one of the pilots heard about the unit from a squib in *Time* magazine—the American Volunteer Group (AVG) never numbered more than 112 pilots, but as the Flying Tigers, they quickly became household words, racking up an astonishing kill ratio against the best the Japanese had to offer.

What ''The Few'' of the Battle of Britain accomplished over England, the Flying Tigers wrought over the jungles of Burma and mountains of China. Not since Baron von Richtofen's ''Flying Circus'' of World War I had there been a unit like them.

In 1931, the Japanese seized Manchuria, and over the next six years picked off the country's great cities—Peking (Beijing), Tientsin, Shanghai, Nanking, and Hankow. By late 1938, China was all but sealed off from the outside world.

China's leader, Chiang Kai-shek, realized that with the Japanese in control of China's ports he faced economic strangulation, and he ordered the building of a 681-mile road to Burma in 1937-1938. The Burma Road became the last and vital link of a supply line that stretched more than 12,000 miles, down through the jungles of Burma to Rangoon and ultimately to the United States. In addition to the road, Chiang had also carefully constructed an important relationship with Franklin Delano Roosevelt. To woo all Americans, he increasingly relied on his captivating wife, Madame Chiang Kai-shek.

By late 1941, however, China's lifeline was endangered. Chiang appealed to Winston Churchill, who in turn warned President Roosevelt. Four days later, the president replied that the best he could do at that point was to beef up Lend-Lease support—and sanction the American Volunteer Group.

Enter the Flying Tigers.

"Why did I join? That's simple. Since I was 12 years old, I have read everything that [Rudyard] Kipling wrote, twice over. And here I am in the navy, flying dive bombers, having a heck of a good time, enjoying life to the fullest. And then, this recruiter comes around at Christmas time in 19 and 40 and asked who would be interested in going over and helping the Chinese defend the Burma Road. 'My God! what a godsend,' I said to myself. 'This is the only way that I'll see Burma—how does that [Kipling poem "Mandalay"] go?—'by the old pagoda, looking eastward to the sea.' 'This,' I said to myself, 'is the chance of a lifetime . . .' I thought all of 10 seconds before I signed up. Truth to tell, I also wanted to smell a little cordite, and at that point was one of those naïve people who said that the U.S. would never go to war."

Edward Rector, the author of those reflections, was a Lieutenant j.g., flying off the aircraft carrier *Yorktown*, then on "neutrality patrols" in the North Atlantic, when China beckoned.

And, of course, because the United States wasn't at war with anyone, nobody could go around signing up army and navy pilots to fight anywhere—unless, of course, they were "volunteers."

Below:
Joe Rosbert sitting on the wing of his aircraft.

Ed Rector.

The legendary General Claire Chennault.

And unless the guy doing the beckoning happened to be a one-of-a-forever kind, name of Col. Claire Lee Chennault, country schoolteacher, hunter, fisherman, fighter pilot, renegade, visionary, schemer, charmer, and—if you'd believe the gritty, gruff, and grand rival he would finally best, Lt. Gen. Joseph W. Stillwell—"the World's Greatest Strategist."

Not quite the world's greatest strategist, maybe, but there aren't many other superlatives that would fail to fit "Old Leatherface." Besides, his pilots believed in this man.

Joe Rosbert remembers the first time the Tigers saw him: "He stepped out of a B-25 and looked for all the world like he had stepped right out of World War I—leg-wrappings, campaign hat, a World War I uniform!"

David Lee "Tex" Hill: "You immediately see the strength of character in that man. He's the kind of guy you know right off you can trust, a man who knows what he's doing."

Not everyone agreed—except when it mattered most. A Louisianian who numbered among his ancestors Sam Houston and Robert E. Lee, Claire Chennault began to raise hackles almost from the time he joined the Army Air Corps in 1917. He became an early critic of the air war doctrine, particularly of the "bomber school" headed in the U.S. by Billy Mitchell, that fast bombers would become so invulnerable as to make fighter planes obsolete.

Among those Chennault tangled with was Colonel Clayton Bissell. Although himself a World War I ace, Bissell argued that the only way a fighter could knock down a modern bomber would be to drop a ball and chain into its propeller.

Humbug, said Chennault. Tactics more than the planes themselves were the problem, he argued. Between the wars, he set out to prove that a group of planes could operate as a tight-knit team. Together with two others, he formed a precision flying team known as "Three Men on a Flying Trapeze." Their barn-storming spectaculars included a "squirrel-cage" maneuver— slow rolls while the planes barrel-rolled around each other—and a finale in which the pilots executed loops and rolls with their wing tips tied together with 20-foot lengths of rope.

In 1937, Chennault retired from the service, partially for medical reasons, as a 47-year-old Army Air Corps captain. His real career was about to begin. He came to the attention of the Chinese, and in May 1937, arrived in China to assist in upgrading their rickety air force.

A few weeks after he arrived, the Sino-Chinese War broke out, and Chennault found himself trying to forge a wartime air force with the pampered sons of wealthy families. When the Japanese began pounding the vital Burma Road and launched raids on Chunking, the Chiangs turned to neutral America for support. President Roosevelt consented, and Chennault was soon recruiting 112 pilots from the army, navy, and Marine Corps.

One of them—"Tex" Hill—sums it up: "The Chinese air force had been decimated. It existed in name only. So the solution was to have instead an instant air force."

Chennault also managed to scrounge 100 P-40 fighters—no easy feat, since they were in heavy demand on several fronts around the world.

According to their papers, many of these noisy, rambunctious, high-spirited young men bound for the Orient worked for the Central Aircraft

David "Tex" Hill poses alongside his airplane somewhere in China.

A truck lumbers along the Burma Road.

John Rossi, in his flight suit, in Kunming, China, January 1942.

Manufacturing Corporation. They answered to names like "Tadpole Smith" and "Catfish Rains" and "Moose Moss." Some, says "Dick" Rossi, were "pretty rough, tough characters. Some were very quiet, calm people, studious types. The average guy was a pretty patriotic American." Their fake passports listed them as salesmen, teachers, tourists, musicians, vaudeville artists, bankers, and baseball players. Just in case, they brought with them their own ground crew, two American nurses, and their own physician, Lewis ("Doc") Richards, himself a self-described "bit of a renegade and a rebel, an outlaw—in spirit."

The first of them reached Burma in July of 1941, the last in November. They travelled in two or three groups, mainly aboard Dutch ships. Before embarking in San Francisco, the word spread that it would be a good idea to bring their own private armories. "Everybody," reports Rosbert, "says, 'Don't take one gun, take at least two.' Some of the guys bought three or four. We looked like a bunch of terrorists coming out of those gun shops."

Joe Rosbert had an unenviable assignment on his slow boat to Burma. "In San Francisco, the man in charge of seeing we all got on the ship in one piece said, 'Now I have to tell you that the man who's going to be in charge of this group is Joe Rosbert.' . . . I thought to myself, 'I don't know whether I can get myself to Rangoon, much less this crowd!'"

One carried a passport identifying himself as a "missionary." As it happened, there were some real missionaries aboard that Dutch ship bound for Rangoon. "You know," Tex Hill muses, "I don't know who converted whom on that trip, but I'll tell you they had a fertile field to work in. Some of us did try to convert some of the younger missionary women. And I think some of us lucked out!"

At one point, Greg Boyington had another kind of mixing-it-up in mind. The same Gregory Boyington, by the way, who became the Marine Corps' top ace in the war with 24 kills, not counting the six he bagged as a Flying Tiger; the same Pappy Boyington who created a legend of his own, the "Black Sheep Squadron"; the same colonel who won the Medal of Honor.

C.H. "Link" Laughlin tells the tale: "Greg had been on the Olympic wrestling team. So he decided he would like to work out a little bit on some of his fellow shipmates. Didn't work out for him though; we ganged up on him."

There was even a bit of tippling on that ship of remarkable fools. "Link" Laughlin confides that "We were each given a hundred dollar bar bill, prepaid." And as Joe Rosbert recalls it, "we drank that Dutch ship out of Heineken beer the first day out of San Francisco. But they got a new supply in Honolulu." Fritz Wolf: "We were on that ship a long time—six weeks, I think. Before we got to Singapore, the captain said he wouldn't take us any farther," but we "convinced the skipper that he better take us to Rangoon because that's what the contract said."

The Burma they came to was a land that would breed heroes. It had to, because from start to finish, the Allied forces fought with never enough of anything except hardship. The war was as much against tantalizing nature as against a fanatical and implacable foe. Slightly smaller than Texas, Burma is a wild place, a terribly country that breeds disease and despair. It is a place of steamy jungles and mountains pushing up past 19,000 feet, a place the British soldiers called the Valley of Death.

British "Tommies"—the spunky devil-may-cares of Kipling's "Road to Mandalay"—took Burma in the nineteenth century, and in the following century it was given self-governing status, while relying on the British for defense. The war years brought men to Burma who were every bit as rich in courage and leadership as Claire Chennault, of course, and his boss and antagonist, then-Lt. Gen. Joseph W. Stillwell, the senior American commander in the China-Burma-India (CBI) theater of operations. His men called him "Vinegar Joe."

Then there was Orde Charles Wingate, dubbed by his men "Brigadier Bela Lugosi" after the ghoulish movie star. Yet another was U.S. army Col. Philip J. Cochran, prototype for a dashing airman in the comic strip, "Terry and the Pirates." And finally Brig. Gen. Frank Merrill, who in 1943 returned from defeat to lead a 3,000-man force in support of Wingate—"Merrill's Marauders," the first American combat force on the Asian mainland.

Stillwell, Wingate, Cochran, Merrill—giants of an unloved and largely forgotten remote battlefield. Once Burma had fallen to the Japanese, Churchill likened its recapture to "munching a porcupine, quill by quill." Yet these greats persuaded him—and Roosevelt—that it could be done. These men took their axes into those swampy jungles and kept an otherwise confident enemy constantly off-balance, edgy. These were the men who dared—and died—when raw courage was about all there was left in the Allied inventory.

Heroes? How about the men of the India-China Wing, Air Transport Command. For three years after the Japanese cut the Burma Road, they were

Gregory "Pappy" Boyington of Black Sheep fame.

the lifeline to China, flying huge C-46 transports over what came to be known as "The Hump," over a spur of the Himalayas, through enemy planes and weather that flipped planes over and caused them to plummet 3,000 feet in a minute. They flew their route with a pistol and a Tommy gun—and a lot of grit and prayers.

"Skip" Adair, one of Chennault's right-hand men, was there to meet the motley American pilots when they arrived in Rangoon in November 1941. On reaching Rangoon, a few looked around and said they wanted no part of this hell-hole. The rest boarded a train for the 150-mile trip to Toungoo, about one-third of the way to the old capital of Mandalay. Bob Layner and a few others laid in "provisions" for the trip. "They called it Australian bourbon. The next morning we were very sad to have found that Australian whiskey— I don't know whether it was made out of potatoes or cactus or what—but wow!"

When they reached their real headquarters, the former RAF air base at Toungoo, they came face-to-face with their new commander. Joe Rosbert picks up the story: "The next morning, I was taken out to the airstrip, and Chennault's deputy, Harvey Greenlawn, said, 'Joe, I want to take you in to meet Colonel Chennault.' So he led me into his office, and there he was sitting behind a desk. Mind you, I had only heard his name. I didn't even know his background. . . . He had a pith helmet hanging on the wall, and was wearing khaki shorts and a khaki shirt. What impressed me right away was that he was a man who looked you straight in the eye.

" 'Joe,' he said, 'I'm very happy you're here, and that you brought your group through in one piece. In the next few days, we'll be getting down to business, and I'll tell you all about the P-40s and the Japanese.'

"That first meeting with Chennault stayed with me. . . . As a leader, that man couldn't be beat."

James H. Howard speaks with some authority on the matter of leadership.

Two P-40s head down the runway, Tungoo, China.

He went on to become a brigadier general—and the other Flying Tiger destined to win the Medal of Honor. "Chennault," he relates, "was one of those characters you read about, that you imagine. He was a terrific individual, a leader. And he knew what he was doing. Not only because he was one of the foremost people in aviation in recognizing the importance of fighters, but because he had been out there for four years. He knew the Chinese, he knew the Japanese opposition. He knew how we should fight them."

"Tough and determined," says Doc Richards. "A gung-ho character!" agrees marine Link Laughlin. "He took no back-talk from anybody, but at the same time, he mixed well with everybody—played softball with us, that sort of thing. We had a lot of respect for him."

Dick Rossi, who heard about AVG through a small article in *Time* magazine, takes over: "The group immediately liked him and respected him. His background as a teacher helped him handle some of the guys 'cause we weren't all that mature at the time."

There was a lot to learn, and Chennault was the man to teach them. First off, there was the P-40. Dick Rossi (John Richard Rossi): "None of us navy guys had ever even seen a P-40, let alone flown one. For that matter, there weren't very many of us who had flown single-seat airplanes. We had people there who had been flying B-17s, flying patrol boats (PBYs)—they hadn't seen anything that small since their training days." Joe Rosbert was among those in that boat: "I had no idea what a P-40 even looked like. I had never even seen a picture of it. We led a rather cloistered life in the navy—naval aircraft, that was it. When I went out that first morning to the airstrip and saw the P-40 for the first time, I thought, 'I made the right decision,' because it was a sleek-looking airplane. I was impressed." Bob Layner agrees: "Our first impression: we were very enthusiastic—but since I hadn't flown anything but multiengine aircraft for a couple of years, the thought crossed my mind: 'Can I handle this?' Jim Howard remembers the nose; so does Tex Hill: "That thing had the longest nose on it I had ever seen in my life—just went on forever."

Howard had flown a number of planes before hitting Toungoo, so it didn't give him trouble. But that nose, "which protruded way out there," was a problem for greenhorns; "taxiing into somebody else—there were a lot of accidents." Link Laughlin remembers lots of accidents, but for a different reason. "The navy taught us to land tail first on fighter planes, but that wasn't so with the P-40. You landed wheels first, like a transport. We lost a dozen planes in training because navy pilots insisted on flying the thing so that the tail touched the ground first." As serious as the problem was for Layner, Laughlin, and the other navy pilots, it might have been worse; fortunately, there were a few AT-6 trainers to ease them into taming this new creature.

Some called the Curtiss-Wright P-40 "obsolete." Obsolete? Not the world's greatest fighter plane, surely, but one of the most reliable. Between the time the first ones rolled off the assembly lines on April 4, 1940, and the last, four years later, the 13,738 P-40s would fly in every combat arena of the world under the flags of 28 nations. The model flown by the Flying Tigers, the P-40B, mounted four .30 caliber machine guns in the wings, two .50 caliber in the engine cowling. Unlike its later principal adversary, the P-40 had thick armor to protect the pilot. Faster (340 mph at 12,230 feet) than the British Hurricane, the P-40 was nevertheless outclassed by its principal nemesis.

That plane was the Mitsubishi A6M2-Type O, the world famous "Zero." "Zeke," to American pilots, it was the Japanese equivalent of Britain's Super-

Another Mitsubishi A6M, in U.S. markings, under performance evaluation after recovery by the Allies.

Inset:
Mitsubishi A6M in flight.

marine Spitfire, Germany's Messerschmitt Bf.109, the U.S.' North American Mustang, P-51. For two years, no fighter plane in the Pacific could stand up to it—unless its pilot had been trained by Claire Chennault.

The Zero was the work of Jiro Horikoshi, Mitsubishi's chief designer and the man who had given the Japanese the A5M—the Imperial Navy's first metal monoplane fighter that routed the Russian Polikarpov I-16s over Manchuria. On September 13, 1940, the Zero had its baptism of fire—and a legend of invincibility was created.

Thirteen Zeros, led by Lt. Saburo Shindo and Sub-Lt. Ayae Shirane, escorted bombers on a raid on Hankow. The raid completed, they left the target with the bombers—or seemed to have left the target. A Chinese formation of 27 Russian-made I-15s and I-16s appeared and, unbeknownst to them, were tracked by a Japanese reconnaissance plane flying high overhead. Alerted, the Zeroes turned, climbed, and reappeared over Hankow, taking the Chinese Chatos and Ratas by complete surprise. All 27 were shot down; the Japanese had four planes damaged.

In the sixteen months until the outbreak of the war with the U.S. and the Allies, the Zeros shot down 99 Chinese aircraft. Two Zeros were lost, both to antiaircraft fire.

The Zero was designed to rigid navy specifications—and exceeded them. It was to have a top speed of 310 miles; the A6M2 topped out at 332 at 14,390 feet. Takeoff distance was to be no more than 230 feet in a 27 knot headwind. It climbed 9,870 feet in nine and a half minutes. It packed heavy armament; two 20 mm cannons, two 7.7 mm machine guns, and two 132-pound bombs. With extra fuel tanks, the Zero had a range of 1,930 miles—more than double that of the P-40, nearly four times that of the Spitfire, five times that of the Me.109. The Allies would soon feel the sting of that awesome range.

Beyond its advantages of range and firepower, the Zero possessed a maneuverability that enabled it to outclimb and out-turn the P-40. But Claire Chennault knew that.

" 'Do not,' he told us, 'dogfight with the Zero.' " Link Laughlin recalls Lesson Number One. "The only thing we had on the Zero was armor plate and six guns." Tex Hill elaborates: "'Don't turn with those guys'—he drilled that into us. 'If you do, they'll be right on your tail. Just try to hit them and dive out and come back up and try to get another shot at them. But don't ever, ever turn with them.' " Hill continues: "The P-40 didn't come off very well in the Pacific because they were using this classical dogfighting which every pilot was trained to do. Chennault changed all that."

Chennault held his classes every morning at 6 A.M. during those first weeks, around 50 hours in all. Ed Rector, who would go on to become the third-scoring Flying Tiger (12 kills, a hair behind Tex Hill's 12 ¼), adds: "We all went—every day."

"By the time Pearl Harbor happened, we felt that we weren't going up against an unknown enemy," Bob Layner interjects. "All those blackboard chalk talks—they paid off. As it turned out, he knew what he was talking about."

Ed Rector, flying with the all-navy Panda Bears Squadron (Jack Newkirk in command, Bob Layner, Tex Hill, Tom Haywood, John Bright, Robert "Moose" Moss, among the 30-plus pilots), was the first AVG pilot to score a victory. Chennault had organized his men into three squadrons: Hell's Angels (with a shapely nude adorning the fuselage), Adam and Eves, and the Panda Bears. Panda Bears and the Adam and Eves were moved to Kunming shortly after the attack on Pearl Harbor, Hell's Angels assigned to aid the British in the defense of besieged Rangoon.

Rector narrates: "We arrived at five in the afternoon. The next morning, we were in combat, against a formation of nine Japanese bombers in a great big V. They had bombed Kunming the day before, so we went up and met them. My plane had been scheduled for a check, so I had them just throw the cowling on and caught up with the formation—our boys were hanging in there, shooting. I got up on the high perch like I had been taught in Pensacola, taught by Chennault, came around and started shooting about 20 degrees off."

A top-rated gunner in training, Rector now discovered the very different feel of combat: "I held the trigger down, closed in, saw my shots hitting, and then I was directly astern and continued to hold the trigger down. At the last moment, I got target fascination—damn near killed myself—shoved the stick foward—you know, I can see it today in my mind's eye: rivets, the camouflage pattern, the dead tail gunner with his jaw shot away. I shoved the stick forward and pulled out to the left, back to the high perch. When I looked back, the plane I hit was the last guy in that V, on the left side, the port side. He was on fire, going straight ahead in formation. Slowly, he nosed down and went in. And my thought was, 'Well, so that's the way it is!'"

A G4M "Betty" in flight.

Above right:
Gun camera footage of an A6M Zero being shot from the sky.

Very nearly, as it turned out, the way it *was* for Ed Rector. "My guns had stopped firing, all except for one little .30 caliber out on the wing. So I went out up ahead of the bombers and came back with head-on passes with my one little .30 caliber popping away, and finally, it stopped, too. So I flew alongside the bombers, took their heading and turned around and flew the reciprocal of [the heading] to go back to Kunming. Except what those bombers had done was fly for about 40 to 50 miles to the east before turning south for Haiphong [Vietnam]. So I ended up 130 miles northeast of Kunming, out of gas and trying to find an alternative airfield on that flimsy little map we had.

"I followed a river, got caught in a canyon—mountains sticking up on all sides. Next thing, I was doing 90-degree turns with a 400-foot ceiling over the river—less canyon now, and wide. Finally, I saw a two-mile straight stretch and threw the throttle to it, floorboarded it—climbed out at 140 miles an hour, expecting to crash into a mountain at any moment, expecting to die." But Ed Rector didn't die; he managed to put the sputtering plane down and was picked up later.

That first combat reinforced another Chennault lesson. Tex Hill describes it: "When they [the Japanese] would come over in those big bomber formations, those big V's, they'd hold formation 'til the last guy would go down. They'd never move. Never break it. If they could carry out an attack without being disturbed, they would come off perfect. Absolutely perfect. Pearl Harbor's a good example of that. Their weakness was that they were not able to accommodate to a new situation. But, as I say, as far as plane handling, they were great. Real good pilots."

The flyers weren't alone in learning new tricks. Lewis "Doc" Richards was just out of medical school, doing his first hitch in the Medical Corps at Fort Bragg, North Carolina, when adventure beckoned. Now in the jungles of Burma, facing exotic diseases he had never seen, he did some fast on-the-job training. "I will never forget," he tells us, "the first time I saw Dengue fever and I didn't recognize it. One of the local nurses came around and says, 'Oh, that's a beautiful rash of Dengue fever.' I was so pleased that she diagnosed it for me.''

The first big success for the Tigers came on February 25, 1942, as the 75-day siege of Rangoon was nearing an end. A force of 166 Japanese planes came to bomb and strafe, determined to wipe out the RAF and AVG flyers. By then, all had been deployed back to Burma for that last-ditch defense effort. Nine Flying Tigers rose to meet the Japanese force. The Japanese lost 24 planes that day, the Tigers two. The next day, 200 planes came. This time, 18 Japanese planes were downed; all six P-40s returned to base. "That one," Dick Rossi recalls, "was right over the field where everybody on the ground, our own group, was watching a lot of it. That one stands out pretty much in my mind."

Being outnumbered—and flying as many as eight sorties in a single day—was a way of life for the Flying Tigers. But here again, Chennault had given his gallant warriors an edge. Tex Hill explains: "Chennault set up a warning net that was very effective. Every little village had a radio, a CW deal. So when we would move into a base, say like Hinyang, we'd put up a map and that would be the center. Then we'd draw concentric circles to 300 kilometers, in 50 kilometer rings. When a village would hear something, all they had to do was report what they heard or what they saw. They'd say, 'Light engine noise, heavy engine noise.' It was refined to that extent. Or, 'I see three,' or whatever you saw.

"Then you'd put a flag in the map at that village. Well, pretty soon, another call would come, and a flag would go over another village. First thing you know, those flags start lining up, and you know they're heading your way. So when they hit the 150-kilometer circles, that'd give us time to launch, and we would get up to about 20,000 feet—ideal for contact with them. This thing never failed."

From 20,000 feet, or higher, the Tigers would execute their most effective maneuvers: diving singly or in pairs at speeds reaching 400 miles per hour, striking, then curling back and away.

(Chennault, by the way, had a private "early warning system" earlier in the war. Ed Rector describes it: "It was back in Nanking. Being the keen hunter that he is, Chennault was very close to nature. Well, he was there three or four weeks when he noticed there was a jackass outside his window. And every time that jackass brayed, within 30 minutes, the Japanese were overhead. Never failed.")

Fact is, they weren't the Flying Tigers at all, at least at first. Dick Rossi says it was not until around February of 1942 that he first heard the "Flying Tiger"

P-40C in flight over an airstrip.

monnicker. When they were recruited they were to become part of the First American Volunteer Group because, Rossi clarifies, there were supposed to be three of them. The second, a bomber group, was en route when Pearl Harbor was attacked and it was diverted to Australia. The third was cancelled after Pearl Harbor when America no longer needed a cover—''volunteer'' outfits—to aid embattled friendly nations. The shark in the nose of the planes was borrowed from a British squadron in Africa in the belief it would help ''spook'' the Japanese pilots. Once again Dick Rossi explains: ''Someone saw in the Sunday supplement, one of those pictorials, pictures of an RAF squadron in the desert that had painted sharks' mouths on their planes. We thought it was a good idea, and so tried it on one plane. Everyone liked it, so they painted it on all of them.'' A Walt Disney artist contributed the unit's symbol—a Bengal tiger with tiny wings leaping through a V for victory—which was painted on all their planes.

For all practical purposes, the shark's teeth and Bengal tigers were about the only things uniform about those swashbucklers. Since they were supposed to be civilian volunteers—and, as far as the State Department was concerned, not even combatants—they weren't to take along their military uniforms. Joe Rosbert confesses that ''quite a few of the fellas'' brought their uniforms anyway, which they promptly mixed with the khaki shorts, mos-

Inset:
American aviators of the 1st Pursuit "Adam and Eve" Squadron.

Group photo of American Volunteer Group pilots of the 3rd Squadron "Hell's Angels."

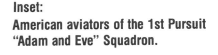

quito boots, and pith helmets issued to them at Toungoo. Otherwise, the first "standard" item was Madame Chiang's scarf. When she flew down from Chunking to Kunming, she gave the men she called "her angels without wings" what Bob Layner describes as "our flying scarves with the generalissimo's stamp on them." Still later, in late March or April 1942, Layner, Rosbert, and one or two others were in India to pick up replacement aircraft. While there, "we went to one of those British tailors in Karachi. So we designed a uniform, a nice light weight gabardine, the kind the British were famous for over there. When we came back, a lot of the guys liked it, and so when they got to India, they had them copied. Wasn't official, but it was pretty good-looking."

Official, indeed! Students of the Tigers cherish a photograph showing the members of the Hell's Angel Squadron lined up in front of one of their planes. Except that all ten were wearing leather jackets (of one kind or another), there was nothing "uniform" about these men: some have goggles pulled rakishly over leather caps, another sports an insignia-less British officer's visored cap, another the American officer's version of it. And yet another photo shows Frank Lawlor of Winston-Salem, N.C., alighting from his P-40 after a 1942 mission—goggles on top, loafers on the bottom.

A cynic might say they were mercenaries. After all: pay was $600 to $700 a month, which in those days very nearly paid for a new automobile. And a $500 bonus for each enemy plane shot down. But mercenaries don't fight like the Flying Tigers did—nor have their motivation, or panache.

Big David L. "Tex" Hill, navy pilot, son of a Texas Ranger: "I was born in [Kwangju] Korea, and my father, being a missionary there, had told me about his experiences in the Far East. I was interested in getting there."

Jim Howard, a 28-year-old ensign flying Grumman F4F Wildcats off the *Enterprise* when recruited: "I was born in [Canton] China, and I felt that I wanted to go back there and defend the Chinese." His parents were also missionaries.

John "Dick" Rossi, native of Placerville, California, a 25-year-old flight instructor at Pensacola Naval Air Station when a Commander Irvine came to call: "It was a challenge, it was going to be a change, it was a chance to do something different, even a chance to enhance my career."

C. H. "Link" Laughlin, one of the Pensacola legionnaires, had only finished flight training in April: "I was a second lieutenant in the Marine Corps, and a

Chinese laborers at work building an airfield for American use in Kunming, China.

flight instructor—a day-after-day grind. It got a little too much, and I was happy to get this offer.''

Robert Layner, who soloed as a navy pilot the day the Nazis marched into Poland: ''We thought when we went into flying we would be in the skies fighting the enemy. Two years later, we were still in the peacetime navy. We were looking for adventure!''

Fritz E. Wolf, attached to Bombing Three aboard the San Diego-based Saratoga: ''I was from a small town called Shawano in Wisconsin. The only time I ever travelled was when I played football with Carroll College and we went out of state. Otherwise, I never had a chance to travel. So for me, it was a time for adventure. I wanted to go to China—an exotic country. I wanted to go.''

And the bonus? ''I'll tell you one thing,'' Tex Hill tells us, ''the bonus was very, very little incentive because people in combat don't think about anything except how to survive.'' Besides, adds Dick Rossi, ''there was a rumor that we would be paid $500 for each plane we destroyed. But it was never in the contract, it was never written down, and nobody knew for sure whether it was rumor or what. And the fact is that up until the time we were disbanded, nobody was paid a bonus.'' Indignation creeps into the discussion: ''At no time,'' emphasizes Link Laughlin, ''were we told we would get a $500 bonus.'' And if the Tigers were mercenaries, how about those American and French and other foreign flyers training the Chinese, at one thousand dollars a month? Dick Rossi poses the question. Fritz Wolf chimes in: ''And they got free room, meals, servants—and weren't even in combat!''

Link Laughlin has the last word: ''It was a game of sorts. If you won, why congratulations: a $500 bonus. If you lose, a funeral.''

At Toungoo, it was steamy hot; up there on the 6,000-foot Kunming plateau, it was cold. In both places, the living was anything but easy. At Toungoo, an entire squadron bunked in long, thatch-type buildings, with mosquito-netting along the sides; at Kunming, there was, of course, the bombing, the infernal shortages.

And then, the quarters. Fritz Wolf describes his: ''My room was smaller than a hotel room, with a floor that was part board, part dirt. It had cloth windows and was heated by a charcoal burner. I slept on a rope cot, with some rice on top of it, and a sheet. The roof was sound, but there was no running water—showers were in another building.''

Later, deployed back for the last-ditch defense of Rangoon, their air field all but destroyed, the men were billeted in private homes. While it lasted, a few of them found themselves in the mansion of the head of Shell Oil in Burma. ''Beautiful home, with seven or more servants,'' Bob Layner reports. ''After a few weeks, that man and his wife had to be evacuated, and they left that big house with all the servants to us.''

Joe Rosbert describes his first combat mission at Kunming. ''We were on alert when we got the report that 10 Japanese bombers had just crossed the Indochina border headed for Kunming. When the time came, we all raced to our planes—in spite of those pictures you see, we didn't waddle along with parachutes on our backs. The parachutes were all prepared in the cockpits. And we just hopped in the plane, strapped the parachutes, and waited for information. We had terrible radio gear in the planes—a constant squawk in your ears—but finally they told us that the planes were at about 14,000 feet. We got up above the clouds—we only had about 12 or 13 planes in the air.

An A.V.G. pilot examines a stripped and abandoned Zero in a Chinese hangar.

P-40s taking to the air.

We saw them, then they saw us, turned around and headed back to Indochina, and that's when we engaged.

"I'll tell you, if you know what happens to your sphincter muscle when you're in a nervous situation like that, you just hope you can hold on and not have an accident.

"But we went in, made passes like we had been told, maintaining our altitude after each pass. In other words, coming back up and getting above the planes. We made several passes, and shot down four of them—confirmed. Afterwards, we heard that maybe only one of those planes had gotten back to its base, but we only confirmed four. I'll tell you: in combat I found you never completely lose that nervous feeling when you are told to scramble and you get into actual action."

Fritz Wolf was there and bagged two of the four "confirmeds" that day. Hear him tell it: "Our guns were bore-sighted for 500 yards. Now, being an old navy pilot, I always carried a scratch pad on my knee. And one of the things I jotted down that day: 500 yards was too far to be shooting from, the 30s anyway. The 50s are the ones that tore up the aircraft.

"Anyway, the first attack was an overhead attack. I was getting some hits, but wasn't doing any damage. So I decided to just go in and mix it with them. The next time around, I cut back on the throttle and stayed with them, just

P-40s taking to the air.

P-40D in shark's teeth regalia.

Yohei Hinoki with sword stands on his fighter in Rangoon, Burma.

switching back and forth, a tail movement, and sprayed three of them. I set two of them on fire. Then I went back up again and came underneath them because I was getting hits. In fact, after I got back, I found I had more American shells in my wings than Japanese!''

On December 7, 1941, the Japanese attacked Pearl Harbor. The Flying Tigers, their training not even completed, were already in a wider war. Link Laughlin sums it up: ''When they recruited us, we got the impression that it was to patrol the Burma Road, much like the highway patrol back home. Nobody said anything about going to war with the Japanese. Pearl Harbor meant for us that we're in a war.'' Adds Dick Rossi: ''It seems kind of funny to say it, but I think we were kind of glad that something had happened. We now knew that we had a real purpose. It gave us a whole new definition. We knew exactly where we were now—we were in it!''

They learned fast. The first combat took place over Rangoon on December 23; the Tigers lost two that day. Bob Layner also nearly bought it, first time out. Rising to meet the heavy formation of bombers and fighters, Layner ''looked up and there were three Japanese fighters coming right at us, firing heavily. Noel [R. Bacon, his wingman] managed to get away, but I'm too late. Those little I-98s could flip over and be on your tail—and man, they were letting go with everything! They hit my radio antenna on that first pass, so I was off the air. By the time I got turned around, they were in position, and all at once I get a very heavy vibration in my engine. I continued firing, but there was no doubt about it, I couldn't stay to see what happened, my engine was vibrating so much. As I came into the landing pattern, directly across from me is a Japanese fighter. 'What to do now?' I asked myself, because I knew if I put power on, the way I was vibrating, I was in serious trouble. Fortunately, he wasn't paying any attention to me, but watching [Robert J.] Sandell landing, with some trouble. And this Japanese fighter pilot tried to crash into Sandell—I mean he dived right into the ground, missing him by about 50 feet. We found out later this Japanese had been raked right across his plane. When I got down, come to find out I had a 20 mm hole in one of my prop blades, which is why it was vibrating so much. I lucked out on my first deal.''

A week later, flying escort for British bombers evacuating personnel from an airfield in neighboring Thailand, Dick Rossi is separated from his AVG wingman and the two RAF fighters. Suddenly: A Japanese fighter is ''coming straight at me, and I'm going straight at him. And I can see his guns firing, and I'm firing. We both turned and came at each other a second time. I realized that these were real bullets we were firing, that it was for keeps now.''

Within the first two months of combat over the skies of Burma and China, the Flying Tigers brought down 60 enemy planes—including a remarkable 24 in a single day. Japanese pilots came to respect them—even exaggerate them—early on.

Yohei Hinoki, a Japanese ace, describes his first encounter with an American early in his war. It was in March 1942, flying out of his base in Thailand, and the Americans were Flying Tigers. ''Their bullets came without stopping—like water pouring out from a watering pot . . . That was the first time I fought against the Americans, and was wounded in that fight. I had the impression that they were tough.''

Hinoki confirms that the Tigers' fame had preceded them, ''but we didn't know it was such a strong force. My unit took a lot of damage from that army.''

Army? The Flying Tigers were lucky to put up 18 planes on a good day. But they and their ground crews, the Americans and the Chinese, were masters of deception. The Chinese built bamboo dummies and parked them on the airfields, camouflaging the real planes in the trees. The ruse not only drew enemy bombs but swelled the count the Japanese made of their planes. They added another ruse: changing the numbers on the fuselages and painting the noses of their P-40s in different colors. In the air, they radioed orders to fictitious squadrons. Joe Rosbert tells how well it worked:

"Towards the end, we shot down several Japanese planes, and one Japanese airman survived. Under questioning at headquarters, one of the things he told us was that Japanese air force intelligence said we had at least a thousand airplanes!"

The Japanese increasingly viewed the Flying Tigers as an infuriating burr beneath their saddle. Warned Tokyo radio: "The American pilots in Chinese planes are unprincipled bandits. Unless they cease their unorthodox tactics, they will be treated as guerrillas." In other words, if captured they would be shot.

"The pilots—we got the glory. We got the notoriety. But let me tell you," Ed Rector emphasizes, "we are *nothing* compared to the ground people. It is beyond belief, even today in recollection, what they accomplished. Mechanics, crew chiefs, armorers, radio people—they kept the airplanes flying and guns firing and radios operating. It boggles my mind. We were just flying the airplanes. Without them, we would never have shot down an airplane."

From the day they arrived in Burma, there were shortages. With the outbreak of war, the shortages got worse. "We were," Rector adds, "at the tail end of the supply line. Truth to tell, there was no supply line." Bob Layner illustrates: "It got so you could see the fabric on the tires. We had to try to tiptoe on our landings." Jim Howard jumps in: "We didn't have spare parts, period. We'd cannibalize other airplanes to get the parts. The one thing that kept us alive was our ground crew people."

The stories multiply: gas tanks plugged with chewing gum, fuselages patched up with adhesive tape, gasoline pumped by hand from 55-gallon drums. Joe Rosbert remembers landing to discover that half of his rudder had been shot up. "My crew chief just got out a bunch of tape, taped it up, and the plane was ready to go."

Sometimes they would perform their "miracles" while the bombs were falling and the bullets impacting—patching up a damaged plane so it could join the fight against the attacking bombers.

Pearl Harbor did bring one small respite to the supply-impoverished Flying Tigers. Around the end of December, a PBY Flying Boat splashed down in Rangoon harbor. Bob Layner: "The plane had a load of supplies and ammunition bound for Manila. We pointed out to them that Manila had already fallen, so they couldn't very well go there. So, we got the ammunition." In the nick of time, too; Layner recalls that days before, they were forced to borrow 7.9 machine guns from the British for their P-40 wing positions because they had run out of .30 caliber ammunition. He adds: "Two or three months went by before we got any supplies—until they started flying them over the Hump."

Respite was otherwise hard to come by for these few. Playing baseball helped relieve some of the tension. Playing poker relieved some of their cash; Chennault, it's said, pocketed his share, and then some. Fritz Wolf remembers shooting geese with a pistol, and fishing like never before. "You'd go to a river up there, hold your hand out with crumbs on it, and the fish would come up and eat right out of your hand." He also remembers exploring the exotic land around them—and making a memorable discovery. "Once, while still in Burma," he says, "we took a trip up in the mountains and found a lady there who was the first woman to graduate from Northwestern School of Medicine. She was around 80 years old, so we asked her whether she wanted to go home. 'Nope,' she said, 'I'm going to die here.' "

The fun got a tad out of hand at times. One story that made the rounds concerns a night in a Rangoon saloon when a few of the Tigers talked the pilot of a C-47 cargo plane into making a night raid on Hanoi. As Don Moser tells the story, they loaded the fuselage with old French, Russian, and Chinese bombs, and, amply fueled with liquor, headed for the target. Reaching Hanoi, the tipsy Tigers simply kicked the bombs out of the open door.

Bob Layner tells another about the time Robert "Moose" Moss, from Bull Run, Georgia, came in after a big night on the town. "Believe it or not, Moose had taken his tuxedo to Burma and was wearing it that morning." Tex Hill continues: "Had lipstick all over him. All of a sudden, there was an alert—the Japanese had been bombing the field and we had the planes dispersed right in the rice paddies. So Moose waded in his tux and flew his plane to Rangoon. It cost him a hundred dollar fine." Tex should talk: one raid caught him lounging in his longee—a sarong-type garment they slept in. With the bombs already falling, Hill jumped "in this damn airplane and barely cleared the ground when a stick of phosphorus bombs went off right under me!"

Even among the high-spirited, some were more high-spirited than others. Most agree with Fritz Wolf's judgment that "there was one character who did stand out—and that was Boyington." Most agree with Bob Layner that he wasn't exactly "a team-player. Now, understand, I'm not taking anything away from his flying—he just wanted to go his own way. Colorful he was. Like the night he shot up the town clock in Rangoon." Most agree with J.R. Rossi that "when Pappy had quite a few drinks, he was a good man to stay away from." And most would agree with Joe Rosbert, who was billeted with him in the last days of Rangoon, that Pappy often had a few drinks and was no stranger to trouble, and that "most of the stories about him are true."

"Were we adventurous?" Ed Rector fields the question with a laugh. "You don't go to the other side of the world and not really know what the hell you're going over there to do or how you're going to do it unless you're a bit adventurous. And a little nutty. And that applied to all our people."

The military situation in Burma was weak from the beginning. Although the British well understood that the fall of Burma would not only cut off the supply line to China, but also imperil their Indian Empire, they were scarcely in a position in 1940 and 1941 to reinforce the region. In India itself, Mohandask Ghandi and his Congress party were urging their followers to a campaign of civil disobedience to pry the war-beleaguered British out of India. To add to British worries, the Japanese had already trained and armed a rebel Indian National Army to fight the British, furthering the image they wanted of themselves as liberators—"Asia for the Asiatics," was their slogan. In Burma itself, a paramilitary group called the Thirty Comrades, also trained by the Japanese, was the core of a ragtag Burma Independence Army. They carried out sabotage, terrorism, and spying for the Japanese.

Having stormed through neighboring Thailand early in December, the Japanese targeted Burma. First to fall was the air field at Tenasserim, about

P-40K cockpit.

400 miles southeast of Rangoon. From there, and bases in Thailand, they began their aerial bombardment of Rangoon. Against Japanese Gen. Shojira Iida's crack 15th Army, the Allies could muster only the 17th Indian Division—trained for desert warfare—and a Burmese division. Shojira was supported by 300 combat aircraft; the Allies had a handful of RAF pilots—and the Flying Tigers.

Dick Rossi remembers: "The Japanese had hoped to wipe us out on those first two big attacks [December 23 and 25], but we gave them a pretty good bloody nose. So, from then on, they went after Rangoon in earnest, sending large fleets of bombers and fighters over there regularly. . . . Their main objective was to wipe out the RAF and AVG in Rangoon."

Joe Rosbert observed an interesting phenomenon about the Japanese attempt: "At first, they sent nothing but bombers, without fighter protection. When they discovered that we were shooting them down, and they weren't shooting many of our planes down, then they started bringing fighters with the bombers as protection.

"When that didn't work, either, a strange thing happened. They started sending fighter plane—with no bombers! We couldn't figure out the reason for that except that they were getting just plain frustrated, and figured there must be some tactic that we can use to shoot these people out of the sky. Only that didn't work, either."

Day after day, the raiders came. Day after day, the Tigers learned—and shared their lessons. Rossi: "When we got to Rangoon and started getting into combat, we started telling each other how it was. Those bull sessions afterwards probably were some of our greatest learning experiences. A man would come back from combat and describe how he almost got it—those things would register pretty well in your memory bank." One lesson unlearned: "You know that saying that if you fly close, you've got twice as many guns? Baloney! That lead guy is looking at a target, and there's no way you can look at him and fly close formation at the same time. Once it gets started, you spread out—each guy pretty much on his own."

Three P-40s in formation.

By the end of February, the end was near for Rangoon. Bob Layner describes those last chaotic days. "They turned all the lepers and prison inmates out. They were running around on the streets begging. Automobiles—they'd give them to you, because you were an American and they didn't want the Japanese to get them. The docks were piled high with jeeps, tires. All you needed was a battery and you could have your own jeep. Trouble is, there were no batteries. At the end, the only way out of there was to fly out. But before that happened, before the Japanese cut off the roads, we loaded every truck we could get our hands on with spare parts—and cases of gin and Scotch, all that we could pile on. The importer had a boat in the harbor loaded with 75,000 cases of Johnny Walker. Rather than let the Japs have it, he sank the boat in the harbor. I heard years later that they went in and retrieved a lot of that.

"Before we left, we loaded all the incendiaries in our magazines and strafed targets like the oil refinery. We also set fire to the drapes in that nice house we were in—we didn't want the Japanese to get it."

Rangoon fell on March 7, 1942. The Allies retreated to a defensive line stretching east-west across the country, about 150 miles north of Rangoon. The Flying Tigers headed north for Magwe, on the banks of the Irrawaddy River in western Burma, about 250 miles northwest of Rangoon. More heavily outnumbered each day, they did what they could. "Sometimes," reflects Link Laughlin, "I think maybe because we were so outnumbered, we had nothing else to do except to fight—or else." Incredibly, they had to do it with even less. Dick Rossi: "The mechanics were doing a wonderful job, cannibalizing planes, but the planes that were left were in bad shape. We had trouble getting spark plugs and ignition. Gasoline trucks were harder to come by. Ammunition was in shorter supply—we had to keep scrounging around for ammunition to keep the guns loaded. So the logistics problem got really bad. And all the time the Japanese were getting closer and closer."

Strafing runs became a staple of their lives. Joe Rosbert describes strafing as "the most dangerous" of their missions: "The Japanese had antiaircraft bristling around every airstrip, and, of course, you lose your altitude advantage. You've got to get down very close to the ground to shoot up airplanes."

He describes a raid on Moulmein, across the Gulf of Martaban from Rangoon: "We had to take off at dawn so as to get over to the east side and come in with the sun behind us. After making a few passes and seeing the Japanese pilots actually trying to scramble into their airplanes, we headed for home. We were down on the water; when I say 'we,' I actually mean 'me,' because everybody was split up and I was alone. I was using the old 'rubber-neck' Chennault had drilled into us—looking behind as well as forward—and never spotted a Japanese plane on my tail. But when I got back to the base, that's when I discovered half my rudder had been shot off."

Doc Richards attests: "These gentlemen were in excellent physical shape." But even men in excellent physical shape fade under such pressure. Dick Rossi relates what happened to his squadron leader, Bob (Robert H.) Neale: "He was down to less than 150 pounds—and he's a big, tall guy! It was stress, days of it. A lot of the guys were on the verge of nervous collapse."

Rossi adds another insight: There wasn't much time to think in combat. But, on a long mission, flying an hour or so, "you had a lot of time to think. And that was probably the worst time."

With the fall of Rangoon, supply lines were severed from the ground forces. The British were surviving on bully beef and biscuits, fortified with what they called "Vitamin W." The "W" was for weevils. To make matters worse, the British forces had been pushed back to the hot, dry central region of Burma. Water became an obsession; Moser tells that men urinated on their hands and passed them over their cracked lips just for a touch of moisture. On April 15, Slim was forced to torch the 5,000 oil wells and power station at Yenangyaung. Next came withdrawal: General Slim leading 25,000 men on what would become the lengthiest retreat in British military history—900 miles through the jungle and over the mountains to Tamu, India. Only 12,000 made it. Meanwhile, Stillwell, cut off from the remnants of his Chinese forces, was setting out with his ragged band on his grueling odyssey ending, finally, in safety. Soldiers weren't alone in leaving. Around 900,000 civilians fled as well. Hundreds of thousands died.

For the Flying Tigers—as for so many others on that forsaken battleground—the war was now ugly, very ugly. "Was there any chivalry in our air war against the Japanese?" Ed Rector asks the rhetorical question. "None whatsoever!" The man who got hooked on flying by reading the sagas of aviation in pulp magazines reflects, then adds: "The idea is to kill as many of them as you can. Air warfare is no place for chivalry."

Hate came early to the Tigers. Several of them saw their buddy Bert Chrisman shot down over Rangoon. Ed Rector relates: "He was hit in a dogfight, bailed out and was killed while descending. Shot up in his 'chute.

When the natives picked him up and brought him in, they confirmed that he had been strafed while he was descending. That's shattering.''

Ed contends that the ''Japanese did strafe. There are a number of instances of them shooting our guys who had bailed out or trying to hit them as they descended by parachute. I don't know of any of our people who did that.''

Tex Hill disagrees. ''I was strafing a field over there after the Japs had run us out of Burma. Pete Wright and myself and another guy. We went down to Toungoo, our old base, and I caught a guy landing. I was strafing him, and when I pulled up, as a matter of fact, the guy jumped out of the airplane when it hit the ground. I steepened my dive quite a bit to get him, and I just raked through him and almost flew into the ground.''

Hill goes on with his account: ''We shot them any way we could find them. Unless a guy was in a position to get captured. See, the Japanese never jumped out unless they were over their own territory. They had parachutes, but they never use them when they are over enemy territory.

''They shot us in our parachutes and we shot them in theirs. One guy came back, he had shrouds all over the gun camera, showing this picture of this guy in the 'chute, and he said, 'God, you know, I forgot to turn my gun switches off!''

Joe Rosbert saw the Chrisman killing. But he read it differently. ''The Japanese actually killed one of our pilots—Bert Chrisman—in a parachute. They had a feeling of getting the pilot, regardless, whether in the plane or in the parachute. We didn't have that kind of feeling. At least I think I speak for the majority of AVG pilots—we never had that feeling.''

''When Bert was killed,'' Tex Hill remembers, ''and we had to bury him— they didn't have any embalmers in those days—you just put a guy in a pine box. And here's a guy that's your best friend and you can hardly stay around the box. We took him out to the cemetery and buried him.''

''A good fighter pilot,'' Bob Layner remarks, ''is like a good poker player. He thinks ahead, leaves an option open, and knows how to make split-second decisions.'' The Tigers played the wretched hand they were dealt—and how they played it. Their kill rate rose to 23 to one.

But the Tigers also played an important role in the ground war. Tex Hill recalled how he and Ed Rector—among five Tigers recruited from the aircraft carrier *Ranger*—taught the dive-bombing lessons they had learned in the navy to other pilots. Outfitted with bombs, the P-40 thus became a dive-bomber as well as fighter-bomber. It also became a supply ship of sorts. Hill explains: ''The Chinese fitted bamboo belly tanks to give us some more 'legs.' Lots of times, we used those tanks to drop food and ammo and stuff to people behind the lines because bamboo is resilient and the stuff would hold together.''

Ed Rector and various others among the Tigers believe they played the decisive role in stopping the Japanese advance at the Salween River on China's border. Says Dick Rossi: ''We blew up their tanks and their bridges. And from then on, they started a retreat.'' ''Had we not done so,'' Rector says, ''the Japs could have walked right into Kunming.''

But casualties mounted. Doc Richards remembers one raid that killed two pilots and numerous ground crewmen. ''Most of the time,'' he recalls, ''I practiced medicine mostly from the running board of my car when these men were hurt and picked up.'' Fritz Wolf tells of a time when he was near death with jaundice and woke in a hospital room to find a Chinese attendant with a big stick measuring his body. ''I asked the doctor—a public health doctor who hadn't been to the States in 18 years—'What's he doing?' 'Measuring you for a coffin,' he said. 'You better get your things in order.' 'No, sir, I'm not going to die here!' I told him. Weak as I was, I dressed myself on the floor and crawled out of that place first chance I got and hitched a ride back to my old barracks.''

"There are two sins you cannot commit in the military." Joe Rosbert, one of the 38 Flying Tiger pilots who qualified as an ace, tells what happened: "One, you don't tell higher-ups how to do things. Chennault did that all the time. Two, you must not prove that you're right. Chennault committed both of those cardinal sins. They couldn't accept that."

But if Chennault had enemies, he also had friends: Madame Chiang, Chiang himself—and Franklin Delano Roosevelt. That would be enough to keep him in the war—for a while. But not enough to save the Tigers.

"We," Joe Rosbert announces, "saw the handwriting on the wall, towards April or May of 1942. Chennault was made a brigadier general, and the word spread that we would go out of existence officially on July 4."

"AVG people," Rosbert adds, "felt pretty strongly that it was strange that they would make Chennault commanding general of the Air Force in China, but wouldn't let him recruit his own group." That was left to the West Pointer Clayton Bissell.

Dick Headman of the American Volunteer Group with his P-40.

"Bissell got us into a hall in Kunming and, among other things, told us if we didn't join the army or navy, the U.S. military in China, then when we set foot on American soil, we would be drafted as pilots." "He was," adds Bob Layner, "about as obnoxious as anyone could be. Not only—he told us—would they have the draft board on our backs within three days of getting home, but we would have no priority on transportation, no help getting home! Well, 75 percent of us got up and walked out." Tex Hill: "That kind of a threat went over like a lead balloon. Bob Neale, for instance, our leading ace, said, 'You let me go home and get a little rest and I'll come back.' But they wouldn't do that. They had offered him a lieutenant colonelcy, and he would have taken it. He just needed a little rest, he was almost having a nervous breakdown."

The upshot: only five Tigers accepted the offer.

"If," comments Link Lavelin, "it had been General Chennault instead of General Bissell, I suspect that most of us would have signed up."

On July 4, 1942, the Flying Tigers passed into history. In just seven months, these men—"trained," as Doc Richards would put it, "to accept tragedy as well as glory"—had destroyed 299 enemy planes, plus 153 probables. They left behind nine pilots killed in action, nine dead in accidents, and four missing in action over Asian jungles.

Ed Rector sums it up: "We were losing our hat, ass, and spats around the world. And here we were, the Flying Tigers, with all those tremendous victories. So, I would say the contribution we made was to morale back home. We were the only people giving it to the Japanese!"

Dr. Lewis Richards, the man who patched them up when they were wounded, healed them when they were sick, believes they made a contribution over there as well: "If they hadn't been there, China would have been lost."

In the years ahead, other pilots, would affect the rakish uniforms, the tiger-teeth snouts. Tex Hill has something to say about that:

"Those bastards—I mean, they use our name! And that name is magic."

5 HELL IN THE PACIFIC

The carnage at Pearl Harbor, December 7, 1941.

NPM 1516
Z OF2 1830 Of3 Of4 O2FO O
FROM; CINCPAC
ACTION; CINCLANT CINCAF OPNAV
AIR RAID ON PEARL HARBOR
THIS IS NOT A DRILL

At 1:50 P.M., Washington time, Sunday, December 7, 1941, the message flashed on the U.S. navy's Washington-Honolulu circuit. The bombs were still falling on Pearl Harbor.

Below right:
B5N "Kate" with pilot.

Walker "Bud" Mahurin in flight gear.

"Yesterday, December 7th, 1941—a date which will live in infamy—the United States of America was suddenly and deliberately attacked by naval and air forces of the empire of Japan." So began Franklin Delano Roosevelt's address to millions of Americans hunched around their radio receivers.

The president's speech finished, Congress, with but a single dissenting vote, declared war on the empire of Japan.

Walker M. "Bud" Mahurin, from Chickasha, Oklahoma, remembers that, once recovered from "the big shock" of the news, he did what countless others across the land were doing in those first, uneasy hours: he took up arms. "We knew," Mahurin says, "we were headed for a big-time war."

Dawn had not yet broken when the first four Aichi E13A "Jake" reconnaissance floatplanes lifted from the decks of two cruisers, part of the flotilla under the command of Vice Admiral Chuicho Nagumo known as the 1st Air Fleet: 183 warplanes were launched from the decks of four of the six aircraft carriers. The first strike planes: 51 D3A1 "Val" dive-bombers, 40 Nakajima B5N "Kate" torpedo bombers, 59 bombers with specially designed, 800-kg (1,760-pound) armor-piercing (AP) bombs, and 43 Mitsubishi A6M2 Zero fighters for escort and strafing duties. Lying at anchor on that sleepy Sunday morning were 94 of the 127 ships that made up the U.S. Pacific Fleet, under the command of Rear Adm. Husband E. Kimmel.

Bunched wing-to-wing on the ground at U.S. army air bases were 400 fighters and bombers. The army commander, Gen. Walter Short, warned by Washington the day before, along with other Pacific commanders, that "hostilities may ensue, subversive activities may be expected," had ordered the planes parked that way to guard against sabotage. It was a logical choice; the only specific war warning spoke of a possible Japanese attack on the Philippines, Thailand, or the Malay Peninsula.

Just after 7 A.M., an army Signal Corps private, manning a British radar unit installed on a mountaintop on the northern coast of Oahu, sighted on his screen the largest formation of planes he had ever seen. The lieutenant he reported this to told him to forget it and shut down the set.

Lt. Commander Nakaya, leading the first wave of fighters, describes the scene as he neared the target: "Pearl Harbor was still asleep in the morning mist. . . . inside the harbor were important ships of the Pacific Fleet, strung out and anchored two ships side by side in an orderly manner."

At 7:49 A.M., the attack began. Zeros raked the American fighters. Before they had finished, 188 were destroyed, 160 damaged — all on the ground.

The attack was only 10 minutes old when the *Arizona* was blown to bits by an AP bomb that penetrated to her forward magazine. The battlewagon went down almost immediately, with her skipper, Rear Adm. Isaac C. Kidd and 1,106 officers and men in a total crew of 1,511.

In those first 15 minutes, the battleship *Oklahoma* had capsized, trapping 415 men below decks, and the *California* was sinking. The target ship *Utah* had sunk; four other battleships were damaged.

At 8:15 A.M., Nagumo launched his second strike: 54 bombers, 80 dive-bombers, and 36 fighters. In the harbor, an enterprising junior officer had managed to get the *Nevada* underway. The second wave, arriving at 9 A.M., attacked her mercilessly, but the officer managed to beach her before she blocked the only Pearl Harbor channel. They finished off the *West Virginia* and inflicted more damage on the remaining battleships: the *Maryland, Tennessee,* and *Pennslyvania.*

Iyozo Fujita, then a 24-year-old ensign flying off the *Soryu*, had his first taste of combat over Hawaii. "We expected American fighters would be waiting and attack us. But, when we went in, the fighters were not in the air. I thought that was very strange—we believed Japan had declared war before bombing Pearl Harbor.

"Anyway, on the way back, after bombing some P-36s, about nine of them flew up in the air and attacked us—we were the only unit in a dogfight that day."

Francis S. "Gabby" Gabreski was now in the right war but in the wrong place. Of Polish extraction, he was a freshman at Notre Dame University when the Nazis invaded Poland. He knew he had to go. "The world situation," he tells us, "was very dismal. It was a very upset world. We had one individual trying to master the world, and that was Hitler. And he was doing a real good job." Gabreski signed on for the U.S. Army Air Corps in July of 1940. First time around, his instructor washed him out. Fortunately, the reviewing officer detected something in Gabreski and gave him a second chance. This time he passed, and the career of a great fighter pilot was launched. After flight training, he was posted in April 1941 to Wheeler Air Force base on Oahu, overlooking Pearl Harbor. But when the attack came, "we never did get up. They strafed the barracks and scared the living daylights out of me. The second wave of airplanes came over the barracks, and after they left, there was absolutely nothing for us to do except get down to where

The P-36 could not match the performance of enemy fighters at the onset of the war.

all the airplanes were parked, wing-tip to wing-tip. The pilots, the airmen, any able-bodied man, went to work moving the burning airplanes away from the good ones. The hangars were going up in flames, ammunition going off. It was like the Fourth of July, the Roman candles, the tracers, and all the bullets started exploding in the hangars." Gabreski didn't get to fight that day—but he would, to the regret of many, many enemy pilots.

The United States lost 2,402 soldiers, sailors, marines, and civilians that morning; another 1,178 were wounded. All seven battleships were out of action, two permanently, three cruisers and three destroyers also suffered heavy damage.

Japanese losses that day were 29 planes and 55 flyers.

At 2:30 P.M. on December 11, Germany declared war on the United States. The United States declared war on Germany and Italy on the same day.

The war in the Pacific was long in coming, but in the end, it was never a question of whether it would break out, only a question of when—and where.

On April 13, 1941, Japan, although now formally allied with Nazi Germany, signed a Non-Aggression Pact with the Soviet Union. With its old nemesis Russia out of the way, only one obstacle stood in the way of Japan's annexation of much of Asia—the United States.

The man who crafted Japan's successful early naval strategies had been educated at Harvard and admired the U.S. Because he knew the country, Adm. Isoroku Yamamoto, commander-in-chief of the Combined Fleet, drafted the only kind of plan he believed would give Japan a chance against the vastly more powerful U.S.: a sudden and decisive knock-out blow of the U.S. Pacific Fleet at Pearl Harbor.

In 1941, the buildup of the woefully inadequate U.S. military was only beginning to gather momentum. Japanese naval aviation, on the other hand, was the largest in the world, with some 3,000 planes and 3,500 pilots. The Japanese navy, only 70 percent that of the U.S. navy, was better prepared for modern warfare and operated in one ocean; the U.S. fleet was spread between the Atlantic and Pacific. America's main strength, Yamamoto knew, lay in its population, twice Japan's, its wealth, and its manufacturing potential.

In December 1941, Japan took the fateful step. That winter day, Yamamoto committed his entire fleet to battle, the main force against Pearl Harbor. The rest of the fleet supported the army in a twin-pronged drive called the "Southern Operations"; 11 infantry divisions and seven tank regiments, covered by 795 combat planes, departed Formosa, Okinawa, and the Palau Islands to strike the Philippines in one attack; the other, mounted from French Indochina and south China, invaded Malaya and the Molucca Islands in the Dutch East Indies.

Malaya was the first struck. Japanese ships shelled the landing area. The Philippines were next. Word of the Pearl Harbor attack had been flashed to Manila. Gen. Lewis Brereton, commander of the U.S. Army Air Corps there, sent his B-17s airborne on unarmed patrol within minutes. They waited almost three hours for permission to strike Japanese air bases on Formosa (Taiwan). Meanwhile, the Japanese pilots in Formosa waited, frustrated, until thick fog lifted. Then, hours behind schedule and the element of surprise lost, 25 bombers took off. They were joined later by naval units: altogether, 108 bombers and 84 fighter escorts.

Francis S. "Gabby" Gabreski in full flight gear preparing for a mission in the European Theater of Operations (ETO) later in the war.

Arriving over Clark Field, they expected to find that the B-17s had escaped. Instead, they found the bombers and fighters parked neatly, bomb bays and ammunition racks loaded. Those aircraft were destroyed on the runway. At nearby Iba field, Zeros found the 3rd Pursuit Squadron of P-40s circling to land after scouting, their gas tanks nearly empty. All but two were shot out of the sky. Between noon and 2 P.M. that day, the Japanese destroyed 17 B-17s, 56 P-40s, and 30 other assorted planes. They lost seven Zeros. Japanese raids over the next two days targeted Nicholas Field and three air bases around Manila. Heavy damage was reported at the navy shipyard at Cavite. A handful of U.S. war planes escaped intact.

The situation was equally precarious on land. Gen. Douglas MacArthur was the commander of U.S. forces and a man with deep empathy for the Philippine nation. In July 1941, the Philippine forces were incorporated into the American army, and MacArthur, who had retired, was returned to active duty as commander of all American army forces in the Far East. He was to learn of the Japanese attack on Pearl Harbor from a commercial radio station.

Saburo Sakai, an eight-year veteran, was there. So, too, was Colin Kelly. They met in the skies over the Philippines. Sakai would go on to become Japan's fourth-ranking ace, with 64 kills. Kelly became America's first song-celebrated hero of the new war. According to the legend, Colin Kelly, flying a B-17, sent the mighty Japanese battleship *Haruna* to the bottom. Some even said that, realizing his plane was doomed, he dove right into her smokestack, blowing her sky high. Sakai, at the controls of a Formosa (Taiwan)-based Zero, tells the story: "It was December 10. We were at a place called Vigan [on the far northwest coast of Luzon]. A cruiser, the *Yura*, and about five destroyers were anchored, supporting a landing by the army. We were ordered to fly down from Formosa and provide air cover for them. A little past noon, I looked down at the sea—*boom*! *boom*! *boom*! Bombs were exploding near the ships. I looked up and saw a B-17, flown by Colin Kelly.

"We were flying at about 6,000 meters. When I looked up, I saw the B-17 about 1,500 meters above us. It had already started flying away, towards the south. Because that was the first time we had seen a B-17, all nine of us chased it. But it was very fast, and it took a while for us to overtake it.

"Finally, close enough, we attacked—but the B-17s were tough. We could not shoot it down easily. Gradually, our bullets began to hit the plane's body. Smoke came out. Then parachutes. One. Two. Three. Four. I confirmed up to

Below:
Nakajima B6N2 "Jill" running a gauntlet of heavy antiaircraft fire.

Isoroku Yamamoto in uniform, with medals.

five. I got closer to it, flying at top speed, and flew around it. I saw that only the pilot was in the plane. A fire had started and he had ordered his men out and flew the plane himself. The cockpit, too, was full of smoke. Grabbing the stick firmly and looking at me, he disappeared into the clouds.

"Kelly's bombs did not hit the ships, but he came to attack with only one plane against these fearful Zeros. He was a very, very brave man. That's why, with the photographs of colleagues who died in action, I placed Mr. Kelly's photograph in front of my Buddhist altar. I respect him."

There were other heroes: the pilots who flew the two glued-together P-40s that remained with the Bataan forces, until they, too, were shot from the skies. On the ground, beriberri, disease, hunger, and relentless air and artillery bombardment ground the defenders down. On March 12, MacArthur obeyed a direct order from the president and escaped to Australia, vowing: "I shall return." On April 8, the "battling bastards of Bataan" surrendered: 9,300 Americans and 45,000 Filipinos. On an infamous, 55-mile "Death March" from Bataan to a railhead, 2,330 Americans and between 7,000 and 10,000 Filipinos died. A month later, the 15,000 defenders of Corregidor surrendered.

Guam fell on December 10. Wake Island's tiny garrison held out until December 23. Hong Kong was bombed on December 8, and the Anglo-Canadian garrison surrendered on Christmas Day. The atolls of Tarawa and Makin in the British Gilbert Archipelago were taken in December. On February 15, the surrender of the British garrison at Singapore was considered the greatest military disaster in British history.

Part of the disaster at Singapore was due to the underestimation of the enemy's capabilities. British Intelligence believed that Japanese airmen and planes were not worth half their British counterparts.

Australia was now virtually defenseless. On February 19, 1942, planes from four of the carriers that had attacked Pearl Harbor struck against Darwin and surrounding towns in northern Australia.

Hopelessly outgunned, Allied forces hit back when and where they could. U.S. naval units raided the Marshall Islands on February 1. Three weeks later, a small American task force centered on the carrier *Lexington* moved to hit the big Japanese navy base at Rabaul, on the northern coast of New Britain. Alerted, the Japanese launched torpedo planes. Navy Lt. Edward "Butch" O'Hare, leading a flight of Grumman F4F3 Wildcats, met the oncoming torpedo planes. One torpedo plane after another went down in flames; O'Hare killed five in as many minutes to become the first navy ace of the war. The mighty *Lex* was saved, only to fight and die another day.

On February 27, the Allies launched an all-out attack on the Japanese invasion force approaching Java. The Japanese sank the U.S. light carrier *Langley*, depriving the force of the ship's complement of 32 P-40s that had been counted on both as air cover and as distant "eyes" to track Japanese moves. Only four destroyers managed to escape to Australia. With no naval or air opposition, the Japanese moved rapidly to seize the East Indies; Dutch forces on Java and Sumatra quickly capitulated.

On March 30, Adm. Chester W. Nimitz was given command of allied forces in the Pacific, General MacArthur in the Southwest Pacific Region.

Roy M. "Butch" Voris of Santa Cruz, California, was fresh from flight training at Corpus Christi Naval Air Station when he was whisked to service aboard the *Enterprise* in the South Pacific. He describes the difference between land-based and carrier-based pilots: "Ground-based, you live ashore, you live

A photo of Saburo Sakai taken during his first stay in Hankow, China, 1938.

The Brewster Buffalo sacrificed maneuverability for strength.

in the BOQ [Bachelors' Officers Quarters], or if you're married, you live at home, and you have your family. But the carrier keeps that squadron very cohesive. You build a camaraderie in carrier aviation that you'll find no other place in the world. The carrier is your home. You have the ready room and you have the sky. The flight deck and the sky. You leave the carrier, you do your mission, and you come back home, really. Making a carrier landing, you don't think of anything else. It's total concentration conducting a carrier approach at maybe five to six knots above stall speed, and grinding around there, and knowing you've got to make it or you're going to end up in the barricade.''

Camaraderie, training, a zest for flying, initiative—these qualities gave the American pilots the edge their machines still missed. The snub-nosed Wildcat, though a vast improvement over its predecessor, the Brewster F2A Buffalo, was still no match for the nimble Zero. As fast as its rival, and with a significantly higher ceiling (37,500 feet vs. 32,810 feet), it simply did not have the same maneuverability. But it *was* strong: ''It was built almost like an iron machine,'' Voris adds. ''I think that's why Grumman got the name the Grumman Ironworks.'' The big test for the two planes was not long in coming: the four-day Battle of the Coral Sea, May 7-11, 1942.

It was the first naval battle in history in which no ship sighted any of the other side; the entire battle was waged by carrier planes, of which the Japanese had three, the U.S. two. The American flyers, many knowing they hadn't enough fuel to return to their carrier ships, fought bravely and stubbornly. Butch Voris, squadron operations officer aboard one of the U.S. carriers, laments: ''We lost over half our aircraft that night.''

Warrant Officer Sadamu Komachi, based aboard the *Shokaku*, then the most powerful carrier in the world, tells what it was like on the Japanese side:

''We took off in formations of three, but after the first attack, we scattered. Looking around, the only planes I could see belonged to the enemy. They were coming from every direction. When I attacked one below, another one came from above. We were not, of course, perfect. Some of us tried suicide attacks to protect our carrier. It was a tough battle. There were many casualties.''

Douglas Dauntless dive-bombers.

This time, the U.S. lost the *Lexington*, 81 planes, and 33 pilots. The *Yorktown* suffered heavy damage, so heavy that the Japanese believed her destroyed. She was repaired in 45 hours at Pearl Harbor. The Japanese light carrier *Shoho* was lost, the *Shokaku* was crippled, 43 planes went down, and with them, 43 of their dwindling reserve of experienced pilots. Losses aboard the *Zuikaku* kept her out of the next major battle. The immediate effect was to blunt the Japanese blitzkreig in the Pacific.

Yamamoto planned to deliver the death blow to the Americans at Midway, a pair of tiny islands 1,150 miles northwest of Honolulu, and so end the war. The Japanese admiral hoped to surprise his enemies, first by seizing Attu and Kiska in the Aleutians, then by seizing Midway as a base from where he could destroy what remained of the American fleet.

He sailed from Hiroshima on May 27, 1942, with almost his entire battle fleet: 7 carriers, 11 battleships, 15 cruisers, 44 destroyers, and 15 submarines. Aboard the carriers were 272 fighters and bombers and the cream of Japanese airmen.

Yamamoto did not know that Commander Joe Rochefort's crew of crypt-analysts working underground at Pearl Harbor had succeeded in breaking the Japanese naval code JN.25 and knew where Yamamoto was headed. Admiral Chester Nimitz stripped Pearl bare and sent his three carriers to sea to lie in ambush northeast of the threatened islands.

On June 3, a navy PBY Catalina flying from Midway spotted the great Japanese fleet while it was still 500 miles away. The battle began on the following day.

The fighting was intense, relentless. Iyozo Fujita, who first saw action over Pearl Harbor and much since, was aboard the *Soryu*. He was ordered into the air in the predawn hours of June 4 to attack B-17s bombing the fleet. The bombers were too high, but while airborne, Fujita was diverted to pursue a flight of American planes returning from a torpedo attack. As he took after them, another message came in: dive-bombers headed his way. "I saw the formation coming towards me—five of them. I was alone. I had to shoot down Americans, or our aircraft carrier would be bombed. I came at them from the right, firing. Two or three fell away, trailing smoke."

Back on deck to refuel and rearm, Fujita remembered he had had nothing to eat and ordered rice balls. "But before the rice balls were brought to me, we had another warning. A new formation came, about 10 American torpedo bombers. I was joined by some Zeros and we attacked. In the end, only three Americans remained. Then we attacked about 15 fighters, and reduced their number to three or four."

By 10 A.M., Nagumo believed he had weathered the worst. Having fought off an attack by *Yorktown*'s torpedo bombers, he prepared to launch his own massive counterstrike. But Nagumo was beaten to the punch.

At 10:25 A.M., a dive-bomber group from the *Enterprise* led by Lt. Cmdr. Wade McClusky dealt the Japanese a stunning and decisive blow. Diving from 14,500 feet, and packing 1,000-pound bombs, McClusky's 37 Douglas SBD3 Dauntless bombers hit the volatile carriers with awesome fury. *Akagi* was the first to go; *Kaga* was next; *Soryu*, left ablaze and dead in the water, was finished off by a submarine; for good measure, the attackers sent a cruiser to the bottom.

Iyozo Fujita watched in anguish. "A bullet hit near my leg. The fuel tank blazed up. I climbed to six hundred feet, rolled over, and jumped out. I crashed into the sea. The impact was immense. Bang! I looked around and saw our carriers burning. I was so tired. I floated around and slept. One of our destroyers finally pulled me out of the water.''

The war in the Pacific had reversed course in a matter of minutes. The 1st Fleet had been destroyed—aircraft and pilots alike.

Hiryu managed to pound the *Yorktown* with two air groups, disabling her. But her turn came at five that afternoon when dive-bombers from the *Enterprise* damaged her so badly she was ultimately scuttled by her crew.

Mauled and battered, Yamamoto headed for the Japanese home island. Air power had turned the tide.

For the next two months, both sides sparred fitfully, regrouping for the big battles to come. Midway had confirmed beyond dispute the potency of carrier-based aviation. The two navies were now equal in carriers—three apiece—but already the *Wasp* was steaming to join the U.S. Pacific Fleet. Still other carriers were in production. Between 1941 and 1944, America built 14 big carriers, compared to Japan's 6. The U.S. also added 9 light carriers and 66 escort carriers.

While Washington debated its next move, the Japanese in 1942 easily dislodged small Australian garrisons from a series of islands in the South Pacific known as the Bismarck Archipelago. And on New Guinea, the Japanese massed huge forces in an effort to drive the Aussies off the island. Casualties in the first phase of the campaign—July 1941-February 1943—were staggering.

Two days after Pearl Harbor, a 33-year-old congressman from Texas became the first member of Congress to volunteer for active duty. He went on to become a lieutenant commander in the navy, seeing action in the South Pacific. (In December 1942, President Roosevelt signed an executive order returning all congressmen then on active duty to Capitol Hill.) Versions vary as to how Douglas MacArthur came to award the former congressman the Silver Star—the second-highest combat decoration—just as versions vary as to how that congressman would later deal with the medal. What seems beyond dispute is that Lyndon B. Johnson, the future 36th president of the United States, very nearly ended his life and career in the skies near New Guinea.

Saburo Sakai, the great Japanese ace, relying on his memory of many years

Lt. J.H. Doolittle with his Curtiss Wright seaplane.

past and with what he later pieced together from other events and sources, gives his version of those days:

"On June 9, 1942, we were based in New Guinea and fighting in Rabaul. Lyndon Johnson visited the front with Mr. Stevens and one more person—I forgot his name; they came from Townsville, Australia, to visit the front.

"They could have returned home from there. But Mr. Johnson and the other men thought their report would not be complete without seeing the Zeros which had achieved a lot of victories. Then they insisted on seeing the Zeros fly. They said to General MacArthur that they wanted to attack our base. MacArthur said, 'Of course not.'

"They were the important men of the country. Such a request could not have been accepted. However, these three gentlemen were very active men. They were told that meeting Zeros meant death. They answered that they were willing to die. If they would not see Zeros, their report would be without 'heart.'

"I was impressed. In Japan, even a chief of staff avoided going to the front. They insisted. So the Americans planned a strategy. The night before was heavy rain. Slightly before 8:00, B-17s were coming from far away. They tried to induce Zeros to come out from the base.

"Then North American B-25s—a five-plane formation, I believe—were attacking from a very low altitude. They let Zeros attack these B-25s and tried to entice Zeros towards the Arabura Sea and Coral Sea. The Americans had hoped that the Zeros would chase the B-25s, and a 12-plane formation of B-26s would follow the Zeros—without being attacked. Mr. Johnson, Mr. Steven, and one more person rode in three different B-26s.

"But we felt something was wrong and cornered a B-25 going towards the mountain, not the sea. It changed its course and started flying towards the B-26s. Then we started bumping into each other. We really bumped each other.

"The B-25 did not have any bullets left, so I attacked the B-26s. One, two, three planes—when they were coming, I shot. My bullets hit one of the planes and its bombs exploded. *Baang*!!! I flew through the formation and shot guns—*dadadadddadd*!

"Someone thought I made a body attack on one of the planes and reported it. But I flew away and looked back; one plane caught fire. I attacked another plane. *Ddddddd*! But there were clouds, and my plane and the plane I attacked flew into the clouds together. That was the plane Lyndon Johnson was in. His plane had a lot of bullet holes, but it managed to get away."

Sakai adds a postscript: "Each time I went to America, I was asked, 'Why did you shoot at this one first, not the other one?' If I hit the other one, there would be no President Johnson, no Wallgate [Watergate], no Vietnam War. So this scene completely changed the world history." He then shows the interviewer a painting done by an American painter "to let the world know that world history was rewritten on that day."

Sakai can be forgiven certain lapses of memory and fact-garbling, such as identifying Johnson with Watergate; Sakai himself was severely wounded in the fighting in Guadalcanal on June 7.

In May 1942, an Australian coastwatcher reported that the Japanese had occupied Tulagi, the British administrative capital of the Solomons and one of the best anchorages in the area. Later reports revealed work on an airfield on the island across the channel: Guadalcanal. American strategists quickly understood that with Rabaul to the northwest and Guadalcanal to the south, the Japanese would threaten U.S. supply routes to Australia and be within easy striking range of the remaining Allied outposts.

The lst Marine Division in New Zealand was hastily embarked on transports with a minimum of essential arms and supplies. At dawn on August 7, the vanguard of that 19,000-man division went ashore at Guadalcanal and Tulagi, quickly routing the 2,200-man construction force at the Lunga Point airstrip on Guadalcanal, subduing the garrison on Tulagi in 31 hours of bitter fighting.

The first American offensive of World War II had begun.

No sooner were the marines ashore than another coastwatcher, Paul Mason, warned: torpedo bombers headed your way.

Squadrons of Grumman Wildcats from the carriers *Enterprise, Saratoga*, and *Wasp* rose to meet the 27 incoming Mitsubishi G4M2 "Bettys." During that raid and others over the next two days, navy pilots and antiaircraft fire brought down 42 of the Japanese raiders.

The air attack was followed on August 8 by another and more ominous report: a Japanese naval task force was steaming south from Rabaul. Not wishing to risk his carriers, Vice Adm. Frank Jack Fletcher decided to withdraw, leaving marine Gen. Alexander A. Vandergrift's transports unprotected. Still aboard were 1,400 marines and more than half his meager supplies.

A few hours later more bad news. The Japanese naval force found Fletcher's cruisers at the western entrance of the sound leading to Guadalcanal and in 40 minutes sent four of them to the bottom, badly damaging a fifth. Not only was the Battle of Savo Island one of the greatest defeats in U.S. naval history, but it meant that the poorly provisoned marines on Guadalcanal were now on their own—"bare-arse," was the way their CO put it.

The airstrip was now the key. With the Americans stripped of naval cover, the Japanese bombarded at will from cruisers and destroyers. Then, there were the air raids. Every day at noon, Japanese planes arrived to bomb and strafe while shells were lobbed on the construction crews. A private named Roy F. Cate in the marine 1st Pioneer Batallion operated a bulldozer abandoned by the Japanese from morning to night to finish levelling the 2,600-foot runway. As he and others toiled, the Japanese began reinforcing their units on the 35-by-90 mile island, landing the first 1,000 on August 18. The marines, 10,000 strong on Guadalcanal, 6,000 on Tulagi, were down to half rations and, at one point, ammunition for four days. Finally, on the evening of August 20, General Vandergrift looked up: "From the east," he recalled, "came one of the most beautiful sights of my life—a flight of 12 SBD dive-bombers."

Led by marine Maj. Richard D. Mangrum, the bombers touched down on a field now named for another marine: Lofton R. Henderson, killed in air combat over Midway with his dive-bomber squadron. Continued Vandergrift: "I was close to tears and I was not alone when the first SBD taxied up and this handsome and dashing aviator jumped to the ground. 'Thank God you have come,' I told him." Later, the SBDs were joined by 19 F4F Wildcats, led by marine Capt. John L. Smith. The "Cactus Air Force," so called for the code name for Guadalcanal, was born.

"Butch" Voris was part of it. "We had battle wagons shelling the fields at night and we were in dire straits," he recalls. "We had to fly fuel and food in—or bring it in by specially converted destroyers. So we didn't have control of much. Maybe a square mile, and that's all."

George Chandler was among those army replacements. And he was one of that familiar breed of World War II fighter aces bitten by the flying bug at an early age. He was ll when a barnstorming uncle, flying a plane leftover from World War I, took him for a ride over Holly, Colorado. "I was so enthralled with flying in that airplane," he tells us, "that I wanted to fly airplanes like crazy." Years later, he flew his first combat mission, a P-38 over Guadalcanal. It very nearly ended in disaster—one engine lost power while he and the others were at 15,000 feet.

"Just about that time," he relates, "the Zeros came over the top of the clouds and down on top of us. And I was scared. My mouth was so dry I had chewing gum stuck to the inside of my mouth. I thought, that guy can't chase me into the cloud. I came out and there he was in front of me, and I gave him a bunch of it, then went back in the cloud and got back home."

The plane he was flying—Lockheed P-38G "Lightning" —was just beginning a combat career that would earn it the respect of aces in both major theaters. German pilots called the Lightning *Der Gabelschwant Teufel*, "The Devil with the Cleft Tail," for the plane's double tail fins. The Japanese dubbed it "Two fighters, one pilot." The Lightning was the first twin-engined interceptor to go into service in the U.S. Army Air Corps (in November 1941), and the first to top 400 miles an hour.

Now combat-blooded, Chandler dove his P-38 after two Zeros headed for the deck to drop bombs. "I thought, now don't dare go after an enemy fighter or you're instantly the target. Instead of the hunter, you're the hunted. How can I get those guys and be sure of it? The first one I was coming up on I let fly and could see the canopy go all to pieces. And when the canopy goes all to pieces, so does that guy's head inside. I went on past him to the second one and did the same thing." (Chandler, later Major Chandler, was credited with five official kills; on Guadalcanal, it was sometimes hard to be sure. "Our gun camera film," he notes, "was not in tropical packing, and it was always so corroded with fungus and mold and mildew of the jungle that none of our gun cameras would work.")

U.S. replacements now streaming onto the island, the Japanese operate their "Tokyo Express" in reverse, gradually evacuating 13,000 men. By the first week of February 1943, Guadalcanal is secure. The fighting is over. Many of the Americans—more than 1,000 of them—didn't make it beyond Guadalcanal. Joe Foss reflects:

"There's no one that, in the short span of life that we have here, that likes to leave ahead of schedule. And of course war will cause you to leave ahead of schedule. I'll guarantee you. I've seen it first hand."

For the Japanese, Guadalcanal meant more, far more, of their men "leaving ahead of schedule": 22,000 died there. The symbolic effect was even greater.

Henderson Field and the coral strip just off the northern tip of the island which they called Fighter Two continued to launch countless strikes in the months and years ahead. None would be more dramatic than the mission on April 18, 1943.

Newspapers of the day called him the foremost castaway since Jonah. That's how widely told was the story of W. Robert Maxwell. Bob Maxwell's love of flying dated from his boyhood days in Wasau, Wisconsin, making model airplanes and bumming rides on the real ones every chance he got while hanging out at the local airport. Enlisting in the Naval Air Corps on April 18, 1941, Maxwell earned his wings and ensign's commission, and on April 26, 1943, he reported for duty on Guadalcanal.

On his very first mission, flying cover for bombers raiding the Japanese air base at Munda, his division leader's engine-troubled plane accidentally clipped his tail, forcing him to bail out from his F4F Wildcat at 18,000 feet. Hear it from Bob Maxwell:

"It was about 4 o'clock in the afternoon when I bailed out. I floated down for about 14 minutes before I hit the water. After struggling with the parachute, I got into the little one-man life raft.

"Once in the raft, I got pretty sick. I didn't realize it at the time, but I guess I was suffering from shock. I was scared to death, naturally, and about ten minutes later, four planes from my division came out in a search mission. They were about 100 to 200 feet off the water and I saw them coming; I flashed my little round signal and they picked it up and circled me for about 10 minutes more to get a good fix. Then they headed off back to Guadalcanal, I figured about 160 to 180 miles away. At that time, I was about 10 miles from a Jap-held island called Tetipari, but I figured that somebody—a PBY or something—would be coming out to pick me up. But what happened was that a storm came up and blocked any chance of that.

"So I floated for four days in my little life raft. For the first three days, I was paddling like mad, using the little hand paddles we had. I tried to paddle towards Tetipari, but the wind was from the north and kept blowing me farther south. The paddling didn't do any good. That little raft was just like a leaf on the water. We had a little canvas sea anchor, so I threw that out and did a lot of praying. About the beginning of the fourth day, the wind shifted from the south and by the end of that day blew me into Tetipari.

"Seeing I was getting in close to land, I was, of course, elated. All of a sudden, I realized that in the big swells that my little raft was riding was a big stretch of coral between me and the sandy beach I was looking at. But, by the grace of God, there were some big splits in the coral, and I went right through one of those and never got injured, except that my flight suit was kind of torn. I was within an inch of disaster.

"I spent five days on that island, working my way to the opposite end from where the Japs were, and spent most of my time hiding in the woods and ridges and climbing up and down. Finally, I got up to the west end of the island.

"This being my first mission, I didn't have an awful lot of background on what to do, but they did tell us when we first came to Guadalcanal to head for an island called Rendova. It had a big tip just across from Tetipari. They said if you get over there, just sit and wait and the natives should come along and they should be friendly. I had some trepidations about that—it was about four miles across, and I didn't like that north wind. But I rigged up a sail out of my backpack, and oars from an old Jap anchor from a barge that had been beached, and sure enough, I made it across. When I came out of the surf, two natives who had seen me coming came up and I didn't know whether they could speak English, so I did a little 'pidgin' English to take me to the big white boss.

"And they said, oh, Mr. Horton. They never would tell us the names of the coastwatchers out there. Ended up that it was this Mr. Horton. Well, they hid me for two days in one of their villages. The Japs had ravished all the natives in that area, taken all their food and apparently a lot of their women, and they were on the run all the time, so they just had temporary villages. While I was hiding, they sent one of the men up into the mountains to see this coastwatcher. And he sent back what he called a constable and a note and some

Robert W. Max in flight gear.

cigarettes. Then this constable got a party of about eight natives together and they got me in a dugout canoe—I think it was the next evening—and started straight across for the north side of Tetipari, which is where the Japs were.

"So, I told this constable, I want you to get me out to sea— I don't want to get close. And he said they had a system: they let one of the natives go ashore in the shadows of the shoreline. What this native does is whistle like a night bird. So long as he whistles, we're okay. Then he told me to get down in the dugout and they covered me over with a bunch of bamboo. And this fellow slipped over the side and he whistled and whistled and we went right through this anchorage, except at one point he stopped whistling.

"I had a little chocolate left over—one of those little army rations—and I thought, well, if I've got to be a prisoner, I'm going to eat this chocolate. So I ate that little chocolate square, and then the native started whistling again, so we continued on our way. At sunup, we went in and camped until night. The next morning, they speared some fish and cooked the fish and, late in the afternoon, we started out. There was a famous coastwatcher named Donald Kennedy at a place called Gagi Point, and the natives paddled me across this open water in this little dugout canoe and got me in there about midnight. There was a native who spoke English, so he had me get all cleaned up and shaved—I had a pretty good red beard by that time—and I went to bed. Kennedy came 'round and asked where I'd been—they had sent all their scouts out to find me and thought either the Japs had gotten me or I had drowned. That's the last time I saw him—he apparently was sick with malaria, I found out later.

"The native who got me fixed up told me the next day I would be picked up by a PBY at 9:30 the next morning and to be ready. Sure enough, the next morning the PBY came in just a few feet off the water, they dumped me aboard and threw some boxes—I'm sure it was liquor—for the coastwatcher, and away we went.

"I was with my squadron in Guadalcanal just briefly before they sent me the next day to a hospital in Auckland, New Zealand, and then, two months later, back to the United States." (Within a year, Commander Maxwell was back in combat—to the regret of at least eight Japanese pilots he shot from the skies.)

The Japanese believe that if one's life is near the end, his shadow will become pale. The image went through Iyozo Fujita's mind that day in Rabaul. He was about to take off when a visitor waved at him. The visitor was the great Japanese sea leader, Isoroku Yamamoto.

"That's what I thought that day, when I saw Admiral Yamamoto. I said to my colleague later: I wonder if Mr. Yamamoto will be all right. His shadow looked pale."

The life of the great sea lord was nearing an end.

Rex T. Barber and John W. Mitchell both entered the service in 1940, before the outbreak of war. Barber went in as a private in the Air Corps, Mitchell as a cadet pilot. Both would end their careers as aces and full colonels. Barber, a native of Culver, Oregon, served six months as an enlisted man before taking flight training at Mather Field, outside Sacramento, California. On January 12, 1942, he sailed with the 70th Fighter Squadron, bound for the Fiji Islands. After the Guadalcanal invasion, he was moved to Fighter Strip #2. In January 1942, Mitchell was aboard the same ship, in his case as second in command of the 339th Fighter Squadron. Also aboard the ship was a stranger to them: 25 spanking new P-38s in crates. Strangers,

Rex Barber and other American flyers.

because none of the 30 pilots aboard had ever flown one, and it would now be Mitchell's job, as squadron operations officer, to teach them. A few months later, Mitchell was tapped to head a very special mission, a mission so sensitive that approval for it had to be bucked all the way up through Admiral Nimitz, on to Navy Secretary Frank Knox, and finally to President Roosevelt. The mission: assassinate Yamamoto.

"That," John Mitchell says, "was the most important mission I flew, and I guess the most important everybody else on that flight that day ever flew."

On April 14, 1943, U.S. intelligence intercepted radio reports that Yamamoto would be flying to Bougainville four days later. Yamamoto, on a morale-building mission, was known to be punctual to a fault. He was due at one of the six airstrips on Bougainville at 9:35 A.M., April 18. Mitchell, by then commanding his P-38 squadron, tells how it happened:

"They assigned me the mission, the Army Air Corps the mission, because the navy didn't have any aircraft that had the range to get up there. The Japanese had about 75 fighters on a base within 15 miles of where Yamamoto was going to land on Bougainville. It was about 350 miles if you went straight up there. But we didn't go straight up because they had coastwatchers all along this chain of the Solomon Islands. So we had to fly a circuitous route, and get down on the water, 50 feet off the water, so we couldn't be seen, or be picked up on radar.

"We started out about seven-thirty in the morning—16 P-38s, instead of the 18 originally planned. One guy blew a tire on take-off and another couldn't get his extra belly [gas] tanks set.

"The ground crews had worked all night long, hanging these big tanks on—they had never done that before. I don't know how they did it, but just as the sun was coming up, they hung the last tank on.

see that when we got to just the position where we were ready to turn in on the bombers that they were going to be right on our tail. So Tom broke 90 degrees to the left and up and into the fighters.

"I continued on in, rolled over and momentarily lost sight of both of them because I backed up so sharply. When I rolled back, I was slightly on the left side of one bomber. I didn't know which bomber because I didn't know where the other bomber went. So I started shooting across into his right engine, pulled over behind the right engine, and was within 50 yards of him at that point. He was smoking very, very badly out of his right engine and going downhill very rapidly — down to three or four hundred feet off the trees. As I got over the fuselage, he cocked one wing up rather rapidly and I almost hit his upturned wing as I went over him. I looked back and could see the black smoke still belching. The three Zeros evidently from the other side of the formation had caught up with us, and they were just ready to start shooting at me, so I hit the treetops and cut to the coast, and saw black smoke coming out of the jungle. I was sure it was Yamamoto's plane that had crashed.

"I continued taking evasive action as best as I could, right on the treetops. A P-38 is faster than a Zero and will run away with it in time. Well, about that time, two P-38s came over and the Zeros scattered. They ran, and I was free then. I went on out toward the sea, and then I saw Holmes and Hine circling out over the water. About the same time, I saw a Betty bomber right on the wave top levels, so low he was kicking up waves with his prop. Holmes and Hine saw him and so they dove down and started shooting. Holmes' bullets walked right up across the water through the right engine and back on out to sea. I could see white vapor coming off the trailing edge of the wing, so I dropped in behind the bomber and got very close to him and opened up. Second after I opened up, he blew up. Black smoke came clear over the top of me. A large piece of the bomber cut my left wing and took out the supercharger on my left wing. Another big piece hit the gondola where my nose wheels were buried and cut a big gash in the skin of the plane, embedded in the plane. Holmes shot down a Zero way up ahead of me—it burst into flame and spun into the ocean. There was another Zero coming along just below that, making a kind of slight bank and turning left; evidently he was looking at what happened to his friend. Because he came almost under me, I just rolled over onto him and had no trouble at all shooting him down. I think he never saw me, my bullets hit him before he ever saw me because he was so interested in this other airplane. So I turned and went home."

Yamamoto's charred body was later found in the jungle; his ashes were buried in Tokyo on June 5. The Japanese navy had lost its most treasured officer.

Joe Foss, the man who started his military career as a private and ended it as a general, looks back now across the rich tapestry of his own heroism, of a later life of accomplishment (including service as governor of South Dakota). Of those men, he says:

"Who could never not win with these guys? Gung-ho. They believed in their country. They believed in what they were doing. You could take them anyplace under the sun and they'd follow you. They believed in it, and they put their lives on the line. Young chaps, 18, 19 years old. I think about them all the time."

6 UNDER ALL FLAGS

The Battle of Britain had very nearly wiped out Fighter Command. But the ranks of The Few began to grow, swollen in part by volunteers, tomorrow's aces, flowing into the island from every corner of the globe, from the conquered nations, from neutral America. RAF fighter strength at home rose from 51 squadrons in 1940, when Britain in those dark hours could not muster even 1,000 pilots, to 78 by the end of 1941. England now carried the air war back to the Continent.

Pat Jameson in full gear in North Weald.

Above:
Pilots of the 71st Squadron scramble for their fighters.

In the conquered nations, a burning need to strike back.
In Commonwealth countries, a desire to protect the beleaguered island.
In America, a compulsion to help the underdog.

Reaching fighter cockpits in England required courage and persistence. Ragnar Dogger was barely 17 when his native Norway was overrun by the Germans. He took a fateful decision.

"I heard about the Battle of Britain and decided I'd try to join up. I tried to get out by boat, but didn't make it. Then I managed to get to Sweden, but they just laughed at me when I told them I wanted to join the RAF because I was so young. They put me in boarding school, instead. But I got some money from an uncle in Japan. We weren't allowed to travel to Japan, but they fixed some papers for me and I got over into Russia and across Russia by railway. The train trip took 11 days. From there, I got to Japan—on the very day Germany invaded Russia. I learned about it in South Korea. They told us we were pretty lucky to have managed to leave Vladivostok, because we would have been interned if we had still been there.

"From Japan, I got on a big ship bound for San Francisco, the *Asama-Maru*. Well, just after we crossed the international dateline, everything stopped. The crew seized all radios and compasses and spoke nothing but Japanese. After three days, we felt cold and understood we were heading straight north. Then the captain came on the radio and said we were going back to Yokohama. And then they stopped speaking again, and soon we crossed the dateline again.

"Just when we thought we were about to arrive in Yokohama, we woke one morning to find the same good service again and the same good Japanese English. They told us everything is fine—we're going to Honolulu. And we crossed the dateline for the third time. When we got to Honolulu, we were supposed to stay there for four hours. I grabbed my rucksack and jumped into a taxi. I asked the driver in my Norwegian English to take me to the highest point around. I had just $50, so I got out of the taxi at that high point and just sat there for four hours.

"When I saw the *Asama-Maru* leave the harbor, I went to the nearest police station and they laughed themselves to death when they saw me, and cried, 'Look at this young man, he's going to beat Hitler!' I thought they'd probably put me in jail, but they were very, very nice, and they gave me $50 and drove me to the Norwegian consulate.

"I stayed in Honolulu a few days, then got a job as a mess boy on an American ship. We sailed through the Panama Canal and on up to Baltimore. From there, I made my way to Little Norway in Toronto. I often tell my wife: I washed more dishes on that ship than she ever would in her whole life!"

Young Dogger began his odyssey on February 1, 1941. It was now around September 1941. America was still neutral, Canada, as part of the empire, was in the war. In Toronto, he joined up. First the dirty jobs—washing windows, scrubbing floors. Then he started in flying school, flying American Fairchilds for three months. Next, RAF training at Moose Jaw, Saskatchewan, and after six weeks, England.

"That," Dogger resumes, "was a bit tough, because until then, nobody had ever asked whether we could speak English. We had about a fortnight to learn; those who didn't were just let go." The training in Moose Jaw lasted four months, then back to Little Norway, now with pilot's wings, flying Curtiss P-40s. Six weeks later, aboard the *Queen Elizabeth* along with thousands of others bound for England.

What drives a 17-year-old boy to leave home and go clear 'round the world, virtually penniless, battering down one language and bureaucratic barrier after another, to fight in another nation's air force?

"Well," he tells us, "it started with the German occupation of our country. That got us all worked up. Then, before the Germans confiscated the [short-wave] radios, we heard interviews with the Battle of Britain boys. That's when we decided we had to do something ourselves."

Patric Jameson, a New Zealander, later commanded the Norwegian flyers, including Dogger. "They were," he says, "simply terrific." Jameson adds a footnote: the *Asama-Maru* did not continue on to San Francisco from Honolulu, but went straight back to Japan. "And all the poor people on it" he adds, "were prisoners of war for the whole war."

Waclaw S. Krol had already paid his dues in his Polish homeland fighting against impossible odds when the German blitzkrieg rolled over his country.

Poland was out of the war; Krol, like so many other Poles, was not. Among them, their top ace, Stanislaw F. Skalski, who shot down six-and-a-half planes with the 142 "Wild Duck" Squadron before escaping to Britain to fight again.

Krol also escaped, first to Romania, next to Marseilles where he joined the French *Armée de l'Air*. His first plane was a Morane-Saulnier M.S.406, billed in 1937 as "the best fighter in the world." By 1940, it was clearly not, and certainly no match for the Messerschmitt Bf.109Es. Next, he was in the plane France got too late: the excellent Dewoitine D. 520. At the controls of a 520, Krol shot down two more Germans before the collapse of French resistance forced him to flee once again.

With other members of his squadron, he escaped to Tunisia. The surrender of France only two weeks later once again left him as a warrior without an army. A French transport plane got him as far as Algeria; a train took him to Casablanca. From there, he managed to board a British ship that took him to Liverpool—and the Polish 302 Squadron of the Royal Air Force.

Ragner Dogger with mascot.

Waclaw S. Krol is decorated with the Distinguished Flying Cross with six kills in the RAF and two previously won in France.

Above:
Polish aces of 303rd Squadron.

The Battle of Britain was underway, and this indominitable Pole was now one of The Few. Within weeks of his arrival, on October 15, he bagged a Messerschmitt. Krol was now flying yet another type of aircraft, the Hawker Hurricane Mk. 1; but, for this tough veteran, adapting was easy. He had already logged 800 hours in the air in Poland, another 200 in France.

Perhaps no foreign group in the RAF fought with such passion as the Poles. Johnny Johnson bears witness: "When they fought together, they fought with an extreme sort of bitterness and cynicism. They showed no mercy and often gave up their own lives, ramming people and so on. That bitterness amongst the Poles—we could understand that."

Group Capt. Duncan Smith admired the Poles' fierce loyalty to their own. "I was leading my squadron back from a sweep over France, and we were well into Kent. I saw these two aircraft in front of me and flew up alongside, and they were Spitfires from the 303 Polish Squadron. The port wing of the one on the right must have been out of action because his chum had his wing underneath him and he was holding him up—which was a very dangerous thing for him to do! It was almost a mid-air collision. Well, he carried him all the way, as far as he could inland, then gave him time to bail out."

Hugh Kennard, who commanded Poles in combat, shares his memories: "When they were in the air, they were suicidal pilots. They didn't care for anything apart from shooting Germans. That's all they wanted to do. They didn't care whether they got killed themselves—they were almost kamikazes, actually. If they happened to see a German in the air, their discipline used to go sky-high. They would break away from the squadron and chase him and if you happened to get in front of them, they'd shoot you down as well. And they were excellent pilots. If they got shot down over the Continent, in France, and they force-landed, they always took two .45s in their boots and used to stand by their aiplane shooting all the Germans coming at them until they ran out of ammunition, and then they would shoot themselves. Nearly all of them, everyone in 306 Squadron, were shot down. . . . It was a great privilege having anything to do with them."

One who survived was Stanislaw Skalski. There is no bitterness now in his words. For example, he relates that he used to tell his young pilots: "If you shoot one German and lose your life, it's no good. If you shoot two, you can go off." Or: "They [the Poles] were very well trained and very keen to fight. [But] we were sportsmen only in one thing, you're fighting for your life. So you're not to kill somebody, but to win."

Adds Waclaw Krol: "We have been very excited. We wanted to fight with Germans, hard, hard. We knew what was happened in Poland. And so we fought very, very hard."

So hard, that during the Battle of Britain, Poles were only 5 percent of The Few but they accounted for 15 percent of the losses inflicted on the Luftwaffe.

The roll call of these remarkable men continues. Meet Miroslav J. Mansfeld, a Czech whose country the rest of the world bartered away hoping to buy peace for themselves. Mansfeld was a pilot in an air force grounded without being able to fire a shot. "France didn't want to help us. England didn't want to help us. Everybody thought, well, it's better to be quiet and let this situation work itself out. I can tell you," he goes on, "we didn't really enjoy it when we see the Germans taking over our aiplanes and telling us, you can go here or there, but first you've got to let us know where you are. You know, every time they wanted to fly our airplanes, they made us go out and test them first, in case someone had tampered with them." Czechoslovakia was occupied by the Germans, but the rest of Europe was not yet at war. Mansfeld wanted out—out. One day, he communicated as much to his CO. "So he said: 'Go to a certain restaurant in Prague and see a Lieutenant Schneider, and he will give you further instructions.' Sure enough, there was Lieutenant Schneider and he was organizing groups of six to leave Prague for Poland and then on to France.

"When we got to France and said we have come here to fight, they said, 'Oh no. That's not necessary. You see, we've got this Maginot Line and nothing can get through it.' We pleaded for a chance to fly, but they said war won't come. But you can go and join the French Foreign Legion.

"So we went to Africa and joined the Legion and, three months later, war was declared. That very day, we were sent to the French air force." But with France crumbling, back they went to Africa, where the British invited them to join the RAF.

It is now late June 1940. At a base near Edinburgh, the Czechs learn to fly the Hurricane and to master enough English to understand the code signals vital to combat operations. On November 13, ground control alerts them to an enemy plane over Aberdeen harbor. "'Tallyho, I can see him!' our [British]

Below:
Skalski's Spitfire in Tunisia.

Stanislaw F. Skalski in cockpit.

Above:
Sgt. Miroslav Mansfeld and Sgt. Olmar Kucera.

Above right:
An Me.109 pokes its nose from under a hangar in France that is camoflaged as a farm house.

squadron leader called out. The German dove right down to the sea. Three of us attacked: Peter Simpson, our leader, Otmar Kuchera, and myself. I was on my second attack when the German dropped his bomb; the explosion splashed water all over me. Next thing I could see, the German was in the sea, slowly sinking. Returning to base, my mechanic pointed out a big hole in the wing, about that much from the propeller. A little closer, and I would have been swimming with the Germans!''

Miroslav Mansfeld puts his war in focus. His father was killed in World War I when he was 18-months old. Later, he would tell his widowed mother: "Don't worry, Mommy, when I grow up, I will look after you." After the war, the Russians made his country captive, and he had to flee, without even being able to say good-bye. "And 50 years, 51 years later, I am still here, fighting for the Czechoslovak freedom, and 51 years later, they still don't know what it is." (He spoke those lines shortly before Czechoslovakia broke through to freedom in 1989.)

Against that backdrop: "I wouldn't say that [we Czechs] were fanatic, but we were trained to kill. It was for my mother, my country. When we have seen the British, they said, oh yes, oh yes, we shouldn't do that and we shouldn't do that, but we said, no, we have to do everything possible to shorten the war. And that was our attitude right from the start, naturally, because we were chased all over the place. France, England, Poland, they were pleased when they got rid of us.''

Many Frenchmen decided they had had enough. Many others fought on, some with the Russians, some with the British. The top French ace, Capt. Marcel Albert, flying with the all-French 1st Escadrille Regiment de Chasse Normandie-Niemen 303rd Air Division, racked up 23 kills over Russia. Wing Commander Jean Demozay bagged 21 with the RAF; Squadron Leader Pierre Closterman, who came to Britain from Brazil to sign on with the 341 Alsace Squadron of the Free French Air Force, got nineteen.

Some came even more circuitously. Take Jim Goodson, an all-around winner (32 air victories). By the time the war ended, Lt. Col. James A. Goodson's chest looked like a showcase for medals. They included the Distinguished Flying Crosses with seven clusters, the Silver Star, the Air Medal, a Purple Heart, and the Presidential Citation. As he tells the story, with war clouds darkening, the U.S. ambassador to Britain, Joseph P. Kennedy told Americans to get out of England "because there was going to be a war, and England was going to lose the war." So, "rather reluctantly," the 17-year-old youth boarded the first available ship, the SS *Athenia*. That was September 2, 1939, the day before England declared war on Germany. A few hours after war broke out, the SS *Athenia* was torpedoed, "and I found myself in the Atlantic. I was fished out by a Norwegian tanker and taken to southern Ireland." Only now, the Germans had managed to get young Mr. Goodson's dander up. Part of it was seeing women and children, innocents all, perish as the ship went down. Part of it because "in those days, we had no doubt in our mind about who the good guys and the bad guys were." But there was more, "the sense of adventure, of joining the battle. And, because I wanted to fly very badly. In those days, flying was the thing for adventurous young men."

So he marched into the first RAF recruiting station he saw and asked to join up. He could, but he would lose his U.S. citizenship. He joined anyway. Goodson was eventually assigned to the 43 "Fighting Cocks" Squadron at Tangmere, on the Channel coast near Portsmouth. Although there weren't very many Americans—only seven from neutral America fought in the Battle of Britain—Goodson "didn't feel out of place at all. The RAF, particularly Fighter Command, was a very international organization. There were Poles, a large number of French, Canadians, Australians, New Zealanders. South Africans, Rhodesians, and everything else."

Some, like the South African Adolph Gysbert "Sailor" Malan—the RAF's third-ranked ace during World War II—liked to send German bomber pilots home with a dead crew, as a warning. The great British ace Johnny Johnson, who flew with him, said of Malan: "He was the greatest fighter pilot we had in the Battle of Britain." Desmond Frederick Burt Sheen of Canberra, Australia, goes one better: Malan was "one of the finest pilots the world has ever known."

Brian Kingcombe, a graduate of the RAF's elite Officer's College at Cromwell, remembers those early war years when foreign volunteers were scattered throughout the RAF. "Each squadron had a handful of Rhodesians,

Below:
Eagle Squadron pilots in flight gear.

James Goodson in flying gear.

Above:
Group photo of first Canadian wing of the RAF to arrive in France (1944). British pilot Johnny Johnson is eighth pilot from right with a piece of paper in his hand.

Inset:
The 244th wing in Italy is shown. (L-R) Squadron Commander Stan Tume (Canadian), 417th Squadron; Squadron Commander "Hunk" Humphries, 92nd Squadron; Wing Commander Duncan-Smith; Group Captain Brian Kingcombe; Squadron Commander Lance Wade (US), 145th Squadron; Major Mosler, 1st South African Air Force.

South Africans, Americans, Canadians, Poles, Czechs. And they got on like absolute houses on fire. Everybody was amazingly international-minded." Ragnar Dogger adds a wrinkle: "Being a refugee from Norway or another country made us more like professional fighters. We didn't have to go home for dinner and have mother tell you to be careful and all that." The veteran New Zealander Patric Jameson agrees: "The best squadrons were the mixed ones, because they seemed to compete with each other. I can't say that I got any 'grizzles' against the New Zealanders I led, and the Norwegians I led, and the British I led; their squadrons were damned good, too. But the international ones had the edge. Yeah."

Brian Kingcombe resumes: "That huge mish-mash of nationalities made for marvelous spirit, a magnificent sort of feeling and *esprit de corps* engendered by the multitudes of nations all gathered today for the common cause.

"And luckily, everybody sort of speaks English. Even the Americans."

Well, not quite everybody. At first, all newcomers were obliged to learn at least basic command codes in English. That applied, at the beginning, even to the high-spirited Poles. Sort of.

Stanislaw Skalski had started studying English in Warsaw, back in 1933. By the time he hooked up with the RAF, he says, he had advanced to "good morning and [ordering] breakfast and so . . . So, during battle, after training and some of that matter, so I was switching off my radio because if they start talk in English fast, so I didn't understand and it, you know, it spoiled my sort of, orientation. So I always switched off radio." Ultimately, the pilots in the three Polish squadrons were allowed to use their own language.

Later, as more Americans joined the RAF, they were grouped together in the first all-American Eagle Squadron: No. 124, which became operational in May 1941. For Brian Kingcombe, the segregation by nationality was "a great tragedy." Some of the Americans weren't wild about the idea, either. By then, the Americans liked their British squadrons, the kind of camaraderie Kingcombe describes. Jim Goodson was one of 133 Squadron's first "volunteers"—shanghaied, really. The Eagles, Goodson remarks, by contrast with the RAF, had no combat experience and "they had very accelerated training and I think probably, looking back on it, for propaganda reasons, they were probably thrown into combat a little too early." On one of 133's early missions, escorting bombers attacking Morlaix near the Channel coast of Brittany, none of their planes came back. "And that," Goodson adds, "if my memory serves correctly, that is when [Blakeslee] and I were not just invited — we were told to join 133 Squadron. When I joined, 133 had been almost annihilated. It was a very dramatic scene when I went to Debden [the squadron's base, about 40 miles northeast of London]. In room after room of the officers' sleeping quarters, there were personal effects and half-written letters, 'Dear Mom, Everything's fine,' and the toothbrushes and shaving cream. All those empty rooms; it really brought it home.

"The remarkable thing is how fast the squadron was reformed—almost overnight. Americans were brought in from other squadrons, and 133 was on missions within a very short period of time."

RAF Ace Brian Kingcombe was on that disastrous mission and remembers that it started out as "one of those lovely, simple, harmless operations. The sort one dreams of." From what he learned later, Jim Goodson pieces together something of how the dream became a nightmare. "The weather got extremely bad. The wind shifted from the south to north, so they were blown farther into France, but didn't realize it because of the cloud situation. [The] 133 had a British commander at that time, and he was determined to protect the bombers and stick with them, and really stuck with them a little too long. Some were shot down by flak— they thought they were coming down into England and actually, they were coming to the Brest peninsula, over the city of Rennes. Others were shot down by 109s and [Focke Wulf] 190s. But in any case, they wouldn't have made it back because they just didn't have enough gas."

Acting wing commander Charles Brian Fabris Kingcombe in flight vest.

Pilots of the RAF's 92nd East India Squadron with scoreboard of aerial victories. Kingcombe is in cockpit.

92 EAST INDIA SQUADRON

92 EAST INDIA SQUADRON

DESTROYED 129
PROBABLE 60
DAMAGED 70
TOTAL 259

Four Eagle Squadron pilots pose with Spitfire.

Me.109 in flight.

Kingcombe, leading one of the three squadrons, thinks it was something else: "The first ever recorded incident of a jet stream. They didn't know there was a jet stream then. They just knew that some phenomenon had blown a few Spitfire squadrons, and one of the [Consolidated B-24] Liberators landed in Gibraltar." After wandering an excruciating time in fog—"we flew and we flew and we flew and I was getting bloody nervous"—he finally sighted a southern coast, said, "Thank God for that," and the Eagle Squadron circled off in the distance. "For no reason at all, except a hunch, I didn't follow them, but continued to fly north, my fuel needle getting lower and lower and I getting extremely alarmed." All of a sudden the radio crackled with a message from RAF control which had picked up his squadron on radar, telling them they were 100 miles south. "But sadly, that was the end of that magnificent Eagle Squadron. They were the cream. We lost quite a lot of them, and, of course, the Germans were handed on a plate a whole lot of intact Spitfire 9s with its marvelous new supercharged engine which, of course, their engineers leapt on."

With experience, the Eagles rapidly become a formidable fighting machine. They also became fighting fanatics. Hugh Kennard commanded a Polish squadron before they moved him to lead Eagle 121 at North Weald, northeast of London in Essex. The Americans, he found, were not "suicidal" like the vengeance-seeking Poles. But they were "enthusiastic, very enthusiastic. If the weather was bad, when one thought, 'I can stay in bed all day, or go to the pub, or whatever,' they wouldn't have any of this. 'Let's go and fly somewhere and find some Germans,' they'd say. I said, 'Well, you know, we can't do that. I mean, you have to have a thing called a Form D, the operational instructions, and so forth.' But eventually, we got permission from Group, if the weather was bad, I could take it into my own hands and go and find Germans."

By the time they were folded into the newly formed 8th Air Force's 4th Fighter Wing in September 1942, the 71 Eagle pilots had shot down 45 German aircraft. They had also produced the first four American aces of World War II's European Theater. And they would go on to become the most successful fighter group in the U.S. Army Air Force.

A British ace says of these buccaneers from the other side of the Atlantic: "They were an exhilirating company to be with, and some of them could almost salute."

The Eagles also learned to hit it off with the ladies. "The Englishmen,"

Goodson avers, "used to go off to the pub and drink beer, and we'd go off with their girlfriends. Sometimes I'd switch to the emergency Mayday channel and hear these people saying, 'Please call Daphne at Mayfair three-six-three-seven and tell her I'll be late for our date at the Savoy." Adds Hugh Kennard: "One flew all sorts of sorties all day, and in the evening, everyone knocked off and went to the pub—mainly Shepherd's in Shepherd's Market. If they had dropped a bomb on Shepherd's in the middle of the war, they would have killed the whole of Fighter Command!"

Others were learning fast, too. Ragnar Dogger recalls that, after the customary six weeks' operational training (OT), he was assigned to one of the two Norwegian squadrons, each with about 20 pilots. "On my first trip [mission], we lost four, before we even knew it. But we got four, too. If you weren't shot down within six weeks, I think you managed fairly well." Dogger sounds another common chord: "We admired RAF pilots very much. They were very calm and cool on their radios." Dogger stayed calm and cool enough to score six victories and win a DFC.

Stanislaw Skalski was an old-timer of 27 when he joined the RAF. "In RAF, they choose very young chaps to be fighters. If you was 26, 'Oh, go away! You are too clever now.' "

Andrew Robert MacKenzie, flying with the Royal Canadian Air Force (RCAF), saw something else to admire: the men leading these youngsters were themselves youngsters. MacKenzie names some he served with: "Buck" McNair, "a remarkably young and gallant chap," led his first outfit, the Red Indian Squadron, and later was inducted into Canada's Hall of Fame; Johnny Johnson; Lloyd Chadburn. "They were all gallant, and only 22 and 23 years old . . . leading so many people with such terrific responsibilities. I don't know how they did it, really. It was fantastic.''

Under the relentless browbeating of Lord Beaverbrook, Britain's minister of War Production, Britain's aircraft factories in 1942 outproduced Germany's for the first time. Britain turned out 17,385 planes that year, the Germans 15,556 (the Americans 45,000). Among the British planes: 3,300 Spitfire Mk.Vs, faster than the nation-saving Mk.1 (374 vs. 355 mph), capable of flying higher (37,000 vs. 34,000 feet), and packing two 20 mm cannons as well as four machine guns (vs. eight machine guns, no cannons). Unfortunately, the Germans came up with a superior craft—the Focke Wulf FW.190, considered by many to be the best German fighter plane of World War II. The fight over the skies continued. The raid on the French coastal town of Dieppe was on.

Gen. Sir Bernard Law Montgomery, then commander-in-chief of Southeastern Command, felt after bad weather caused delays that the raid on Dieppe ought to be cancelled. Churchill insisted otherwise: he felt—and the military backed him up—that until such a large-scale operation were undertaken, the main invasion would be impossible to bring off. And so the order was given: Operation JUBILEE must go forward.

Planning had started in April 1942 after a spectacular commando attack on the huge drydock at St. Nazaire. JUBILEE was more ambitious: 5,000 British commandos and men of the Canadian Second Division went ashore at dawn on August 19, 1942, supported by 252 ships, 60 squadrons of RAF fighters, and seven squadrons of bombers. The attacking force included all three Eagle Squadrons, as well as three USAAF fighter squadrons, the 307th, 308th, and

Pilots of JG.1 in Holland ready to scramble against British pilots at a moment's notice.

309th. Advance intelligence said the area was defended by no more than 1,400 "low-category" German troops. From an air cover standpoint, the choice was questionable: within 50 miles of Calais, there were no fewer than eight Luftwaffe fighter plane bases—the heaviest concentration along the entire coast. For the battle, the Germans drew on 190 serviceable FW.190s, 16 Me.109s, and 45 Dornier 217 bombers.

Churchill relates that the Canadian army had been waiting impatiently for action. They got it at Dieppe. Instead of 1,400 ho-hum troops, the attackers faced a full division, and on alert, to boot. All told, of 5,000 who went ashore, 3,614 men and 215 officers fell dead or wounded.

The Luftwaffe was slow on the trigger that day. Peter M. Brothers, commanding 602 Squadron, arrived at first light "looking for trouble" at 5,000 feet, but he found none. Later that morning, at 10,000 feet, [we] "got quite a lot of fun, a lot of activity. One of my flight commanders was shot down, bailed out into the sea. I circled around his dinghy until he was picked up."

Brothers' squadron darted back home for a quick lunch, rearmed and refueled, and back across the Channel a third time, now at 15,000 feet. "Interesting thing about aerial tactics," Brothers comments, "is how everybody's struggling for height. He who's got the height is on top in a big way." They did their fourth and last patrol that day at 25,000 feet. By then, "things had really hotted up. The Luftwaffe had bombers attacking the ships, the fighters roaming the area just as we were doing."

For James Edgar "Johnny" Johnson, the top-scoring (38 kills) British ace of World War II, Dieppe was "an absolute bloody shambles." Leading Fighter Squadron 610 on one of the nearly 700 missions he flew in World War II, he found that, on getting to Dieppe, "we couldn't even contact the headquarters ship, there were no communications—they had gone." As for the ground battle, "I caught a glimpse of the shattered tanks, just complete chaos and devastation. The planning was bad, the intelligence was bad, security was very lax—it was a bloody disaster for all concerned, and especially the Canadian army."

Patric Geraint Jameson, a native of Wellington, New Zealand, had been flying in the RAF since 1936. He apparently had an angel on his shoulder: Early in his combat career, during the Norwegian campaign (May-June 1940), he landed his aircraft aboard the aircraft carrier H.M.S. *Glorious*. A few days later, the German battle cruisers *Scharnhorst* and *Gneisenau* blew the carrier to bits. Not only was Pat Jameson one of the few survivors, but he was one of only 29 aboard a tiny raft to live through their ordeal at sea before being picked up.

Dieppe found Jameson commanding the Wittering wing: Johnny Johnson headed one of his squadrons, a Canadian squadron was in the middle, and Jameson led No. 485 New Zealand Squadron. Though he had seen action in Norway and Britain, "I had never seen so much activity, not before, not since" as he did that day over Dieppe. "There were a tremendous number of bombers . . . the bombers didn't survive long." He was moving in on one bomber formation when another squadron came in and shot them all down. Later, he nailed an FW.190 from below. "He was a flamer—flames coming up, surrounding the cockpit. The chap didn't get out. I think he was killed when I fired. Unfortunate for him, but that's the way it was." Viewing the butchery down below, Jameson learned an important lesson: "Before the army could do anything, really, they had to have air superiority over the battle area. Otherwise, they didn't have a hope."

Group Captain Johnny Johnson sitting on the wing of his plane with a mascot.

Sir Harry Broadhurst in the cockpit of his fighter plane as he prepares to lift off from the first Allied airstrip in France.

Sir Harry Broadhurst was a wing commander covering the withdrawal from Dunkirk. Now he was back over France, only this time at Dieppe on the offensive, 90 miles down the French coast from the scene of 1940's painful retreat. He really shouldn't have been in the air at all, because as operations chief of the key 11th Fighter Command Group, he covered all of southeastern England. But "I rang up [Squadron Leader] Duncan Smith and borrowed a Spit-9 from him and went over to see the arrival of the first troops at Dieppe and to see what was going on. Being a careful chap, I flew up to Calais or somewhere and got a brilliant sun and came down in the sun to Dieppe and saw four 190s doing exactly the same thing. So I attacked behind them. They went down and bombed the ships and then shot off at naught feet into France. Meanwhile, another lot were forming up. They seemed absorbed in bombing our ships so I got in behind them, the chap in the back end, and [shot him]. He bailed out and landed by a destroyer and I talked to him afterwards, actually."

Back in England, Sir Harry rang up the Operations Room for 11 Group with a suggestion: "Why not divert a squadron or a flight, put them up-sun over Calais at about 18,00 feet, and you might get a bit of business." The RAF pilots followed Broadhurst's lead and flamed an entire formation of four German 190s.

Broadhurst with fellow pilots.

Broadhurst flew sortie after sortie that day—he's not sure whether there were four or eight. What is clear is that he added four more German swastikas to the cockpit of his plane.

Shortly after the raid, Broadhurst was asked to brief senior commanders on the lessons of Dieppe. One of them "asked me all sorts of silly questions"— "silly," because they weren't about Dieppe, they were about how to invade Fortress Europe. The questioner was Gen. Sir Bernard Law Montgomery. One month later, Montgomery was given command of Allied operations in North Africa. A month after that, Broadhurst joined him as his air commander in the desert. "Probably this Dieppe experience," Sir Harry speculates.

For Reade Franklin Tilley of Clearwater, Florida, it was almost foreordained that he would be fighting alongside the British in an Eagle Squadron. Five Tilleys, he tells us, came over to America on the *Mayflower*. "So," he says, "we're pretty partial to England." It took a special circumstance to seal his rendezvous with destiny. "I had planned to be a racing driver, but that didn't work out too well, so I started looking around for something else important to do. There were a few wars going on, and I decided to pick this one."

Joining the RAF early in the war, Tilley was posted to 121 Eagle Squadron when it was formed in 1941. On March 26, 1942, he scored his first kill, an FW.190. But he found defensive fighting dull. By contrast, newspapers spoke of "hundreds of enemy airplanes over Malta every day." So, off he went, aboard the American aircraft carrier USS *Wasp*, in April 1942. It didn't take Tilley long to find Germans.

"On my first combat mission, I managed to pick up about half a dozen Messerschmitts on my tail, several times, and all in a matter of minutes. The intensity of the combat, the odds against you— that's something you have to get used to. I had a hard time staying in one piece on that first mission. After that, they came easier." Tilley shot down a 109 right out of the starting gate.

Tilley wasn't alone in courting danger over Malta. Another Eagle pilot he calls "Tiger" Booth "had a habit of lagging back, straggling. Now that you're not supposed to do, because that's where you get attacked. It took me a long

Colin Gray returning after a kill.

time to find out why he did that—to be sure he'd get into combat. He was shot down about three times, but survived all three times."

Other pilots didn't have to look for danger. It came stalking them. Colin Gray, who flunked the physical on his first two tries at joining the RAF, recalls one five-plane patrol along England's south coast. Suddenly: "I saw this gaggle of aircraft coming over, masses of them. In we went. I never saw the other four aircraft after that. Spent all my time trying to get out of trouble."

The best way to handle the "quite aggressive" Germans? "The best way to get rid of them," the New Zealander tells us, "was to shoot them down." It was a lesson Gray learned well: he bagged his first plane, an Me.109, over Dunkirk, and before being sidelined in July 1943, had run his score to 27½, making him New Zealand's highest-scoring ace of the war.

Andy MacKenzie, a Canadian, had to settle for a three-way share for his first kill—and that on his tenth mission, August 26, 1943. Two months later, he scored his first clean kill, an FW.190. But, by then, he had some help. Made gunnery officer of 421 Squadron after his first kill, Andy confesses that at that point, he knew "bugger-all about shooting." Fortunately, there was an expert at hand, the legendary George Frederick Beurling, top Canadian ace with 31 kills. He was then serving with 403 Squadron at the same base. In two intensive weeks, Beurling taught MacKenzie deflection shooting: how to shoot an enemy aircraft down while firing at an angle. "Deflection shooting is leading the aircraft. Like when you're shooting ducks, you have to swing your gun around so you lead the duck and he flies into the fire. Same idea."

Two months later, on December 20, MacKenzie put those lessons to good effect. Facing a formation of 50 German planes, he violated the cardinal rule

A group of British Typhoon pilots pose before the barracks with the squadron's mascots.

of fighter combat: he left his wingman and tore into the formation alone ("I was so young and keen, I couldn't resist the temptation"). With the whole wing watching, he proceeded to shoot down two FW.190s and an Me.109. Good thing: "It got me an immediate DFC; but if I hadn't shot anybody down, I probably would have been turfed off the wing and back to Canada as a bad boy."

MacKenzie discusses Luftwaffe pilots. "Quite gallant and very well disciplined. I remember getting on the tail of two aircraft. In the fighter world, you fly in pairs. And the number two looks after number one. They were so well disciplined that I was lining up my aircraft to shoot down this number two and only about 50 feet away from him. Instead of breaking off and leaving his number one to be shot down, he preferred to die. He was looking right at me when I shot him, covering his number one where he should have been."

One great ace, Johnny Johnson, discusses another, "Screwball" Beurling. Beurling had already made a name for himself in the desperate battles over Malta where, before being shot down and wounded in October 1942, he scored 28 kills. Awarded the DFC and DSO, he was sent on a triumphal tour of his native Canada. Johnson tells what happened next: "The Canadians rang me up and asked whether I could give Beurling a chance in the Canadian wing. [He] had the reputation of being difficult to control, a loner, not a team man. I said, of course he can have a chance. But we couldn't do a thing with him.

"He flew with us, but he'd peel off from 30,000 feet, go down after something, come back, all the rivets popped out of his airplane, eyes bloodshot with the G forces he put on. He was just not a team man. And so he had to go."

Bristol Beaufighter.

When the Battle of Britain ended, the two air forces jabbed at each other across the Channel. German night raids continued but no longer worked so well against the increasingly sophisticated RAF. The most effective British weapon was the Bristol Beaufighter, armed with four 20 mm cannon in the nose and six .303 machine guns in the wings. And, with the Russian, Mediterranean, and African fronts draining Wehrmacht resources, the Luftwaffe could no longer mount huge raids on Britain. The alternative was to send small formations of Me.109s or FW.190s on fighter-bomber missions, flying either so low as to evade radar, or so high the pilots could make prolonged diving attacks across the Channel. Many pilots took off without pre-identified targets; the German pilots called them "reconnaissance with bombs." In every case, the emphasis was: hit and run. The low-flyers soon bashed into a British nemesis: the Hawker Typhoon. The "tank-basher" was not only good in ground support roles, but was faster at low altitudes than either the FW.190 or the Me.109, and with its four 20 mm cannon, it was an awesome adversary. Harry Broadhurst comments: "Fortunately for us, they [the designers] didn't develop [upgrade] the Hurricane. They designed a new aircraft based on the Hurricane which became the Typhoon."

On the Allied side, the pilots called their sweeps "circuses" or

Famed legless British ace Douglas Bader is greeted by JG.26 officers at the Schlageter wing's headquarters in France. Bader meets here with Colonel Joachim Huth, who lost a leg in the previous war. Pilots from left are Adolph, Schopfel, Galland, Causin. To the right rear of Huth stands Eschwege, and at Huth's right shoulder, Horst Barth.

"rhubarbs"—offensive sweeps up and down the French, Belgian, and Dutch coasts, taking the war to the enemy. They began in earnest on June 22, 1941, the very day the Germans invaded Russia.

New Zealander Robert Spurdle began and ended his combat career in Europe, with the Pacific sandwiched in the middle. Now he discusses rhubarbs: "During the Battle of Britain, with 74 Squadron, we flew as a squadron of, say, 12 aircraft. Now, with 91 [Squadron], most of our work was solo flying, shipping, and reconnaissance. One plane flew south, and one north. The two planes took off and it was up to ourselves as to what height we flew and which direction we took. So it was extremely dangerous, and so they [the missions] weren't extremely popular with us. We had to fight over enemy territory now, flying machines which were no faster than those of the enemy. In fact, I think they were slower. It was extremely dicey. We lost a lot of pilots."

Stanislaw Skalski remembers rhubarb sweeps taking the pilots as far as their fuel would last. He also remembers Doug Bader, the legless ace, working to perfect four-plane, finger-four formations during those sweeps, the same fighter formation introduced by the German ace Werner Mölders in Spain. To Brian Kingcombe, rhubarbs meant flying the Channel "at wave-top height underneath radar and picking opportune targets wherever we found them— gun placements, military lorries or whatever. We'd just have a bash!"

Robert Spurdle relishes one particular episode from the rhubarb days of 91

Spurdle leaning against his plane named Nigeria.

Hawker Hurricane in flight.

Squadron. It happened on July 26, 1942. He and another pilot were flying patrol off the white cliffs of Dover, keeping an eye out for stragglers returning from sweeps into France. "Off Dungeness Point, at about 5,000 feet, we found these four strange aircraft above us. Focke Wulf 190s. We were flying the old Mark-5 Spitfires, much inferior to the 190. For a very shameful second, I thought, you know, shall we or shan't we? I called out on the radio, expecting to get some sort of assistance, but the sweeps over France were occupying the controller's attention. So I led my number two up and we kept on climbing and the four Jerries on top saw us and dropped down on us. It was very difficult because they had the speed and height. All we could do was make head-on attacks, and eventually I managed to shoot the leader down. I must have hit him in the oxygen bottle. There was a big white cloud and his tail fell off, and down he fluttered and bailed out. My Number Two damaged the other aircraft.

"But the best part," Spurdle says, was yet to come. He learned that the German was Horst Benno Kruger, who had shot down 17 Spitfires and was a *schwarm* leader of some note. Spurdle and his wingman went to see Kruger in Dover Hospital. Spurdle describes himself as "short, bald, and scruffy and [wearing an] old uniform." His Number Two: "a nice, tall, handsome Englishman. So in we marched and this German said, congratulations, and held out his hand to my friend. My friend stepped aside and Kruger saw me and it was like a pin in a balloon to be bested by such an insignificant little person."

Brian Kingcombe recalls a more dramatic rhubarb incident. A man named Victor Beamish was out one foggy morning on a rhubarb when he happened to see "these three enormous boats going up the Channel." Beamish didn't know it, but he had stumbled on Operation THUNDERBOLT, a daring German plan to do what no enemy of Britain had succeeded in doing since 1690: move hostile surface forces through the English Channel. Kingcombe resumes the narrative: "So, he [Beamish] called Control and said, I think *Scharnhorst* has escaped! 'Absolute balderdash, my dear fellow,' they said. 'These are bottled up and can't escape.'

"What happened was that the Bomber Command the night before had sent over reconnaissance aircraft to photograph the German capital ships at Brest harbor, and the report was that they were so badly crippled that they would not be able to leave for some weeks. So the submarine on permanent surveillance was called off, and they were just written off. What happened, we discovered later, was that they had very carefully covered the ships with debris and made them look as though they were a mess."

What Beamish saw was the culmination of a plan over one month in the making—to move the 26,000-ton battleships *Sharnhorst* and *Gneisenau* and the 10,000-ton heavy cruiser *Prinz Eugen* to safer anchorage at Wilhelmshaven in northern Germany. For the operation the Luftwaffe committed 252 Me.109Fs, FW.190s, and twin-engine Me.110 night-fighters. On the night of February 11, 1942, the ships, escorted by three destroyers, sailed. At dawn, nearly 60 torpedo boats and other smaller escort vessels joined them. They were opposite Dover before they were sighted.

Finally, the alert went out. Kingcombe's squadron was advised that German E-boats (torpedo boats) were "rushing up and down the Channel." Three times came the counterorder to stand down. Then, on the fourth alert, they were ordered into the air to escort a flight of Fairey Mk.1 Swordfish, that old, low, slow, awkward biplane, but nevertheless one of the finest torpedo bombers in history.

Pilots of 71st Eagle Squadron crowd around Congressman J.B. Snyder.

Kingcombe's squadron was supposed to rendezvous with two other squadrons of Spitfires at Manston in Kent, then cover the Swordfish. But there were no other Spitfires. Into action anyway. But they found not only E-boats, but "a bloody great battleship. The Swordfish came down to sea level and the *Prinz Eugen* turns all her guns around and puts up a wall of water in front of them. Most of them made it through, though."

Next, the air attack begins; Kingcombe saw a 190 for the first time—and was impressed. The Swordfish fared less well with the curtain of fire put up by the German ships, shredding the wings, killing the gallant crew that launched their torpedoes before dying. Adds Kingcombe: "The sad end of the story: all six Swordfish were shot down, the leader killed, most of them killed. It was a tremendous coup for the Germans."

More so than Kingcombe knew. The British continued to hit the flotilla with Westland Whirlwinds, Bristol Blenheims, Bristol Beaufort bombers, Vickers Wellington bombers, Handley-Page Hereford bombers. Altogether, the Fleet Air Arm, Coastal Command, Strategic Bomber Command, and Fighter Command put up 250 aircraft. Of 15 fighter squadrons in action, bad weather and the heavy flak meant only 39 planes managed to get close enough to launch attacks. The Luftwaffe lost 17 aircraft that day, shooting down 49 British planes, plus 13 probables. The three ships managed to escape and make it to Wilhelmshaven.

For Patric Jameson, now in his sixth year in the RAF, the rhubarbs had a very special meaning: "When we started on those offensive sweeps, farther and farther into France, Belgium and Holland, it was pretty obvious that we had beaten them."

But, inevitably, taking the war to the enemy was costly. In 1941, the RAF lost somewhere between 850 and 950 fighter planes. In 1942, the figure was

900. The Luftwaffe, in those two years, claimed losses from all causes on the Western front of 450 fighter planes.

David Cox steams up discussing sweeps: "I've always considered they were rather a waste of time. It was Churchill's idea. Germany had attacked Russia, and he decided we must show some effort. We couldn't open a second front, obviously. So all right if we do fighter sweeps, it will tie up some of the German fighters.

"Well, I think it only tied up about a couple hundred. The Germans used to sit on the ground and watch us go over the top and we were wasting a lot of very valuable fuel. Then they thought, well, we'll put a few bombers in and perhaps bomb the odd railway yard in France, which I don't think did very much because I sometimes used to drop the bombs in the field, or perhaps kill a few Frenchmen.

"But it perhaps brought the Luftwaffe up a little bit. They were at a great advantage, because unlike us in the Battle of Britain, we would want to take off and intercept the bombers quickly. They weren't defending their own homeland, so they would quietly take off—Galland was one of them—and get superior height and have a look at us and just come down and pick the odd straggler off. We used to get the figures: six fighters lost, perhaps two of the Luftwaffe gone. We lost some very good pilots. I've always felt that was an awful waste of time."

Cox then adds a common lament: to placate the Russians, Churchill deprived his own forces, diverting fighter planes headed for the embattled garrisons of southeast Asia to Russia. "We were about to lose Singapore," Cox continues, "and I remember reading several books on this, that three or four Spitfire squadrons out there might have saved the *Prince of Wales* and *Repulse*. So I was not in favor of those sweeps."

The Germans had their version of "sweeps." They called them *Jabos*, or fighter-bomber raids. Herbert Ihlefeld explains: "*Jabo* is any aircraft equipped for ground support. It has all sorts of weapons—machine guns, cannons, shrapnel bombs, what have you. My group flew several *Jabo* missions over England, which was essentially a tertiary mission: we were pursuit pilots, we were escorts, we flew *Jabo* missions, we were rather poorly equipped, carrying only a 250-kilogram bomb which we dropped from high altitude practically without sighting in order to devote ourselves to other more essential missions—protecting the other combat aircraft and engaging the enemy fighters."

Reflections of fighter pilots.

Desmond F. Sheen joined the RAF before the war because he thought he would like to see the world. The sights he saw were mainly violent but, says the Aussie ace, "I have never regretted it." Nor does he harbor rancor against the Germans. "They had a job to do, which was to shoot us down, and we had a job to shoot them down. It was a gentlemanly war, we were all gentlemen."

Colin Gray, who was bitten by the RAF bug after seeing the World War I film epic, *Wings*, amplifies: "One was never really conscious of the enemy pilot flying the aircraft. We weren't trying to hurt him, just shoot down the aircraft. I remember being quite pleased when I saw one of them bail out, thinking, oh well, he's all right, anyway."

Andy MacKenzie viewed the war in a similar vein: "There was no animosity between the two pilots, just a game. You never thought about his next of kin, or whether he had kids or anything like that. Most of the young people like myself had utter confidence. I never dreamed that I would get a hole in my airplane —I was so good at what I did.

"We never thought about the blood and gore that's in the cockpit. We just looked at those crosses on the aircraft and tried to hit the cross. It was almost like a pinball machine."

Patric Jameson aimed for the gas tank, just below the pilot's seat. "Almost certainly it would be a flamer then."

Ragnar Dogger on aiming: "The first time I shot at a German, I never hit it. The squadron commander who flew alongside me told me I'd been too far away. You have to see the white of their eyes to be sure to kill them."

Jameson remembers a moment of terror when he got separated from his squadron while chasing Messerschmitts. One of the Germans got on the radio and answered in English ("those rascals did that very thing"), tricking him into climbing to rejoin his boys. Only they weren't his boys: "I could see the cannons as they came on, winking. I screamed! I thought, God, I'm going to get a cannon shell through my tummy. I thought it might not hurt so much if I screamed. But I didn't panic, kept slipping and skidding so as to get away. I was terrified, of course." The slipping, skidding, steep dives helped—briefly.

Then: "To my horror, there was a fellow formatting me, a German. I looked on the other side, there was another one." Fortunately, their guns had iced up, as had his. The ordeal wasn't over. "I got on the deck and opened up the throttle flat out and went out over the sea, towards England. On and on and on. No England. God, that's strange, I thought. Then I noticed a bubble on my compass, which had led me astray. Then I saw a great big bluff, and I realized it was Cape Gris-Nez. I was back to France again, getting shorter and shorter of gas. So I got the sun on my left shoulder and steered with that and eventually landed at base with just a trickle of petrol in my tank."

Planes were faster, deadlier. But they weren't much more comfortable. Jameson: "We had a dinghy on top of our parachute that we used to sit on. And if that wasn't packed properly, it was very, very lumpy. And, of course, the Spitfire cockpit wasn't pressurized, so it was very, very cold in the wintertime up around 30,000 feet where we had to go sometimes." The lumps, the cold— the terror.

Jim Goodson has the last word: "We were very young, and very full of fun and enthusiasm. Because, of course, it was always the other guy who was going to get shot down, not you."

As 1942 ended, there were approximately 20,000 U.S. airmen in Britain, mainly in the East Anglia area. Americans in the Eagle Squadrons were phased into this new U.S. phalanx.

"It was a gradual thing," Jim Goodson explains. "We went down to London by twos and came back as American officers. But we even continued flying the same planes. We simply painted out the British roundel [insignia] on our Spitfires and painted on an American star. And since we'd all been in the RAF, including most of our officers and commanding officers, there was really very little change in things. Of course, eventually we changed our Spitfires for longer-range Thunderbolts, and then the remarkable P-51 Mustang. But the spirit and so on, I think we carried on the spirit of the RAF."

There was, of course, a mite more to such a huge emotional change, particularly for veterans like Jim Goodson who had been in the thick of it with the RAF long before America entered the war.

"We said we wouldn't transfer unless we could keep our RAF wings. So we

Australian pilot Desmond Sheen in cockpit of his fighter plane.

FW.190s in flight.

got permission from King George of England and the president of the United States, and we wore our smaller RAF wings here, and the U.S. Air Force wings there, and were very proud of those. We were able to wear our RAF decorations, too. They were very tolerant of us.''

''They'' had good reason to be: ''It's true, of course, that our British wing commander was replaced by an American general. But we were very lucky with our generals in the American air force. They understood that we who had been brought up in the RAF were a little different from their people. They also realized that we had an enormous amount of experience. I remember, for example, when we painted the roundels off, I said it would be nice to do a mission now to show Spitfires with the U.S. star on them. So I called up and said, 'Can I do a mission, low-level, so that people can see the star?' And our general said, 'Well, Jim, if you think you can get away with it, okay, but don't get yourself shot down because we need you.' So, although we expected things to be very different, really we were left to continue our RAF methods.''

Goodson remembers one particular ''tolerant'' American general: Dwight Eisenhower, by then the four-star commander of all allied forces in the West. ''In one of my books, *Tumult in the Clouds*, there's a picture of Eisenhower and his staff at my base. And I'm talking to him, and Eisenhower was asking my opinion on what we should do. He did that. He'd go all around the table and get all those impressions and then at the end, he would make the decision. He was a great diplomat. Most of the American generals were that way. They were outstanding."

There was, actually, one difference: "We also got a greal deal more money. I don't think this affected us very much because we never had enough time to spend the money we had. Although we got practically nothing in the RAF, I never remember being short of money. However, it did cause some resentment, particularly with British males because they felt we Americans then had so much more money to spend on our girlfriends." It translated in a refrain familiar to tens of thousands of American GIs in wartime Britain: Americans, it went, "are overpaid, oversexed and over here!" But, Goodson adds, the "resentment was not reflected in the general public, and I don't think it affected us."

Reade Tilley reflects: "When I was in the RAF, I felt part of a big, old, traditional organization, a very important one." He would learn to adapt well to his new one: he went on to serve until 1965 in the U.S. air force, retiring as a colonel.

Those Eagles would go on to create their own legends, their own traditions, in the 4th Fighter Group.

Stanislaw Skalski of Poland: "The RAF is the finest organization I met during my life."

Desmond Sheen, Australian: "We were a mixture of English, Canadian, Australian, New Zealand, you name it, they were there. They paid their own way over, too, by the way. Everybody wanted to fly. A very hilarious bunch. Good-natured. We took the 'Mickey' out of everybody else and we thoroughly enjoyed life."

Jim Goodson, American: "I was privileged to fly with some very outstanding, unique, and wonderful people. A lot of them didn't survive the war. After the war, I felt that was very tragic. I went to see their next of kin and I realized that these boys had no grave, no memorial—they'd just been blown away. I felt they should have a memorial, so I wrote a book about them."

Desmond Sheen, half a century later: "It's very difficult to explain the spirit you found throughout the war. It was pretty hard going. A lot of people got killed. But everybody made the best of it. The camaraderie was terrific. We made terrific friends, and we stick together, even to this day."

Reade Tilley, American: "I found that the war years, my time in the RAF, probably are the best years of my life. I thoroughly enjoyed every minute of it. You know, I'd love to do it again."

The Americans are gone, but the RAF remembers the international organization—the Poles, the Czechs, the French, the Norwegians, the men from the Commonwealth countries, and the Americans.

7 MEDITERRANEAN SHOWDOWN

At 6:57 A.M. on June 11, 1940, the 300,000 inhabitants of Malta heard the high-pitched wail of air raid sirens. Minutes later, 10 Savoia-Marchetti 79 bombers in two V-shaped formations approached the island at 14,000 feet. The unopposed (as expected) raid completed, they set course back to Sicily. Suddenly, the rear plane in the tidy Italian formation was stitched by machine gun fire. Faith, Hope, and Charity were in the air. In all of the annals of aviation, there has never been anything quite like them—for raw courage, for inventiveness, bravery, dogged determination, for the measure in which so few, so very few, could affect so much the fortunes of war—for the unbelievable, preposterous, mind-boggling improbability of it all.

M.T. St. John's Gladiator shown in flight.

As war approached, Air Commodore Maynard, the air officer commanding Malta, found he was a flight leader without any planes. One day, he learned that some mysterious packing crates on the dock at Kalafrana contained some dismantled biplane Gloster Sea Gladiators. Not one of the dozen or so pilots on Malta had ever been trained as a fighter pilot, but to a man they volunteered. Four planes miraculously escaped damage on that first day of combat, one was thereafter cannibalized for spare parts, leaving three planes for combat. *Faith*, *Hope*, and *Charity* symbolized the intrepid knights of yore, the historic Sovereign and Military Order of the Knights of Malta.

With France collapsing and Italy in the war, the balance of power in "the Med" shifted dramatically. Italy's *Regia Aeronautica*, the first of the independent air arms among major powers, went into the war with 3,295 aircraft, of which 1,796 were frontline: 783 bombers, 594 fighters, 268 observation planes, and 151 reconnaissance planes. They had overwhelming numerical superiority in the Mediterranean, and the advantage of geography.

And they were more than a match for the three Gladiators, single-bay biplanes more reminiscent of the Sopwith Pups, Camels, and S.E.5 scouts of World War I than the new generation of fighters and bombers. Though sturdy and highly maneuverable, the Gladiator was even slower (257 mph, top speed) than the Italian bombers (267 mph).

That first day, the Italians sent over 150 unescorted bombers against Malta in eight separate raids. But after being stung by *Faith*, *Hope*, and *Charity*, the Italians guarded the bombers with fighter planes: Fiat C.R.42 Falco (Hawk) open-cockpit biplanes and Macchi M.C. 200 Saettas (Arrows).

Each time they came, *Faith*, *Hope*, and *Charity* rose to meet the dense formations of attackers, shooting down one of the bombers the very first day. Against the Italian fighters, the Gladiators had one advantage: superior armament. The Gladiators mounted four machine guns; the Italian fighters only two.

For tens of thousands of Maltese watching the air battles overhead, the mere fact that their side was fighting back turned despair into defiance. Day after day the Italians bombed and strafed. Day after day, the Maltese risked injury to watch—and to cheer their gallant fighter pilots. On July 16th, the inevitable: one of their planes, piloted by Peter Keeble, was shot down, Keeble killed. All Malta mourned.

The two remaining planes—battered and abused beyond all imagination, as were the pilots—fought on. At one point, Flying Officer Collins and the bedraggled ground crews improvised an impossible solution: fitting engines intended for Blenheim bombers into the fuselages of the Gladiators, giving the planes a new lease on life.

July became August, and the planes continued to fight against 50-to-1 odds. Furthermore, the Italians began sending far more fighter planes than bombers, obsessed with shooting down the infernal Maltese falcons. Along the way, the Gladiators not only shot down somewhere between 30 to 40 of the Italian raiders, but repeatedly broke up the bomber formations, causing thousands of tons of bombs to miss their target. And their bravery was catching. But pilots and planes were near the end of their endurance.

Then one day in August, four sleek monoplanes streaked in for a landing. The first of the long-promised Hurricanes had arrived, flying off the deck of the ancient British carrier *Argus*. By the end of the month, eight more had come.

The Italians immediately intensified the ferocity of their raids. By October, only one Gladiator and four Hurricanes were left. More would come—but at a high price. Still, by the fall of 1941, the British, by now on the offensive in the Mediterranean, had managed to ferry 300 fighters to Malta from the carriers *Ark Royal* and *Victorious*. In the first five months of combat, the handful of defending fighter planes shot down 37 Italian and German aircraft.

By late 1941, Malta had come to the attention of Adolf Hitler. So long as the island survived, Malta's aircraft and ships foiled Axis efforts to supply their forces in Africa. In December 1941, Air Army 2 (Luftflotte 2) was transferred from the Russian front to the Mediterranean to reopen the supply route by blasting Malta into submission. Now it was the turn of flyers like Reade Tilley, "Screwball" Beurling, "Tiger" Booth, the American James A.F. MacLachlan,

Three Hurricanes shown low in flight.

and many more like them to meet the new and grave threat. Percy Belgrave "Laddie" Lucas was among them.

Laddie had been flying with RAF 66 Squadron in Fighter Command Group 10 since August 1941, mainly escorting bombers on cross-Channel raids. All in all, Laddie had just about had his fill of over-water flying, which he mentioned to a good friend, Ron "Daddo" Longley, whose father had been a distinguished officer in the Royal Air Force. "He said to me one day, 'You know, we really ought to go abroad.' And I said, 'I wouldn't mind going.' It's a great thing to have a friend with a friend in the RAF. Well, almost the next day, a signal came through to 66 Squadron: Post two pilots to Burma. So Ron nudged me and said, 'What about it?' The agent was standing there, so we put our hands up. About a week or ten days later, we were in Malta. Not Burma, but Malta.

"The conditions in Malta when we got there were totally different from what we expected. First of all, we were Spitfire pilots and we had been told that there were Spitfires there. There weren't. A Canadian named Stan Turner—who was one of the great operators in the Battle of Malta, just as he had been in France, and the Battle of Britain—flew us out there. I think there were 13 or 14 of us. No sooner did we arrive than the sirens started up and we heard the sound of single-engine motors and looked up, and here were five antiquated, tapped-out old Hurricane IIs clambering up, trying to get height. Within a moment, high above there were the 109s, going like the clappers.

"And old Stan, who'd been through it all by then, looked up and said, 'Good God!' And that's how we got started."

At that point, as Lucas indicates, the Germans were flying Messerschmitt Bf.109Fs, considered by many the most exceptional of the various 109s produced during the war. The 109F was capable of 389 mph against 340 for the Hurricane IIs. Although the Hurricane had far greater firepower, it was not nearly so maneuverable as the lighter Messerschmitt.

"Then," Lucas continues, "there was the tactical problem. They were coming from Sicily, 60 miles away, which meant they always had the height. We flew those Hurricanes for about a month before we finally got Spit 9s, and it was a tortuous affair. But I'm glad we did it, because it made one realize how good those Hurricane pilots were."

Shortly after Lucas reached Malta, he took over 249 Squadron from "a marvelous squadron commander, Stan Grant. They always used to say in the RAF, never take over a squadron from a good squadron commander—you can only make it worse." One of the new CO's first responsibilities was selecting five pilots from among ten who had just flown in from the aircraft carrier *Eagle*; the other five to go to his old outfit, 603. Among the ten was the inimitable Screwball Beurling. The commander of 603 was David Douglas Hamilton. "'David,' I said, 'let's flip a coin to see who chooses first.' I won, but before we started choosing, a friend of mine who had flown with Screwball Beurling in the North Weald Wing tells me, 'If he's anything like he was in North Weald, we'll have our hands full.' I asked him how he thought Beurling would fit in with us, and he said, 'Well, either fit in well, or else buy it!' So, I said, 'Well, he sounds all right to me,' and went to Hamilton and said, 'David, I'm going to have Sergeant Beurling.' And that's how he came to 249 Squadron."

And just who was this fellow whose fame had spread so far, and would yet spread farther as he went about shooting down 26 enemy aircraft? "A quite extraordinary character," Lucas responds. "He was of Scandinavian descent.

Laddie Lucas.

His eyes were a piercing blue, they pierced through you when he looked at you. He was very fair, and untidy—almost unkempt.

"And he never called me 'Sir.' He used to call me 'Boss.' After we had flown once or twice, he started to go off on his own, as he had in England. 'Now, look here,' I said to him, 'we fly in pairs here. Two airplanes in line abreast, for preservation. And you are flying on your own, and you can't go on doing that. You've got ability here, much above the average I think, and I want to see real advantage taken of it. If you overstep the mark now, you are on the next plane to the Middle East.' And he looked at me—I can see those eyes looking at me now—and said, 'Boss, that's fair.' You know, after that, he was always marvelous.

"He had this wonderful eyesight—he could see things before the rest of us. Then, he used to get in very close, he never used to shoot from more than 200-250 yards, sometimes less, and he was very quick. He had another advantage: he flew an airplane beautifully, he could maneuver it all over the sky.

"And he always wanted to fly, never wanted a rest day. One day, I think it was in June 1942, the squadron had ten airplanes up, and there was a raid with three Italian bombers covered by about 100 Messerschmitt 109s. We were vectored onto this formation, and I said to the three sections, we'll take the airplane to port, the other section on the right take the one on the starboard side, and the middle section will take the middle aircraft. We did this, and we actually shot all three of the bombers down, and the 109s never even saw us. Screwball, who was supposed to be on a day off, was in the old dispersal hut, and as I walked in, absolutely soaked through with perspiration, he looked at me and said, 'Boss, I couldn't fault that one.'"

Lucas tells how George Beurling actually came by his nickname: "When we were on dawn alert, we used to have our breakfast—bully beef and hard biscuits from the last war—sent down to us. No one ate the bully beef, and it was chucked away. Screwball would throw a piece of his bully beef on the

Top RAF pilots in Malta during the summer of 1943, just prior to the invasion of Sicily. (L-R) Squadron Leader and Canadian ace George Hill, Squadron Leader O'Neill, 143rd Squadron, Squadron Leader Jackson, 126th Squadron, Wing Commander Wentworth, and Wing Commander Duncan-Smith.

floor and as the sun was coming up, so were the flies, and they would start to settle on top of this.

"As they settled, maybe a hundred of them, he'd get his flying book up and pull his chair up alongside the flies and squash those flies, a terrible mess, and he'd say, 'the goddamn screwballs.' And that's how Screwball became Screwball and he was always Screwball."

Squadron Commander Lucas—credited with somewhere between six and 12 combat victories—compares German and Italian pilots.

"The Italians always treated the fighting over Malta like a flying display—like the Hinden flying display before the war—doing aerobatics and all that. It was great fun. They could fly, just as they could drive motor cars, very well, too.

"The Germans were different. They flew beautifully, they were ruthless. Once, we went to see in hospital a German that Norman McQueen of 209 had shot down. His name was Kurt Laing, a nice man, from southern Germany. Spoke English very well. 'Daddo' Longley was with us, and he said to the German, 'Kurt, how do you get on with the Italians?'

"Kurt had broken his leg, but he leaned over and he got a torch and switched the torch on and shone it under the bed here and there, and said, 'You can never find them!' "

Mussolini had not waited for Malta to fall. On September 13, 1940, Italian legions streamed out of Fort Capuzzo in Libya and into nearby Egypt. Within four days, they had advanced 60 miles to Sidi Barrani. The vastly outnumbered British—36,000 vs. nearly 300,000 Italians in Libya—had withdrawn 80 miles to Mersa Matruh. For the air war, the Italians had 151 first-line aircraft; the British had only three squadrons equipped with the sluggish (257 mph) and outmoded Gloster Gladiators, the RAF's last biplane fighter.

Though badly outnumbered in the Western Desert, the British had pilots of the guts and genius of Flight Lt. T. Marmaduke St. John "Pat" Pattle. In the tradition of such great fighter pilot innovators as Oswald Boelcke in World War I, Werner Mölders in Spain, and Adolph "Sailor" Malan in the Battle of Britain, Pat Pattle jotted down notes of enemy strengths and weaknesses, lessons he not only applied himself but passed on to his men. A thinking pilot, Pattle flew Gladiators with 80 Squadron in the first days of the desert war, later taking the squadron to Greece to help them repel the Italian invasion. In only four months beginning in November 1940—at the end, flying Hurricanes—Pattle shot down between 40 and 50 aircraft, to become the top-scoring RAF pilot of the war. On March 4, 1941, his concentration on a target allowed two Me.110s to get on his tail and knock his Hurricane into the water in a storm of cannon shells.

Far to the south, Italian forces seized undefended parts of the Sudan and Kenya and all of British Somaliland. The dream of a great empire appeared within Mussolini's grasp.

But Sidi Barrani was as far as the Italians got in Egypt, and the British recaptured the other lost African territories within a year, adding Italian Somaliland, as well. The bold British torpedo bomber attack crippling the Italian fleet at Taranto struck one heavy blow to Mussolini's plans, while on land Maj. Gen. Richard Nugent O'Connor launched a counteroffensive. The Greeks struck their own blow, driving Italian invading forces back to Albania. Once again, Hitler came to the rescue of his floundering ally: Enter the man they would come to call "The Desert Fox," Erwin Rommel, Germany's hero.

But after a score of brilliant victories, Rommel faced a new and determined enemy commander, Gen. Bernard Montgomery, and a vastly stronger British 8th Army: 230,000 men and 1,230 tanks compared to the Axis's 80,000 men and 210 tanks. In the air, the proportions were worse: 1,500 Allied fighters and bombers against 350 Axis planes. On November 3, the British broke his defenses at El-Alamein. And, in no small measure because of Malta, Rommel was increasingly starved for men, munitions, and fuel. The Desert Fox was on the run.

Shortly after 1 A.M. on November 8, 1942, the biggest amphibious invasion in the history of warfare was getting underway. Code-named Operation TORCH and commanded by Lt. Gen. Dwight D. Eisenhower, it put 107,000 troops ashore at nine coastal points stretching 900 miles from Oran in Algeria to Casablanca in Morocco. Three-quarters of the troops were American, the rest British. For the Americans, it would be the first taste of full-fledged combat in the European war.

Capt. Jack Ilfrey ran into trouble en route to North Africa. Ilfrey was flying with the 94th "Hat in the Ring" Squadron, the one Eddie Rickenbacker, America's top ace in World War I, had immortalized. The squadron was one of the first equipped with the new Lockheed P-38Fs and the first fighter squadron to make a mass overwater flight from the United States to the UK early in 1942. Now, early in November 1942, the squadron left England with a flight of B-26 bombers to support the invasion forces in North Africa. En route, one of the drop tanks carrying extra fuel fell off, forcing Ilrey back to his main tanks.

"But," he relates, "we were following a B-26 that kept flying farther out into the Atlantic Ocean, dodging thunderstorms, when it hit me that I'm not gonna have enough gas to make Gibraltar. So I took off by myself and hit the

Below:
Four P-38s in formation.

Jack Ilfrey in his flight gear.

coast pretty close to where the Tagus River goes up the Portuguese coast to Lisbon. Not knowing whether to bail out or land on the beaches, I saw the beautiful concrete runways of Lisbon's airport, and I landed.

"Six horsemen with plumed hats galloped out with guns and all to escort me back toward the ramp. I parked and got out, and the Portuguese immediately told me that me and my P-38 would be interned, because they were neutral. We had some pleasant conversation—some spoke English. They had me talking with a Portuguese pilot and he wanted to know something about this P-38, its operations. I didn't see much wrong about that—it was not going to be used for combat, after all.

"A couple hours went by when we walked back out to the ramp and they asked me what kind of gasoline it took. A hundred octane, I said, and they said all they had was 80, so they put that in. And I said, you're going to have to get in and make adjustments to your spark plugs and all to burn 80. By now, I'm sitting in the cockpit with the horsemen all around and the Portuguese pilot on my left wing here. I was showing him this and that when, in the distance, I heard the familiar whine of a P-38, coming in on one engine.

"All the horsemen ran off to meet him. And I'm sitting there and thought, 'Well, I've got gasoline—what am I waiting for?' Now, if you were good and lucky, you could energize both engines at the same time. If you didn't make it the first time, you're out of luck because your battery's gone. I energized both of 'em at one time, set the proper controls. Meanwhile, the Portuguese guy was trying to reach in to keep me from doing it. The left prop fired and I gave it all the gas I could and just blew him off the wing, down between the twin booms, turned it around, blew a lot of hats off, and just took off."

Landing in Gibraltar, Houstonian Ilfrey discovered he had created an international incident and was in deep trouble. The colonel who met him "read me up one side and down the other and said that Eisenhower's headquarters wanted to send me and my plane back to Lisbon. Here I am now, a first lieutenant talking to a full colonel. I said, 'Colonel: do you think that if I get in that P-38, I'll go back to Lisbon?' I thought he was going to hit me—but he didn't." Probably just as well: Ilfrey went on to become the first American ace in the Mediterranean Theater, this time earning a commendation from Eisenhower's boss, army Chief-of-Staff George C. Marshall.

He got a chance to prove his mettle early on. On November 29, 1942, Ilfrey was on patrol with his flight leader, Capt. Newell Roberts, "a real gung-ho leader." "On our way back," he says, "we spotted two Messerschmitt 110s, a twin-engine, three-person fighter bomber, at about one o'clock position. 'Jack, I'll take the first one and you take the second one,' Captain Newell told me. At that time, I had never shot at anybody in my life, and wasn't even familiar with guns, as such. It seemed very easy just to fly up behind this Me.110, which was by this time pouring out black smoke, and just pull the trigger. But, at the time I was doing this, I saw little orange balls coming out the back of his airplane, and I thought, 'Well, what in the devil is that? Well, hell!—it's a tail-gunner!' So, this Me.110 belly-landed in the desert, and the one that Captain Roberts shot crash-landed and exploded.

"The three men in my Me.110, the one I shot down, jumped out and started running. I thought to myself, to God knows where, out here? It was real 'desert-y,' you know. So, just as a lark, frivolous or devilish—whatever—I circled around and set that Me.110 on fire. And then I headed toward that crew. They were running one behind the other. And I gave them a few sharp bursts, just off to the side. I wasn't about to shoot them. Well, they fell down and raised their fists at me, and I got the biggest kick out of that in the world!''

That devilish streak nearly cost Jack Ilfrey his life on another mission. ''Four of us were assigned to strafe the airdrome at Gabes, on the Mediterranean coast in southern Tunisia. Captain Roberts led and he pretty much hand-picked the men flying with him. We came upon the airdrome 50 feet off the ground, the four of us in our P-38s, just as six Me.109s were taking off, leaving dust tracks as they did. Captain Roberts said, 'I'll get the first one. MacWordie, you get the second one. Jack, you get the third one, and Lovell, you get the fourth one.' Well, we did exactly that—shot down all four of those. But the thought in my mind was, 'Well, how about those other two? They got off, too.'

''Foolishly, I turned around and went back, and got shot up pretty bad by guns from the airdrome. Then the 109 taking off came head-on into me firing and knocked out my right engine. I, in turn, was firing at him, and he went down. But I'm sitting on one engine, trying to get the hell out of there. One engine on the P-38 was just not as fast as the 109. I was yelling on my radio for my friends, and the next thing I knew, the radio was all gone, and two Me.109s were making passes at me. Sounded like a severe hailstorm on my wings. I kept hoping the thing [the engine] would quit so I could sit it down on the desert and get out of this. But it didn't—kept right on performing. That's the beauty part of a P-38. But my friends did see me and came over and scared off those other two Me.109s and escorted me back to base.

''I knew I was severely shot up; hydraulic fluid was all around my feet from broken lines and tanks. And I thought, 'Well, I'm going to have to make a belly landing in the thing,' but just as a matter of procedure, put the wheels down, but got no indication they were down. So I was preparing myself for a belly landing on this one good engine. Oh, I forgot to say: there were several 30 mm cannon holes through the prop, which had vibrated all the cowling off the engine. But it kept running. So I came in for the landing, hitting the ground, and me wondering what was wrong, because the prop kept turning. It so happened the nose wheel was down and locked, and I was on the nose wheel and the two back rudders, shuddering to a stop.''

Douglas Ian Benham discovered early on how difficult it would be during the first days of the war to distinguish friend from foe. Ever since the surrender of France in June 1940, France's fighting forces had been divided among those few who had joined the Free French led by the proud and petulant Charles de Gaulle and those loyal to the Nazi-subordinated Vichy government.

At dawn on November 8, Benham's Squadron 242 took off from Gibraltar immediately behind Squadron 81. Extra tanks gave them just enough gas to make it to their destination, the Maison Blanche airfield in Algiers, ''a one-way ticket.'' Reaching the field, ''we were horrified to discover that the French were using their antiaircraft guns against us, all around the airfield, trying to stop us from landing; 81 Squadron was first in and 242 followed about three minutes later. We parked our aircraft on the far side of the airfield, away from the French hangars, and we pilots had a conference about what to do because all we had was our Smith & Wesson, three revolvers, and six rounds of ammunition among us. Seeing how little fuel we had left, we decided to siphon what we had to get four planes flyable, in the event of us having to scramble to get airborne. Our group captain negotiated with the French who to that point were noncommittal—they hadn't made up their minds whether to put us in prison or whether we would be putting them in prison. So it remained a stalemate until the French figured out whether the landings by the army would be successful or not against the French army. In the event, it was, and the French decided we were all friends.''

Benham, like tens of thousands of others in the landings, had just collided with the first unknown of the new war: would they or wouldn't they? ''They'' were the considerable French forces garrisoned in the Moroccan, Algerian, and Tunisian French territories. By keeping the British invisible in the invasion—the French felt bitterly about Britain's scuttling the French fleet—the Allies were hoping that many of the French defenders would surrender without a fight. In the event, French reactions varied from garrison to garrison.

After a series of battles, with the fortunes of war seesawing between the Allies and the Axis, Rommel found himself in a huge vise inside Tunisia's borders: the Americans to the west and south, the British closing in from the east. Allied tanks were not alone in being outclassed. Although the Allies held a commanding lead in the numbers of planes on the Algerian/Tunisian fronts, the German Me.109Fs and Focke Wulf 190As easily outclassed the Spitfire 5s and Curtiss P-40Bs that initially made up the backbone of the Allied fighter forces.

Some refused to be outclassed. Catapulted from the American aircraft carrier *Chenango*, American Capt. Phil Cochran organized his American P-40 pilots into what amounted to a guerrilla squadron, draping the pilots with red scarves, conducting wild and woolly air-to-ground and air-to-air operations. The Red Scarf Guerrillas destroyed 34 German and Italian warplanes in a five-day period. His deputy, Capt. Levi Chase, ended the campaign with 14 confirmed air-to-air kills to become the top-scoring ace in the Northwest African Air Force.

David Cox reveals an early countermeasure, developed by Spitfire pilots back in Britain, to engage a very dangerous enemy: ''The Focke Wulf was much superior, but we did get around that by the tactics of a very famous chap called Wing Commander Jamie Rankin. He worked out a system that, instead of climbing up from our bases and letting the German radar see what we were going to do, we'd go off at naught feet right across the Channel until we got

Spitfire Mark is on the flight line.

within sight of the coast, underneath German radar. Then we'd climb like hell and by these tactics hoped we'd be above Abbeville or Sainte Mere when the 190s were taking off. And we'd have a dirty dart at them and then away."

In Africa, Douglas Benham practiced a variation on the "dirty dart"—wait until the 190 was about to bottom out from his dive, then cut across and get close enough behind him to shoot him down. In January 1943, Cox and other RAF pilots didn't have to resort to tricks; they flew back to Gibraltar and picked up Spit 9s, the great equalizer in the air war. Says Cox, "Its greatest value was that when you got to, say, 20,000 feet, when your performance on the Spit 5 would normally fall off, the 9 had a two-stage blower which would come in with a *woof* and you got this sudden surge of power, like a kick in the pants. When we met the old Luftwaffe at 25,000-26,000 feet, we were at a bit of a disadvantage. Suddenly, we had the advantage. In fact, I have an entry in my logbook—meeting the Hun at 37,000 feet, and getting above him!"

The Germans had their own tricks. Once, Benham remembers being scrambled from the Bône airfield in northern Algeria to meet an incoming flight of 190s. No sooner were they dogfighting at 17,000 feet than another group of 190s swooped down on them from 25,000 feet, forcing them to break off the action. He managed to escape; his number two wasn't so lucky. "Looking over the top of the canopy, I could see this Focke Wulf trailing us behind. When he was about 90 degrees, he fired and the engine of my Number Two— a Canadian by name of Masters—was very nearly blown out of the Spitfire. Incredibly good shots, those German pilots."

Eisenhower had the foresight to find out enough about life in northwest Africa to order long underwear for his men. Such touches made a difference. Life during that winter of 1942-1943 was raw. For some, too raw.

David Cox recalls that "Living conditions were part of the great strain—we all lived in one tent, 20 of us with our feet to the middle." The Luftwaffe added its own torment, reminiscent of the Japanese tactic on Guadalcanal. "They used to send a couple of 88s over, round and round the airfield, and drop one bomb about every quarter of an hour. Only a small one, but still it was a bomb. And obviously, you didn't get any sleep, and that made us very irritable and didn't do morale much good, either. We had a flight commander at the time, and poor old chap, one of those nights it was going on, it got too much for him and he got a hurricane lamp, and rushed out and waved it, shouting, 'Here I am, you bastards! Here I am.' Needless to say, he was sent home."

Douglas Benham recalls the bully beef and the dog biscuits—day in and day out—and being cooped up in small tents. And the small things: "The first thing that a pilot did as soon as he woke up was to empty his flying boots because he was frightened that there was probably a scorpion gone in there during the night."

Benham remembers the khaki-colored battle uniforms to match the desert sand, a sort of camouflage. "It never got dry-cleaned or washed and pilots used to grow their hair very long. But there were no girls around, so I don't think it mattered very much how we looked or how we smelt."

Lack of girls was not always a disadvantage. The great German ace Johannes "Macki" Steinhoff believes that the female factor may have had a lot to do with the phenomenal success in Africa of one of the most extraordinary fighter pilots of all time. That man was Hans-Joachim Marseille who, in four brief years as a fighter pilot, flashed across the skies of Britain, France, and North Africa with such brilliance that he became known variously as the

Squadron Leader R.W. Oxspring and Flight Lieutenant David Cox (R) congratulate each other at an advance RAF fighter base in North Africa after receiving honors. Oxspring has been awarded a second bar to his Distinguished Flying Cross (D.F.C.) and Cox received his D.F.C.

Hans-Joachim Marseilles smiles as he watches a ground crewman add another kill to his plane.

Star of Africa, Young Eagle, African Eagle, Yellow 14, and Star of the Desert. Before he finished, he had shot down 157 planes to become one of a dozen men in the Luftwaffe awarded the Knight's Cross with Diamonds, and one of only three to receive Italy's Medal for Bravery in Gold.

Born in Berlin's Charlottenburg district, the son of a World War I pilot, the rebellious and fun-loving Marseille was not quite 21 when assigned to Steinhoff's JG/52 4th Squadron in France. The time was August 1940, and the Battle of Britain was just firing up. "Marseille," Steinhoff recalls, "was an extremely good-looking young man. Back at our post, during rest periods, he had far too many girls. Basically, I had nothing against this. But it did have an effect on his performance." In under six months he shot down seven planes— and was shot down four times himself, each time belly-landing on a French beach near Cape Griz Nez. "Finally," Steinhoff continues, "I told him, Marseille, I really can't work with such an undisciplined fellow. He was transferred to Africa and was very successful there. And the secret of his success was the fact that there were no girls in Africa!"

And such success it was: between April 22, 1941, and September 30, 1942, Hans Marseille shot down an even 150 Allied planes. On June 3, 1942, he shot down six South African Curtiss Kittyhawks in ll minutes. Before going home on leave at the end of that month, he ran his score to 100 and became a national hero and an idol to German women. One, Hanneliese Bahar, won his heart, and they made plans to be married at Christmas.

Back in North Africa, with the Luftwaffe now outnumbered six to one, he again became a scourge of the skies. On his first day back, August 31, he shot down 10 planes. The next day, Marseille shot down a stunning 17 planes, including 5 Kittyhawks in 7 minutes. On the morning of September 30, he climbed into the cockpit of his Messerschmitt Bf. 109G-2 "Gustav Two" with a yellow 14 emblazoned on the side for the last time. Flying over Imayid, he radioed that his engine had caught fire and that his cockpit was filled with smoke. Ironically, engine failure and not enemy fire ended his career; bailing out of his crippled and inverted fighter, Marseille was struck by the tail fin of the plane. His parachute unopened, he plummeted four miles to the desert floor near El Alamein. The Italians erected a pyramid over his grave at Derna with the inscription: "Here lies undefeated Haupt. [Capt] Hans Marseille." He was not quite 23 years old.

Comrades-in-arms speak of this remarkable young man. Walter Krupinsky went through fighter pilot training and "often raised hell" with him on their off-hours in Vienna. "You can't imagine a wilder daredevil."

Herbert Ihlefeld, Marseille's first combat commander, said, "He had to be led. He had to be spoken to after every mission, so that he would stay close to the formation, so that he wouldn't become a lone wolf."

Hans-Joachim Jabs called Marseilles "The best flyer, the best gunner, the best fighter pilot. He personified the boyishness, the nonchalance of a fighter pilot. And he had an unbelievably good eye and could shoot exceptionally well in a bank. He was, without doubt, a man who possessed a definite greatness."

Gunther Rall: "I think many will agree with me if I say that Marseille was the most talented of the fighter pilots—and also the most ambitious. He even trained between sorties in North Africa. And, according to the statistics, he had the most number of enemy downings using the least amount of ammunition."

Adolf Galland: "Marseille was one of the best. No one could follow him."

The war in the desert wasn't always what it seemed. To begin with, in the west, it wasn't always desert. David George Samuel Richardson Cox was with RAF 72 Squadron, the first sent to the "desert" war in Tunisia.

"Only," Cox sputters, "there wasn't a desert. This is where everybody made a mistake. So we got out there in November [1942] with our lovely sand-painted Spitfires for the desert and operated over lovely green country, so we could be seen a mile off. The Luftwaffe knew better, because they were all green and blue. The first month, it was very dry, and then it was rain and rain and rain and mud and mud and mud!" (The real desert was to the east, in Libya.)

But Cox and his cohorts of the 72nd did discover something familiar about their new setting: the enemy. A Turkish delegation came to see them after visiting the Germans at Bizerte in Tunisia, and, Cox resumes, "the German fighter pilots sent us a message. Seems they had fought against us over the Channel and remembered our call sign, so they sent their best regards to 72 Squadron."

Rain and mud notwithstanding, within a few days of his arrival Cox was credited with a probable on an Me.109, a definite kill the next day, November

Below:
Honor guard at Marseilles' grave in North Africa.

Hans-Joachim Jabs in uniform.

26, a probable on the 27th, a definite shoot-down of a Ju.88 dive-bomber on the 29th, and a definite on another 109 on December 4. That record was enough to earn him a DFC and promotion to flight commander.

Douglas Benham expands on the picture of life on that forlorn front. "One was permanently on duty, flying seven days a week, 365 days a year. In fact, Christmas day was treated by both sides as a working day. The squadrons were given a week's rest in rotation at a little French-Arab town called Setif, which was down in the desert, but there was very little there, really. It was just getting away from living in a tent; there, we generally lived in a French school."

Even the lighter moments were bizarre: "An Italian pilot used to come across in his Fiat [C.R. 42] fighter and do aerobatics for us first thing in the morning. We always would come out and watch him and clap and wave our hats in the air. Then, one day, he came over and the ack-ack guns shot him down, and we were absolutely incensed and really desperately sad, because we'd got used to this Italian and we loved him dearly."

David Cox, the lad from Cambridge who was rebuffed as medically unfit the first time he tried to join the RAF, tells another. "One of our pilots shot down the equivalent of a German wing commander. This pilot, a Canadian chap called Hussey who was killed later on, was a very brilliant young pilot—he shot down half a dozen 109s in about a month—but he was a sergeant. It was rather amusing because the German wanted to meet the pilot who had shot him down, in a head-on attack at that. The German was disgusted to think he was shot down by a sergeant pilot. He thought that was terrible."

There's a sequel to the story: the British flight leader who, in Cox's phrase, had "gone over the top" because of the German's nightly bombing of their airfield, was detailed to escort the wing commander back to prison camp in Britain. As Cox tells it, although he will not swear to its authenticity, they got as far as Gibraltar and the Briton "forgot the wing commander and wandered off and went a bit nutty again. And the German wing commander got hold of him and took him home to bed."

Darker moments were, of course, the rule. Jerry Collingsworth first tasted combat flying out of Biggin Hill in England during the Battle of Dieppe in August 1942. But because he was a rookie, he wasn't able to get into position to fire a single shot. Attached to the USAAF 31st Fighter Group, Col-

(L-R) Adolf Galland, Gunther Lutzow, Werner Mölders, Viek, Osterkamp, V. Maltzahn, and Teichmann.

Focke Wolfe-190 in flight.

An aerial view of a wartime air field.

lingsworth was later based at Fariana in Tunisia. One day, at the tail of a three-man formation, he was suddenly jumped from above by a flight of Focke Wulf 190s. "I could see the gun sparking, and then it hit me: That man is trying to kill me. And it made me angry, which is better than fear. So I said, okay you, if you can dish it out I can, too." Minutes later, "I could see the sparks hitting his right wing, and they hit an ammuniton box or something. There was a big flash of blue and his engine started windmilling and he went skidding into the desert." Ignoring radio discipline, the excited tyro hollered, "I got him, I got him, I got him, and one of my buddies said, 'Shut up,' which I did." It was the first of six kills.

Collingsworth remembered another even more vividly. Until then, March 8, 1943, he was not "shooting with the express purpose of killing anyone. I was shooting for the express purpose of shooting that airplane down. If the man got killed in the process, it was either him or me. He was doing what Hitler told him to do and I was doing what Roosevelt told me to do."

All that changed when he saw his good friend and wingman—Woody Thomas from Little Rock, Arkansas—go down in flames and explode on the ground below. Then Collingsworth saw the FW.190 that had shot Thomas down "rocking his wings to keep me in sight, trying to slow down, so he could slide down behind me. So I zoomed up under him. I couldn't get behind him, but I pulled under him and into the clouds. Couldn't fly instruments though—I was only six months out of flying school. I gently eased up on that Spitfire—what a great airplane!—and gently touched the inside rudder to come back down out of the clouds, and the first thing I see is a flight of three in a 'Lufbery' defensive circle right on the deck. Then I see this Focke Wulf that had shot Woody down, and I have to make up my mind: Do I go down there, or do I go for this man. There wasn't any choice in my mind—I was going for the man who had gotten Woody.

"He saw me about that time and I could see the black smoke coming out of his engine. We had a booster on that Spit, to emergency override for about five minutes before it would damage the engine, and I broke that wire and

Sir Harry Broadhurst brings in his Spitfire for a landing.

Inset:
Head on view of FW.190.

then held the throttle and we went screaming down to the desert. I didn't know where we were. About 15, 20, 30 feet off the ground. He was 'wide-out' and I was too.

"I began to gain on him just a little bit. He got nervous down there, broke into a tight turn, and I could see the contrails coming off him, and I remember thinking, friend, you ain't about to out-turn a Spitfire, 'cause I knew he couldn't.

"So I started shooting one cannon. There was a cannon on each wing, and it made what we called a seesaw, the recoil made the wing jerk back. I don't know whether that hit him or not, but he snapped over on his back and I thought, if I pass over him, then he's going to do a split-S and come up behind me—forgetting we're only about 50 feet above the ground and doing about 350 miles an hour.

"So I rock over to keep him in sight. I rock this way, 'cause we're in this kind of a turn, and then I see him explode.

"Our leader was shot down, my wingman was shot down. Two out of the four of us got back. It was the only time I ever had animosity toward the enemy."

Collingsworth reflects on the deeper meaning of those frenetic times. "You know, you develop intense friendships in combat situations. The chips are pretty high. I developed a very, very intense relationship with a classmate of mine. We graduated from flying school together and we asked to fly together. It got where I knew what he was going to do almost before he did it. I'm sure he felt the same with me."

Collingsworth illustrates the psychic nature of the bonds forged during those intense times. "We [he and his classmate] got separated in a fight over Tunis one day and were attacked by six 109s, just the two of us. With the Spit model we had the time, we could out-turn the German, but he could outdive us, outrun us, and outclimb us. That left us one thing: out-turn him. Two against six. He shot down one, and we'd worked our way near the surface and as we started climbing out, I looked behind and saw two Focke Wulf 190s coming up behind him and called and said, 'Johnny, there are two 190s coming up behind you. If you sit still 'til I tell you to break, maybe we can get one in a compromising situation.' Now that's what I mean about trust, and intense friendship. He sat there and said, 'OK, I'll sit here,' knowing those two fellows were coming up behind him. Takes a lot of faith in that other guy over there, because you can't see behind as well as the fellow who's at an angle.

When Johnny broke, I was hoping the lead German would follow Johnny, then I would get behind him, too, but he didn't. He turned toward me, and we met head-on. I could see him firing, and I was firing, though I don't know whether I hit him or not—I didn't knock him down, I know that. When I got home, I had a bullet hole in the tail, and that was the one time I picked up my one bullet hole. But that illustrates the close relationship among people who are betting on each other to protect them."

Jack Ilfrey agrees: "Friendships forged in combat are never forgotten. I'll tell you that. Better than brothers."

The war in the real desert, 1940-1943, in Libya, Egypt, eastern Tunisia, brought a new dimension to aerial combat. There was no mass bombing, nowhere to hide in those vast spaces during air attacks—and accidents happened.

"When we got to the desert," Colin Gray reports, "one of the first things that happened to me was we bombed the [British] army instead of the Germans. So I called up the chap commanding the bombers, 205 Group, and told him to go and apologize to the general, a Scotsman commanding the Highland Division—a pretty rough bunch, actually. So I said, you go along and say how sorry you are, and so on. No need to remind him their own guns sometimes shell their own troops. When the RAF chap eventually got to see the general, the general said, 'If you don't get out of here immediately, I'll have my Jocks after you, and they'll have your 'this and that."

To a large extent, the British knew exactly what they were going for, thanks to ULTRA intercepts obtained by cracking German codes encrypted by their ENIGMA machines. Sir Harry Broadhurst says the system "helped us to sink their ships with petrol and oil and ammunition and so on." But he came to have his doubts about the believability of some of Desert Fox's reports.

"At the end of the day's fighting, we submitted a report, how many aircraft we had lost, how many pilots, to get reserves up from Cairo. They were doing the same, and we were picking it up. But, as I say, you couldn't necessarily trust Rommel too far because he was signaling Hitler and Hitler was a rather temperamental boss and didn't want to know the bad things, only the good things. So, you couldn't necessarily trust entirely what Rommel was saying to Rome and Berlin. But the shipping movements, you did get." Indeed, ENIGMA intercepts enabled the War Cabinet to alert Gen. Sir Archibald Wavell, commander-in-chief of British forces in the Middle East, of Rommel weaknesses in his siege of the Tobruk garrison in 1942.

Allied air superiority was a long time in coming in the east, not until the fall of 1942. Among the RAF's early reinforcements was the 112 Royal Australian Air Force Squadron, arriving in September 1941 with its "shark-mouthed" Curtiss P-40B Tomahawks. The squadron boasted such aces as Britain's Neville Duke (whose 26 kills tied him with Beurling as the second-highest scoring ace of the Mediterranean campaigns) and C.R. "Killer" Caldwell (an Australian flyer whose 20½ victories ranked him sixth in the theater). The Squadron's shark's mouth, painted on the fuselage, inspired the Flying Tigers a few months later to borrow the symbol and make it famous half way around the world.

The Tomahawk itself made its first appearance over the desert skies on June

N.F. Duke exiting his Spitfire.

Postcard photo of Hans-Joachim Marseilles.

D.I. Benham is shown in flight gear somewhere in Tunisia.

16, 1941. Although consistently bested by the 109s, the Tomahawk's six guns made it a serious adversary, and especially valuable in ground support roles. In 1942, a later version, the P-40D Kittyhawk, joined the air war. Slightly faster, it was also outfitted with wing racks for six 20-pound bombs, as well as a 300-500-pound bomb beneath the fuselage.

The newcomers faced formidable foes: the pilots of JG.27 had already seen combat in the Battle of Britain, the Balkans, and the Mediterranean (Crete, Malta). The Germans, including a young cadet named Hans Marseille, arrived in North Africa on April 14, 1941, and saw their first action five days later against RAF 274 Squadron. In six weeks, the 37 pilots of JG.27's Squadron I had destroyed 63 Allied aircraft, themselves losing only six killed and two wounded, nearly as many planes as the entire Italian air force had shot down in the first eight months of the campaign. The wing's greatest day coincided with Marseille's: September 1, 1942. On that day, Air Chief Marshal Arthur Tedder's fighter pilots flew 674 sorties in support of the 8th Army. And on that day, JG.27 shot down 20 Kittyhawks, 4 Hurricanes, and 2 Spitfires, losing one pilot killed, one captured, and one reported missing.

On June 1, yet another first-line *Jagdgeschwader* arrived: 26, commanded by Maj. Joachim Muncheberg, whose 40 victories up to then included 19 Hurricanes shot down over Malta. (American fighter pilots shot Muncheberg down on March 23, 1943, on his 500th mission of the war. By then, he had fought in France and Russia and had 135 kills. With Marseille and the duke of Aosta, he rounded out the three persons awarded Italy's Medal for Bravery in Gold.) Muncheberg was succeeded as *Kommodore* of JG.77 by another great ace, "Macki" Steinhoff, who only a few days before had scored his 150th victory of the war.

In November 1942, JG.27 was pulled out, Squadron 1 back to Germany, 3 to Greece. In 18 months, Squadron 1 had shot down 588 planes; 3 had destroyed 100 in ll months. Their replacement, the JG.77, had scored more than 1,300 victories in Russia and Malta.

By late fall of 1942, the tide had turned decisively against Rommel in the desert. German fighter strength in Africa was down to 80 planes, only half of which were serviceable. But the Luftwaffe was reinforced for Rommel's final battle in Tunisia.

The great New Zealand ace Colin Gray was among the Allied pilots in for the kill. He was posted to North Africa in January 1943 to command RAF 81 Squadron for the final battle. He remembers: "During the sweeps over France, you didn't see very many enemy aircraft. In North Africa, there were plenty of them." On February 25, 1943, an Me.109 fell before his guns, his 18th kill of the war. With another probable and another kill (a Macchi 202) in between, on March 25, Gray shot down another Me.109. The pilot who bailed out and was captured turned out to be Rudolf Müller, who claimed more than a hundred victories of his own.

Another legend was there in those closing days: Stanislaw Skalski, leading a unit known as the Polish Fighting Team, more informally, "Skalski's Circus." The CO of their RAF 145 Squadron was an American named Lance Wade. Wade had joined the RAF early in the war and fought in the Battle of Britain. Skalski remembers him as "a terrific leader and fighter pilot, the 'wildcat of Texas,' or 'cowboy in the air,' I think they called him." Skalski was some pilot himself: between his arrival in March 1943 and the end of the campaign two months later, he managed to add two more Me.109s and a

Ju.88 to his score. It was enough to earn him the right to lead 601 Squadron—the first Pole to command an RAF squadron.

Waclaw Krol was one of the pilots in Skalski's Circus. "There were 15 of us, and in six weeks' action there, we scored 28 German aircraft." Three of those kills were Krol's, running his RAF score to six, added to the two-plus he shot down over Poland.

The powerful vise was closing. Nearly half a million Allied soldiers battered the Axis from three sides. The Germans tried a new gambit: giant six-engine Me.323 motorized gliders. On April 22, Allied fighter planes shot down 16 of the 21 flying boxcars bearing fuel for German tanks and planes. Allied pilots called it the Palm Sunday Massacre. On May 8, the Luftwaffe, facing an Allied air armada of 4,500 combat planes, abandoned Tunisia altogether and fled to Sicily. On May 13, it was all over: 275,000 German and Italian soldiers were taken prisoner in scenes so pathetic that the German general commanding the 15th Panzer division wept as he surrendered.

As the end came in North Africa, the pressure eased on Malta. But while it had lasted, the siege was an ordeal with few equals in modern warfare. Reade Tilley, there during the last of the dark days in mid-1942, remembers the rationing, "a sort of starvation rationing," although, "pilots did better than anyone else because they thought it was a good idea to keep us in fighting shape." Some didn't survive, despite the care; others, only barely. James MacLachlan, one of the great fighter pilots of the Battle of Malta, had his left arm shot off. A few months later, he was flying again.

So unbearable was the siege, so great the courage of the people of Malta and of their defenders, that in 1942 King George awarded the George Cross for Bravery—to the entire population of the island!

Mussolini's vainglorious dream of empire was dead, the Duce's days numbered.

On June 11, 1943, a gigantic naval bombardment signaled the onset of an offensive to capture the Italian island of Pantelleria. A young American pilot named Michael Russo got his first taste of combat that day, flying a new P-51 fighter plane outfitted as a dive bomber. At that point, Russo had a total seven hours of combat training. Flying over from the recently captured Luftwaffe base at Cap Bon, Tunisia, Russo describes what it was like being a dive-bomber pilot in the Army Air Corps in those days: "You flew over a target at 14,000 feet, turned upside down, pulled the nose back in so that you dove straight down toward a target, dropped two 500-pound bombs, then pulled up, heading back to your base." He was among a swarm of Allied pilots who did that to Pantelleria that day. With that obstacle removed the way was now clear for Operation HUSKY, the invasion of Sicily.

The weather turned foul on July 9, forcing Lt. Gen. Dwight D. Eisenhower, from his command post on Malta, to take the kind of momentous decision he would face eleven months later: He ordered the operation to continue despite gale force winds. The first British forces ashore south of Syracuse were largely unopposed; the defenders believed no one would dare risk an invasion in such foul weather and had lowered their guard. But American units at Gela faced heavy opposition. J.D. Collingsworth was overhead:

"We were patrolling at about 10,000-12,000 feet, two of us, when I saw a flash on the ground. Our first thought was that it was artillery, because I knew our troops were down there, someplace. Then I saw a reflection off a canopy—it was in a turn—and I called to Bill Brison and said, 'Bill, I've got

Mike Russo.

Neville Duke resting on the nose of his Spitfire.

one going,' and he said, 'Got you covered.' So I dove down on this man, in a turn right on the deck, and as I approached I could see it was a Focke Wulf 190 and he apparently had just dropped a bomb, the first flash I had seen. I was gaining on him because I had dive speed and as I approached within shooting range—I normally shot from 300 feet down—I could see the bullets kicking up dirt behind him. He was only about 10 feet or so off the ground, so I elevated a bit and began to hit him. With that, he put his airplane into about a 45-degree climb, and at about a thousand feet or so, I was pretty close behind him, when he jettisoned his canopy. Now a Focke Wulf's canopy slides directly back, so it missed me by about 30 feet.

"When he did that, I figured he was going to bail out and I stopped shooting, and he did bail out. I was really surprised to see his 'chute harness come loose from him. Apparently he hadn't locked it properly, and so his 'chute went one way, his airplane went one way, and he went another way. At 22, you don't feel too much one way or the other; I felt, too bad, but that's what this business is all about."

Collingsworth and his cohorts, by then encamped at Gozo, one of the tiny islands off Malta, continued to fly ground-support missions while the fighting lasted in Sicily. In the air, the Luftwaffe and *Regia Aeronautica* were virtually blown out of the sky on D-Day.

On August 17, after frequently fierce fighting, Lt. Gen. George S. Patton, commanding the U.S. 7th Army, entered Messina.

The two armies now glared at each other across the 10-mile expanse of the Straits of Messina, each side readying for the next and dramatic phase of the war.

For Michael Russo, it was a providential pause. Russo was a student at Ohio State when Pearl Harbor was attacked, picking up pocket change running the projector for noonday movies at a local movie theater. One day he saw an air corps recruiting "short" featuring Jimmy Stewart—"be an officer and a gentleman by Act of Congress, country club living, parties, all that. If I was going to fight a war, I decided that was the place to do it." Flight training finished in February of 1943, and Russo joined 46 other pilots flying their P-51 A-36A dive-bombers from Miami in stages to Casablanca.

Russo was among the Allied pilots covering the invasion, flying ground-support missions. One day, in northern Sicily, he found himself in company with a Pole who had been imprisoned early in the war, then escaped to join the U.S. Army Air Corps. "He asked me, what religion are you? 'Catholic,' I told him. 'But you don't go to church,' he says. We didn't have any priests there, so he said, 'Why don't you go into town with me?' I did, and got friendly there with this old priest. He wanted to buy an organ, so I drove him up there to where we could get one. When he went to pay for it, it was the equivalent of $65. So I reached in my pocket and gave him the $65. The next week, they came out from the parish and blessed my airplane. I always said, if there is a God, he got on my shoulder that day, because I never got another bullet hole in my airplane. My airplane was blessed by a village."

The Allies were ashore in Sicily only a few days when Hitler left his Russian front headquarters and flew to a July 17 meeting with Mussolini. With the decisive battle of Kursk raging in Russia, the Führer was in no mood to temporize, and for three hours he raved about the utter failure of Italian arms. Six days later, the Fascist Grand Council demanded Mussolini's resignation. On September 3, the Italians signed the armistice, and a new Italian government was set up at Brindisi.

The Allies now welcomed Italy, not as an ally, but as a co-belligerent.

Several Allied aces speak highly of the flying abilities of the Italians. Wilfred G. Duncan-Smith, who shot down 19 planes himself, recalls mixing with them while based at Malta in 1943: "The Italians were excellent pilots for my book. They also flew very good airplanes. If they had a fault, which I think is a nationalistic fault, it is that they tend to give up rather easily. Whereas the stoicism of the British character is such that you go on until you drop. You know, the Spitfire could turn just as well as a 'Mackie' [the Macchi M.C. 205], so when they realized they weren't going to shake us off and we weren't going to go away, they would roll on their backs and disappear back into Sicily. In other words, give up."

It began in earnest on September 8 when Gen. Mark Clark led the American 5th Army ashore at Salerno. The Allies were now back on the European continent, back to stay. At the beginning, the Allied advance was rapid. The great naval base at Taranto was taken on September 9. Group Capt. Wilfred Duncan-Smith was there. "I took the surrender of the air base there, and they were delighted to see us. The first thing the [Italian] colonel said was, 'Of course, we were enemies—but we're not, are we?'"

But in October, the Allies ran into the twin terrors of top-notch German troops and the unforgiving Italian terrain. The endless mountains, heavily ribbed and ridged, were a honeycomb of natural defensive positions.

Sir Harry Broadhurst: "You couldn't see the target." Learning to coordinate tactics in that setting was difficult—and accidents did happen. Broadhurst recalls:

" 'Bimbo' [Lt. Gen. Sir Miles] Dempsey was commanding a brand new corps, and they hadn't worked out all their routines. One day they asked for us to attack a target. Our chaps rushed off to attack it. But while all this was happening, the Germans had retreated, and the British army had moved in to capture that village. Dempsey was absolutely livid. Next thing, I have Monty [General Montgomery] on me, telling me to go and see him. So I arrived there with my alibi, and Monty said this is getting a bit old-fashioned. After I told Monty what happened, I've never seen a general get such a rocket from another general in all my life. He really tore poor old Dempsey apart. As a result, Monty used to lecture the army about this kind of thing. In fact, he wrote a letter to all the divisional commanders, including the Americans, before the invasion of Normandy, calling their attention to the absolute necessity of keeping in touch with the air force."

In Italy, as in North Africa, RAF spotters increasingly were assigned to ground units to prevent just such accidents from happening. Hugh Dundas reflects: "The army had a very, very tough job in Italy, because the terrain is far from easy, and because the Germans were fighting every inch of the way. The ground-support mechanism developed between the RAF, particularly, and the army was a very good one. We'd fly about 8,000 feet and we had special maps which were gridded. What used to happen was we'd get a call from our RAF people right up with the artillery observation people on the front line. They'd report that some battalion was being harassed by a particular lot of German guns or something of the kind. Then they'd tell us: 'If you look at grid such-and-such, you'll see there's a little lane, and a farmhouse with a haystack and some outbuildings, and just behind that, we think you'll find some German guns, so would you please attack them!' We got pretty accurate, actually.

"Until the beginning of 1944, none of us had ever aimed—we just used the

Looking down on a well-armed B-24.

Mustangs of the 375th Fighter Squadron of the 361st Fighter Group, England.

ordinary gun sight for the two bombs we carried in our Spitfires. You just used to roll over and put the bead on the target and then gradually pull through and you got to judge when to press the button. We got so that we were getting very close, nine times out of ten.''

Michael Russo describes another ground-support role, strafing. Cruising over Avezzano, west of Rome, he spotted a column of German soldiers marching north. Overflying them to get organized, he put wheels and flaps down to slow the airplane and rigged the six 50-caliber machine guns in the ''down'' firing position. Then, approaching so as not to be seen, ''I strafed the road and killed some 300 men. When I got back, they gave me the title of 'The Killer.' But it's different. It's not like looking a person in the eye and shooting at 'em. It didn't bother me at all. Where I saw friends of mine get killed, it did bother me.''

Another time, it was Russo's turn to cringe. Eighteen Messerschmitts chased him all the way back to Naples. ''On the ground, I jumped off my airplane and that was the first time I realized that I could get killed. And I laid on the ground and cried like a baby.''

Russo was, by then, himself an ace—the only A-36A ace. As he points out, dive-bomber pilots weren't supposed to go out "looking for fights." With the exception of a German plane he caught taking off once at Avezzano, all of his kills were defensive, after getting "jumped" while on a bombing run. After 146 sorties and 80 missions in six intensive months of combat, he was burned-out and heading home on a hospital ship. He was lucky: of the 47 men who came over with him, he was the only one of the original 47 pilots to make it home.

Johannes Steinhoff, commanding JG.77, already had more than 150 victories to his credit when he shot down four P-38 Lightnings raiding the airfields in Foggia. "One of the shot-down pilots," Steinhoff tells us, "was a Canadian. It was my birthday, so I took him to my tent, and we celebrated my birthday. He drank along and by midnight, he was just as drunk as we were. I had to take him to a prisoner-of-war camp, but first blew up an air-mattress and had him lie down in my tent. Around 3 o'clock in the morning, I awoke and thought, 'Oh, my God, if he runs away, I'll be in trouble!' So I felt his head with my feet and he woke up and said, 'Sir, don't worry, I won't run away. I am too drunk!' Unfortunately, I never saw him after the war.''

Despite numerical superiority and control of the air and seas, it took the Allies eight months to cover the 100 miles from Naples to Rome. It was eight months of unrelieved misery.

Italian bases made shuttle bombing unnecessary. Now, from those newly captured airfields around Foggia, beginning on October 9, swarms of four-engined B-24 Liberator bombers and escorting P-51 Mustangs thundered over Italy on round-trip raids against targets in southern Germany, only 500 miles away.

In the cockpits of many of those new Mustangs in action over North Africa and Italy was a group of young Americans who had to fight for the right to fight. They were the men of the all-black 99th Pursuit Squadron and 332nd Fighter Group. Already blooded in North Africa, it was their proud boast that no American bomber was lost on a mission they escorted to target.

New planes, new pilots.

Some of the "new" pilots were veterans. Jim Goodson, for example, had been fighting Germans since the early days of the war, first in the RAF, now in the USAAF. As the 15th Air Force was forming, he was detailed to help the change-over from P-39s to Mustangs. "Things were much easier down there," he recalls. "I think I shot down three planes on the first mission or something, because the Luftwaffe pilots down there were also less experienced." What concerned him was the lack of experience of the American pilots. With men like Goodson teaching—an ace with 32 victories—these rookies were in good hands.

Take John J. Voll, a 22-year-old farm boy from Goshen, Ohio, victor in 17 dogfights with the Luftwaffe. Voll was on his way back from Germany with a shot-up radio. He dove after a Ju.88, got it, and was bounced by a dozen Me.109s and FW.190s. Voll turned into his attackers, got three of the fighters, then "scrammed, eluding the other five." It was his last mission, and he returned home with 21 kills, making him the top ace of the 15th Air Force in the Mediterranean.

And those planes, the red-and-blue-nosed Republic P-47 Thunderbolts, pouring heavy machine gun fire into anything marked with a black cross. The Thunderbolt was the largest and heaviest (19,426 pounds) fighter plane in the war—"the seven-ton milkbottle." Between 1942 and 1945, 15,683 "Jugs" were built, more than any other U.S. fighter plane. Despite its weight, the Thunderbolt could climb to 15,000 feet in five minutes, careen along at 427 mph at 30,000 feet, and pack a mighty wallop: six to eight heavy machine guns, plus 2,500 pounds of bombs. And it was tough, able to take a heavy beating and still get the man in the cockpit back to base.

But if the Thunderbolt was a champion, the North American P-51 Mustang was the grand champion of all, deemed by some the best fighter plane of the war. In its most successful version, the 51D, this sleek, bubble-canopied aircraft combined American aerodynamics with a matchless British Rolls-Royce engine. That pushed the P-51D along at 436 mph (at its 25,065-foot peak), and allowed it to climb to 20,000 feet in just under six minutes. The incomparable "D" version came out in 1944. And it revolutionized the air war because, with its 949-mile basic range, double that with drop tanks, bombers no longer had to brave it alone over Germany. The P-51 flew under the colors of 50 countries. For the USAAF in Europe alone, P-51s flew 213,873 missions, destroying 4,950 enemy planes, 4,131 of them on the ground—48.9 percent of all enemy aircraft destroyed in Europe during the war.

With such men, with such machines arrayed against them—and with such crises at home—the Luftwaffe all but vanished from the skies of Italy. For Hugh Dundas, "the air-fighting side of the war pretty well ended over Sicily. After the end of 1943, really, the German air force pretty well pulled out."

Now, more than ever, the fighter pilot became an aerial ramrod for the forlorn foot soldier. And he did so at great risk, for lacking the fighters to throw up against them, the Germans increasingly filled the skies with menacing curtains of lethal antiaircraft fire.

"We were," Dundas adds, "absolutely under fire—20 millimeter, 40 millimeter, even 88 millimeter—the whole time. And there was nothing you could do—just go down, and if you were hit, you were hit."

Many more would be. The war was far from over.

H. Spencer Dundas in his RAF uniform.

8 BIG FRIEND, LITTLE FRIEND

B-17 Flying Forts as far as the eye can see.

On the morning of August 17, 1942, a dozen four-engine B-17E Flying Fortress heavy bombers of the U.S. 8th Bomber Command thunder from an English airfield and head across the Channel for the French marshalling yards at Rouen. They are escorted by short-range British Spitfire 9 fighters. The bombs explode, the bombers return undamaged, if you discount cuts to two bomber crewmen caused when a pigeon smashed against one of the bomber's Plexiglas noses.

A B-17 burns furiously as it streams towards earth.

Inset:
An early model B-17 with its wing shorn off inverts for its final dive.

Behind this first all-American strategic daylight strike by the fledgling bomber command lies controversy. British Bomber Command and the German Luftwaffe tried daylight bombing with unacceptable losses. From 1940 forward, they bombed at night. American generals—first, Maj. Gen. Carl "Tooey" Spaatz, commander of the 8th Air Force in 1942, and then Maj. Gen. Ira Eaker, who took over in December of that year, strongly supported by their boss, Army Air Force chief-of-staff, Gen. H.H. "Hap" Arnold—stubbornly persisted in the belief that daylight precision bombing would shorten the war. Arnold's opposite number, RAF air chief-marshal Sir Charles Portal, who had headed RAF Bomber Command until 1940, felt equally strongly that the war effort would be better served if the Americans would join the British in night raids on the Reich and the occupied territories.

At the Casablanca Conference, Eaker confronted Churchill privately, and the matter was resolved: the Combined Bomber Offensive—Americans by day, the British by night—became policy. The question: Could unescorted, heavily armed American bombers withstand the onslaught by Luftwaffe fighters to and from industrial targets deep inside Hitler's Reich?

Bombers formed up in the sky and headed for Germany. Fighter pilots climbed into Spitfire, P-38, and P-47 cockpits and stacked themselves over the Big Friends, only to peel away and head back for England a short time later, low on fuel, leaving the B-17s at the mercy of cannon-firing Me.109s and FW.190s.

Douglas Benham, rested up after the African ordeal and by now commanding RAF 41 Squadron, describes what it was like to be a fighter pilot watching the maimed and mauled bombers limping home alone: ''We couldn't escort them all the way to their targets—even with drop tanks—the Spitfire's range was only about 500 miles. So we used relays: fighter pilots who would take them as far as they could, then another relay to meet them on the way back. When they came back, it was quite heartrending to see them—engines on fire, part of the wing gone, shot up and not able to keep up with their formation, straggling back and losing height. The air crews I admired most during the last war were those B-17 crews, the Flying Fortress crews.''

A major raid beginning at mid-year would look something like this: Sleepy crews assemble in the operations hut just before 5 A.M. Briefing officers expose a huge wall map on which a red string stretches from the base in East Anglia to the target, deep inside Germany. Lifting off in darkness, the 150 planes form up around circus-colored lead ships. It takes about an hour to collect in stately formations, each group 1,000 feet below or above the lead group, a parade of aircraft often stretching out 15 miles across the sky heading out on an aerial highway plotted to their targets.

The patterns, designed to give the bombers maximum coverage for their nearly 2,000 machine guns, are basically the same ones worked out 20 years before in an era of 85-mph bombers by Brig. Gen. Hugh Knerr. As they break through clouds into the rising sun, the 1,500 men manning the big planes realize they are already registering on German radar screens across the channel. Gunners, some perched on bicycle-type seats in cramped and icy-cold turrets, test-fire their .50-caliber machine guns, causing the huge ships to shiver and shudder, filling the cockpits with the smell of burnt cordite. Within minutes of crossing the Dutch coast at 17,000 feet, flak fills the sky with exploding shells.

A few minutes later, the first yellow-nosed Me.109s flash toward them, their cannon and machine guns spewing death and destruction. One copilot watches a rectangle of metal sail past his right wing, recognizes it as an exit

Photo taken on a hunting trip in France, 1940. (L-R) Wilhelm "Wutz" Galland, two enlisted beaters, Adolph Galland with Johannes Seiffert at his left shoulder. Gerhard Schopfel (at Galland's left shoulder), two flak officers, Hptm. Joachim Munchelberg at far right rear. Hptm. Janke (left, back to camera). Major Helmut Wick (center, back to camera).

door. Then a black lump hurtles through the formation. It is a man, clasping his knees to his head, so close the flyer sees a piece of paper blow out of his leather jacket—but the copilot fails to see a parachute open. Next, in that macabre maelstrom, he sees a B-17 falling out of formation, suddenly vanishing in a brilliant explosion. But they fly on through the debris of shattered, disintegrating planes, the skies filled with the puffs of spreading parachutes as the air battle rages. The sight, though commonplace, never fails to pain those still aloft, flying doggedly on course through the haze of destruction.

And the Luftwaffe's worst is yet to come. As the meager fighter cover peels off and heads home, the big bombers are left alone to face the desperate effort of men determined to stop the bombing of their homeland, no matter the cost.

The losses on such mission after mission mount; planes straggle back to England with holes in their sides big enough to shove a sheep through. At Cambridge, fresh graves are dug for dead American airmen removed from the bloody interiors of the shot-up bombers. But the bombs take their toll: as the year wears on, scarcely a corner of the Reich is not scarred by ruins and rubble.

The man whose job it was to parry the round-the-clock aerial ravaging of the Reich tells how it looked from his embattled command post. Adolf Galland, since 1942 chief of the Luftwaffe's Fighter Command: ''The fact is that Fortress Europe was a fortress without a roof over it.''

The Combined Bombing Offensive was born in controversy, the product of sometimes heated negotiations between the British and American military and political leaders assembled at Casablanca, January 14-24, 1943. The RAF had been flying night sorties inside Germany since May 15, 1940, sporadic at first, intense beginning early in 1942. Now they would enter a strategic phase. With the increase in tempo came an increase in the sophistication of Germany's defenses. And with that, an increase in losses suffered by the RAF's unescorted night bombers. Fighter escorts began in June of 1943. But, even then, losses were heavy, though within the ''acceptable'' 5 percent range.

Daylight bombing was a starkly different story.

The first American bomber to reach the UK—a B-17E named ''Jarring Jenny'' by her crew—touched down at Prestwick, Scotland, on July 1, 1942. Francis S. Gabreski, earlier at Pearl Harbor, was there to meet it. Gabreski was among the first twenty officers who put together a headquarters for the U.S. 8th Fighter Command in London. Despite the loss over the next year of 1,261 of the four-engine behemoths—and most of their crews, or more than 12,000 flyers—those numbers had grown by year's end to 19 B-17 and seven B-24 groups. Even more impressive were the statistics on the number of sorties flown: from 279 in January to 5,618 in December. The huge jump at year's end reflected the appearance in the skies of Little Brothers capable of covering the vulnerable bombers all the way to and from their targets.

Medium bombers—the Martin B-26s—were especially vulnerable in the first half of 1943. The newly formed 322 Medium Bomber Group, based at Great Saling, sent 11 aircraft on its second sortie, May 17, against Ijmuiden and Haarlem in Holland. One plane was forced to turn back early because of mechanical trouble. The remaining ten and their 60 crewmen were shot out of the skies by flak and Me.109s.

The bombers arrived first; the fighter planes followed. Among the newcomers was the 56th Fighter Group, the first to fly the plane featured on a cover of *Life* magazine: the Republic P-47 Thunderbolt. Walker M. ''Bud''

Mahurin has something to say about that: "In those days, *Life* was a big deal. And it showed this giant airplane with a pilot standing in front of it, and said, 400-mph-plus fighter. And the thing I was flying, it didn't seem like it even wanted to get off the ground!" The men of the 56th found much more to squawk about. In part, Mahurin explains, because they were attempting to fly these pachyderms by the Army Air Corps book ("don't abuse the equipment"). That translated as flying on power too low for such a hefty plane. Before leaving Mitchell Field, Mahurin adds, they were convinced that "we were going off to fight a war with an airplane that really wasn't that good."

Things didn't get any better when they touched down at their RAF base in 1943. Seeing the big "Jugs" for the first time, RAF pilots poked fun at them: "'You guys,' they said, 'better go home with those trucks—you'll never survive.' That was a terrifying experience, and we were scared to death already." Mahurin and his mates recovered quickly when they discovered that the Jug was really a juggernaut.

For a while, they had a breather. Gabby Gabreski had by now hooked up with the 56th as a flight commander. "We had one advantage. Our job was to escort the B-17s and the B-24s. The Luftwaffe's job was to destroy the bombers. We were more concerned with the fighters, and so we were the aggressors, always on a tail of the Germans, shoot them down as they went in to attack the bombers. However, when we did tangle with the Germans, they did fight back. But they didn't stay with us long, because once we had them up at high altitude, we had them. The P-47 had a turbo supercharger, giving better performance up at 28-30,000 feet than the 109 or the 190."

One of Gabreski's charges, a rambunctious free spirit named Robert S. Johnson, claimed an early victory by flaming an FW.190 on June 13, 1943. Gabreski bagged his first on August 24, flying high escort for bombers hitting marshalling yards in France. The fighters went out ahead of the bombers; looking down, Gabreski "saw a bunch of 109s milling around, trying to get themselves into position to attack the bombers. I was in perfect position because I was between the sun and the 109, so I came in with altitude also to my advantage and caught this 109 in a climb, came in from behind, and went right on by with my eight guns blazing. I practically blew him up. But it was sobering. I had to think that I did that to that airplane, there are other German airplanes that could do the same to me. It was adjusting your thinking and your ability and everything else to a more positive attitude. It's like an

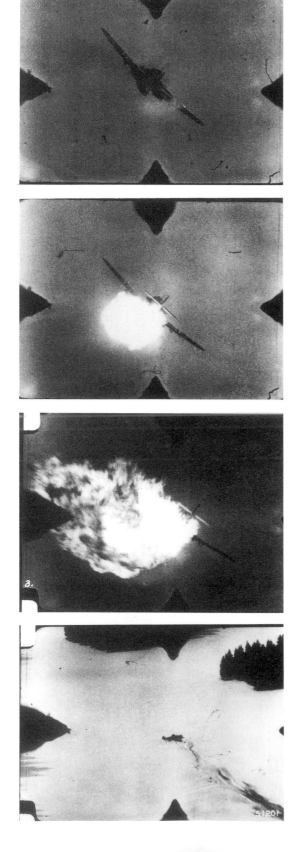

Another Me.109 being removed from the Luftwaffe inventory.

amateur boxer. You get into the ring, you're slow, you're not sure of yourself, you're probing. But as you become proficient, gain experience, you hit the other league, the professional league. Fear is no longer there. You are part of your profession and I felt that my profession as a fighter pilot was to destroy the German Luftwaffe.''

By the fall of 1943, both Johnson and Gabreski were professionals, among the first Americans to become aces. Thereafter, these two flyers, together with Bud Mahurin, were the men to beat among the pioneer USAAF fighter pilots in the ETO.

From the beginning, the men of the 56th were locked in a spirited competition with the pilots of the 4th Fighter Group, many of the latter veterans from the Eagle Squadrons. Bud Mahurin, of the 56th, talks about it: ''It's hard to say how it started, other than the fact that the most notorious fighter group was 4th Fighter. These were the guys who had flown in Royal Air Force uniforms before we got into the war. And of course, they came on board [the U.S. Army Air Force] with a number of victories they had generated flying Spitfires and Hurricanes during the Battle of Britain. There was a great deal of animosity involved in that one because these guys ran around more British than the British were. They spoke with British accents and wore offshoots of Royal Air Force uniforms and whatnot. And since they had experience, they disdained us. We liked to look at the scoreboard, like we do today at all of our games. And the first time you got a score, that added prestige to your squadron. As time went by, the more you got, the more prestige, and the more envy other fighter groups would have of your organization. So it became a competitive thing, trying to outdo each other! I think that's the American way!''

All fighter planes in the ETO, including the American, were still under the control of the RAF, and given the fighters' short range, earmarked for the relatively short missions into France and Holland. They were also under strict orders: ''RAF headquarters,'' Gabreski tells us, ''had put out a directive that our mission is principally, primarily to escort the bombers. We're not supposed to follow the German fighters down below 16,000 feet.'' During 1942, American bombers concentrated on targets within fighter-cover range.

Walter C. Beckham didn't find anything to shoot at during the first month or so he was escorting bombers on those sweeps across the Channel. But in the cockpit of a P-47 assigned to the 351st Fighter Squadron of the 353rd Group, he found plenty of action. In just six months, on 56½ missions, Beckham shot down 18 German planes to become the highest-scoring American ace in the European Theater. Says he of his job escorting Big Brothers: ''I was just lucky they put me into fighters. I would have been frightened to death of flying bombers, four-engine bombers. Those poor guys, when they were attacked, about all they could do was pray! They had to just sit there and hope they make it home. We could at least pull the stick back or kick a rudder, climb or dive or turn or maneuver. At least we could do something.''

On January 27, 1943, a new and portentous era dawned in the war. On that day, a force of B-17s and B-24s, escorted by P-38 Lightnings, bombed the German shipyards at Wilhelmshaven. It was the first U.S. raid on Germany from bases in Britain. Only three planes were lost.

Round-the-clock bombing stirred Hitler, at last, into heeding Galland's insistent pleas to strengthen the homeland's air defenses. Air divisions were brought back from Russia and Italy and new tactics were introduced, including ''bombing the bombers.'' On March 22, Lt. Heinz Knocke dropped a 250-

kilo (600-pound) bomb from his Messerschmitt and destroyed a B-17. Luft-waffe fighter planes were also outfitted with powerful 30 mm heavy cannon and wing-mounted rockets; it was estimated that it would take about 20 hits from 20 mm ammunition to bring down a Flying Fortress. The 30 mm cannon—the Mk.108, firing an 11-ounce high-explosive shell— could do it with three rounds. The trick was for the fighter pilot to get close enough to fire one of his 55 rounds, and do it in the roughly five seconds usually available to him. (By 1944, the twin-engine Me.410A-1/U4 fighter-bomber had mounted a 50 mm cannon to knock down bombers.)

Rockets were deadlier yet: A single hit from any one of the four 210 mm rockets slung beneath the wings of an Me.110 or Me.410 was enough, even if it exploded 50 feet from the target. A B-17 hit by such a rocket, packing an 80-pound warhead, on occasion would bring down another bomber as it exploded in those tight formations.

The disadvantage of the heavier armament was that it slowed the German planes—a factor of increasing importance as Allied fighter cover joined the bombers. As the grizzled veteran ace Walter Krupinski put it: "After '44, we called the new models the 'Bumps,' because after '44 every new model had another bump or hump on the fuselage, which naturally was particularly bad for the flight characteristics of the aircraft."

Beefed-up armament on the deadly FW.190A-5 and Messerschmitt Bf.109G-6 gave those agile fighters the ability to pummel a B-17 with as much as 70 rounds per second of tracer, armor-piercing and high-explosive ammunition. To counter such withering fire and the frontal attacks, the B-17E and F were phased out during 1943 and replaced by the new B-17G. Besides longer range, the G added a chin turret below the nose mounting twin 50-calibre machine guns, raising the Fort's total to thirteen. On the ground, the Germans added monster antiaircraft guns.

Weapons or no, Adolf Galland points out: "A bomber is a large target, but every four-engine bomber the Americans had had at least 11 to 12 heavy machine guns. The firepower around the bomber is tremendous, and could be overcome only at great risk."

Macki Steinhoff was already a veteran at running those risks: "I first

The FW.190, one of the two mainstays of the Luftwaffe's fighter assets.

Consolidated B-24 Liberator "Briney Marlin," piloted by 1st Lt. Lester C. Martin, returns to its base escorted by a P-47 Thunderbolt. Seven feet of the right wing and the aileron sheared off in a collision over the North Sea during the formation of an assembly.

encountered these four-engine planes in 1943. They flew out of North Africa, over Naples, Rome, Milan. And I had experienced them also within the borders of the Reich. There was a theory that the best way of attacking them was through a collision course. The speeds of the two planes were, of course, then combined, so there was no time to shoot. Only great experts were able to do this, shoot several salvos and bring the plane down." Although he was among the great experts of the Luftwaffe, Steinhoff preferred "the conventional attack—from the back—shoot and set them on fire." The idea was to "attack with a higher speed than they. There was no other tactic for flying up very close to the bomber. They flew in very narrow formation. If you approached them, you would fly through a snowstorm of missiles, projectiles from 30 to 40 machine guns. You would close your eyes. Young pilots, by the end of the war, could survive only two such attacks on the average—and then they were dead."

Fritz Losigkeit speaks of the danger and adds the element of motivation. "When you think of fighting the four-engined aircraft—four of them together, each of them with 12 machine guns, that's 48 machine guns, all firing at one fighter plane—you don't see anything but tracers. But you also know that he has been dropping bombs, so you try to shoot the aircraft down, because the aircraft is the bomb-carrier. When it starts to nose in, and you see three, four, five, six guys jumping out, then you say, 'Thank God, they're out, they're gonna be with us now [captives], they won't be able to do anyone any more harm and their plane is, thank God, destroyed!'"

Erich Hartmann, who shot down more enemy planes (352) than any man before or since, had his own rules: "I would attack only if I had 2,000 meters of clearance above them. Then I would come down with great speed—I would come down out of the sun so that he wouldn't see your approach. Because most downings are effected through surprise. And then I would shoot them down. I would always tell my colleagues that when your windshield was filled with enemy aircraft, that was the time to pull the trigger and shoot!"

Beginning in May of 1943, German fighter plane losses exceeded those of the Allies for the first time since 1940. The 8th Air Force's General Eaker decided the time had come to make fighter plane production the primary target. Out of that came Operation ARGUMENT—the first deep penetration raid into Germany made by American bombers.

That first real moment of truth for unescorted daylight bombing was on August 17, with 376 planes taking to the air. The primary target—the ball-bearing works at Schweinfurt, deep inside the Reich, some 900 miles from the bombers' British bases—was assigned 230 bombers. The rest went to the secondary target—the Messerschmitt factory at Regensburg.

Even if the mission had gone according to plan, it would have been a killer: the bombers had to fly the entire over-Germany leg without fighter escort.

But it didn't go according to plan. Poor visibility forced the Regensburg groups to delay their take-off an hour and a half. Both formations paid a frightful price. Between the two, 59 bombers were shot down, another seven crashing on return; more than 600 men dead, maimed, or prisoners-of-war; 138 bombers damaged.

Bud Mahurin was among the fighter pilots who sortied that day to cover the stricken Schweinfurt bombers on their last leg home. He describes the scene as he saw the bombers come into view from his P-47. "The German fighter pilots were making buzz-saw runs parallel to the bombers, from some distance out. They'd go way out in front of the bomber stream, then turn in and make head-on passes, flying through the bombers. We were flying over the top of the bombers; I could see the flickering flashes from their guns, and see the guns of our bombers flickering back. And all I could think of is, 'They're hurting our boys!' The old gang spirit came up, and I thought, 'I've got to try and stop that.' So I went out to where they [the Germans] were queuing up and went in there and got two of them."

With that, Mahurin had squared accounts. On an earlier mission, he had collided over England with a B-24 which sheared off the tail of his Thunderbolt. A sheepish Mahurin parachuted to safety. "It was all my fault. And so I felt duty-bound to make up for that somehow or other." (Mahurin made up for it handsomely: 21 German planes; later in the war, a Japanese plane in the southwest Pacific.)

The Regensburg raiders were led by Col. Curtis LeMay, who would go on to become one of the most colorful men ever in air force blue. His flight plan that day took his planes into southern Germany and Regensburg, then south over the Alps through the Brenner Pass. At the pass, LeMay circled the division to round up the strays before leading them low over the water down the Italian coast past Corsica and Sardinia, finally to an air field in North Africa—an 11-hour aerial agony.

That raid cost the lives or made captive more than 200 American airmen.

In June, the Luftwaffe pulled two more groups back to Germany, this time

George-Peter Eder demonstrates how to attack a B-17.

Above:
(L-R) Otte, Reinhard Seiler, Herst Adameit, Walter Krupinski, Erich Hartmann, August Gerger, and Adolph Hitler.

FW.190 groups based in France. As a result, the Allies in late August launched Operation STARKEY, a series of coordinated "ramrod" raids over France and the Low Countries. Fighters, fighter-bombers, Martin Marauder B-26 light bombers, B-17s, and B-24s were used, mainly at air fields around Paris. The objective was to draw the Luftwaffe back closer to the Channel coast, where superior Allied airpower could mangle it. What the sweeps proved was that neither side yet enjoyed the clear-cut power to clobber the other. Between August 25 and September 9, British and American pilots shot down 51 German planes, damaging 30 more. Forty-three Luftwaffe pilots were killed, about 20 percent of those still based in France. The Allies lost 49 fighters and fighter-bombers, 8 British medium bombers, 7 B-26s, and 65 B-17s and B-24s.

Gunther Rall, a veteran of both the Eastern and Western fronts, learned early on how futile it was for bombers to fly unescorted. The day after arriving at Mamaia, assigned to guard the Romanian oil fields at Constanta on the Black Sea, his squadron was scrambled to meet an incoming flight of unescorted Russian bombers. The German fighters made mincemeat of them. "You simply can't fly such missions," he insists, "without fighter support."

Still, the daylight raids went on, men and planes falling from the shell-scarred skies. Heavy losses prompted Robert A. Lovett, U.S. assistant secretary for war, to push hard in August of 1943 to outfit Lightnings and Thunderbolts with improved drop tanks. Finally, in November, with 200-gallon drop tanks, the P-47 gained about 70-80 miles of range and could fly missions of up to 650 miles. The Lightnings and Thunderbolts were able to escort the bombers on shallow penetration raids into Germany.

Jack Ilfrey, having trained pilots in the U.S. after becoming America's first ace in the Mediterranean Theater of Operations, is back in action as commander of 79th Fighter Squadron, 20th Fighter Group. He explains how it worked: "We had three types of missions. One was known as 'penetration': to rendezvous with the bombers at a certain time and escort them into the target. Then another group would pick them up and give them target area support. Then another group would pick them up and give them withdrawal support. As a fighter pilot, seeing those bombers disappear into clouds of black flak upset me, knowing that there were ten men on each one of those bombers. Here I am, in a fighter, I can evade, get around—but they couldn't. They had to stay on course and drop their bombs."

If the target was not too far, Lightnings or Thunderbolts would fly directly to it ahead of the bombers—the "target area support" Jack Ilfrey spoke about—fending off German fighters which had taken to ganging up on the bombers as they made their final approach to the target. The Germans had observed that when the bombardier in the lead plane in each group triggered his bombs, so did all those following. Those lead planes took severe punishment.

Other Thunderbolts flew with the formations but, forced to weave and bob to remain with their slower charges, used up their fuel faster. Walter Beckham was among the pilots who chafed at the restrictions: "The instructions said, 'If you're escorting a box of bombers and a German fighter or fighters dives away, don't follow them; stay with the bombers.' This was a mistake, because if you shoot down a German fighter plane, he's never gonna shoot down another bomber. If you just chase him away, he may be back 10 minutes later after you've left and destroy one or more bombers. Our job, really, was to destroy the German air force."

Postcard photo of Gunther Rall.

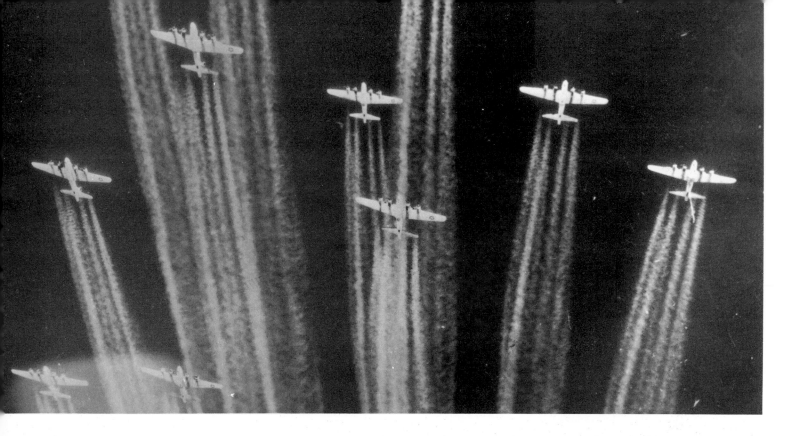

As the American pilots gained experience and confidence with the "Jugs," they discovered that they held a commanding advantage over both the 109s and 190s any time they met them above 22,000 feet. At those higher altitudes, the Thunderbolt not only was faster but had a superior rate of roll and turning radius and could outdive both of the top two German fighter planes. In a gentle dive, the Thunderbolt could reach 400 mph, and, recovering, climb back equally impressively.

Walter Beckham tells how it took some friendly persuasion to get bomber pilots to let the Little Brothers gain those advantages. "The bomber crews— bless their souls—liked to have us 'close by,' close to them. There were two things wrong with that. One, we looked a little bit like the 190s, so they may shoot at you. Second, and more important, if they're attacked by some 109s or 190s, and we're at bomber level, we're in a bad position. We should—and did—fly about 5,000-feet above the bombers. We could still see the bombers, and we could see any German fighters making an attack. And we can quickly swap that altitude for speed, position. I suspect a lot of the crews, because we were 5,000 feet over them, would never see us, and then say, 'We didn't have any escort!'"

Beckham speaks almost ecstatically about the Jugs, but with an element of family pride. The first time he ever went up in an airplane was with a first cousin. That same cousin was the test pilot who flew the P-47's first trials at Mitchell Field on Long Island, back on May 6, 1941. Beckham brags about the high-level performance and its awesome armament. "We had eight .50-caliber machine guns, and that's a tremendous amount of firepower. My recollection is that each gun fired about 800 rounds per minute, so that made 6,400 rounds per minute. Now, we didn't carry 6,400 rounds, of course—we had enough for about 16 or 18 seconds—but that's still a lot of firepower. The 51 only had six machine guns, and earlier, four. Just for a fight, I'd rather have the P-47 than the P-51." But then he adds: "Overall, the 51 was a better airplane. No question about it."

The P-38F Lightnings—which had given a good account of themselves in

An increasingly familiar sight over the Third Reich: Flying Fortresses generating contrails.

Loading the P-47's eight .50 caliber browning machine guns.

the low-level dogfights of North Africa—had a greater range than the Thunderbolts and so flew longer escort missions. The Js, which entered service in August 1943, flew even farther: 721 gallons in external tanks were added to their 433-gallon internal tanks, giving the Lightnings a phenomenal 2,598-mile range. But in the savage dogfights over German skies, usually well above 20,000 feet, they were outclassed. Ask Gerald "Jerry" Brown. After finishing his flight training on Lightnings in mid-1943, his 38th Fighter Squadron, 55th Fighter Group, was shipped to England in early September 1943. The first time out, a sweep over France on October 15 "to see if we could stir up anything," they stirred up only flak. Combat came a couple of weeks later: "That taught us a good lesson, what we were going to be up against, because there were only about half a dozen of 'em, 109s, and they tied up a whole group of our fighters! We lost three or four on that one."

On November 5, the 38th was assigned its first distant bomber escort mission, then another on the 15th. On the latter, the idea was to rendezvous with the bombers at Hanover (800-miles round-trip). "There were about 16 of us, and when we got there, there were about a hundred 109s and 190s attacking the bombers. My flight commander, Joe Myers, and I both got shot up very badly. I had an engine shot out, on fire. This 109 had me just dead to rights . . . sittin' right under my tail boom, about 100 feet back, just shootin' the bejesus out of me! And when you're on fire and on a single-engine, and that guy is back there with a better airplane—well, there's just no place to go! I'm just doin' a spiral, down toward the deck, tryin' to keep him from getting more of a deflection shot at me and hopin' the fire would go out after I feathered the engine, and thought, 'That sonuvabitch isn't gonna shoot me down!' But he's hitting me all the time. I had lost about 10,000 feet and was down to around 20,000 feet. Meanwhile, Joe had worked himself around, and he just shot him off my tail—shot him down! I owed my life to Joe Myers."

Joe Myers shepherded Brown, two other crippled P-38s, and a stricken B-17 home and was awarded the Distinguished Flying Cross (DFC). Back at base, they counted more than 200 bullet holes in Jerry's plane. A time for reflection: "You know, you hear guys say, 'Oh God! I was scared, and I froze,' or something like that. That didn't happen to me. I just said, 'No way that this mother is gonna shoot me down.' And that's the way I felt. I had been up against better pilots in my own squadron, you know, just playing 'grab.' But up there, that was air combat!"

Jerry Brown: "Joe was the best flight commander in our squadron. Everything I knew about fighters, about the P-38, he taught me. How good you were as a fighter pilot, you could lay basically to how aggressive and how good your flight commander was. Later on, he became our operations officer and squadron commander. I just thought he was one of the best fighter pilots I ever flew with." And, like Jerry Brown, Joe Myers went on to become an ace. And, like Joe Myers, Jerry Brown went on to collect a chest full of medals: DFC with 4 clusters, Distinguished Service Medal (DSM), Air Medal with 13 clusters, and the French *Croix de Guerre*.

Increasingly outnumbered, the Luftwaffe sought new ways to fight back. Two special squadrons formed originally to foil the fast and high-flying British Mosquito fighter-bombers now met the American daylight raiders in their "souped-up" Messerschmitt 109Gs. These "Gustavs" tangled not only with the bombers, but with the Thunderbolt and Lightning escorts, typically flying

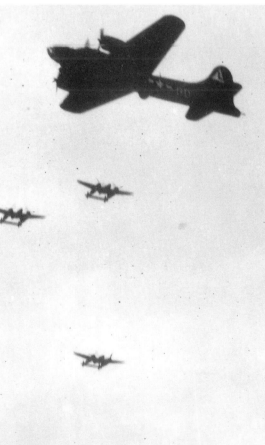

No better sight for a weary bomber crew: Lockheed's twin-tailed P-38 Lightnings.

Harley Brown.

Above:
Laden with fuel and high explosives, this Liberator disintegrates quickly after being hit with German antiaircraft artillery.

8,000 feet above the bombers. Maj. Herbert Ihlefeld bagged 18 of his 130 kills while commanding one of the special squadrons.

But the ace-of-aces against bombers was a 27-year-old noncom who had already fought on the Eastern front and in the Mediterranean before he was pulled back to join in the defense of his bomb-blighted homeland in the fall of 1943. Herbert Rollwage shot down more Allied daylight four-engined bombers—44—than any other Luftwaffe pilot. (Given a battlefield commission later, Rollwage ended the war with 102 victories and a Knight's Cross of the Iron Cross with Oak Leaves.)

Operation ARGUMENT raids caused German fighter production to drop back from 700 in July of 1943 to 350 by December. But the American attackers paid a terrible price. On July 26, 92 B-17s bombed Hannover while 50 hit Hamburg; 16 were shot down over Hannover, eight over Hamburg. On the 28th, 22 Fortresses were shot down, eleven of them by one-eyed Capt. Gunther Specht (Specht had lost an eye in combat over the North Sea in December 1939).

By the autumn of 1943, it seemed that the Luftwaffe was winning a major victory over the 8th Air Force. Attacking Bremen and Vegesack on October 8, the 8th lost 27 Flying Fortresses, three Liberators, and three Thunderbolts; 25 more B-17s went down in a raid on Marienburg the next day. On the 10th, the target was Munster; 30 more went down. The last great shocker came on October 14, the second Schweinfurt raid. This time, the Germans were waiting for them.

Walter Beckham, a top American ace, was in the cockpit of a P-47 that day with the 351st Fighter Squadron. "Several fighter groups failed to make the rendezvous with the bombers because of bad weather. My group did make it, and we discovered that the Germans were making an all-out effort. They even met us over the English Channel—I'd never before seen that. They were trying to break up the fighter escort so they could have the bombers all to themselves." As it was, the fighters could only make it a little more than a third of the way. All told, the Germans threw up 300 interceptors to meet the bombers. Of the 291 B-17s on that raid, 60 were shot down; another 17 among the 138 damaged had to be written off. The Luftwaffe lost 38 fighter planes. The 8th's loss rate on that raid—26 percent—was far, far above the RAF's "acceptable" standard for a single mission. Follow-up raids in October on Bremen, Danzig (Gdansk), Marienburg, and Munster cost 148 more bombers—nearly 1,500 men. For the month, the command's loss rate was 9.1 percent.

Fallout from the Schweinfurt raid reverberated all the way back to Washington, to the halls of Congress, the Pentagon, the White House. Deep penetration raids by unescorted daylight bombers became a dead letter.

In November, the raids were scaled back to closer-in targets. P-47s escorted B-17s on a raid on Wilhelmshaven (a roughly 800-mile round-trip) at the beginning of the month. On the 13th, they were in the air again over 600 Fortresses dropping 1,600 tons of bombs on Kiel, a 1,100-mile round-trip. But in both instances, the fighters had to turn back not long after crossing the German frontier.

The bombers would return to Schweinfurt, to Regensburg, to Kiel, would range the length and breadth of the Reich. But they would no longer fly alone.

There was debate in Germany, as well—secretive, cautious debate, out of earshot of the dreaded Gestapo. But as the devastation intensified, the talk grew bolder. Johannes Steinhoff, who fought about as hard for his country as any man ever could (over 900 missions, shot down 12 times, 176 victories), reveals his contempt for Goering: "In the fall of 1943, a narrow circle of squadron leaders began to ask whether it wouldn't be possible to stop this amateur, this charlatan leading the Luftwaffe. We were of the opinion that the bomber attacks could be stopped. After the Schweinfurt attack, the Americans did stop bombing for three weeks. The Americans had lost 800 men, and there was debate in the American Congress. So we believed we could stop this pulverization of German cities. We blamed this charlatan who, at this time, was capable only of collecting diamonds and paintings. We regarded it as his fault. Our plans came to naught, not least of all because we were betrayed. We already had a successor picked, someone to succeed him. When this was discovered, he had us come to Berlin. There were five of us, five *kommodores* [group leaders, commanding 120 planes]. He listened to what we had to say, and then he left the room saying, 'I'll have you shot.' You couldn't just shoot highly decorated officers. We were just transferred, for disciplinary reasons."

This was not Macki Steinhoff's first meeting with Goering, nor was his aversion to the man new. "It began," he continues, "at the end of 1939. I was stationed at Bonn as the only night-fighter squadron leader. I was ordered to go to Berlin, the English were flying over Berlin dropping leaflets that said, 'Now we're dropping leaflets, but soon it will be bombs.' So I was ordered to meet with the leadership of the Luftwaffe to discuss strategy. General [Ernst] Udet was there. He committed suicide because of Goering. The chief of the general staff and Goering entered the room. He was really fat. He sat down in a huge Germanic chair and began to describe how he imagined an air battle. Well, this description was right out of World War I. The way it was fought over Flanders, when you see the whites of the enemy's eyes. I couldn't stand it any longer and said, 'I'd like to have the floor. I have to fly at night. We have no navigational tools. We don't know where we're going. We have no lighting. We have only one-engine planes. We can't go on like this.'

"While I spoke, Goering waved his cigar and said, 'Young man, sit down on your little behind. If you want to talk with us, you have to have much more experience.' And I said, 'Well, what's going on? I *am* the only one with experience.' Since that time, I hated this man, and that hatred continued throughout the war. During the Battle of Britain, which was also the result of bad strategic planning, I realized that I had to find like-minded friends who would agree with me that this man has to go. It was clear to me that it really

Herman Goering with Adolph Galland examining papers.

P-47s on patrol.

had to happen or we had to witness the destruction of the cities. The culmination of this was when Goering accused all the fighter squadron leaders of cowardice. At the time, we didn't have the courage to get up and throw our [Iron] Crosses at his feet."

But, as Macki Steinhoff points out, one man did: Adolf Galland. Galland relates what happened: "It was in 1943, and Goering was going on about the alleged lack of bravery of German fighter pilots. He cursed the fighter pilots and claimed that they got their decorations undeservedly. I was very angry, so I tore my decoration from my collar and banged it on the table." The tension between the two men did not abate; a little over a year later, in January 1945, Goering fired the feisty Galland as head of Fighter Command.

Between January 1 and December 31, 1943, 135,000 tons of bombs had been dropped on Germany—most of them by the night-flying British. Although the bombing had not yet crippled Germany's armament industry, it had forced highly significant shifts in priorities. More and more men were assigned to antiaircraft weapons, which claimed an ever-larger share of the overall output, and the Russian front was stripped bare of these weapons to cover the mounting needs of the fatherland. The relentless bombing was also taking its toll on the nerves of the German leadership.

As 1944 dawned, there were two U.S. air forces in England: the 8th, as of January 4, commanded by Lt. Gen. James H. Doolittle; and the 9th, moved in October of 1943 from North Africa.

Harley Brown had been flying since age four with his barnstorming uncle Earl Beech, back in El Dorado, Kansas. But Harley Brown had never seen anything in the sky like America's airpower in 1944. "On one mission I remember, there were over 2,000 bombers—in box formations—over 300 miles long! Can you imagine? Astounding! And over 1,000 fighters, counting ours—Jerry [the Germans] had sent up about 500 of theirs. Our group, free of escort—on free-lance—saw 'em and headed for 'em. In the next 30 minutes, I was lucky enough to get three destroyed and one damaged. It was a spectacle! All these bombers, as far as you could see in both directions. All these fighters, and the bombers are being hit, exploding—in every direction you could see, parachutes going down, bombers exploding—a lot of the time, there'd just be a big flash and you'd see pieces trickling down. And fighters fighting from sea level to 30,000 feet. And they were so thick, there were several midair collisions. You had to watch out to keep from runnin' into each other. You can't imagine—Hollywood couldn't reenact that."

A wingman flying a P-47 photographs with his gun camera another P-47 attacking a flak tower.

Perilously low to the ground, another dramatic shot. Two P-47s beat up a runway with their guns.

Bud Mahurin witnessed similar sights. "Awe-inspiring! Those guys got up four hours earlier than we did in the morning for a mission. We could hear them droning around over the skies in England, trying to assemble. Then we'd get up there, Little Friends with the Big Friends—they always referred to us that way—and we were a protective envelope that surrounded them. Then you realize you've got a job to do, and then you realize that you're really protecting lives."

Gabreski recalls a variation on that crowded-skies theme: "There were eight of us, coming in behind a bomber, when we noticed about 12 Me.110s beneath us, coming in to attack. It looked like a perfect setup for the whole squadron, and I said, 'Let's prepare to attack!' When I nosed my plane over, somebody didn't get the word or somebody got confused, but two of my airplanes were crossing over and ran together. As I looked out, I could see the flaming pieces go through the sky, and the first thing that hit my mind was, 'Oh my God!' But then I saw that Focke Wulf 190s were shooting us out of the sky from behind, so I broke off my attack on the 110s and went up to survey the situation, and it was obvious to me then that some of my own people had run together." Times like that, he said, test leadership—"when your emotions are under control and your professionalism takes over."

Gabreski also remembers that when Doolittle took over the 8th he told his pilots: "Anything in Germany is fair game." They took him at his word, strafing and bombing everything in sight. "We had reached the point by then," Gabreski adds, "where we had a tremendous number of aircraft—backup aircraft, attrition aircraft. We had so many airplanes coming in that we went from a 12-airplane squadron to an 18-airplane squadron. We went from 35 to 55 pilots per squadron." Germany was also being hit from the south by the 15th and the 12th Air Forces. An ominous silhouette was, moreover, about to complete the picture, a picture of far greater devastation than anything yet seen.

They could fly faster, farther, and higher than anything the Germans could put up against them. They became the "dominator of the skies" over Europe. With them, Big Brothers would never again need go out alone. They were the Mustangs, that hybrid of American aerodynamics and a British power plant—the 1,612 Rolls-Royce engines—that sent the Mustang soaring to 20,065 feet in five minutes and 54 seconds, hit a top speed of 439 mph at 30,082 feet, and climb to a ceiling of 42,111 feet. Even more importantly, 110-gallon drop tanks added to the 269-gallon internal tank gave the Mustang a range of just over 2,000 miles. Says Jerry Brown: "By the time the first Mustang group became operational, they were very, very welcome, because by that time, we [the 55th Fighter Group, flying P-38 Lightnings] had lost, oh, maybe a third of our group, either due to enemy action, enemy fighters, flak, or bad weather." (The Lightnings increasingly were assigned ground-support missions, a role in which they excelled.)

Lt. Col. James A. Goodson, late of the RAF, later of its all-American Eagle Squadron, now with the USAAF's 4th Fighter Group, puts the Mustang in perspective against the Spitfires and Hurricanes he had flown. "The big difference is that the war had changed. The Hurricane and Spitfire were designed as defensive fighters, with only a couple hours' range. After the Battle of Britain, when the Germans were no longer coming over here, we had to carry the battle to them, and of course, the idea of the American bombing effort was daylight precision bombing. But the big bombers soon

James Howard in his Mustang
emblazoned with Japanese and German
kill marks.

found that it was suicide for them to go against the Germans in daylight
without a fighter escort. The Spitfires could only take them a few hundred
miles on their way to Germany, and the P-47 helped a bit, but it could really
only just get to the edge of Germany. It was when we got the P-51 Mustang,
which had this extraordinary performance and this enormous range, that
things changed. We used to fly that plane eight and-a-half hours, all the way
to Berlin and back.''

Now, the Reich was nowhere safe.

The British, who had commissioned the plane in the first place, called it the
Mustang Mk.1. They had been flying them since the spring of 1942, mainly as
tactical reconnaissance planes. Alan Geoffrey Page, shot down and so badly
burned during the Battle of Britain that he was hospitalized for nearly two
years while he underwent 14 operations, returned to duty in 1943 with RAF
132 Squadron as a flight commander. The squadron itself was commanded by
the remarkable J.A.F. (James) MacLachlan, who lost his left arm when shot
down over Malta. The plane they flew was the Mustang Mk.1. And their
tactics were pure guts. Page describes what they did:

''We had worked out a scheme so as to penetrate in daylight—low-level,
treetop height—to attack German airfields, where the German night fighters
would be doing their daylight testing before going out and attacking RAF
Bomber Command in the heart of darkness. This is 1943, before the invasion.
It was an interesting game because, to give one example, if we came across
high tension cables, we'd have to fly under them and not climb because just
that little bit of altitude would give our position away. MacLachlan was quite
extraordinary. He was senior to me, and so he was leading, with his one arm,
flying his airplane and map-reading. You try map-reading at treetop height
and getting to the airfield you want several hundred miles away—it's quite an
achievement. We didn't use radio, of course, because he hadn't got the hand
to work a radio, so we did an immense amount of practice flying before we set
off in earnest.'' On one such ''earnest'' mission, these two indomitable warriors between them destroyed four trainers and two Ju.88s within ten minutes near Paris, which earned them both DFCs.

The 354th Fighter Group of the U.S. 9th Air Force was the first to receive
the P-51B and C Mustangs on December 1, 1943. On December 5, the

North American P-51D Mustangs on patrol.

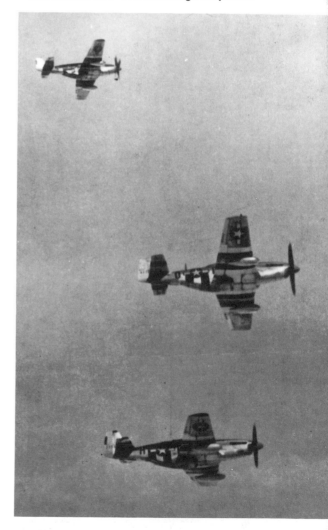

British pilot Geoffrey Page and these five other RAF pilots were part of a group of Spitfire pilots to fly alone into Germany for the first time, April 26, 1944. They shot up Nazi fighters and gliders, railway wagons and locomotives, and returned to base without a loss after a trip of 800 miles.

354th—destined to become famous as the Pioneer Mustang Group—accompanied bombers on a "shake-down" raid on Amiens, about 75 miles north of Paris. The first big test came on the 13th when P-51s of the same group, bolstered by P-38 Lightnings of the 55th Group, rode shotgun with the bombers all the way to Kiel and back, the longest mission yet flown by fighter escorts. Other fighters were in the air that day with bombers over Bremen, Hamburg, and Schiphol Airport at Amsterdam. A total of 1,462 aircraft took part in those raids, the biggest American effort so far in the war.

James H. Howard—a veteran of Claire Chennault's Flying Tigers—now a major, commanded a P-51 squadron in the 354th. Over Hamburg that day in January, he spied a Messerschmitt "tooling behind a B-17 which was lagging behind. I gave him a shot and he went right on in. He didn't even see me." The German was the first of nine-and-a-half victories Howard would rack up in Europe, added to his six-and-a-half with the Flying Tigers. Scoring victories was important, but, along with his men, Howard insisted that "our job is to protect the bombers. Each bomber has ten men in it. And of the, say, 800 bombers—you figure it out yourself—how many men depend upon our being there to protect them? Instead of tooling off and flying off by yourself, our job is to escort. Escort these bombers and knock down the fighters before they get to them."

Another great ace of the 8th, Maj. George E. Preddy, Jr., gave the same advice to his men before he himself was shot down. "In escorting bombers," he wrote, "it is a good idea to range out to the sides, front, and rear and hit enemy fighters before they can get to the bombers unprotected." Preddy was commanding officer of the 328th Fighter Squadron at the time of his death. Earlier in the war, he had fought against the Japanese, damaging two Japanese aircraft. In the European Theater, he scored 28 kills between December 1, 1943, and his death in combat on December 25, 1944. On that Christmas day, Preddy was down on the deck in hot pursuit of a FW.190 when he flew into American flak meant for the German. His Mustang disintegrated into flaming chunks.

Several months after reaching the ETO, Preddy was asked to put on paper his advice to pilots. A key priority was the need for close teamwork between a flyer and his wingman. His own wingman, Lt. William T. "Whis" Whisner, learned his lessons well: Whisner ended the war with 15½ air-to-air and three ground kills. (Later, in the Korean War, he added five-and-a-half Migs.)

Like Preddy, Jim Howard was a solid teacher as well as a great ace—so solid that the 354th Group, which he later commanded, ended the war with the greatest number of aerial victories of any American fighter group in any theater of any war before or since.

Though severely weakened, the Luftwaffe was not finished, as it soon demonstrated. On January 11, 1944, 663 U.S. bombers escorted by P-51s set out for aircraft production centers at Halberstadt, Brunswick, and Oschersleben. Bad weather forced two of the three formations to strike alternative targets and head back. The remaining bombers and 49 P-51s were challenged by 200 German fighters; 60 American bombers and five Mustangs went down, the Luftwaffe lost 39 fighters.

Jim Howard, who led the mission, practiced what he preached—Little Brothers protecting Big Brothers. Taking off in an overcast, he led the P-51s straight for the rendezvous point. "We could see the bombers in a long stream stretching over miles and miles and miles. I dispatched one squadron to them as we approached the [bomber] stream, and then a second squadron, and then my squadron approached towards the head of the stream. Then we broke up in flights, and then elements—you know, you don't attack by squadron or anything like that. You have to break it down into individual airplanes or flights."

In that fierce fighting, Jim Howard became what they would later call "the one man air force," single-handedly fighting off 30 German fighters making attack after attack on the 401st Bomb Group of B-17s. He shot down three of them. About as far as Jim Howard will go is to say that "there were some 30 enemy airplanes descending upon the bombers. And when they got back, they said that they had been saved by my actions."

For what he did that day, James H. Howard was awarded the nation's highest decoration for bravery, the Medal of Honor—the only American fighter pilot so honored in the European Theater.

Gerald Brown was riding shotgun on one of those January raids when he also noted that the Luftwaffe still had plenty of sting in its wings. "We picked the bombers up, a usual mission, over the North Sea and were gonna escort

432nd Fighter Group pilots. (L-R) James Mayden, Willie Jackson, George Preddy, and John Meyer.

A P-51 suffered this damage in the air and safely returned its pilot to base.

'em down near Nancy, France. We were at about 28,000 feet, the box of bombers at about 25,000, when they got hit by about 200 German fighters. By the time we had chased some of 'em off, there were only about 16 of us left! We had to set up a defensive maneuver—the Lufbery Circle. Well, in this particular case, we set up, one goin' one way, one goin' the other, and with a thousand feet separation between the two circles. We did this strictly for defensive purposes, so that the Germans wouldn't pick us off piecemeal. In about ten minutes, they had picked off four out of the original 16. One of 'em wasn't fast enough, and he tried to get in behind somebody in one of the circles. When I saw that, I dived down on him from the upper Lufbery Circle and was able to shoot his tail off. That was my first victory against the 109. And it was very memorable for me.''

Things looked quite different from the cockpit of German planes now that the air war had been carried to their homeland. Hans-Joachim Jabs had been a fighter pilot for eight years and flying combat missions for four. None of that prepared him for January 18, 1944. ''I was flying above Magdeburg—my wife's hometown—and it was a burning inferno. My family was down there. It was a horrible experience.'' He adds: ''When you're flying above a city, and bombs are falling and the city is burning, you felt rage because you were unable to stop the destruction.''

Rage—and determination to fight even harder. Heinz Marquardt remembers looking down from his fighter plane on ''the destruction of the cities, refugees fleeing. We felt that we had to do our duty, to help those on the ground. We were like hunted rabbits, but we did our best to save as much as we could. We had known for some time that we couldn't win the war.''

Fritz Losigkeit likens the situation of the Luftwaffe's pilots from 1943 onwards to that of the RAF pilots of 1940-1941. ''When the fighter pilot knows, my hometown has been reduced to rubble, there's no question of fear or cowardice. The English Hurricane and Spitfire pilots flew better, were more courageous and resolute after they saw their cities being destroyed.''

On February 8, 1944, Lt. General Spaatz, now in overall charge of American strategic bombing, ordered Operation ARGUMENT ended by March 1. It was to end with a bang: "Big Week" opened February 19 with the biggest combined bomber-fighter raid of the war. Covered by 700 fighters—17 U.S. fighter groups of Mustangs, Thunderbolts, and Lightnings, backed by 16 RAF squadrons flying Spitfires—940 bombers blasted fighter plane factories and 12 synthetic fuel plants. So powerful was the armada that only 21 bombers were lost. All told, 3,800 heavy bombers of the 8th and 9th blasted a dozen targets in Germany that week, some as far south as Ratisbon and Augsburg. A total of 226 bombers and 28 fighters—2,600 men—was lost; the Germans lost some 600 fighter planes. By then, the Germans had only 350 single-engine and 130 twin-engine fighters left to defend their homeland.

On February 22, 1944, Walter Beckham's luck ran out. His squadron of 16 Thunderbolts was heading home when Squadron Leader Glen Docking spied a Focke Wulf taxiing at an air field at Ostheim, Germany. Taking a closer look himself, Docking radioed up to Beckham, cruising at 25,000 feet, that there were seven or eight more real planes parked below. Beckham nosed his Thunderbolt down through "a lot of flak; they can't hit anything much, but they shoot so many bullets that it's dangerous." At about 12,000 feet, he "felt a little boop and heard a little pop." He realized only later that his engine had been hit. Undaunted, he joined Docking in strafing the field, ending with a pass at the first plane Docking had strafed.

"There was a man in a white suit trying to put out a fire, and I tried to bend around and shoot at him and the airplane, but couldn't quite make it." Heading home, smoke belching from his engine, Beckham opened the canopy of his plane and unhooked the seat belt, shoulder harness, and oxygen mask—just in case he had to jump in a hurry. Suddenly, "fire burst into the cockpit, flames underneath the rotor pedal." With smoke filling the cockpit, he stood on the seat of the plane and tried to jump out head first. No dice—something was restraining him. "So I sat back down, and don't want to try that again, 'cause if I try and get hung up again I'm a dead man! I could just barely see the stick through the smoke and I took my foot, turned it sideways so I don't miss, and jammed the stick forward. When you do that, the plane continues in a straight line, but starts a sharp dive, and that's when I ejected. I bumped into the tail but not too fast, because, you see, I'm going the same speed as the airplane. At about a thousand feet, the 'chute opened very nicely and I see below a road with a line of trees. We had been told to avoid trees, and so I pull the strings on the parachute to maneuver, but the wind is blowing and I landed in the top of one of the trees. You know, if someone told me to do it, to land in a tree, I couldn't do it. Anyway, I remember putting my feet together, and the branches stopped the 'chute, and I stopped with my feet about two feet off the ground."

The next thing Beckham knew, he was surrounded by German civilians. "And this," he adds, "was very unpleasant. I can remember one guy had a switchblade knife, the long-bladed kind, and he had it open." Through Beckham's mind raced images of flyers on both sides killed by civilians because "people didn't like folks to bomb them. I would never have made it except the police arrived." After a few hours in a police station, Luftwaffe MPs arrived. The next day, with "some dozens" of Allied airmen, Beckham was taken to an interrogation center at Obersurel, near Frankfurt. He spent 27 days, most of it in solitary confinement, discovering that "they knew more about everything than I did. They knew my call sign, my squadron, my group, my base. They had a roster of all of the pilots in my squadron. They knew the armament officer had a big German Shepherd dog. They knew its name.

A pilot exits his damaged P-47 somewhere over Europe.

Adolph Galland.

Suppose I had wished to cooperate with the Germans, changed sides—I wouldn't have known what to tell them.''

Interrogation over, Beckham was given an overcoat, a Red Cross parcel—and the opportunity to discover what it was like on the receiving end of air warfare. ''That first evening, the British came over and bombed, and the U.S. bombed during the day. Happily, they made us all go down into shelters, because a bomb or two landed in the camp and totally destroyed the building that we were in. We spent a miserable night in the cold air raid shelter, with water on the floor, so you can't sit down or lie down.'' The next day, a train took Beckham and his fellow prisoners to their home for the next 14 months—Stalag Luft 3 at Zagan, southeast of Berlin. The war was over for Walter Beckham.

Two German aces describe their last missions. For Heinz Marquardt, the day he was shot down for good, May 1, 1944, was the day ''I celebrate as my birthday.'' Marquardt had shot down as many as 12 planes in a single day (his total was 121). How did it feel to blast so many out of the skies? ''When we returned from a sortie, we would fly victory rolls, but it didn't matter whether we shot down five, what was important was that I knew those aircraft couldn't bother us anymore. That's what mattered.'' Now, on what would be his final mission, his group was jumped by Spitfires just west of Hamburg. Attempting to attack from below, he was shot down but bailed out.

For Gunther Rall—the world's third-ranking ace (275 kills)—combat, but not the war, would end on May 12, 1944. ''I was engaged with a large American bomber, and was successful, when a Thunderbolt chased me from a height of 8,000 meters [26,500 feet]. My plane was totally shot up, my thumb shot off, and I had to get out.'' It was the fifth time in 621 missions that Rall had been forced to bail out. Now, as before, he parachuted safely, but the wound failed to heal. By the time he returned to duty in 1945, the war was winding down.

The pounding continued, now against Berlin. Poor weather on March 3 prevented the force of Fortresses and Liberators from reaching Berlin; only the escorting P-51s did. Three days later, they did it right: 609 B-17s and B-24s, escorted by 90 Mustangs with old RAF hand Jim Goodson leading the way, raided the capital. For three hours, harrowing duels were fought high over Germany's skies: 68 bombers went down, as well as 11 fighters; the Germans lost 37 fighters.

Jim Goodson learned later that on that first Berlin raid he had faced an extraordinary adversary when he chased an Me.109 until, low on fuel and out of ammunition, he broke off and returned home. The pilot he had been chasing was none other than the head of the Luftwaffe Fighter Command, Lt. Gen. Adolf Galland.

Patric Jameson, the New Zealander who had flown with the RAF since 1936, speaks of what the arrival of American flyers meant to the war effort:

''When the Americans started their operations, it made a tremendous impact. Our bombers weren't so heavily armed, and they couldn't possibly survive if they went over enemy territory without fighter escorts. But the American B-17s had very good defensive armament, and although they took pretty hefty casualties, they were able to continue on. And then, of course, they got those long-range fighters, like the Mustangs, and they had escorts all the way to Berlin. That did make a tremendous impression on the enemy. So there was bombing by day, bombing by night . . . it kept them 'on the hot' the whole time. A tremendous difference.''

9

STRUGGLE FOR SUPREMACY

A Sopwith Camel in flight.

In the sky over Flanders in 1918, American ace Elliott White Springs in his Sopwith Camel was vying with a new Fokker D.VII German fighter to see who would live, who would die. He later wrote: "I could have given my shirt for two more horsepower."

At about the same time, Capt. Eddie Rickenbacker was futilely urging his Spad to climb another thousand feet to bring a German Rumpler artillery observation plane within range of his guns. The enemy plane sailed overhead unmolested, calling down artillery fire.

A generation and a war later, the fate of battles and pilots still hinged on technological advances, large and small.

Berlin was rapidly becoming a wasteland of rubble when the first American bombers arrived. RAF raids, begun in 1940, were desultory until the night of November 18-19, 1943, when British Gen. Arthur "Bomber" Harris launched his Battle of Berlin. Now, American daylight bombing would wreak even greater havoc on the city.

Against the marauders, Adolf Galland, head of the Luftwaffe Fighter Command, turned increasingly to technology to fill the void created by dwindling manpower and aircraft. Into the frenzied fray, he threw up five-ton aerial "tanks"—specially outfitted FW.190A-8/R8s. These *Sturmgruppen* planes added 5 mm to 12 mm steel armor plates around the pilot and engine cowling, and 50 mm thick bullet-resistant glass for the cockpit windscreen. To the two 20 mm cannon were added two 30 mm cannon. These fighter-monsters targeted the bombers, while lighter fighter planes tangled with the American fighter escorts.

The appearance of Mustang fighters over Berlin in March 1944 dealt a heavy blow to Luftwaffe morale. Jim Goodson says it all: "I understand that Goering, when he saw our red-nosed Mustangs over Berlin, said: 'Now I know the war is lost.'"

Jack Ilfrey led his Lightnings on a leg of one of those Berlin raids, escorting what he called "a flock" of B-17s. "Well, we got jumped by 50 to 60 German fighters. When they come through you like that, you pretty much get mixed up. I had a real good shot at one Me.109 and he burst into flames; my camera caught it, and I was given credit for that one. About then, someone screamed on the radio, 'Jack! Look Out! Somebody's right under you, trying to ram you!'" Ilfrey threw the Lightning into a fast turn. "My right wing tore about four and-a-half to five feet off the cockpit of that plane." The German was down, but Ilfrey was in trouble. He had lost the gas tank for the right engine and the impact had thrown him into a spin. Recovering, he looked around,

Captain Eddie Rickenbacker by his Spad.

Clayton Kelly Gross and his aircraft, "Live Bait."

"didn't see a soul, so, I'm by myself, and now have to get back to England by myself—on one engine. Everybody else is gone. So I thought the best way to do it would be to get into the overcast and fly instruments, fly in the clouds."

Flying an estimated course to England, "I suddenly start seeing these big, black puffs of flak right at me. Now, I had seen a lot of flak before, but when they're right at you, they're red inside. Some of the shrapnel was peppering my aircraft, and I said, 'I gotta get out of here.' So I dove down as fast as I could and busted out [of the clouds] right over the middle of Hamburg, Germany. They had all those guns firing, plus barrage balloons up in the air. I spotted a river—I can't think of it now [the Elbe] that Hamburg's on—got right on that river, and made just like a motorboat going out to the North Sea and finally got myself home. Now that upsets your constitution!"

Clayton Kelly Gross, out of Walla Walla, Washington, came to the 354th Fighter Group and was one of the first 12 pilots to fly Mustang escort for the Big Brothers—and it was no picnic. "When I saw big bombers go down, I felt terrible because you knew there were ten men in each one of those. We watched a lot of them go down, from enemy antiaircraft fire, and sometimes from fighters, though we were pretty successful at keeping fighters off them. It really hurt me to watch them go down.

"The bombers were very vulnerable in daylight bombing," Gross adds. "They were given a target deep in enemy territory and they had to maintain a straight and level course while the enemy fighters were able to pick and choose the areas where they could attack. Bomber losses were tremendous until we were able to have fighters with them at all times, one group relieving another. Since we had the long-range fighter, we usually took them on the final run into the target and back out again, then turned it over to some of the shorter-range fighters, such as the P-47s."

Captain Gross's journey to a combat cockpit deserves a clarifying word. Veronica Lake was a celebrated actress of the day, whose trademark was hair pulled over one eye. Gross "thought all pilots got girls with hair over one eye, and I wanted to be a pilot." Next "I read *God Is My Co-Pilot* and I wanted to fly alone, to be a fighter pilot." The young pilot got married the day he won his wings. "We were marched into an auditorium and given forms with three lines on them. Told to fill out our first top three choices, and then they said, 'If you are 5'11" or over you may not apply for fighter pilot.' And I was 5' 11½", so I thought, as long as I had just been married, I'd stay home for a while. So I wrote down instructor, then, for second choice, heavy bombardment, and third choice, medium bombardment. So, they sent me to fighters! Which is the way the air corps operated in those days: just exactly the opposite of what they said." Clayton Gross went on to become an ace with six kills, earning a Silver Star, DFC with cluster, and Air Medal with 15 clusters.

On March 4, 1944, the Luftwaffe managed another triumph in the savage but unequal contest for control of the skies. The Mustangs got lost in clouds near Hamburg. Aided by ground control, JG.1's first squadron stalked them and shot down 11. Back from the Russian front, Walter Krupinski—"Graf Punski" to his cronies—prowled those hostile skies with the instincts of a hunter where game was abundant. "My mission," he says, "was to combat the enemy escort fighters, not the bombers. My first impression on my first sortie over Germany was 'Oh my God! Look at all those targets! This is gonna be a lot better than Russia.' In Russia, you sometimes really had to search for an opponent. But on that first sortie I shot down two Mustangs, and a Thunderbolt on the second. On the third sortie, I was the one who had to bail out. Then I realized this was a completely different kind of combat than in Russia—although I had to bail out there twice, too, and made at least half a dozen belly-landings. Still, there was no comparison between Russia and what we now faced in the West."

Krupinski was back in the sky after that shoot-down. He explains his job: "As a fighter pilot, one doesn't fly against a huge formation, but rather seeks to gain the best position in relation to the other aircraft and you try to attack them. Naturally, if they attacked first, then—as an experienced pilot, which I was by then—you found yourself in a fight for position which ended in a dogfight, taking place at any altitude, with lots of possibilities for survival."

In those desperate days, Krupinski tried to spare young pilots the rough time he had had four years earlier in the Battle of Britain. "I was thrown into that fight, and no one told me what to do. That's why I tried to show young pilots what to do, how to do it. At the end of a dogfight, when there would be only one enemy aircraft left, I'd tell my wingman, 'That one's yours,' and I'd give him instructions over the radio how to do it, like, 'Closer, get closer, don't shoot yet. OK, shoot, shoot NOW!' "

Those tips applied in spades when it came to the devastating 30 mm cannon. Although they could blow a bomber out of the sky with just three hits, pilots had only five seconds in which to shoot. And planes carried only 55 rounds per gun. That, plus the cannon's relatively low muzzle velocity, which meant that accuracy diminished rapidly as the range increased, made it imperative that it be fired up close, and in short bursts, typically from 100 yards or less.

The problem was, there simply weren't enough Krupinskis left.

Luftwaffe strength continued to wane. Between January and April 1944, the Luftwaffe was losing an average of 50 fighters per raid; more than 1,000 pilots were lost in the first months of 1944. Galland, struggling to repel the onslaught, scrounged reinforcements when and where he could find them. By the end of May, the Luftwaffe had only 250 single-engine fighters left,

A B-17 Flying Fortress disintegrates after a direct hit by German flak.

facing an enemy capable of hurling as many as 1,000 fighters against them on a single mission.

Now a lieutenant general, Galland knew that his was an impossible mission. "No fighter pilot in the world had as many opponents as the German fighter pilot. On the Russian front, they faced enormous numbers of aircraft. The English and Americans had 20 times superiority over the Germans. The German fighter pilot had to continue his mission for as long as he was physically capable, or until he was wounded. But even if he was wounded, he had to return to duty."

Galland knows whereof he speaks. He crashed the first time during basic training, suffering an eye injury so serious that he passed his eye examination only by memorizing the chart. Still, among the many admiring fighter pilots who served under him, a number—Fritz Losigkeit, for example—would rank him the best fighter pilot they had known. And Losigkeit speaks of Galland's "amazing eye. Galland could see things . . . unbelievable." Galland also knew what it meant to be shot down in combat and return quickly to duty; he did it twice in a single day over France.

Now, with Germany's back to the wall, Galland held his tattered command together the only way he could, extracting every ounce of service out of every man. "Our fighter pilots flew a thousand sorties each. The Americans and the British flew 80 to 100 sorties . . . and they were pulled out and used at home. Our opponents could afford this . . . they had the resources, the aircraft, the men. So those veterans could share their experiences with the new pilots, and their experience could be multiplied. We couldn't do it, but had to provide on-the-job training, a very dangerous kind of training. Most of the novice pilots perished within the first five sorties."

Many of the *Experten* did what they could. Walter Hoffmann says it was "my job to share my experience, to train young crews, to warn them of dangers, to give them the tactics necessary to be able to fight successfully."

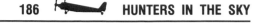

Famed German fighter ace Adolph Galland between flights with his dog.

Wolfgang Spate, whose World War II victory count was 99 planes shot down, saw it happening, too. Noting the constant shortening of training time, he reports: "By the last year of the war, the replacements that were sent to the front were, in all probability, doomed to be shot down."

If in those dark days for the Luftwaffe a man had a right to talk about "burnout," that man was Fritz Losigkeit. Ever since his tenth birthday, he had wanted to be a pilot; by 1939 he had joined the Luftwaffe. He fought in Spain, was shot down, held captive, and escaped over the Pyrenees into France. He fought in the invasion of France and the Battle of Britain, and when that became too boring, volunteered to take the Trans-Siberian Railroad across Russia to train Japanese pilots. He then flew on the Russian front. And now he is fighting against a vastly superior enemy to defend the homeland. "The Americans," he states, "didn't know what 'burnout' meant. They flew for a limited period of time, then went home. Our pilots were constantly on duty. A service record of 500-600 sorties among those survived was perfectly normal."

Walter Beckham, American, confirms: "Our rule, at that time, was that if you put in 200 operational hours, that would be your tour and you'd go home. And you might not ever come back again."

The survival rate for German newcomers plummeted: one half were dead before completing their tenth sortie. Another veteran, Walter Hoffmann, provides an insight: "The new pilots—and I met quite a few in my squadron—were not sufficiently trained. They had considerable difficulty in bad weather. It was rarely the result of enemy action which killed the younger generation of pilots."

Martin Becker's service record goes back five years. At this point, he commands a night-fighter group: "The younger pilots didn't receive the same quality of training we had; that's not difficult to understand. We had suffered considerable losses. Our younger pilots were put through a so-called accelerated fighter training course. But they didn't have the flight hours, the practical flying experience."

In fact, to turn out replacements as fast as possible, ten new Luftwaffe training schools were opened in 1944, but training time was cut to 150 hours—one-third the time given U.S. pilots.

Facing such staggering odds, even *Experten* fell before the guns of Allied fighters. In the first half of 1944 alone, Mustangs flamed Luftwaffe aces Wolf-Dietrich Wilke (162 victories) and Josef Zwernemann (126 victories); and Thunderbolts ended the lives and fighting careers of Egon Mayer (102 victories), Kurb Uben (110), and Hans Philipp (206). Another great ace, Horst Ademeit (166 victories), was killed by infantry fire; Anton Hafner (204) crashed into a tree; Albin Wolf (144) was brought down by antiaircraft fire; and Leopold Munster (95 victories) died while ramming a B-17. Obviously, no air force could lose so many men of that caliber and remain a vital fighting force.

The Luftwaffe would be hurting increasingly in other ways. Satisfied they had throttled aircraft production (they were wrong), the Allies concentrated on oil, and hydrogen and synthetic fuel installations. Increasingly, an impressive number of new planes remained grounded because there was no fuel to power them.

By contrast, American strength grew steadily, in numbers, in quality, in the skill of the pilots. The P-51Bs and Cs were rapidly phased out and replaced by the P-51D, the bubble-top model. The Ds mounted six machine guns instead of the former four and a cut-down rear fuselage that enhanced maneuverability.

Jim Howard speaks of an important lesson learned: "Hit them [enemy fighters] *before* they get to the bomber formations. You see, ahead of them. And that's what we did."

Walter Beckham tells how American pilots learned what aces had been learning, and relearning, ever since Oswald Boelcke's *Dicta Boelcke* way back in World War I. "See," Beckham confides, "I should have understood it sooner: the critical point is if you cut your range in half, you double the solid angle into which a bullet will hit the target. Not only do you hit him lots more times, but the kinetic energy of those .50-caliber bullets is much greater because they slow down in the air—'air drag' reduces their speed. And they were not explosive, so it was only the kinetic energy that would do the damage. If you got close enough, you didn't even need the gunsight. I didn't know that at first. You see, we're all new at this game."

Goering called them the "Debden Gangsters," Debden for their base northwest of London. They were the pilots of the legendary 4th Fighter Group. And none more so than the "Terrible Twins," Don Gentile (23 kills) and his inseparable wingman, Johnny Godfrey (18 kills)—first at the controls of Thunderbolts, later Mustangs. Gentile came out of the equally legendary 133rd Eagle Squadron. Between them, they developed a tactic American pilots in Vietnam mimicked more than a quarter of a century later. Whichever of them first spotted a target and was in a better position, the other would fall back to cover the attack. To work, the pilots had to have complete faith in one another; they had almost to be able to predict each other's maneuvers, hook

Major Woerner Hoffman had 51 night and one day victory during the air war.

into each other's minds. The Terrible Twins, between them, destroyed more than 60 enemy aircraft in the air and on the ground.

Before the team had solidified, in one furious battle, Gentile flamed two German fighters before being bounced by a third. The relentless duel lasted 15 minutes with Gentile shouting for help, fearful that if he were downed, he would not get credit for his kills! Out of that came a song composed in his honor, to the tune of "Tramp, Tramp, Tramp the Boys Are Marching":

> *Help, Help, Help! I'm being clobbered*
> *Down here by the railroad track.*
> *An FW.190 chases me around,*
> *And we're damn near the ground.*
> *Tell 'em I got two if I don't make it back.*

At one point, General Eisenhower buzzed up to Debden in a two-seater P-38 to award Distinguished Flying Crosses (DFC) to Gentile and his commanding officer, Don Blakeslee. Not long afterwards, stunt-flying low over the field, the irrepressible Gentile banged up his Mustang, the fuselage adorned with "Shangri-la" and a passel of swastikas. Blakeslee sent him home to sell war bonds.

Over at the 56th Fighter Group they had hot-shots, too. Robert S. Johnson, who shot down 28 German fighters in only 91 combat missions over 11 months, was among them. Like Gentile, Johnson had a strong independent streak. His first kill, mentioned earlier, came shortly after he arrived in England, on June 13, 1943. But he broke away from his group to make it. That

Lt. Godfrey (left) and Captain Don Gentile pose for the camera in front of a P-51 Mustang.

earned him a reprimand. Beginning early in 1944, American fighter pilots escorting bombers were given greater latitude, enabling Johnson to act on his axiom: if you see an enemy, go after him. (Jerry Brown felt the same way. Once fighter pilots were allowed to break away from the bombers, he tells us, that's "when the Luftwaffe bought the farm!")

Between January 1 and his last mission on May 8, 1944, Johnson bagged 18 German planes, including four double kills (two in a day), and a triple (on March 15). On one mission, he found himself bleeding, half-blind from hydraulic fluid, trapped in a riddled P-47 that could barely fly, hunched down in his armored seat while an FW.190 calmly emptied his cannons into the big Thunderbolt. But Johnson made it home to fight again. Johnson went home a hero, tied for air-to-air kills (28) with his first flight commander, Gabby Gabreski, the same Gabreski who became the European Theater's top American ace with 31 total victories.

Like those of other top American aces who became familiar to American schoolboys through newsreel coverage of the war, the image of the 4th's Kid Hofer survives—bear-hugging his dog, climbing into the cockpit of his Mustang and heading for enemy skies to bag his 17th Hun. Hofer was never seen again, and his Alsatian looked for a new master.

Despite decisive superiority in the air, the skies were still dangerous for an Allied fighter pilot. As Gabby Gabreski put it, "We viewed the Luftwaffe as the most professional group in the world. We took precautions, designed our own tactics around the airplane and around the mission to be performed." Allowing the fighter pilots to do a little target free-lancing while flying bomber escort created opportunities, but perils as well. Bud Mahurin was flying escort on a bombing mission to Tours, southeast of Paris: "We had orders to leave the bomber formation after they'd dropped their bombs and head toward Paris to strafe targets of opportunity. And of course, in March of 1944, there was no question but what eventually we were going to invade—so targets of opportunity meant anything that moved.

"As we headed toward Paris, I happened to look down and saw a Dornier 217, a twin-engine German fighter, flying along a railroad track to the south-

Don Blakeslee in his Mustang.

Above:
Francis "Gabby" Gabreski in his P-47.

Crowded airspace: A P-47 captures another in its gunsights as they all but battle one another for an Me.110.

west, and we were flying northeast. Now comes the competitiveness part: you learned pretty quick that you didn't call in the sighting of an enemy aircraft until you were pretty sure you could get there first. If you did, there were going to be hordes of P-47s there ahead of you. So I didn't call it in until I was pretty sure that I was out in front, and made my attack. It had been equipped with four equivalent-.50 caliber machine guns [12.7 mm] in a top turret. It had never occurred to me how to attack something that had a turret facing the rear, so I went boring in and began to shoot at it. And I could see that the guy was shooting back at me, and as I'm headed toward him, a big blob of oil appeared on my windscreen.

"I had to pull up, because I was overriding him, and I called the rest of my flight and said, 'Get out of the way, I'm coming back in,' and went down and sat behind this bomber until finally it caught on fire and the crew bailed out. It was at low altitude, and I found out later from the French underground that they didn't survive that episode. At any rate, I turned away after the bomber crashed and started to go back toward England when, to my horror, I looked down at the ground and the sun was approximately on my left side, up high in the sky, and as I looked down I could see the shadow of my airplane with a great long trail of black smoke following me. So I knew something was wrong.

"I got to what I think was about 800 feet and, all of a sudden, there was an explosion and fire started coming through the cowling of the engine. At the same time, the group leader called and said, 'Watch out, boy, you're on fire.' The last word I heard was 'fire' as I was going over the side, bailing out. I hit the ground in a total panic, in a plowed field—wide open farmland— sure there would be 10 million German soldiers around me any minute and I'd be off to prison camp.

There were 35 P-47s hovering over me like bumble bees. And the only thing you can do is tell them to go away. I found out later they were debating whether or not they should land and try to pick me up; it had been done before, a single airplane would land, the pilot would throw out his parachute and the guy on the ground jump in and sit on his lap and fly the airplane home. Fortunately, they decided not to do that, and I kept waving for them to go. And since it was broad daylight, I started to run. I thought I saw some trees in the distance and started to run toward them, only the trees when I got there were about as tall as I am. So I had no place to hide, and quick dumped my escape and survival gear and my pistol and all that. You can't imagine how a .45 pistol grows to where it's about a 155 millimeter howitzer when you're in enemy territory.

"Then I found a place to hide, and hid all night and the next day—it sounds like a grade Z movie you see on Channel X at one o'clock in the morning—but I found a haystack, climbed on top of it, burrowed down and hid 'til about four the next day. I saw a single peasant working in his garden, went over and gestured—the typical bad acting, you know, 'Psst, psst, je suis Amerique aviateur,' which he didn't understand at all, of course. And when he came over, I gave him my class ring, my watch, and some British coins, and he said, '*Cachez ici*,' and I know what that meant. Hide here. He ran off and got the village elder and they came back.

"I stayed with the French underground for about three weeks. Moved a couple of places. They asked me what rank I was, and I told them I was a major. They had no equivalent rank in the French army, and so they considered that I was a sergeant major, which put me substantially below the list of guys they were going to get out through the French underground. I felt like I was stagnating. But fortunately, the Allies dropped leaflets all over Europe with my picture and name and that I was a victorious ace. The underground guys came home so excited they could hardly see straight. I flew out of France on a special mission airplane about two days later."

Regulations in those days were that anyone rescued by the underground anywhere in occupied Europe had to be rotated out of the theater to guard against the chance they might be shot down again and forced to betray their rescuers. Mahurin was sent home—but not out of the war. He would later command the 3rd Air Commando Group fighting in New Guinea and Okinawa. In his career as a fighter pilot, Walker Mahurin accumulated official confirmation orders for 21 German aircraft shot down, one Japanese plane, and 3.5 Mig-15s during the Korean War. He has his own "confirmation" for the Dornier he shot down—and which shot him down at the same time: The French underground brought him pieces of the wreckage while he

Trains, such as this one destroyed near Luxembourg, Belgium, became sought-after targets as the Allies gained air superiority over the Continent.

The P-38 was joined in the reconnaissance role by a British Spitfire, also stripped of its armament for speed on photo missions.

Above:
A Lockheed-built P-38 swapped its guns for high speed cameras as a reconnaissance platform, providing the Allies with much needed intelligence on Wermacht deployments.

was still in hiding. He also was "credited" with four American planes lost: three when he was forced to bail out, one which he crash-landed.

He's Major Gabreski now, commanding 61st Squadron. On May 8, 1944, Gabreski shot down one plane on the day Bob Johnson got his last two. Johnson's score now stands at 27, to be raised to 28 when a "damaged" claim is upgraded to a kill. Gabreski has 19. On May 23, he spurts ahead. "My squadron went out with 16 planes—I was leading one section of eight. As the bombers did their job on the submarine pens at Bremen, it was a pretty clear day and I noticed a steam engine rolling along the tracks with a good lot of freight cars behind it. So I told one of my sections to go down and destroy the train while we went down from 28,000 feet to 16,000 feet to give top cover. Reaching that altitude, I was making a turn to the left when I saw an airdrome with 190s taking off and landing. So I immediately got on the radio and told my four airplanes that we will bounce the airdrome while the others destroyed the train.

"I took off on a steep dive on the airdrome, and as I came in, there were four planes taking off in front of me. With my throttle wide open, I must have been overtaking them at about 150 miles an hour or so. I had just a split-second shot at the first one, but with eight machine guns, so long as you are in close and are on target, it doesn't take but a split-second to destroy a target. Pieces of the airplane came off—I think even a wing came off—and the airplane went over on its back and hit the ground. I moved over. The second one—sort of the wingman for the first—was accelerating and moved over. I got in behind him and shot him down, flames coming out of the plane. Looking off to the left at my wingman, he was doing his shooting, too. But as he broke off, he said, 'Gabby, there's one coming in on your tail.' And there certainly was one coming in on my tail. So I broke off from the second one I destroyed and went into a tight spiral turn to the left. As I looked off to my left, why I saw the airplane and the guns blinking—those 20 millimeter cannons. Of course, he had a hard shot because I was in a corkscrew, climbing and pulling back on the stick as hard as I could without stalling the airplane, and he went right on by me. I climbed to about 20,000 feet, took another look to see whether my tail was clear. My tail was clear, and all the action was down below and my wingman was still with me.

"We could still see airplanes milling around the airfield, so I went down for another shot. I saw green flares go up for some reason or other just as I was approaching the field—I guess their control tower was trying to guide its own airplanes in and for the gunners to cease firing. So I went over the airfield without a shot fired on me. I pulled up behind another airplane that was in a left-hand turn, came in behind him, shot him down and went up to see what my wingman was doing. My wingman, in turn, picked out another airplane and shot him down. Both of us climbed up to about 15,000 feet and the whole show was over in a matter of about a minute and a half, two minutes."

There was a sequel to those three victories. Heading home, Gabreski spied a 190 zooming off in the opposite direction. With his wingman covering, Gabreski dove down on the Focke Wulf, guns blazing, "with devastating results." But the German disappeared into a cloud, so Gabreski went home with three kills, and "all I could do was claim a damage on that one, or a 'probably destroyed.' "

"Wingman"—the word comes up again and again. Gabreski explains: "The wingman is absolutely indispensable. I look after the wingman. The wingman looks after me. It's another set of eyes protecting you. That's the defensive part. Offensively, it gives you a lot more firepower. We work together. We fight together. The wingman knows what his responsibilities are, and knows what mine are. Wars are not won by individuals. They're won by teams."

The aerial combat team included another kind of player—reconnaissance pilots. They were truly the eyes of those who would carry the war to the enemy, and in many ways, the memory of what had been done. Though spies could often provide important clues, aerial reconnaissance was almost always essential to provide accurate images of targets to be bombed. Afterwards, the reconnaissance planes returned to reshoot their photographs in order to estimate the damage done. Aerial reconnaissance was also vital for effective ground campaigns. More often than not, missions were flown in unarmed planes.

Desmond F. Sheen was a boy in his native Canberra, Australia, when the duke and duchess of Kent came to visit in 1927; the Royal Australian Air Force (RAAF) put on a flying show, and the youngster's fate was sealed. He would be a pilot. A dozen years later, he was given the choice of serving with the RAAF or the RAF. Sheen chose the latter because "I thought I'd like to see the world." The summer of 1940 found him seeing it from the cockpit of an RAF Spitfire reconnaissance plane.

"The photographic development unit, as it was then called," Sheen explains, "was a fairly secret organization, set up to take photographs over enemy territory. The aircraft were unarmed, had no radio, and special bubble hoods. They were painted in a pale duck blue to make them less conspicuous against the blue sky. The idea was to fly flat out and at high levels—30-32,000 feet—to avoid any combat. We flew by dead-reckoning or visually. We needed a clear sky over the target area to get good pictures. The one thing you had to do was make sure that you didn't 'contrail' because a short contrail was all right, but a condensation trail a mile behind was too much of a giveaway. To avoid that, we had to fly either a little bit higher or a little bit lower."

Sheen was a fighter pilot; he came by his new (temporary) vocation by volunteering, except he didn't know for what. "They asked for a qualified pilot. They gave no details. We drew lots and I was the last man out."

Sheen began flying out of Heston, now better known as Heathrow Airport, then was shifted to the south of France with two other pilots. "We operated over Italy for quite a long time, from Corsica and from a base in the south of France. Then when the Italians came into the war, we had to duck back quickly to Le Luc. A few days later, they [the Italians] came across and destroyed our support aircraft, so we left in a hurry with the help of some naval people based at Hyeres, not far away. We spent three days on a destroyer headed for Casablanca [to join] the enormous French battleship, *Jean Bart*. From there, on a refugee ship to Gibraltar, then back to England, arriving at Liverpool on July 12, 1940.''

Regrets? ''Flying in an unarmed Spitfire went a bit against the grain—particularly when I saw some very good targets in Sardinia I would have liked to have attacked. But the only time I ever had any concern was when I was crossing the Dutch border going towards Germany and saw another aircraft coming almost head-on. Fortunately, it turned out to be one of our own chaps going back.''

Martin Becker flew reconnaissance for the Luftwaffe in the early days of the war. In his case, he flew a two-seater with two machine guns—but the rules and the risks were the same. ''When you fly reconnaissance,'' he remarks, ''you fly alone. Just you and your observer. You have to fulfill the mission given you: aiding in artillery spotting, checking troop movements, effectiveness of bombardment. Then bring these reports back to the base. The pilot's job is to insure that the observer can do his job.'' Becker had developed his own survival tactic when discovered by fighter planes. ''We would just cut our speed—the fighters usually came at high speed from above, or out of the sun. We would then make ourselves scarce. A dogfight was out of the question.''

Wolfgang Spate was a lieutenant in the reserves when he got orders on August 15, 1939, ''to participate in exercises. To our astonishment,'' he relates, ''the 'exercise' lasted for another six years!'' Spate began his active duty career in a long-distance reconnaissance group, flying the brand-new Heinkel 70, first over Poland, later in France. Even as a reconnaissance pilot, he felt ''a certain amount of combat spirit. I remember once, returning from a reconnaissance flight and with only 15 minutes of fuel left and still a good distance from the airfield, I saw a Potez 631, a twin-engine French aircraft. A fighter had already shot up one of his engines, but he was still able to fly, so I turned back and readied my machine guns, intending to attack the Potez from behind. Suddenly, I was hit in the back of the neck. That was my observer—he didn't want to get involved in a dogfight! And he reminded me that we had to get our report back to base ASAP.''

Along with the frustration, Spate observed another quality of life as a reconnaissance pilot: ''This was a rather hazardous occupation. In France alone, we lost 14 crews out of 20. So, I considered my predicament and decided I had to fly something a little faster. I had noticed at our airfield in France the fighter pilots flying off to England, engaged in constant combat, sometimes with losses, sometimes victorious. But I realized that they would need replacements, so I took a couple days' leave and went to see a general I was acquainted with and told him that with my experience flying reconnaissance, I would make a good fighter pilot in a hurry.'' A few weeks later, Wolfgang Spate was in the cockpit of an Me.109 on the way to a combat career which would see him shoot down 99 enemy planes.

Reconnaissance flyers often were the unsung heroes of aerial warfare, but there were others even more anonymous. A sharp-eyed British photo interpreter set in motion a series of events which profoundly affected the nature and direction of the war. The photo revealed that Nazi Germany had a guided missile almost ready for service. Since 1939, a team of nonpolitical German scientists, engineers, and inventors had been experimenting with various

Martin Becker flew reconnaissance for the Luftwaffe early in the war.

types of rocketry at secret installations. They were headed by Werner von Braun (later central to America's space program). By June 13, 1942, they made their first test-firing of a missile four-stories high. And on December 22, 1942, Hitler gave the order for mass production of the rockets.

Once British intelligence confirmed the reconnaissance information, a go-for-broke attack was ordered. Pilots were told that if they failed to destroy the target, they would be sent back, regardless of losses. On the night of August 16-17, 1943, 597 Bomber Command heavy bombers dropped 1,500 tons of incendiaries and explosives from a low 8,000 feet. Forty bombers were lost, 32 others crippled, but the damage done was great.

Pilots needed to guard against something other than the enemy without—hubris, overconfidence, got to the best of them. Gabby Gabreski tells what happened to him.

Gabreski had dawdled behind in his Thunderbolt after shooting down an Me.110 over Germany. Now, low on fuel, "I saw a 109 go underneath me, but I had to get home, so I let him go. But he didn't let me go. He made a 180-degree turn and started after me. Because of my fuel status, I decided to run him out of ammunition, so I gave him one of the most difficult shots—pulling up the airplane, kicking it off to the side, a very difficult shot. See, at that point, I felt I was master of my airplane, and with the experience that I've had, I could give the enemy the worst shot and he'd still have a hard time hitting me." But this German was tenacious, staying with Gabreski on three dive-climb-and-kick maneuvers, Gabreski's throttle running at 45 inches of mercury, near the 52-inch maximum.

On the third one, "just at the moment I saw flames coming out of his 20 millimeter gun, I heard an explosion in my cockpit. My rudder was shot away. My boot was burned. And my airplane started to lose speed because my turbine supercharger was knocked out. My oil tank was hit. My rudder pedal was hit. And my foot was numb due to the 20 millimeter explosion. The foot was numb, and I hated to look at the foot for the simple reason that when you see the blood, it's a sudden shock and you pass out. I decided I would bail out; I still had my parachute, the only survival-alternative.

"So I got the nose down and opened the canopy about a foot or so, and just as I was about ready to come out of the cockpit, I looked at my RPM gauge and my RPM, my engine, was still ticking over. I looked at my manifold pressure and I was decelerating, it was building up. So this meant that I still had control of the airplane. So I decided to close my canopy and looked at my foot and my foot was still in one piece. I kicked it around a little bit, then rolled the airplane over as steep as I could to get to a cloud beneath me. There was a very thin cloud level, and I wanted to get there before the 109 could finish me off. I made it—it was a very thin layer, but enough where I could hide myself, heading west toward England. At one point, I popped out of the cloud, just to see what was going on behind me, and the 109 was circling back and forth above the clouds, hoping to have me pop up in front of him, but I was still a long ways from him, and I went back into that little cloud cover and stayed there until I came to the English coast. Once there, I sent out a May Day alert for air-sea rescue 'cause I didn't think I had enough fuel to make it. I was living in trepidation all the way across, until I landed at Manston, the closest base to the Channel, there to retrieve wounded airplanes like I had. When I landed, the airplane was out of fuel, out of oil. In other words, there was no way I could have flown any farther. And I was frightened.

Wolfgang Spate went from reconnaissance pilot to fighter pilot and ultimately was credited with 99 kills.

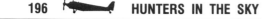
"That night, I didn't sleep very well, thinking of what could have happend that didn't happen. In other words, I shouldn't be here today, and I knew that what I did probably was not the brightest thing I could have done. Perhaps I was tired. Perhaps I had what you call combat fatigue."

The British began night-bombing in earnest early in 1942. Throughout that year, improved electronics enhanced Bomber Command's ability to strike with greater precision. First came "Gee," a navigational aid similar to the "beam" system the Luftwaffe used in 1940-1941 to hone in on British targets; then in December, "Oboe," followed in January by H2S, a radar set which gave the navigator a "picture" of the ground beneath the bomber. In August of 1942, the command fitted "Oboe" to a special Pathfinder unit flying an airplane that became one of the "immortals" of aviation history: the de Havilland Mk. IV "Mosquito." These twin-engine thoroughbreds served— and excelled—as night fighters, fighter-bombers, bombers, and reconnaissance planes. Of all-wood construction, Mosquitoes were a near-perfect blend of weight (21,823 pounds) and power (twin 1,250-hp Rolls-Royce Merlin engines), which meant they could outrun (close to 400 mph) and outclimb everything the Germans had at that point.

In March 1943, "Bomber" Harris ordered a three-stage strategic bombing campaign. The first was the Battle of the Ruhr, aimed at the greatest industrial complex of the Reich. Phase Two was called Operation GOMORRAH, and it would become the most controversial. Between July and November 1943,

Air interceptor Mark VIIIB radar installed in a Mosquito night fighter.

Gabreski taxis towards the runway in his P-47.

the RAF flew 17,021 sorties against Hamburg, to that point by far the most heavily defended German city. Despite those defenses, losses were low (695 bombers shot down, 1,123 damaged), due in part to a new British tactic code-named "Window": jamming German radar by dropping thousands of strips of tin foil which confused the Germans' Wurzburg system for directing anti-aircraft fire and fighter planes. The RAF also managed to break in on German ground control and fighter plane radio traffic, mimicking exactly the ground-controller's voice.

Martin Becker explains how the system worked before the British threw massive monkey wrenches into it: "The night fighter must learn to fly blind, by instruments, in the dark, through clouds, to take off and land in bad weather. In that, you are guided to a particular sector by the ground control-lers. There is a difference between a Wurzburg-red, and a Wurzburg-green. The ground controllers gave us a set of coordinates and we were then ordered to fly in a specific direction towards a radio beacon, along an azimuth of X number of degrees and there to intersect with the bomber formation.

"Guided night-flight consisted of more than one set of instructions: it was an air control system for an entire sector. Those night bombers were not flying in a huge formation the way the Americans did with their daylight raids, packed together like sardines, but spread out over a large area as a matter of security. So the night fighter doesn't know how large a formation is, only what his radio technician or radioman tells him based on the data coming from the on-board equipment—electronic sensors like the *Lichtenstein* radar which leads him in, until he actually sees the bomber himself. Or finds them through the turbulence produced in the wake of the enemies' propellers, which tells you, 'A-ha, there's something out there!' Until you actually see them."

Joined now by day by the American bombers, Hamburg was subjected to a merciless bombardment beginning on the night of July 24. That night, 374 Lancasters, 246 Halifaxes, 125 Stirlings, and 73 Wellingtons saturated the city with incendiaries and high-explosive bombs, many with delayed action fuses.

Werner Hoffmann, who had joined the Luftwaffe in 1936 and scored his first kill over the beaches at Dunkirk in 1940, was now a night-fighter pilot relying on radar to find and engage the marauders. "But we were being jammed by the English and then one felt a hideous sense of inferiority and desperation." The air waves on those first nights of "Window" were filled with the curses of pilots and controllers as they groped to find the raiders. British bomber production outpaced even the staggering losses suffered by Bomber Command during 1943. That year, the RAF received 28,000 aircraft—4,614 four-engined bombers, 3,113 twin-engined bombers, and 10,727 fighters and fighter-bombers. Bomber Command's daily operating strength—planes actually available to fly—stood at 515 in January of 1943; early in 1944, that number had grown to 974, including 58 Mosquitoes and 594 of the big Avro Lancasters, capable of dropping bombs as big as the 22,000-pound "Grand Slam."

So strengthened, Harris was ready to launch Phase Three—the Battle of Berlin, November 1943-March 1944. Bomber Command flew 20,224 sorties against Berlin during those months, losing 1,047 bombers, with 1,682 more damaged, as well as 3,640 air crewmen killed or missing.

For many, the damage was far too great. Walter Hoffmann had always fought "the opponent's aircraft, not the individual crew member in the cockpit. I wouldn't say that I developed feelings of hate, but after my parents'

A woman in a factory fashioning aluminum strips into the radar spoofing "chaff."

The radar unit fashioned into the nose of the Mosquito night fighter.

home was reduced to ashes in Berlin, I wanted to avenge myself on the English Crown.''

The first British night bombers had barely left their targets over Germany on May 15, 1940, when Hermann Goering appointed Gen. Josef Kammhuber to create a night-defense organization. The network he created used giant Wurzburg radar pairs at each installation, one to track the enemy intruders, the other to guide fighters to their targets. In airborne radar, the Germans lagged two years behind the British. Their *Lichtenstein* airborne radars didn't enter service until 1942 when Bomber Command tonnage dropped on Germany trebled. By early 1943, all German night fighters had *Lichtenstein*.

And by 1943 the Germans had introduced the most potent night fighter of either side: the Heinkel He.219 A-7 *Uhu* (Owl), flying at 416 mph with two 1,750-hp Daimler Benz engines. Some believed that, with an adequate supply, it could have determined the outcome of the war. As it was, because of the obtuseness of the Luftwaffe high command, only 300 Owls were built.

Its first operative mission, while still in the development stage, was over the Netherlands the night of June 11-12, 1943. Werner Streib, at the controls of an owl, shot down five Avro Lancaster bombers headed for Dusseldorf in 30 minutes. With the bubble cockpit over the nose of the plane, its radar antennae protruding from the nose, the twin-tail Owl was an ungainly machine, more nearly resembling a grasshopper. But there was no mistaking its power: two 20 mm cannon and four 30 mm cannon. The pilot and his radio/radar operator sat back-to-back, giving them a remarkable field of vision. They also sat on ejection seats, a first. And the plane was equipped with a tricycle landing gear, another first. On its first ten missions, He.219s shot down 20 British bombers, including six previously untouchable Mosquitoes. It was, indeed, the success of the He.219 which drove the British to resort to their radar-scrambling ''Window'' tin foil.

To slam that window closed, the Germans turned to *Wilde Sau* and *Zahme Sau* (''Wild Boar'' and ''Tame Sow''). The tactic involved using single-engine night-fighters, specially equipped Me.109G-6 Gustavs, outfitted with a radar warning and homing receiver that had a thirty-mile range. They flew above and tracked the incoming bombers and then, with running commentary, pinpointed their location allowing free-lance night fighters to strike at will, rather than in the previous box formations. Successful only on moonlit nights at first, *Wilde Sau* missions later were aided by flares dropped by planes, improved ground searchlights, and the glare of the burning cities themselves.

New armament was also added, including a device code-named *schrage-Musik* (shrill music, a euphemism for jazz): A pair of 20 mm cannon (later 30 mm) mounted amidships on twin-engine Me.110s, Ju.88s and He.219s. They were mounted so as to fire obliquely, at an angle between 70 and 80 degrees, enabling the fighters to hit the bombers' soft underbellies, fuel tanks, engines, and bomb loads.

Of that group, one bears special mention: the Messerschmitt Bf.110 G-4, a vastly improved variant on the earlier night fighter. The G-4 began its combat career early in 1943 and would bear the brunt of the Luftwaffe's bomber defense campaign. Like the He.219, the 110 mounted ungainly but highly effective *Lichtenstein* radar antennae in its nose. It also mounted two 30 mm cannon, two to four 20 mm cannon, two machine guns, and 1,540 pounds of bombs. Manned by two or three crew, the 110 reached its top speed of 341 mph at 22,998 feet, but had a relatively low ceiling of 26,069 feet, well below that of the Allied fighters.

Hans-Joachim Jabs—some would say he "wrote the book" on German night flying—was one of the "jazz players." Jabs joined the Luftwaffe in 1936 and not only survived the Battle of Britain in the early Me.110s, but shot down eight Spitfires and four Hurricanes. And that despite his opinion of the plane he flew: "We saw that the 110, the destroyer, was GREATLY inferior to the British, at least to the Spitfire."

Jabs explains the dual meanings for *shrage Musik*: "In the late '30s and '40s, jazz was forbidden in Germany. Shrill music was then any form of music which sounded like that forbidden 'ape music,' or jazz, or swing." Whatever you called it, Jabs says "it wouldn't express the unconventionality of the roof-mounted cannons, which essentially shot the bombers in the belly without allowing themselves a chance to defend themselves."

The bombers kept coming; the fighters kept shooting them down. The Lancasters, Short-Stirlings, and Handley-Page Halifax B II's were sitting ducks. Lumbering through the skies at speeds of 260 to 287 mph, these four-engine behemoths were easy prey for the fast, cannon-firing fighters. Comments Martin Becker: "It was very easy to see the enemy in those formations. That's an immense weapon flying through the sky. We were operating on a much smaller scale, as night-hunters, and the element of surprise was decisive. The enemy doesn't see us, unless you're spotted by the tail-gunner or the belly-gunner. We were flying 'blind' against the night sky, always in the dark. The upper half of our aircraft was camouflaged with a cloud pattern, and the lower half painted black so that our own AA searchlights wouldn't pick us out."

New night-fighter *Experten* emerged from the deadly duels over German skies: Maj. Heinz-Wolfgang Schnaufer, in the cockpit of an Me.110 G-4, scored 121 victories in 164 sorties; on May 25, 1944, he shot down five Lancasters in 14 minutes, and the following year, on February 21, he shot down two in the early morning hours, seven more that night. The first night-fighter to score 100 victories was Helmut Lent (102)—also a 110 pilot—before he was killed in a crash in late 1944. Martin Becker, who flew with both, speaks admiringly of their "unimaginably high number of kills." Third-ranking was Prince Heinrich of Sayn-Wittgenstein, with 83; on a single night of 1943, he shot down seven bombers, and on January 1, 1944, six. He had just shot down his fifth of the night when, on May 21, 1944, he was shot down himself.

To counter the carnage, the British sent Bristol Beaufighters Mk. Xs and Mosquitoes to fly with the bombers, beginning in July of 1943. The Beaufighters, whose bristling armament including rockets, four 20 mm cannons, and 7 machine guns, were intimidating foes, but were limited to four to four and-a-half hours flying time. The British got lucky when a German Ju.88 night-fighter fell into their hands, enabling them to study the on-board *Lichtenstein* radar unit. British fighters were thereafter provided with a small receiver called *Serrate* which could pick up *Lichtenstein* signals, enabling them to distinguish between German night fighters and their own bombers. That did not help them against the Wild Boar fighters, since most were not radar-equipped. Furthermore, unbeknownst to the British, the Germans learned how to intercept the AI (Airborne Interception) signals emitted by the bombers. As the operators switched on their AI sets at the beginning of their missions, German monitors relayed the information to Wild Boar fighter planes.

Beaufighters were two-seat aircraft. To fight at night successfully required finely honed teamwork between a pilot and his radar operator. RAF Squadron 141, led by Wing Commander J.R.D. "Bob" Braham and seconded by such outstanding AI operators as Sergeant "Sticks" Gregory and Flight Lieutenant "Jacko" Jackson, was among the units that raised teamwork and tactics to the highest level. In the last two years of the war, Braham's squadron disposed of some 200 German night fighters. Mike Allen, who flew with the 141st, recalled: "We also achieved much confusion among the Germans who knew we were around and were concerned that while they might be going for a Lancaster, one of us might be behind them." Braham himself ended the war tied with Group Capt. (Col.) John Cunningham as the RAF's second-scoring night-fighter pilot (19 kills) after another squadron commander, B.A. Burbridge (21 kills).

The tactics these pioneering pilots developed included patrolling between German night-fighter airfields and the path of the bomber streams to catch the interceptors on the way up or down; flying free-lance patrols at the edges of the bomber streams, waiting for the German fighter pilots to be vectored in for their attacks; and, for large target areas such as Berlin, timing their arrival for the end of the bomb cycle, knowing that by then the milling night fighters would be illuminated by the light of the fires and their own searchlights.

A test pilot before the war, John Cunningham was already a legend when he took over Mosquito-equipped RAF 85 Squadron in January 1943. Back in 1941, at the height of the Battle of Britain, the press had dubbed him "Cat's Eye Cunningham" because of his remarkable performance in the embattled night skies over Britain. Between November 19, 1940, and May 31, 1941, Cunningham shot down 15 German night raiders, the last two while King George VI was in the RAF control room following operations. In truth, Cunningham tells us, "my night vision was only average."

The term "Cat's Eye" was concocted by Fighter Command after Cunningham's second night of combat to explain how he had shot down two German aircraft while no one else had managed to intercept anything. Cunningham—and his erstwhile radio operator James "Jimmy" Rawnsley—

John Cunningham's skill in the air at night against the Luftwaffe earned him the moniker "Cat's Eyes."

did, in fact, have special vision: their Beaufighters were among the first outfitted with airborne radar. Cunningham—who would remain the top British night-fighter (19 of his 20 kills were at night) until overtaken in 1945 by Bransome Burbridge—liked the Beaufighter, and especially ''its marvelous armament, four 20-millimeter cannons which were fired beneath one's feet.''

As for the radar, they had to do on-the-job training because they were barely installed when the German bombers began blasting Britain. ''We had no opportunity to train other than to use it against this stream of aircraft that came in across the country.''

Cunningham described his first night kill as ''a bloody miracle because the [radar] sets were extremely unreliable. It was also not very easy for the radar operator to interpret the picture and then tell the pilot where the target was.'' In the end, identification did involve a more ancient ''radar''—human eyes— and that meant mainly coming up below the aircraft, hoping ''we could identify by a plain view of the wings, against starlight. The right way to go about attacking anything at night was to make sure that you got an indication with one's own eyes of the aircraft, most usually from the flicker, the exhaust flames from the engines. The only place you could identify an aircraft at night—and we always had to identify whatever it was that we had intercepted—was from almost vertically underneath. A gunner in the aircraft was very unlikely to be looking downwards. So we felt fairly secure identifying what our target was and then it was rather a slow business because we had to come up gently and at exactly the same speed as our target to a position fairly close behind, at its own level, and that, of course, was when the rear

Above left:
Night fighter radar antennae on the nose of a German Me.110.

Above right:
An RAF fighter pilot exits the cockpit of his radar equipped Bristol Beaufighter after a sortie over Anzio. He is credited with nine kills.

An English radar installation somewhere near the coast.

gunner should have shot us, or shot at us. So we came up very slowly, looking through the top of our canopy and maintaining visual contact—our night [gun] sights were rather inadequate then —and then shooting at the target from its own level."

Cunningham portrays his principal adversary, the Heinkel 111, as "a most lovely looking airplane with an elliptical wing that made it very easy to identify." Even shooting required stealth: "When we fired our guns, there was no flash or light from our own guns. And, if we missed as I did on occasions, I was fairly happy that I hadn't given my position away. I never used any tracer. We used only armor-piercing and some explosive ammunition. Having fired and seen no hits on my target, no response from the target, I was able to take aim again and hit and shoot the target down.

"The Mosquito was a much faster aircraft than the Beaufighter, and the radar operator sat beside me in the cockpit, facing forward. And I could actually look across at his radar set. It was a remarkable airplane because with its two Rolls-Royce Merlin engines which seemed to go on almost indefinitely, it had a fine performance which could deal with any aircraft we were up against. And it also, with its water-cooled engines and radiators, allowed us to have heating in the cockpit. In the earlier airplanes, we used to have to wear very heavy flying clothing because there was no heating."

Along with a better plane came better electronics: the Mark X Airborne Interception (AI) radar, a 10-centimeter unit which Cunningham describes as "more reliable, more accurate, and [which] would enable us to intercept aircraft at a lower altitude without losing radar range." The range of the earlier MK IV AI was governed by the plane's height; the MK X did not have that limitation, but a uniform range of five to ten miles.

Meanwhile, Cunningham reports, the Germans had moved ahead in another area: "Countermeasures were used pretty extensively from 1943 onwards. I can recall a number of occasions when I was totally unable to close to a firing position on my target because it obviously had a tail-warning radar that could inform my target of the distance that the fighter was behind him. That plus very skilled flying on the part of the Germans made it impossible for me to close to a firing position."

The British would later respond with "Monica," their own rearward-looking radar. Says Cunningham of that long process he helped shape: "The introduction of radar in the autumn of 1940 was, of course, a tremendous step forward. And Fighter Command was helped on it by some of the best technical brains in this country, who used to come and visit us in 604 Squadron to find out what our difficulties were, what advances we needed, and how to make use of the capabilities of the radars we had. It was a tremendous joy to have, from the highest level on the air staff through the most competent technical people in the country, full backing to see that we could have good equipment and to learn from us how best to improve it."

Men like Cunningham helped make the Luftwaffe pay a high price for its aerial siege of England. Yet, even as its strength ebbed away, the Luftwaffe did not give up. "In that period—1943–1944—the main activity in the area where I was operating, southeast of London, was high-speed, hit-and-run raids on London, many of them with fighters, the Focke Wulf 190. But by that time, the squadron had been reequipped with the Mosquito, and the Mosquito had the performance to deal with these high-speed attacks. The Beaufighter simply wasn't fast enough for the newer German fighters."

They're a special breed, these fighter pilots who hunt by night, guiding their aircraft stealthily toward that blip on the small, green-glowing screen, until closing on the prey they trigger a thunder of cannon. When the shot is true, a darkened aircraft is ripped apart, fire and explosion following, and then all is darkness again while the hunter slips warily into the night lest he now become the hunted.

Hear John Cunningham, a night-fighter through and through, describe some of the hazards: "By far the greatest number of casualties among night-fighters was due to flying accidents or bad weather—flying into the ground perhaps when trying to return in bad weather to one's airfield with virtually no landing aid at all. The number shot down was quite small compared to the number lost due to bad weather and failures in instrument flying. Midair collisions at night were always a risk and I went very close to one or two aircraft. One man in my flight had the misfortune to hit the trailing aerial of a German aircraft which was going in the opposite direction and he came back with the aerial wound around his propeller. That was rather close."

On night-fighters: "There's a big difference between the person who is going to be successful at night and the one who's successful by day. First, he's got to be confident of his own flying ability—to be relaxed and capable of flying safely at night, so that he can use his head, or brain, to absorb the picture that's given to him by his radar operator and figure out how best to approach this target so that he doesn't give his own position away.

"You've got to think of the cloud cover beneath you. Whether you should come in from the side. Or, if you're coming in over water and there's a moon, not to put yourself in the position where you're outlined by the moon against the water. It's a very slow, long, rather drawn-out business, interception by night, as opposed to by day where you can see and take immediate action. It was vitally important that we know how to use our equipment and aircraft well and achieve our object—which was to stop whatever was coming in to attack this country. And a determination to keep that target in view the whole time."

As the inevitable assault on Fortress Europe neared, the Allies massed 5,400 fighter planes in Britain. The Germans had, by then, pulled back virtually all of their remaining strength to Germany. Scarcity stalked the homefront, as well; only one group (30-48 aircraft) in each of the three *Wilde Sau Jageschwadern* (fighter groups, roughly 120 aircraft) had their own planes. The others had to share their aircraft and airfields with day fighters.

Martin Becker tells how he dealt with the stress: "There was always some tension, the risk was always present—engine loss or whatever, or the airfield raided by the enemy. But afterwards, when you were in the air and saw the burning cities, or when you were harassed by your own AA fire, were shot at, too—that was the last straw! And so you said to yourself, 'That's the one I want!'"

With the loss of so many experienced pilots, Becker adds, "we tried to fill our ranks by transferring older, more experienced fighter pilots to our units. We didn't need the 'hunting instincts' you need to win a protracted dogfight during a daylight raid. We had to take off, find and engage the enemy, and return, no matter what kind of weather or how great the enemy resistance."

New aircraft continued to appear. On the British side, the most notable were the Hawker Mk. V Tempest and the Spitfire XIV, in service by January 1944. Reaching a top speed of 450 mph at 26,069 feet, the Spit 14 could operate all the way up to 44,615 feet, while down at sea level it reached a respectable 368 mph. The new version mounted two 20 mm cannon, four

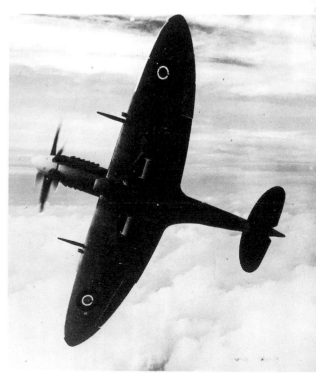

The late model Supermarine Spitfire Mark XIV in flight, a marked improvement over earlier production variants.

The rugged Hawker Tempest, in flight, distinguished itself in the air-to-ground role.

.303 mm machine guns, and a 500-pound bomb load. With Luftwaffe resistance rapidly waning, ground support became more crucial and a later "E" variant substituted two, heavier 12.7 mm machine guns for the original four, doubling the bomb load to 1,002 pounds. The Tempest, capable of 435 mph, went into service in April 1944, and was outstanding as an interceptor and high-altitude fighter as well as in ground attack missions. The Tempest took over where the Typhoon had failed as an interceptor. As RAF ace Roland Beamont puts it, "The Tempest is a Typhoon with the bugs ironed out." But the Typhoon, with its 12 machine guns, was outstanding as a tactical support aircraft for ground operations and was even faster than the FW.190 at low altitudes.

First operational in September 1941, the Typhoon was plagued by mechanical problems which claimed the lives of many pilots. By late 1942, most had been solved. Pilots who flew them compare the merits of these planes.

Roland Prosper Beamont, who had joined the RAF in 1938 and had six kills to his credit at this point, was among those who test-flew the Typhoon. Later, he was posted to Duxford to command 609 Squadron, one of the first three squadrons to get Typhoons. After "train-busting" days along the French coast, in 1943 he went back to break in the Tempest. In March 1944, Beamont became wing leader of the first Tempest squadron, made up of 3, 486, and 56 Squadrons. Few could discuss the three planes—the Hurricane, which he had flown in the early days of the war, the Typhoon, and the Tempest—more authoritatively. Beamont begins with the Typhoon:

"It was designed to be a hundred miles an hour faster than the Hurricane, and it just about made it. The engine—a big, powerful 2,000 horsepower Napier Sabre—was underdeveloped at the beginning of the Typhoon's life. When we got it into service, it was liable to stop and the Typhoon wouldn't glide very well. We lost a lot of airplanes and had one or two fatal accidents. And then, just as we were getting the squadron up to being operational, we started to have fatalities from another source—tails falling off in unexpected ways. In fact, over the next six or seven months, something like 20 Typhoons were lost with the tail breaking clean away and all but one of the pilots killed. But once we got it sorted out, the Typhoon proved to be a very potent, very powerful, strong, low-level fighter airplane. It was obviously not as maneuverable as our Hurricane, because it was so much bigger. But it was very much faster and carried more of a punch.

"We took the 609 to Manston, one of the airfields most closely positioned to the enemy coast. Our main task there initially was what was called 'Channel Stop,' which was to patrol around about mid-Channel to intercept low-level FW.190 and 109 raiders. We were pretty successful with that. Parallel to this, I got permission from my headquarters to experiment with low-level operations over France, first in pairs, later with larger units—low-level against railroad and military installations. The Typhoon proved to be ideal for this. It would go in very fast and could take quite a lot of punishment if you got hit by flak. Perhaps more importantly, it had extremely good gun-aiming characteristics with those heavy cannon and we could knock out trains and vehicles extremely well. And if we met FW.190s, as we soon began to do, then we found that the speed was tremendous, a lot faster than a 190 down low, and you could out-turn the 190 as well."

Beaumont describes how the Typhoon evolved into the Tempest: "It took a year or two of working very hard at the factory and in service to get the Typhoon into an operational condition. Having done that, it still wasn't the airplane we wanted. We wanted an airplane that would be just as maneuverable as the enemy, higher up and faster still. Hawker set about refining the Typhoon, putting a new wing on it, taking the advice that we fighter pilots had fed in over those two years. The Typhoon cockpit had a lot of metal work all round it and the vision from it was very poor. The Tempest had a one-piece sliding canopy which gave you perfect rear vision. And all sorts of improvements like that. A new thin wing, slightly upgraded engine. We ended up with an airplane that was still basically as rugged and as powerful and strong as a Typhoon, but much faster. We could do 435 miles an hour with it at the best height and well over 400 miles an hour at deck level—a unique thing at that time. Nobody could match the Tempest at low level, until the arrival of the new jets, that is. When those new Tempest fighters were coming out of the factory, I was lucky enough to be given the job of forming the first wing and we had just time to work them up to operational efficiency in the weeks preceding D-Day. The Tempest was a beautiful aircraft!"

At this point in the war, New Zealander Patric Jameson is a group captain

Roland P. Beaumont, pipe in teeth.

on the planning staff preparing for the invasion. Shortly afterwards, he would command another wing—122 Wing—flying Tempests, and, after D-Day, P-51 Mustangs. Since joining the RAF in 1936, Jameson had flown combat in everything from the old open-cockpit Gloster Gauntlets to Hurricanes and Spitfires. He shares his thoughts on those planes:

"The Spitfire was a more agile animal. And it was capable of being developed so that it was a very formidable airplane at the end of the war and much better than it was at the beginning. The Hurricane reached its limit very early on, really. The Typhoons were the development from the Hurricane, only much faster and a better airplane, and from them was developed the Tempest, which was an even better one. The Tempests were a great airplane, but they had a fault, too. The engine, for no apparent reason, suddenly cut on takeoff. They carried out all sorts of trials, but don't think they ever did find the cause of it." The Mustangs gave him a bigger problem: "We used to do a lot of dive-bombing and that sort of thing, dropping two 1,000-pounders. On five occasions, they exploded just underneath the aircraft. Eventually, we found out after a lot of experimenting that it was one of the fuses that was faulty. We lost five planes, but some of the pilots got back. They got in touch with the French underground and walked or cycled back."

Jameson on Spitfires vs. Tempests: "The Tempest was very good low down, very fast, much faster than the Spitfire. But the Spitfire could climb much faster, and the turning circle of the Spitfire was better. In fact, the Spitfire could out-turn nearly all of them, except perhaps a Hurricane. The Tempest

A bulldozer clears away the remains of the Luftwaffe as a P-38 snaps overhead.

could carry rockets on each side, about 16. And bombs. It was marvelous for both air fighting and for ground attack—particularly ground attack. A great airplane."

Fellow New Zealander Robert Spurdle agrees: "I don't want to denigrate the Spitfire—it was a beautiful airplane. But the Tempest was a vastly different aircraft. The Spitfire was more maneuverable, and certainly a lot more maneuverable than the Kittyhawk [the Curtiss P-40]. But the Tempest, with its much greater fire-power and higher speed, was a superlative aircraft . . . a marvelous machine for targets of opportunity: railway trains, light tanks, cars, anything you could find. There was nothing to touch us—other than the jets."

Stanislaw Skalski rhapsodizes about the Spitfire: "We called it not an airplane, it's a flying newspaper. Because it was so good, if pilot make a fault, so the airplane itself will sort of correct him. Fantastic airplane! But Mustangs—you have to be careful because it was very heavy airplane, so if you make a fault, immediately you would spin down and you can kill yourself during the landing even!"

Another Polish pilot, Wing Commander Waclaw S. Krol, who had also flown Hurricanes, Spitfires (all the way from Mark I to Mark XXII), sees it differently: "American Mustangs, they were the best aircrafts I think during the Second War!"

An enemy, Wolfgang Spate (99 kills), views the planes he fights: "Of all my many air battles and adventures, I would have to say I had the most respect for the Mustang. The Mustang's armament and equipment were superior to ours. They had better sighting equipment—their sights could automatically compensate for our movements; they could attack from higher altitudes, and in high-speed dives, they'd fly through our formation and still be able to pull

Inset:
Hawker Tempest II.

Above:
The North American "Donna Mite" of the 352nd Fighter Squadron, 353rd Fighter Group, touches down at its base in England, February 1945.

out at low altitudes. Thanks to their high-performance engines, they would still be able to attack our formation again from *underneath*. So, we really had to look out for those Mustangs.''

The Germans, never laggards, unveiled a few surprises of their own: The Messerschmitt Bf.109H, introduced in 1943, capable of reaching 465 mph at 32,894 feet. Then, in September 1944, the ''K'' version with its ''Galland'' bubble cockpit, giving the pilot a wider field of vision. In April 1943, the Luftwaffe began flying the twin-engine Me.410 A-3 *Hornise* (Hornet), a fearsome heavy fighter, fighter-bomber, and (in its A-2 version) heavy bomber. Developed to replace the Messerschmitt Bf.110, it never managed to equal it. But it was a powerful machine, reaching 387 mph at 23,026 feet and mounting two 20 mm cannons and two 7.9 mm machine guns in the nose and wings plus two 13 mm machine guns in remote-controlled side turrets. By the end of 1943, the Me.410 was armed with huge 50 mm cannon, capable of bringing down a heavy bomber with a single blast.

Gunther Rall flew Messerschmitts and Focke Wulfs, though for almost six years this ace-*extraordinaire* (275 kills) flew mainly 109s in combat. ''This was my plane, with all its advantages and disadvantages. I always compared the 109 with a stiletto and the 190 with a sword. You had to know how to fly the 109 very elegantly.''

Stanislaw Skalski had seen it all, from the blitzkrieg in his native Poland, to the Battle of Britain, to the North African war in the desert, and finally to the skies over occupied Europe. He sums up: ''They used to come to the air-dromes and ask us: 'What kind of airplane you want?' So we used to say, 'We like to have a cannon. The same, like a Messerschmitt.' And the guy on the other side of the Channel, they said, 'We'd like to have a Spitfire.' You know, because during the war, you look at your enemy, he is better.''

Then: ''You know, during the war, I always saying, 'Napoleon used to said, if you want to go on war, you need three things. First of all, money. Second, money. Third, money.' I think you need, luck, luck, and luck.''

''An enemy,'' Sophocles observed, ''should be hated only so far as one may be hated who may one day be a friend.'' One need only attend a reunion of World War II fighter pilots to see how many one-time enemies learned later to become fast friends, perhaps because there was something among them which went beyond hatred: bonds, invisible, metaphysical, formed by the very nature of what it is to be a fighter pilot.

The time was the spring of 1944, a few days before D-Day. Alan Geoffrey Page, now commanding RAF 132 Squadron, led a formation of six Spitfire Mark XIIs, outfitted with special long-range drop tanks ''to penetrate as far as we could, just to shoot at anything we could.

''Well, now,'' he recalls, ''I told my pilots at the briefing, 'If we come across any Messerschmitt 110 aircraft, don't do a head-on attack because they have four very lethal cannons in the nose of the aircraft. Attack them from behind.' So we set off, the six of us, and after a few hundred miles, we were flying over Germany and along came this Messerschmitt 110, flying in front of us. And one of my pilots, a very nice New Zealander called Johnny, peeled off and promptly did a head-on attack on this enemy aircraft.'' Page would learn later that the man in the enemy cockpit was Hans-Joachim Jabs; ''Johnny'' learned it then. ''Well, with his experience, Jabs hardly diverted course, he just shot Johnny down and went on his way. Johnny crash-landed in a field and survived.

"Well, I chased off to Jabs' aircraft and started firing and I could see my cannon shells and bullets hitting his aircraft. But it was very unkind of Jabs. He hadn't read the book. He didn't explode and do all the things which should happen. Instead, he calmly put his wheels and flaps down and I could see in front of him as I continued to fire that he was going to land at an airfield. The courage of the man—just to sit there and be shot at and then land his aircraft.

"As he touched down, I, of course, was going too fast. I went over the top of him and alongside me I had my wingman—sadly, he was hit by this mess of antiaircraft flak and he was killed."

Jabs picks up the tale:

"That happened in daylight, after I had visited Schnaufer's group. I was flying back towards Arnhem to my squadron HQ in Dehlen. At that time in the war, there were no more German fighter aircraft stationed on the Western front—they had all been pulled back to Berlin due to the American daylight bombing raids to protect against enemy entrance and enemy escape.

"We had 100 percent cloud coverage, and I flew in the clouds with my weapons ready and thought that nothing much could happen—although it was against orders to fly in daylight. When I reached the vicinity of Arnhem, we lost the cloud coverage and I then began to descend and fly as low as possible, 20-30 meters off the ground, in order to reduce risk to a minimum. Nearing the airstrip at Arnhem, my navigator—who had been with me as a corporal during the Battle of Britain and would end the war with me as a captain—said, 'There are fighters circling the field!' 'What! They're risking everything. They're supposed to be in Berlin!' But we had jumped to the wrong conclusion. They weren't ours—they were Spitfires, the most modern Spitfires.

"They turned in my direction. I didn't have enough time to return to the cloud cover. I had to fly into their formation. They shot at me and I was lucky enough that my plane was only lightly damaged. I was able to activate the landing gear using compressed air, and, well, by God! I just threw that plane onto the runway and my crewman screamed at me, '*Raus! Get out of the plane!*' We jumped out and threw ourselves into a trench, next to the AA guns, and we dug our heads into the dirt and waited. I can remember it like it was yesterday. It started to explode around us—not English bombs, but my plane. It was burning and the fuel and ammo had started to explode.

"In the meantime, a car drove up, picked us up and we were told that an English fighter pilot we had shot up had crash-landed. We drove over there, picked up the pilot—it was John Colton, now a good friend of mine who has visited me many times. The situation was rather unpleasant because I think a Dutch soldier was there with a rifle which he was waving around, and they wanted to do something with him. So I took him with me into the canteen and wrote a note saying that I had shot him down and that he should be treated well during his captivity.

"During my leave that day, I'd picked up a side of ham and some cognac snifters. They were still in the plane."

The plot thickens. The time is now more than 40 years later, a meeting of the Flying Aces Association in Munich. Jabs is there. Page is there.

"Geoffrey was one of the guests. He was the leader of this group of fighters, the formation I had seen over the field with the other aircraft. I saw him standing there, and he asked me, 'Are you Joachim?' 'Yes,' I said, 'are you Geoffrey?' When he said yes, we hugged each other, then exchanged our stories. He told me how he had experienced that fight from above. I told him how I had experienced it from below.

" 'Geoffrey'—I told him—'I don't resent you destroying my plane, that was war. You were also in danger. But the side of ham that was burned up in the plane—that was nasty, because we were all so hungry and my family was even hungrier. I had one son at the time and another on the way. Boy, that ham, I do resent that!' "

The next Christmas, a package arrived at the Jabs residence. The sender was Geoffrey Page. With the package, a note: "I'm sorry about destroying your plane—that, I'm afraid I can't replace. But you should at least have your side of ham back."

Before they parted on that first occasion, Page introduced Jabs to "his lovely American wife, Paulina Bruce. She said, 'Geoffrey, I would never have married you had you killed this nice man.' "

Adolph Galland speaks of the bombing. "The Luftwaffe overextended, overtaxed itself in various theaters of war—from Italy to Africa, France, Norway, Finland, the Russian front, down to the Crimea and the Caucasus. This situation was exacerbated over the years, exacerbated by the tendency of the Americans to attack during the day and strike bomb-specific targets such as power plants, fuel production facilities. They destroyed strategic objectives such as roads, railways, one after another. And they were able to maintain an ever-increasing air superiority over us. At the very least, they had 1,000 four-engine bombers coming from the west, 800 from the south. In addition to that, there were 800 to 1,000 night bombers from England. This was the program which German arms faced on a daily basis. It wasn't air superiority. It was complete domination. As soon as a German plane appeared on an airfield, immediately there was an Allied fighter right on top of it. All the airports were bombed, the fuel tanks destroyed. Our defense industry capability was destroyed. We were building only fighters, but we had no more fuel. By the time of the invasion, we were completely bled white."

It was painful for the men of the outgunned, outnumbered Luftwaffe. But their sense of duty was different from Hitler's, the man who refused to visit his bombed-out cities, the man who made this war.

The ace Wolfgang Spate speaks: "I saw the destruction of the German cities and realized that with this much devastation on the ground, then Germany could never prevail and win the war. I realized that we were fighting only in order to postpone the end of the war, but a victory was now unthinkable."

American fighter pilot Clayton Gross: "Strategic, daylight bombing of specific targets in Germany, wounding their ability to make war, was what ended the war. We were able to get the bombers in to wipe out their factories, ruin their transportation system."

New Zealander Patric Jameson: "Well, there's one big lesson that was learned during the war, and that was that before the army could do anything, really, they had to have air superiority over the battle area. Otherwise, they didn't have a hope."

To the 2.8 million men in the mightiest military machine ever assembled, marking time anxiously at bases and camps and aboard troop transports, from one end of the British Isles to the other, crushing, devastating air superiority guaranteed ultimate victory.

Geoffrey Page waving from his Hawker Hurricane.

10

CRUSADE IN EUROPE

Dawn had not yet broken that day, a day like none before and none since, when Andrew Robert Mackenzie settled into the cockpit of his Spitfire fighter plane and took off from Tangmere, England, heading due south for a place across the Channel code-named UTAH.

Those who lived through that day would never forget it.

Those who were not there cannot begin to imagine it. Mackenzie remembers:

"It seemed," he said, "that if I were a giant, I could have walked across the Channel on the boats. There were thousands and thousands of boats, from England to Cherbourg. We were so fortunate to have this seat at 3,000 feet, like a loge seat, above those ships. It almost looked like the continents were joined with ships."

Geoffrey Page was experiencing similar emotions: "At first light, what was called H-Hour, I was leading my squadron of Spitfires flying cover over the American beaches of Omaha and Utah. We'd stay there for about an hour and then we'd go back to England, and, of course, a replacement squadron would come out. And I must say that, to be there, was the most fantastic experience. Seeing all those ships and troops going ashore on the beaches.

"It had a particular significance for me, because I had flown at the time of Dunkirk and had watched the remnants of the British army being taken off by rescue ships. So, to see them going back, and our American allies and Canadians and everybody else, it was a great thrill."

The day was D-Day, June 6, 1944. The event was the long-awaited Allied invasion of Hitler's Fortress Europe, the first cross-Channel invasion of the Continent since 1688. It was code-named OVERLORD. Never before had man mobilized such apocalyptic power.

Planning for this day began shortly after President Roosevelt and Prime Minister Churchill met at Casablanca in January 1943. (As far back as May 1942, Winston Churchill had recognized the decisive place of the fighter plane in planning an onslaught against the entrenched Wehrmacht.) Heading the planning was British Lt. Gen. Sir Frederick E. Morgan, chief of staff to the Supreme Allied Commander, or COSSAC. Because Eisenhower was a strategic rather than a tactical commander, another Britisher, Gen. Bernard Montgomery, was appointed to command ground operations.

Crucial to Morgan's planning was the operational range of the Spitfire, the fighter plane still most in use among the Allies in Britain. And that was short: from 434 to 460 miles. That limited the invasion options to the French coast from the Pal de Calais to the Cotentin peninsula in Normandy. The Germans expected the blow would fall at Pal de Calais; the planners zeroed in on the Cotentin peninsula area.

When Adolf Hitler realized that an invasion was inevitable, he turned to the Desert Fox, Gen. Erwin Rommel. Within six months, much of the French coast bristled with underwater obstacles, pill boxes, barbed wire entanglements, tank traps, land mines, artillery emplacements. Those obstacles were intended to compensate for the virtual impotence of the Luftwaffe: there were only 300 fighter planes left in France against some 12,000 aircraft available to the Allies in Britain. Against 39 Allied divisions earmarked for the invasion, the Germans deployed 58 divisions, but only 14 of them in Normandy and Britanny.

Originally set for May 1944, OVERLORD was put back a month to June 5 because of an (imaginary) shortage of landing craft. Foul weather then forced another delay to the 6th. Meanwhile, tens of thousands of men had already spent anxious days and nights aboard darkened transports, while airborne paratroopers and glider forces waiting to go in ahead of the main strikes endured nerve-wracking off again-on again hours at full alert.

Finally, Eisenhower gave the order. The time was 4:15 A.M.

The invasion flotilla was made up of 6,483 vessels: 1,200 warships, includ-

ing seven battleships, two heavy cruisers, 23 cruisers, 104 destroyers, 98 minesweepers, 63 corvettes. Those ships flew the flags of Britain, the U.S., France, Poland, Norway, Greece, Holland. To take the troops ashore, there were 4,126 landing vessels, and over 1,000 merchantmen and auxiliaries. The landing craft included LCTs armed with 1,000 five-inch rockets fired in salvoes of 24 each; anyone within the target area—roughly 750 by 160 yards—was on the receiving end of 17 tons of high explosives.

The initial landings—from 6:00 to 7:30 A.M.—were made by 176,000 men: the American 1st Army, under Lt. Gen. Omar N. Bradley, and the British 2nd Army, under Lt. Gen. Sir Miles Dempsey.

In the air, the Allies had 5,409 fighter planes and fighter-bombers, 1,645 twin-engined bombers, and 3,647 four-engined bombers under the overall command of Air Marshal Sir Trafford Leigh-Mallory in the Allied Expeditionary Air Force. In addition, the Allies had 2,355 transport planes for paratroopers and towing 867 gliders carrying about 27,000 troops and their equipment, including light tanks. Luftwaffe Gen. Hugo Sperrle's Third Air Fleet had 169 fighters available on the Channel coast, a handful more inland in France.

During the night and early morning, Bomber Command and the U.S. 8th Air Force blasted German defenses in the immediate vicinity of the beaches with 5,000 tons of bombs. Jack Ilfrey was in a P-38 flying top-cover for those bombers on D-Day. The American ace tells what it was like: "Believe me, it was the most spectacular thing I have ever seen. Thousands and thousands of boats converging, and those bombers that had been in a few minutes earlier to do everything they could before the ground troops landed."

Veteran of the Battle of Britain, Peter Brothers looks over a combat report with a flight lieutenant. Brothers was credited with 12 destroyed enemy aircraft when this photo was taken.

In the weeks preceding the assault, the heavy bombers, joined by the medium bombers of the U.S. 9th Air Force and the British 2nd Air Force, had all but destroyed the railroad system in northern France.

"You know, we'd waited a year or so for D-Day and we were so keen," relates Andy Mackenzie, picking up the narrative. "I remember so well: at about twelve o'clock midnight, they called a briefing at this tent in Tangmere, and we were so excited. As a matter of fact, I thought that I would shoot down so many airplanes on D-Day that I was conceited enough to put a navigation pad on my knee to keep track of the airplanes because I figured I couldn't remember how many I had shot down."

Instead, it was very nearly the opposite case for Mackenzie and his mates. "The whole navy, protecting the beaches, started shooting at us. And at the time, Lloyd Chadburn, who was leading our squadron, called them over the radio and said, 'You know, Christ, chaps, we're Spitfires from England to cover the beaches—stop firing!' Well, they didn't stop, so we had to turn the whole wing around and go back towards England. Chadburn contacted control, and they said, 'Well, terribly sorry, old chap, we made a mistake. Come on in again.' Well, we did and it happened three times. We didn't do much patrolling that day, we were busy avoiding our own flak. I guess they were a little bit trigger-happy. But that happens in war."

Harry Broadhurst blames it on something else—that old bugaboo, lack of coordination. "On your [the American] side, they flew in over the fleet which was busy shelling the beaches without telling them they were going to do it. So they lost more aircraft to the ack-ack guns from their own fleet than they did to the Luftwaffe."

Roland P. Beamont, commanding the first Tempest wing, grappled with another kind of confusion, inevitable in such a mighty enterprise. After patrolling the beaches all day, "around 10:30 in the evening, with the weather worsening, low cloud and rain," he reports, "I suddenly got an operations order to scramble two squadrons of Tempests to the beachhead. And I said, 'Fine, but you know it's just about dark.' And the voice at the other end said, 'Yes,' and so I said, 'Furthermore, we've got a weather system coming in which is going to clamp the base.' And the voice said, 'Yes—you don't have any time to lose, do you?' So off we went and we ended up flying a two-squadron wing formation at night, over the beachhead. We obviously had turned our navigation lights out as we got there, so we saw nothing except the gun flashes on the ground. And then we got diverted to another base and ended up after an hour and-a-half's flying landing at a strange base

Battle dressed P-51 of the 361st squadron, with wheels and flaps down, returns from an interdiction mission over occupied Europe.

where 200 other fighters which had also been in the same predicament were also landing. There wasn't one of those 200 fighters which hadn't had an accident that night. But we all got down safely."

Two days later, on June 8, Beamont's wing was scrambled to do a sweep behind the beachhead. "Somewhere around mid-Channel, I started to get radar warning of unidentifieds in the area between Rouen and Lisieux in northern France, on the flank of the battle. As we closed in, they said the formation is thought to be five to ten aircraft, altitude unknown. We were at 15,000 feet. As we were approaching Rouen, they said the unidentifieds, probably bandits, are five miles ahead of you, crossing left to right. You should see them. At first, I thought they were Mustangs, and I told the top squadron to stay up and cover and I went down with my squadron. As we dived on them, we were doing about 450 [mph] and closed on them very, very quickly. They saw us, because they immediately started to stream their overboost smoke. As soon as they went into overboost, streaming smoke, we could see they were 109s. We went in on this particular bunch—five of them, there were five more somewhere else but I hadn't seen them. Anyway, we shot down four of them without losing one of ours, although something from somewhere came around and knocked a 20-millimeter shell hole in my starboard wing. I've always suspected my Number Two because I never saw another one in line behind me. But that's another thing."

Another, which Beamont neglected to mention: two of those kills that day were his, his first in four years, raising his tally to nine.

Ragnar Dogger, the Norwegian who had made his way clear round the world to fight the Nazis, was in for "a great disappointment. We didn't see any German fighters the whole day." But Dogger did carry away a rare memory: "We went out at around three o'clock in the morning, just when the battleships opened their barrage. That really was something to see!"

Although the Allies flew 4,600 sorties on D-Day alone, very few Allied pilots got to see German fighters. Reports vary, but it would appear that no more than 50 German planes managed to engage the Allied planes that filled the sky that day. Of those, American ace Jim Goodson reports, "only two managed to get through to the beachhead—Pips Pillar of JG.26 and his wingman. We did a lot of ground strafing just before the invasion because we had to eliminate the Luftwaffe before the troops came in. Which we did."

Peter Brothers was among the few to engage an enemy in the skies—but had mixed feelings about it. Commanding the Exeter Wing at that point, he remembers it was "awesome to see the number of aircraft [we had] in the air.

Twelve P-51 Mustangs demonstrate the unequivocal air superiority that Allied flyers enjoyed during the liberation of France.

Beamont enjoying a moment of reflection away from battle.

And the opposition was awfully disappointing. One felt rather sorry. I got tangled up with some 190s and the chap I shot down obviously didn't know the first thing about it. He was just gently turning from left to right as though he was peering over his left shoulder and right shoulder wondering what to do. It was rather sad. I wondered whether he was on his first sortie or not.'' Recovering from his squeamishness, Brothers went on to do what most pilots did that day: ''shoot up everything you could see on the ground. Train-busting was great fun. We kept ourselves busy by ground-strafing everything that moved outside our own area—tanks, cars, trucks. We also used to go and beat up the airfields at Le Mans, and that sort of thing.''

D-Day left the pilots with another kind of memory. Andy Mackenzie: ''Mind you, we also saw an awful lot of people die on the beaches. You could see them falling and you knew they were just dying by the hundreds. Most of my beachhead work was over the American beaches, and of course, those were American soldiers that I saw dying.''

Sir Harry Broadhurst—now Air-Vice Marshal Harry Broadhurst—was transferred from Italy to take command of RAF 84 Fighter Group two months before D-Day. The group spearheaded the RAF's 2nd Tactical Air Force (TAF) during the invasion.

''Well, we'd allowed for the Luftwaffe being there. But,'' Sir Harry adds, ''they weren't. They were involved with Russia. They were involved in Italy, and they were losing Italy fast. They were stretched to hell and we had air superiority. Nevertheless, we expected they would oppose the invasion, particularly on the beaches. But they didn't.''

Ask Adolf Galland, head of the decimated Luftwaffe Fighter Command: ''The Luftwafe was destroyed by the time of the invasion, thrown completely out of the air.''

But, as Galland knew better than anyone, as down as they were, they were not yet out.

To say that Galland ''knew'' is not mere idle chatter. His combat career began flying with the Condor Legion in Spain in 1937 as a member of the legendary JG.2 Richtofen Wing. He later flew sorties over Britain and France. With the suicide of Ernst Udet and accidental death of Werner Mölders, Galland was catapulted in 1941 into the leadership of the Luftwaffe's Fighter Command, the youngest general in the German armed forces. A constant cigar smoker—20 per day—it is said that he actually wrote orders giving himself official permission to smoke while flying on a mission. Because of Mölders' death in a plane crash, Galland, as his successor, was forbidden to take part in combat.

That order neither could nor would ground Adolf Galland. He explains: ''When I downed enemy aircraft afterwards, I was sort of a poacher because I flew those missions without letting my superiors know. If you ask me whether I flew those unreported sorties out of a feeling of insolence, then I have to say, no, not at all, but because a fighter pilot leader who thinks he can do things from the ground is mistaken. He will lose in the shortest period of time the trust of the men. Of him it will be said, 'Oh, the old man doesn't know what's going on anymore.' And I really wanted to know what went on in the air. A leader of a fighter pilot unit, especially of fighter pilots, is forced from time to time, a few times a month, to experience a battle. Otherwise, he cannot be a leader anymore.''

Galland practiced what he preached. Officially, he had 104 air victories. In reality, there were others, "but I couldn't let my superiors know because I would have been reprimanded for it."

Those experiences made him a teacher as well as a leader. Once, while attempting to attack a Flying Fortress, his FW.190 was jumped by four Mustangs. Realizing the futility of engaging them, he dove to escape. The Mustangs dove with him. He then tried a trick that had worked before: firing his guns. The spent cartridges and streams of smoke wafting over their aircraft seemed to induce the American pilots to believe they were taking fire from backward-firing guns. At all odds, they broke off and Galland escaped—to pass along that ruse to others.

With the assault forces on D-Day went specially trained officers and men of the RAF's Beach Squadron. Within four days, they had scraped and clawed together the first Spitfire base on the Continent. Within three days, they had added five more. Progress lagged in the days ahead. Still, during the first month following the invasion, RAF Fighter Command alone flew 21,000 sorties over Normandy. Altogether, the Allied Expeditionary Air Force (AEAF), under Air Chief Marshal Sir Trafford Leigh-Mallory, flew a total of 268,054 sorties from D-Day to the end of August, dropping 103,000 tons of bombs. During the first 70 days of combat, 2,990 German aircraft were destroyed in air combat, another 651 on the ground; the AEAF lost 2,959 aircraft.

Geoffrey Page was among the first to use one of those "little mud strips" on the Continent. "The main purpose of being there," he reports, "was to take off and attack any form of German ground transport. But you got a little bored with that, so you'd phone up your sector control and say, 'I'm having trouble with my guns and I'd like to do a cannon test.' And they knew that you had no trouble with your guns, but they'd say all right. So you'd take off and usually take either one or two pilots with you and just go out looking for trouble. On one of those occasions, I found 70 Focke Wulf 190s, fairly far inland. Well, we were so far above them that we could dive right down and knocked off a couple of them, climbed up again, and went home. Hunting is a great game!"

Page wasn't always so lucky. On another flight over Normandy, "two of us attacked 30 German 109s. The sensible thing of course would have been to go

The Allies increasingly applied tactical air power against German ground targets as the Wermacht was pushed back across Europe. A Tiger and Panther tank here were caught in the open by Allied cannons.

on home, instead of which I got a bullet in my leg. But I managed to destroy one of the German aircraft.'' Page was by then commanding RAF 132 Squadron, previously led by the legendary J.A.F. MacLachlan. A bullet in the leg would not prevent Page from remaining in a cockpit right to the end of the war, ultimately claiming 15 kills.

Supplies—German supplies—were very much on the minds of Allied planners. With the immense fighter armada unopposed over the beachheads, Allied bombers once again began pounding targets inside the Reich. On June 22, raids succeeded in knocking out 90 percent of the production of airplane fuel. That left the German war machine tottering. But they held an ace in the hole: reserves of 574,000 tons of aircraft fuel.

Harley Brown, out of El Dorado, Kansas, tasted combat for the first time on one of those strategic bombing missions. On August 24, his unit was assigned to fly top cover for bombers striking the German rocket facilities at Peene-munde. Doing follow-up strafing, Brown's plane took some flak hits. It was the baptism of fire he needed for what would prove to be one of the toughest of his 57 missions. It took place only three days later.

"We were escorting bombers to Berlin, but because of the cloud cover, they couldn't drop their eggs there. So they diverted to their secondary target, Esbjerg in Denmark. They laid their eggs on this German field there, and did a beautiful job. The field was burning and smoking, and they left and headed for England.

"I was flying the colonel's wing—Col. Cy Wilson, a very famous pilot, highly respected, a real go-getter. I was flying his wing because usually a new pilot flew the commander's wing in the first two or three formations so he could check you out, tell you what you did wrong. But poor Cy didn't get to tell me what I did wrong.

"We went down on the field there, after it had been bombed, and it was just great! But we just got to the edge of the field and all hell broke loose! Guns and tracers and the sky was almost black with flak. I heard the colonel holler, 'Hit the deck!' And boy, did I hit it! I'll bet my plane went three feet off the ground. Cy—the colonel—went over the center of the field, and his two wingmen were kinda at the edge of the field. They both got hit so bad that they went down.

"I strafed a couple of machine gun nests, with tracers flying over my head. This was about 10 miles inland from the ocean. Just as we hit the coastline, I saw a boat about 40 feet long and gave it a 'spray job' and then started pulling up. At that point, Cy asked me to come and check him over. 'I've been hit,' he said. I pulled up, got real close to him, and said, 'Gee, Colonel, you've really been riddled.' Then his engine caught fire, his canopy went off, and he bailed out. His parachute opened, and I was circlin' to see that he got into his dinghy okay. And I'd make some passes and wave to him, wobbling the wings, and he'd wave back. Then I saw a ship a few miles from me. So I circled it, trying to guide it over to him, to help rescue him.

"It turned out later that it was a Danish ship, but when they got back to the shore, why, the Nazis had got him. So he was a POW for the rest of the war. That's why the poor colonel didn't get to tell me what I did wrong!

"We lost four men on that mission, three on the one pass over the airdrome—that's how heavy the flak was.

"Later, this bloke from Denmark came over and interviewed some of us, and he wrote a book all about that one day, because it was the most damage done [in Denmark] in one day of the whole war—from the bombers, and from our strafing. And from two other squadrons; seeing how bad we got shot up on one pass, they just spread out all over Denmark afterwards that day, shooting up everything they could find."

To counter the renewed bombing menace, Luftwaffe chieftain Goering resorted to a macabre solution: the formation of Sturmstaffel 1, made up partly of volunteers, partly of pilots out of favor for one reason or another. Before each sortie, every pilot was required to sign an oath pledging to bring down at least one Allied bomber, by ramming, if necessary. To ram, a pilot needed only pull up slightly, then aim to shear off the B-17s huge tailfin with a wing, or smash one of the B-24s' large tailplane rudders. Of the relatively few rammings, about half the pilots survived unhurt. The threat of being accused of cowardice was effective. Equipped with specially armored FW.190A-Gs, this unit formed the nucleus of an expanded IV (Sturm) JG.3. On July 7, 1944, the unit downed 32 American bombers over Leipzig, losing only two fighters. But the tension on the pilots was nearly unbearable: the first commander, Capt. Wilhelm Moritz, was compelled to give up his command because of exhaustion. By the end of 1944, the Germans would have a far deadlier answer to the menace.

The Germans called them *Vergeltungswaffen*—"Revenge Weapons." The world knew them as V-1s, "flying bombs." Londoners knew them as "buzz bombs," for the ominous sound of their engines, which, when it stopped, triggered terror. They were the first jet-propelled weapons used in warfare. On June 13, a week to the day after the invasion, the first FZG 76, carrying 1,870 pounds of high explosives, exploded near Gravesend, England.

From June 13 to September 5, when the Allies overran the last launching site in Pas de Calais, about 7,250 V-1s hit targets in Britain, Belgium, and France—the great bulk of them striking in southern England.

Fighter pilots now had a new and urgent priority. Destroy the launchers. Destroy the rockets in the air. Fighter planes were put in the air round-the-clock.

Miroslav Mansfeld, now a flight commander, remembers his first encounter with a buzz bomb. "We were stationed near Cambridge; ground control told us that flying bombs were coming over in the direction of Cambridge. I took off and had made only half a circuit when I saw it. So I just went after it and shot it down. It went down into a field and exploded. I just came back on the circuit and landed—seven minutes from start to finish. I was always proud of that."

Although Mustangs and the RAF's new twin-jet Meteor fighters were also pressed into service against the rockets, two other fighters planes would prove their real nemeses: the Spitfire 14 and the Tempest. Fourteens accounted for no fewer than 300 of the nearly 2,000 rockets shot down. And three squadrons of a single wing of Tempests blasted 638 V-1s out of the sky and produced the top scorer, Joe Barry, who shot down 60 of them.

Roland P. Beamont commanded that wing. "We thought we had the war at our feet, and then all of a sudden, it went quite the wrong way for us—the flying bomb attack started. Now my wing was a well-trained organization, and we had been placed where we were, on the southern tip of Dungeness, deliberately to be in the path of the expected attack by unmanned flying bombs. We didn't have any technical detail about them, except we just knew that they were going to be launched across the Channel and aimed at London, sometime during the summer. It was first anticipated that the enemy would launch them before we were able to start the invasion. Well, for various

Below right:
A P-51 of the 353rd fighter group burns furiously after crash-landing at its base in England, January 10, 1945.

The powerful Spitfire XIV was equipped with an unconventional five-bladed prop and a 2,000 horse power engine for high speed performance. The XIV was successful at destroying V-1 buzz bombs and could even do battle with the Me-262 under ideal conditions.

reasons, most of them being the USAAF bomber command and RAF bomber command and our Typhoon rocket-firing force, the Germans were delayed. We were in place right in their path and we were immediately taken off our air support role to fly defense against the flying bomb.

"The Tempest proved to be ideally suited to it. It was extremely fast. It was an extremely accurate gun platform and the four 20 mm guns were just the right sort of gun for attacking the flying bombs. The V-1s were a very small target, and travelling nearly 400 miles an hour, so that our 410-420 in the Tempest was only a small margin above them. This caused immediate problems for all the other fighters which weren't actually as fast as the V-1 at low level and could only reach most of them by a dive attack. With the Tempests, we didn't need a dive attack—we could actually overhaul. So within the first two or three days, the Tempests were knocking these things down quite fast. The air became full of airplanes—every other pilot in Fighter Command and some not in Fighter Command who could find or borrow a Spitfire or something, flying over Kent and Sussex trying to have a go at these V-1s that were coming in by the hundreds."

Indeed: in the first two weeks alone, the Germans fired around 2,000 of them. It took fighter pilots only a few days to master tactics for destroying the marauders, tactics which included closing to within 300 yards of the fast targets. But first, there needed to be a little "traffic control." Wing Commander Beamont explains:

"All those planes in the air were causing chaos in the air space. I was called on to go up to my command headquarters and make recommendations as to how the battle was to be developed. The first thing I asked for was to have the area cleared of all uncontrolled fighters and to concentrate a number of squadrons of the best airplanes for the job—which were the Tempests, Mustang P-51s, and Spitfire 14s with the big [2,078 hp] Griffon engines. This was done within a week or ten days—and our score started to rise—very quickly!"

After a few days, Allied fighter pilots—the right ones, that is, in the right planes—were shooting down 50 percent of the incoming V-1s; near the end, they were destroying 80 percent. One of the big scorers was Roland Beamont: 32 V-1s shot down. The overall kill: nearly 2,000 by Fighter Command, 1,560 by antiaircraft fire, 279 by barrage balloons.

With the French launching sites captured, the Germans resorted to using obsolete He.111 bombers to fire the V-1s from the air. Of 1,200 air-launched, only about 250 reached British soil. Says Beamont of this phase of the attack: "They were a nuisance, not a menace."

But there was another and graver menace. On September 5, 1944, Paris was hit by a new kind of rocket—the V-2. London's Chiswick section was next, on September 9. Beamont: "Our Tempest wing, by the end of August, was full of very good marksmen, because all our guys had been shooting at small, fast targets every day for six weeks. And they were very good shots. We were put onto daylight escorts of bombers to the Ruhr—some exciting jobs, taking out radar stations, other ground attack missions. Then we were given another job: problematical missions to strafe V-2 sites, the second of Hitler's V weapons, except that this big rocket was supersonic. There was no way of intercepting it. Ack-ack command couldn't hit it. And we couldn't intercept it."

No mere airplane could. Much bigger than the V-1s—46 feet long, 5 feet 6 inches in diameter, weighing 12 tons—the V-2s could fly farther—220 miles. And higher, far higher—peaking at about 60 .MDBO/miles above the earth's surface. And faster, *much* faster, a top speed of 3,600 mph, or five times the speed of sound! To make matters worse, they were fired from rudimentary, mobile sites. Roland Beamont tells what it was like in the frenzied search to find and destroy the launchers:

"Some of our units, my own included, were assigned to strafe suspected V-2 sites. I think you could classify this as a problematic mission because we had no target information in the sense of photographs or anything like that. There was just intelligence information as to where a suspected site might be. And it would generally be in a wood, possibly at the confluence of a cross-roads or something like that.

"We'd be given the map coordinates and we would go and find them if I could map-read that well, which wasn't often. And then just attack there, unless I could identify something else like vehicle tracks going through a wood. Then I'd make a pinpoint attack on that. We did two or three of these attacks.

"On the last one, I had two squadrons with me—24 Tempests on a ground-strafing run means you could put a lot of firepower down on a target—providing you could find it. We were operating in Holland, north of the Hague somewhere. Nice, fine morning. I found the map reference all right, and then I saw what I thought were some tracks going through the wood and converging. And so I thought, well, elementary deduction suggests you should aim at the confluence of the tracks. And I went in and, all of a sudden, a lot of flak came up.

"This obviously was a target and it got very hot. I did a strafing run through and then the rest of the guys came through and there was a tremendous explosion. I looked over my shoulder and there was a great mushroom of cloud, and then a shockwave and a lot of flames came up. We reckoned we must have either hit a V-2 on its launcher or else the storage tanks for the fuel."

In the end, the V-2 represented another of Hitler's pig-headed blunders.

The rockets simply didn't do adequate damage. Moreover, the human and material resources poured into the V-2 and the even bigger intercontinental missiles drained resources from a far more promising and viable weapon. That was the ground-to-air missile which carried 660 pounds of explosives along a directional beam to heights of 50,000 feet—and with great accuracy. Had they been produced by the thousands, entirely feasible, these missiles might have nullified Allied air power over Germany.

During those first weeks after the invasion, Allied fighter planes concentrated on disrupting German transport and communications. Jack Ilfrey records that his 20th Fighter Group became known as "the 'loco bunch' because we had shot up so many trains." Actually, he explains, "we shot at anything that moved—troops, trucks, anything. And this is where we had our losses, from ground flak shooting at us."

Borrowing from the Soviet success on close ground-support missions with their rocket-armed Ilyushin-2 Stormoviks, the British developed a "cab rank" tactic for their Typhoon fighter-bombers. Radio-controlled from friendly forces on the ground, they would swoop down one after another in a line, raining rocket and heavy machine gun fire on armored columns.

Back from combat in the Pacific, Robert Spurdle was in the cockpit of a Tempest in the weeks following the invasion. "For a while," he relates, "they held us back because, at that time, the Tempest was a secret fighter—really silly because the war was obviously going to be won and it didn't matter how the Germans evaluated the plane. During the Battle of Britain, we had flown at over 30,000 feet. Now we were cruising at about 4,000 feet on our search-and-destroy missions. To fly at that height seemed suicidal, but the Germans by this time were so pressed for antiaircraft ammunition, they realized we were no real threat unless we came down. So we just free-ranged over Germany, destroying anything we could find—railway stock, railroad engines, staff cars, armored cars, half-tracks. It was one of the most rewarding times of the war for me."

In a sense, it was one of the more frustrating times for Jim Goodson, who came to be known as the "King of the Strafers." He talks about how he came by that name.

"Foolish is probably the right word because everybody was well aware of the fact that because of the German flak, strafing was extremely dangerous. And I did more strafing than anyone else. Unfortunately, at one time, the U.S. air force decided not to count aircraft destroyed on the ground in rating the score of a fighter pilot. I thought that was a very bad decision because then people said, 'Well, to hell with that, I'm not going to risk my neck destroying aircraft on the ground if we don't get any credit for them.' I went on doing it anyway."

The rugged P-47 was ideally suited for the demanding ground attack and interdiction missions that were required over Europe late in the war.

A P-47 flies through debris blasted aloft during a perilously low-level ground attack mission.

Fellow American Joe Gross was proud of the fact that, though hit by enemy aircraft, he had never been shot down by one. Then, one day, "strafing, ten feet off the ground, I was hit by rifle fire. One bullet through the engine. Cut the coolant line. In-line engines won't run without coolant and mine—stopped. I had about 50 miles, according to the radio controller, to get to our lines when I jumped and hung in the parachute, thinking I was destined to go to a prison camp. When I landed, General Patton's tanks were on the ground below me. I came down in the middle of a battle, and got a ride back on a tank. I loved General Patton and the Third Army forevermore after that day!"

Jack Ilfrey wasn't quite that lucky. "I was leading my squadron one day on a mission, diving on a well-known railroad bridge over the River Loire, near Angers. As squadron leader, it was my privilege to say, 'I'll get the locomotives.' And my wingman was supposed to go down with me for protection. Because we knew that, right behind the locomotive, was a big flatcar with eighty-eights mounted on it. Well, I can't say exactly what happened. This train was parked in a little station, right outside this big city. I went down, with one of my friends—we're still good friends today—and he said there was a field of eighty-eight guns camouflaged, right outside this little station. And he said they were just snapping at my ass as I was going down getting the locomotive.

"Shooting a locomotive was no problem. You just dove down and fired your guns and the steam boiler exploded. It billowed way up, and just as I was flying through the steam, I was severely hit on the right side. The whole right engine burst into flame, and smoke started coming from my cockpit, and they were yelling at me to bail out.

"I knew I was very close to the ground, so I immediately pulled up until the aircraft was about to stall and bailed out. The fellows with me later said I bailed out around 600 feet, which is rather low. One fellow told me he saw me pull the ripcord, do about half an oscillation, and hit the top of a farm-house, bouncing down into the yard.

"They flew around some—one of my good friends was trying to find a spot to land, to try to pick me up. But he couldn't because of trees and a lot of barriers that had been erected, posts and things, because of gliders. So, one minute I was hearing my engines, hearing the roar of my guns, smelling smoke, and the next thing I'm lying on the ground, dead silent. What the hell am I going to do now?"

Consolidated B-24 Liberators attempting to struggle to friendly bases, trailing smoke and fuel after taking cannon and flak hits over Europe.

The date was June 12, 1944—Ilfrey has no trouble whatsoever remembering the date. The time was around 8:00 P.M.—still very much daylight in those northern latitudes. "I got myself together and figured there was nothing wrong with me physically. I had on heavy flying boots. I threw them off. I had on a Mae West. I threw that off. I threw the helmet off. That left me in my flying suit over my regular clothes.

"I saw three little kids in this yard. And I saw an old man over at the barn, with a pitchfork in his hand. I ran up and asked the kids which way was north—made them understand that I wanted to go north. Instead of taking the normal escape route—down through the Pyrenees Mountains and over into Spain—I just said to myself, 'I'll go north and try to meet the troops.'

"I ran off through the hedgerows, got exhausted, and sat down in some tall grass to kind of hide myself. I took off my flight suit and all my insignia and just left it there. At about dusk, I got on a little road that I knew was going north. I had not walked very far when two boys on bicycles came up behind me. One of them spoke in a broken English and wanted to know if I was the American aviator who had jumped out of a P-38, and I felt like saying, 'Well, hell, take a look! What do you think I am?'

"Anyway, he said the Germans had been around the airplane and were trying to find me and to come with him and his cousin to their little village, which was nearby. So he put me on the handlebars and pumped for a while. When he got tired, I did the pumping. When we neared the village, he told me to hide in some tall grass until he went and talked to his father. And then he came back and said, 'Come on.' It turned out that he was about 17 years old and they lived upstairs in a two-story building—downstairs was a restaurant. So they brought me in and discussed it amongst themselves, in French, of course, which I did not know much of. There were two older sisters. Finally, they decided they would. The father was against it, but one of the older girls spoke up and said, 'Well, the Germans do come here, for a glass of wine at the restaurant, but there's no big garrison around here.'

"Then they provided me with clothes—a French beret, and some old pants and shirt and shoes. After a while there, I got restless, so one day the girl handed me a broom and I swept out the restaurant. They had to go half a block to the square to bring water, and I'd help out with that and chopping a little wood for the stove. And I was as close to the Germans as just looking out the front window and seeing them coming up and down the street. One day, I'm sweeping out front in my little French outfit, and some young German boys came in to get some wine. I tried to be as inconspicuous as possible and just kind of swept back toward the kitchen until I got out of their line of sight.

"The electricity was off most of the time, but it would come on for eight to ten minutes, three or four times a day, and I would have a chance to listen to the BBC [British Broadcasting Corporation] talk about the war. And then the French news would come on, but it was, of course, run by the Germans and the father got the impression that the Germans were pushing the Americans back into the sea!

"I thought, well, hell, I better get up there before there's another Dunkirk. I didn't realize it at the time, but they were very much in jeopardy for hiding an Allied airman. The girl provided me with a bicycle. And they fixed me up a basket with some kind of chicken and a flask of wine in a worn-out leather-type thing. The kid went to the town hall and brought back an identity card—all French were registered with the Germans.

"When I first saw it, I thought, this looks pretty new-looking, you know. How's this going to go over? But I set out for the main road, a couple miles away. While I was still with them at the house, the kid found a French-English dictionary, and I sat down and, using it, asked them for directions and then memorized the road I was going to take and all the cities I was going to go through to get to where the old man thought the British were at the time. And the Americans.

When I first hit the main road, I saw some German trucks parked down the road. When I turned to start going north, I pedaled on a few miles and there was a German truck parked on the side of the road. A German jumped out and started gesturing, talking to me—I got the idea he wanted to know if I had seen some trucks back down the road, and I said, 'Oui,' and that seemed to pacify him so I went on my way. I went through several cities that were literally flat on the ground—bridges knocked out so you had to work your way around, carrying your bicycle. I saw a lot of Germans on the road and a lot of French people, refugee-type of thing, heading south. There was one occasion where the Germans and their highly camouflaged trucks were going real slow and they passed me several times. They'd stop, and I'd go on. To me, they were just kids—looked like boy scouts. They motioned to me to kind of hang onto the truck, and I did, hitching a ride. And I was laughing to myself hilariously, 'What if they knew who I am!'

"Another time, I hadn't had a bath in quite a few days and there was a nice stream way off to the side of the road and I took off all my dirty clothes, scrubbed myself as good as I could with some of the sand on the bottom and tried to get the clothes a little clean. Two French boys came along and were pretty mad about this. Turned out they thought I was on their property to rob them or something.

"I kept on pedaling. I stayed one night at a monastery. And they were *real* nice to me. In fact, they brought out a package of Lucky Strike Green [cigarettes]. They brought out a pint of—what was it? Green River?—that we used to buy for 98 cents a pint. We just had a real fine time. I was going to stay a while, but the next morning, a priest came up the road on his bicycle and said I had better get going because his parish had been very badly hit and a lot of his people killed.

"So I got out of there—I knew the Germans had a curfew on from daylight to dark, so I was always off the road by dark. One time I slept in a hayloft. The chickens woke me up before dawn. I remember that. Another time I was in a barn that had one of those two-wheel drays that you hook a horse up to. It got pretty cold that night. The kid had given me a knife before I left, and this little dray had a canvas-type top. So I cut out that top and wrapped up in it, saying, well, at least a Frenchman contributed to the Allied war effort.

"I was on the road four days before I finally made contact with the British, between the cities of Caen and Bayeux. They didn't believe me. For one thing, I did not have my dog tag on me. Finally, an American liaison officer with this British outfit shot me enough questions to know I was a Texan. I had gone to A & M. I knew who won the New Year's Day game of 1940, 'cause I was there. And a few other little things. One final thing: when I was able to tell him that Pegasus, the flying red horse, is the big symbol sitting on top of the Mobil Building in downtown Dallas, he said, 'Well, you are bound to be a Texan to know all those things.' "

On August 25, 1944, French and American forces entered Paris. On September 3, freedom came to Antwerp, then Europe's largest port, and to Brussels, where a delirious citizenry gave the liberators their most rousing welcome of the war. Capture of Antwerp had been expected greatly to ease the Allied armies' growing supply problem, but the Germans not only blew up port installations, but held tenaciously onto the approaches of the Schelde estuary, rendering the port unusable. As a result, supply problems intensified. On August 31, Patton's Third Army literally ran out of gas at the banks of the Meuse River.

On the German side, the fuel shortage was reaching calamitous proportions. At an airport in Werneuchen, east of Berlin, the commander of a training company reported that his student pilots could have flight practice only for an hour every week because of fuel shortages.

The employment of the Me-262 marked the first use of jet aircraft in combat. Its performance was better suited for combatting Allied bombers than dogfighting Allied single engine fighters.

Johannes Steinhoff comments: "Our young pilots, during the last six months of the war, flew two missions and then they were dead. Only the veterans survived."

Remarkably, Germany's shattered industry continued to turn out airplanes. The problem now was pilots, more than fuel or planes.

Galland had calculated that, on the average, it took one German fighter plane lost over Germany to shoot down one bomber. But where many Germans could parachute to safety to fly again, being downed spelled death or captivity for virtually all of the Allied crews. And indeed, in 1944 alone, the U.S. 8th Air Force lost 2,400 bombers; RAF Bomber Command lost 55,000 dead—more British officers than in "the lost generation" of World War I's trench warfare slaughters.

In an attempt to put pilots in their fighter planes during August virtually all Luftwaffe bomber units were disbanded and their pilots rushed through fighter training. Galland worked methodically to build up his force to 2,000 fighters, holding them back from force-emasculating combat with the gargantuan Allied fighter armadas. His goal was to strike a series of mighty blows against the American bomber armadas. He believed that if he were to destroy at least 400 four-engined Fortresses and Liberators with each concentrated attack, the stunned Allied leadership might back off on the bombing raids grinding down the German war machine.

On September 2, 1944, JG.52 veterans of the Battle of Britain and countless Russian campaigns scored their 10,000th victory. The wing had among its alumni such aces as Erich "Bubi" Hartmann and Johannes "Macki" Steinhoff. (For comparative purposes, though such comparisons are necessarily imperfect, one of JG.52's old adversaries, RAF 11 Group, which bore the brunt of the fighting during the Battle of Britain, ended the war with 5,524 victories.)

The old ways of dueling and dying in the skies would continue down to the end of this war. But a new era was about to dawn.

"Well, the classical battle which took place at the beginning of the war, where you would see the whites of the eyes of your opponent, that was gone forever."

Macki Steinhoff goes on to describe the last great dramatic development of the air war over Europe—the introduction of the jet aircraft. The plane was the Messerschmitt 262, the world's first jet to see aircraft-to-aircraft combat. The Me.262 represented the culmination of a desperate race with the British and, to a lesser extent, the Americans. The British actually won the race, but it was the Me.262 that would dominate among the jets of World War II. The Me.262 actually could have—and should have—seen combat much sooner.

Adolf Galland, who had so much to do with making this plane happen, tells the story: "Very early on, we had a secret project in effect—the development of jet fighters and missiles. We were hoping, and I was hoping, that this would lead to a balance of forces. We could never have achieved or approached the sheer mass of Russian, English, and American aircraft. Any attempt to do so would have been condemned to failure."

The Me.262 project was launched in 1938 and the first test flight was made on March 25, 1942. Adolf Galland flew his first test flight in the plane in May of 1943. "It was," he recalled, "a really grandiose experience. I knew this was the beginning of a completely new age, a new generation of aircraft." Three months later, on July 23, the aircraft was presented to Hermann Goering, and

Steinhoff was lucky to have escaped this Me-262 late in the war.

Inset:
The Luftwaffe could have severely damaged concentrated Allied bombing efforts over Germany had Me-262 production and deployment been limited to the fighter version rather than the fighter-bomber version wanted desperately by Hitler.

on November 26, to Hitler. Adds Galland scornfully, "At one point, this project had even been banned by Hitler because it couldn't be realized within one year." Actually seeing the jet in flight changed that.

"I was present," Galland continues, "when Hitler was shown the 262 in East Prussia. It was very impressive, a low-level flight doing speeds of about 850 kilometers per hour. Hitler was surprised and asked Messerschmitt, 'Is this plane capable of carrying bombs?' Messerschmitt answered, 'Yes, Mein Führer, yes, a 250-kilogram bomb.' 'Good,' said Hitler, 'then this is the blitz bomber with which I will beat back the invasion.' Then a struggle began to negate the use of this aircraft as a bomber, for which it wasn't at all suited. It had no mechanism for dropping bombs. It didn't have the right center of gravity. The right sighting device could not be installed. All these things would still not have converted this jet fighter into a blitz bomber.

"What happened then was that all bomber groups had to give up their bombers and the jets were introduced instead. The squadrons were gathered around Prague towards the middle of 1944 and an attempt was made to rearm with the 262. Everyone who came before HItler discussed the question of the 262.

"The fact of the matter was that the only way to counter the absolute superiority in sheer numbers that the Allies possessed was through a technological superiority. And this the 262 possessed. It was at least 170 kilometers faster than the fastest propeller fighter. But Hitler issued an order that any use of the 262 other than as a blitz bomber would be forbidden and couldn't be discussed.

"Well, how many 262s were produced? About 1,400. But they weren't all flight-ready. Most of them were destroyed on the ground, and most of them weren't equipped properly. Only 20 to 30 aircraft were used as fighters. We were never able to get more in the air than that. Those that weren't destroyed on the ground, the bombers used them to train, except for one unit. One unit did drop a few bombs during the invasion, but without causing any effect or damage. So this technically superior weapon was completely useless. And this came as a result of Hitler's short-sighted orders.

"If you asked me if Goering took part in this, I would have to say yes. Even though he knew this was the worst possible decision, his position was so weak that he couldn't afford to resist any of Hitler's orders. So he played along with this nonsense only to maintain his position.

"Now, you can ask me, please, what would have happened if all the jet planes were utilized as fighters, the 262s, the 163s, what would have happened then? It could have been done earlier, it was technically possible to do this earlier. Their development hadn't been given priority. We conducted some studies and we came to the conclusion that if we had 200 to 250 jet fighters, we could have stopped the daily raids by the Americans."

That, Galland says, is the good news. The bad news: "If we had done that, the invasion would have been postponed, and the Russians would have conquered even more German and European territory. So although the Führer's orders were completely wrong from a technological, technical point of view, they were actually to the advantage of Germany and Europe!"

Others have argued that Hitler had the right idea—a bomber which could strike targets anywhere in Britain with impunity—but at the wrong time. And he persisted because of his obsession with inflicting damage on the British rather than preventing the continuing destruction of his own country. Trouble was that by the time the plane was operational, Germany was about to lose its cross-Channel ports, and by then, had suffered not only overwhelming air power inferiority but needed most of all to protect what was left of its bomb-shattered armaments industry. "That shortsighted order," Galland goes on, "caused further delay in the design and building of the jet fighters and the rocket fighters. The result was to further delay production."

It was not until late summer of 1944 that the first Me.262-A1 appeared in the skies over Western Europe.

Cunningham, middle, with S/L W.P. Green and S/L E.D. Crew.

Galland managed to assign a few of the new marvels to take on the impudent Mosquitoes on their night-bombing runs on Berlin. RAF Wing Commander John Cunningham observes: "If the war had gone on a bit longer, it [the Me.262] would have wreaked havoc at night against the Mosquito. The Mosquito had had almost a free run to Berlin and back by virtue of its speed alone. But the Me.262 would have given it a bit of a hard run. It was an impressive aircraft."

Canadian ace Andrew Mackenzie recounts seeing the first one: "We were flying along at about 350 to 400 miles an hour, and this jet came down through our formation, and I just saw this thing go by. He didn't shoot at us, I think they were just harassing—a morale thing or something, trying to show us what a fast airplane they had. We all said, 'What the Christ is that?!' Back at debriefing, we found out that it was the first German jet we had ever seen."

Mackenzie was right to be startled. The Me.262 whizzed through Allied fighter formations fully 100 miles an hour faster than they were flying. And he was lucky they didn't open fire on him that day: The Me.262 packed four, fuselage-mounted 30 mm monster cannons, later adding 24 of the new, high-velocity R4M air-to-air rockets, ripple-fired to form a dense pattern. One salvo was usually enough to finish off a Flying Fortress. Peak speed, generated by twin Junkers Jumo engines, was 539 mph at 13,425 feet, range 652 miles, and the ceiling 37,664 feet. It could climb to 30,000 feet in only seven minutes.

Although only 1,430 were built, and most of those not until 1945, no fewer than 22 Luftwaffe pilots became jet aces in the waning months of the war. Tops among them was Col. Heinz Bar. Born in Leipzig in March 1913, "Pritzl" Bar flew some 1,000 missions in just about every theater of the European war: France, the Battle of Britain, Malta, North Africa, Russia, and now the Western front. Second only to the great Hans-Joachim Marseilles in downing the most British and American aircraft, Bar pushed his overall tally to 200 in April 1944, including 20 four-engined American bombers. Shot down and shot up repeatedly, he ended the war with 220 kills—including 16 at the controls of an Me.262.

Like Bar, most other jet aces were veterans of pistons. Macki Steinhoff added six jet victories to the 170 he had already racked up in piston planes. He tells what it was like to make the transition:

"Transition? We were ordered to an airfield near Munich. We trained for one day. We were told where the gas pedal is, and the next morning we got into the plane and flew it!"

He adds: "But I have to emphasize that these were all extremely experienced veterans. Younger pilots had problems. And I have to emphasize also that the aircraft was not operationally ready. It was very risky to fly this thing." Steinhoff refers to engines hastily developed and not fully tested. But there were other perils.

"When we started," Steinhoff explains, "the plane took about 3-4-5 minutes to achieve battle speed. At this point, we were vulnerable. American fighters would keep a lookout over the airfields and they would make use of this early phase when we were vulnerable to get at us."

Jim Goodson was among those predators, leading a squadron of P-51 Mustangs. "When the jets and rocket planes turned up," he relates, "we realized the only way we could catch them was on the ground. So I would take my group down to the deck and just spread out, looking for airfields. On my last mission, we found an airfield with two rocket planes on it and I went

down to take them out. But, of course, the flak from German airfields then was just like a curtain coming up, and I got hit, and that's how I got shot down.''

Americans weren't the only ones waiting to pounce. Ragnar Dogger, flying a Spitfire in one of the RAF's Norwegian squadrons, remarks: "We had standing patrols where they [the jets] were stationed. So we tried to shoot them down when they landed, without any engines going."

Once airborne, it was a different story. RAF Wing Commander John Wray—flying Tempest Vs—comments: "You'd got to be above them, by at least 3,000 feet, because all we could do was open everything up and dive. But as soon as they knew you were there, they were off like shit off a shovel, so we just had that moment when you could catch the chap, when he couldn't see you, when you came down going like the clappers hoping to get close enough to get in a burst before he saw you. He just had to open his throttle and he was gone!'' (Still, Tempests managed the best score against the jets, downing 20 of them.)

Steinhoff resumes: "But please bear in mind, the 262 was a fantastic technical breakthrough. We were taking off from grass fields with low-pressure tires. We had fantastic armament. We had functioning air-to-air [radar] identification. But it was not operational in our model sense now. We had quite a few losses.''

Indeed, Me.262 losses were greater than its victories, mainly because, while it was superb against bombers, it was not agile enough for fighters. The 262s were only a few weeks in the air when a Spitfire 14 shot down the first one on October 5, 1944. Steinhoff, one of Galland's hand-picked jet fighter pioneers, clarifies: "To kill a fighter with a 262 was difficult. The turning radius was miserable, and aerodynamically, the plane had a very high surface stress. Against fighters, he shot immediately, because his turning radius was less cumbersome than ours.''

Allied fighter planes had another advantage. RAF Wing Commander Douglas Benham—flying a Spit 14—describes it, reinforcing Steinhoff's point about the precarious state of development of the 262's engines.

"The Spitfire 14's ceiling was about 41,000 feet, incredibly high. At that

The Gloster Meteor.

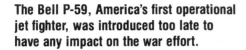

The Bell P-59, America's first operational jet fighter, was introduced too late to have any impact on the war effort.

The Me-163 Comet.

altitude, it's incredibly cold. We had no pressurized cabins or cockpits and everything used to freeze up on the inside of the cockpit, and you'd get ice forming on the inside of the cockpit canopy, for example.

"On one of those trips, we were vectored onto an Me.262 and he was at about 36,000 feet. Now, if we timed our dive right, the Spitfire could almost get up to about Mach.9, which is well over 700 mph and faster than the 262 flying straight and level. So as long as you timed your descent to come up straight behind him, you had a fair chance of shooting him down because he couldn't get away. He couldn't outmaneuver you and he couldn't outspeed you because you were coming down from 5,000 feet above him.

"If you failed to get your tactics correct, we used to just chase the 262 as long as we could because we knew that after about ten minutes of flat-out, his jet engines would just blow up because they couldn't stand the high revs for any length of time. We knew this and we deliberately would go flat-out after him, gradually losing, going farther and farther back, of course. But, never mind, we knew eventually he would blow up, which he invariably did. Our 41 Squadron shot down about 6 or 7 Me.262s, and we never had a shot fired at us by them."

Steinhoff clarifies: "We didn't think of this aircraft as a fighter against fighters. It was the best weapon to kill a bomber, and bombers were our enemies. We had to do everything in our power to prevent the last German city from being pulverized. We attacked mostly in formation of three to six aircraft, from the rear, because on collision-course approach, our speed was too fast. Having this fantastic armament, to kill a B-17 was not difficult. If you placed the B-17 in the reticle of your gunsights, and let the rockets go at a distance of a thousand meters, making sure that the rockets covered the entire breadth of the bomber, this was a kill. It was relatively easy."

At least one Allied pilot rejoices at Hitler's meddling with the development of the Me.262. The great American ace Francis S. Gabreski speaks up: "Yes, I'm very happy the Me.262 didn't come out, say, about two or three years earlier, because if it had, the outcome of the war may have been a little different." Gabreski was a P-47 pilot. How would his plane stack up against the German jet? "If you were going to match one against the other, the ultimate result would be disastrous for the P-47."

As indicated, the Me.262 was neither the only nor the first German jet. On July 3, 1939, test pilot Erich Warsitz flew a rocket-powered Heinkel He.176 for onlookers who included Hitler and Goering. On August 27, 1939, a Heinkel He.178 took off from an airstrip near Berlin to become the first jet-propelled airplane to fly. Goering missed that and didn't bother to attend another demonstration two months later.

The Me.262 was the world's first jet fighter in combat. The Arado Ar.234 was the world's first jet bomber. Nicknamed the "Blitz-bomber," its appearance in the summer of 1944 eased Hitler's resistance to producing 262s for their intended role: fighter plane.

A twin-engine, high-wing monoplane, the Arado could make only 460 mph, but that was fast enough to outrun Allied fighters, as it demonstrated effortlessly on its first combat missions: reconnaissance flights in July of 1944. Mounting two 20 mm cannon, the Ar.234B carried a 4,415-pound bomb load. Range was relatively long (1,012 miles), but ceiling low (32,894 feet). Only a couple hundred were produced, in variations designed for pure reconnaissance, photo-reconnaissance, target search and signaling, and, of course, bombing.

During the last three months of the war, the Germans put another jet fighter in the air: the Heinkel He.162 Volksjager (People's Fighter), code-named "Salamander." Fortunately for the Allies, once again it was a case of too little, too late. Even lighter than the Me.163 (5,480 pounds), its top speed was 521 mph. And Allied pilots could not count on hounding this plane until its engines exploded: it could operate for 85 minutes at full throttle at 36,000 feet. Though produced at widely dispersed plants, with Allied planes plastering Germany around the clock with bombs and Allied tanks already pushing into key industrial areas, only 116 were built.

The British got a head start on jet engines; Frank Whittle demonstrated one successfully in 1937. But it took the German aerial onslaught against Britain in 1940 to spur a jet fighter project into being, and it was not until May 1941—two years behind the Germans—that the British flew their first jet airplane, a Gloster E.28/29. A twin-jet like the Me.262, the first Gloster Meteor's maiden flight was in March 1943. The Meteor flew its first mission against incoming V-1 bombs on June 27, 1944, downing the first buzz-bomb on August 4. Armed with four 20 mm cannons, the Meteor had a top speed of 492 mph.

The U.S. entry in the World War II jet race was the Bell P-59. Eighty of these 412-mph fighters were produced, going mainly to the specially created 412th Fighter Group, but none in time to see combat action.

By the second week of September 1944, Allied armies held all of Belgium and Luxembourg, as well as a piece of Holland and much of France. American 1st Army patrols had actually crossed the German border near Aachen. Allied aircraft now operated from scores of bases on the Continent itself. During the August encirclement of 100,000 German troops in the Normandy hill region, the RAF's 2nd Tactical Air Force's Typhoons and Spitfires destroyed 3,000 German vehicles. As the German remnants fled in disarray, the TAF was taking out approximately 1,000 German vehicles per day. The rocket-firing Typhoons concentrated on the tanks, the Spitfires on the ''soft-skinned'' vehicles.

Roland Beamont led his wing of Tempests across the Channel when the

The 120th regiment, 30th Infantry seized this Luftwaffe airfield at Detmold, Germany for eventual Allied use.

order came to join the Second TAF. He recalls: "It was the order we were waiting for. I led the formation—48 Tempests, four squadrons line astern—from Norfolk across to Brussels. People on the ground said they looked rather good when we got there —obviously we wanted to show the flag a bit. Harry Broadhurst, the famous Battle of Britain fighter pilot who by that time was commander-in-chief of the 2nd Tactical Air Force, came to meet us, to greet his new wing. He told me to get all the guys together in a hangar, and then he got up and made a typical sort of Broadhurst speech which ended up by saying words to the effect that 'You guys better remember that over on this side, when you shoot at somebody in the air, he's liable to turn around and shoot back at you.' A reference, of course, to our home guard duties against the V-1s.

"At that very moment, the station intelligence officer came up with a telex and he passed it to me. See, I had sent off an element of 56th Squadron on a sector reconnaissance to find out what the war was about. I did that as soon as we got there, without waiting for Broadhurst. And the telex said that 56 engaged, claimed three FW.190s destroyed. So I passed it to Harry Broadhurst. He looked at it, grinned, and didn't say a word."

Beamont's own combat days, reaching back to November 1939 when he was posted to France, were about to end. On October 2, he shot down an FW.190, raising his score to ten. He was offered the opportunity to go back to Hawkers, where he helped in developing both the Typhoon and Tempest fighters. But he decided he would like to fly an even 100 missions before "retiring." On his very next mission, number 95, he was shot down over enemy territory and spent the rest of the war in Europe as a prisoner. Freed by the Russians, he returned to England to form a Tempest wing to fight in the Pacific, but the war ended before it became operational. After the war, he went on to become chief test pilot for English Electric, flying the prototype Canberra and Lightning, setting a cross-Atlantic record in the Canberra.

At this time, Sir Harry Broadhurst was mainly occupied trying to help unscramble another mess—the same kind he had faced as far back as North Africa, where he helped create the first RAF Tactical Air Force. The idea then, and now, was to coordinate air cover closely with ground operations. It didn't always work. This one was called MARKET GARDEN, the biggest air drop of troops ever made. It was Field Marshal Montgomery's bold (and highly controversial) plan to leap-frog over the German armies and seize a foothold on the North German plain beyond the Meuse and lower Rhine. From there, his British, Canadian, and American forces would be able to strike swiftly against the Ruhr, the heartland of Germany's war economy.

The idea was to send the American 82nd and 101st Airborne Divisions against the bridges at Eindhoven and Nijmegen, the 1st British Airborne, backed by a Polish brigade, against the more distant Rhine bridges at Arnhem.

The first part of the plan—MARKET—worked. The second—GARDEN—was a disaster. When it was over, nine days later, the British 1st Airborne Division had ceased to exist: more than 1,000 dead, 6,000 prisoners-of-war.

"MARKET GARDEN," Sir Harry relates, "was the biggest disaster. The problem was that airborne never planned with the Tactical Air Forces. I made myself very unpopular, which I was inclined to do—too young, really, to worry much over that." In fact, the failure of radios in RAF "control cars" had much to do with the agonizing spectacle of Typhoons circling helplessly overhead while desperate troops on the ground were unable to guide them to targets.

Broadhurst continues with a tale reminiscent of the moves he had made in

Lt. Forrest Fegan from Kankakee, Ill., a 9th Air Force P-47 driver, destroyed this -109 during the Third Reich's failed counteroffensive through Belgium. The -109 is burning from direct hits.

North Africa, three years earlier, to fuse air to ground power: "Once we crossed the Rhine, I insisted that we would have experienced squadron leaders in gliders with RAF radios so that, as soon as they landed, they could hop out, be in touch with what was going on, and talk to us, talk to the rocket Typhoons overhead. I went down there to watch it happen myself. That was the first time we'd planned the Tactical Air Force in with the airborne drop."

Bad weather in October and November limited Allied air operations, aggravating the monumental supply problems. The interlude gave the Germans the respite they needed to reinforce their West Wall defenses and prepare for a bold counteroffensive. The goal was the capture of Antwerp, 60 miles to the west, and with it, the isolation of the British 2nd and Canadian 1st Armies from their American allies, as well as the protection of the German V-2 rocket launch sites. Beginning on December 16, 1944, and raging for one full month, it would go down in history as the Battle of the Bulge.

Not only did Hitler throw newly reinforced Panzer divisions into this bold lunge, he also ordered Galland to commit the entire fighter forces he had been saving for his mighty blow against the bombers. The 2nd TAF alone was able to fly 15,000 sorties, many in weather which normally would have grounded them. Before it was over, the Germans had lost 100,000 dead, wounded or captured—as well as 1,000 aircraft.

Galland: "Of course, the morale of the fighting troops diminished. The assertion that by the end of 1944 the morale of the Luftwaffe was still very high cannot be taken seriously."

Allied pilots quickly learned how heavy the attrition had been on the ranks of their enemies. Ragnar Dogger relates an incident which took place on December 29, 1944: "In the morning, it didn't turn out so very good—we lost four pilots and shot down four just inside Germany. And then in the afternoon, we had another sweep with 12 planes. Halfway along the German border, we suddenly saw a large group of planes above us. The controllers hadn't said anything and we were certain they were Allied planes.

"Then suddenly, we discovered they were Germans. We attacked from below and shot down 12 of them and didn't lose any of ours. Later, we found out these planes were being flown to forward bases by inexperienced pilots, so it didn't take very much to shoot them down, which was a pity."

There was a sequel to the story: "When we landed, there was a telegram from the other Norwegian squadron, the 332. They had been sent on rest for a week in England and to take some kind of course. The telegram said something like, 'Happy New Year, we made the best score ever on this course.' So naturally, we sent them a telegram that said, "We are proud of you—and we just got 16 Jerries today.' They never forgave us for that."

With that final great gamble lost, Hitler left his last field headquarters and returned to Berlin on January 16, 1945. With the great marble walls of his massive Chancellery now in bomb-blasted ruins, he went to his final headquarters—a warren of underground bunkers, 50 feet below the Chancellery. In a very real sense, the tomb in which he lived out his last days symbolized the larger one his country had now become.

11 CLOSING THE RING

On August 15, 1943, the Japanese ended their occupation of two small islands near the tip of the Aleutians, that chain of volcanic islands arching 1,600 miles into the Bering Sea from Alaska. It was as close as they would ever come to the North American continent.

Takeo Tanimizu had just graduated from the 17th Flight Training Course when he was posted to the 6th Air Group. For him, the Aleutians were a blessing in disguise.

"Our unit," he explains, "was supposed to land on Midway, along with army pilots. But two days before the main group sailed, we were assigned to a decoy force aboard the aircraft carrier *Kosuga Maru* in the Sea of Japan bound for the island of Attu in the Aleutian Islands. The plan was to let the enemy attack us and draw them near to the Aleutian Islands.

"But they did not attack us, they attacked our main force instead. So we returned. We went there as a decoy, and we—the decoy unit—survived."

With the Americans now back on those remote outposts, bombers would begin attacking Japan's northernmost Kurile Islands.

Into the skies over the far-flung battlefields of the vast Pacific Ocean and in the sprawling China-Burma-India (CBI) Theater came new and deadlier aircraft.

On January 16, 1943, the first Grumman Hellcat touched down on the flight deck of the big aircraft carrier *Essex*. The plane more than answered the prayers of U.S. carrier pilots, badly mauled during the 1942 Battles of the Coral Sea and Midway, for a fighter that would stand up to the Japanese Zeros. With a top speed of 375 mph at 20,052 feet, the Hellcat was slightly faster than the Zero in level flight, and faster at altitudes above 10,000 feet. Despite its great girth, the Hellcat could actually outclimb the Zero, thanks to its 2,000-horsepower Pratt & Whitney engine. Moreover, it not only could outdive its Japanese opponents, but could take punishment the frail Zero could not. In firepower, too, the Hellcat was a dramatic improvement over the Wildcat: each of its six .50-caliber machine guns fired 400 rounds of ammunition.

The Zero, in fact, retained only two advantages against the Hellcat: the ability to out-turn the American plane, and, at speeds below 230 mph, to outmaneuver it.

The Hellcat first saw combat on August 3 striking the Japanese air and naval outpost of Marcus Island, an isolated spit of land in the central Pacific. David McCampbell, commanding Air Group 15 aboard the *Essex*, said that for him, the Hellcat "was the finest fighter plane we had during the war unless the plane was shot up so bad and they had to push it over the side or something like that."

McCampbell knew what it means to be that badly shot up. He describes Air Group 15's first combat. "For two days, we hit Marcus Island, but there were no planes there at the time. It was very discouraging actually because what we were doing was giving those people on the ground gunnery practice—and they did shoot the hell out of us. I lost my wingman on the second mission over Marcus, and I got shot up pretty badly myself. I had a belly tank on fire, and the fire then got up into my fuselage, burned up all my hydraulic fluid, my radio gear, and a couple of my control wires. When I got it back to the ship, they took one look at my plane and pushed it over the side."

It was during these operations that the Hellcat got on the victory scoreboard. One piloted by Lt. Richard L. Loesch, seconded by his wingman, shot down a large "Emily" (Kawanishi H8K) flying boat on September 1, 1943. Within a few weeks, 47 carrier-based Hellcats raided Wake Island in a predawn raid. They were met by 27 Zeros. Robert W. Duncan downed three, while a fourth was shot down by a man who knew his target, Lt. M.C. "Boogie" Hoffman; Hoffman had test-flown a captured Zero some months before. Still another was flamed by Alexander Vraciu, flying his first aerial combat mission.

Though a novice, Vraciu was well prepared. After finishing flight training, he had the good fortune to fly wingman to the navy's first ace of the war and winner of the Medal of Honor, Lt. Comdr. Edward H. "Butch" O'Hare, in Navy Fighting Squadron 6. Now he was an element leader in O'Hare's division. Vraciu's radio was out when they spotted the Zeros.

"There were three of them headed for Wake and we had high cover on them. The way my wingman waggled his wings and turned in, I knew I would take the inside plane and he would go after the outside plane. I was, I guess, pretty eager, so I think I opened fire a little farther out than I was taught to do. If you fill up your gunsight, that's in close. Opened fire and pieces started falling about and burning. I felt like I fired right straight through the airplane.

"Butch and his wingman went after the left plane and they ended up below the cloud cover. My wingman and I, by the time we finished the run, were still above the cloud cover, and I looked to see where he was, and he wasn't there. So I still kept my eye on the number one plane and saw it land and skid off the runway over at Wake Island. And not knowing what had happened to Butch and having gone below the clouds, my wingman and I went on and strafed, and I burned the plane on the ground. Then I saw a 'Betty' [Mitsubishi G4M2, a twin-engined land-based Japanese navy bomber] as I was zigzagging across the field to avoid antiaircraft fire. I made another run and burned it also.

"Then I went back to the ship and caught royal holy hell for not keeping my eye on what happened. He was right—I deserved it."

Deserved or not, Vraciu was one of the first Hellcat pilots privileged to paint the symbol of the Rising Sun on the fuselage of his plane.

Of 6,477 Japanese aircraft shot down by carrier-based planes, 4,947 were downed by Hellcats. If land-based and marine Hellcats are added, the total becomes 5,156 victories.

The Japanese uncorked a surprise or two of their own. In trials during the summer of 1942, the Kawasaki outclassed the Bf.109E, Nakajima Ki-43-II, Nakajima Ki-44-I, and a captured Curtiss P-40E. Yet its remarkable performance was marred to the end by engine-tuning problems, causing frequent breakdowns.

The year 1943 saw another American plane enter the war, although navy obtuseness kept it off carrier decks until April 1944. (The navy wrongly believed the plane was unsuitable for carrier operations.) The plane was the Vought F4U-1 Corsair, an inverted gull-winged craft that would go down in history as one of the best fighters of World War II. Corsairs flew 64,051 wartime missions—54,470 from land, 9,581 from carriers—destroying 2,140 enemy aircraft against the loss of only 189 Corsairs.

By the time the Corsair was in combat, it could reach 424 mph at 20,052 feet, had fairly long "legs" (a 1,041 mile range), and packed four 20 mm cannon. A later variant, the F4U-4, introduced at the end of 1944, was even faster: 445 mph, a very high ceiling (41,710 feet), with six machine guns as well as a 2,000-pound bomb load.

The first time Roy M. "Butch" Voris saw the USS *Saratoga* he was eight years old. He was hooked for life. The next time he saw the *Saratoga*, he was a navy pilot making his first carrier landing. One of the first planes he flew was a Curtiss Helldiver. Later, he went on to Wildcats. "Now that was a tremendous

Kenneth Walsh, medal of honor winner, downed 20 enemy aircraft during the war, emerging as the Marine Corps' fourth highest-ranking ace.

Above:
Satoshi Anabuki said Americans lacked a strong will to fight after setbacks at the outset of the Pacific war.

fighting machine," Butch states, "responsible, I believe, for 75 percent or so of all aircraft shot down in the Pacific during the war."

Butch Voris is no idle commentator on the matter of aircraft. After the Hellcat, he flew Corsairs—"the hose-nose," as he describes it—and still later Grumman's Bearcat ("a beautiful machine, all engine, propeller, and performance"). Next he flew the F8U Crusader, until tapped to organize, train, and direct the navy's demonstration flying team, the "Blue Angels."

Satoshi Anabuki began his combat career against the U.S. in the Philippines. He went on to become the highest-scoring Japanese army ace of the war, and seventh overall Japanese ace—51 kills in all. "At the outbreak of the war, Zero fighters had beaten the Americans badly. And that defeat had unnerved them. In the Philippines, the U.S. air force lacked the will to fight."

Now, a year later in Burma, he found a different enemy—hardened in battle, flying new and better aircraft. Anabuki explains: "In Eastern India, the Royal Air Force's will to fight was greater than the Americans'. However, at Kunming [China], Maj. General Chennault and the U.S. air force and his unit were tough opponents. He commanded organized battle very well. So we had to be on guard against his attacks."

Chennault was a master teacher of tactics, unequalled anywhere in the war. The core of those tactics was the formation of four echelons of four planes each. The leading flight was the assault flight, the others were support flights, each capable of breaking into pairs when engaged in combat. Anabuki concurs in their effectiveness. "The British, with their Hurricanes, chose to engage us in dogfights. So they played into our hands. But the China-based U.S. air force launched organized attacks, with their mass power and by formation flight. We suffered greater losses from them because of that."

Manpower, resources, and strategic commitment were all in short supply in the Allied camp in Southeast Asia. To remedy this, the dynamic British vice admiral Lord Louis Mountbatten was appointed supreme commander of the South East Asia Command (SEAC), with "Vinegar Joe" Stilwell appointed as his deputy.

Meanwhile, Washington settled a long-festering interservice dispute, and in April 1943 Operation CARTWHEEL emerged: Adm. Chester W. Nimitz was given command of the entire Pacific Theater, General MacArthur was left with his Southwest Pacific Area, and Adm. William F. ("Bull") Halsey headed the South Pacific.

But by the time they were ready to move, they faced a vastly more frightening challenge. From his headquarters at Rabaul, Gen. Hitoshi Imamura had been busy fortifying his island redoubts. Sometimes he succeeded, sometimes not.

On March 2, 1943, Imamura's 51st Division was en route from Rabaul to Lae when U.S. reconnaissance planes spotted it. B-17 Flying Fortresses attacked at high level, sinking only one ship. But the next day, tactics taught by MacArthur's new air chief, Gen. George C. Kenney, paid off. Kenney urged his pilots to forget the rule book and be innovative. Taking over the 5th Air Force in August 1942, Kenney began by establishing rapport with his men. (He is shown with his pilots outside their officer's club on New Guinea in 1943 with a sign: "Beneath these portals pass the hottest pilots in the world.") He also coached his pilots to go in low, fight in packs, and attack with guns and fragmentation bombs. His men were the first to perfect a tactic called "skip bombing"—bouncing bombs off the water and onto their targets. He later specialized in "parafrag" bombing—small fragmentation bombs attached to parachutes—a technique that ultimately enabled the 5th to claim more than 1,000 enemy airplanes destroyed. They did so well, Tokyo Radio dubbed him "the Beast" and his men "a gang of gangsters."

Now, with that Japanese convoy virtually intact, Kenney's men pounced. When the Battle of the Bismarck Sea was over, the 5th's planes had sunk all the troop transports and four of the eight destroyer escorts to boot.

By mid-1943, the Allies realized that Japan could not be strangled into submission by choking off its supply lifelines. Men and machines would have to do the job on the home islands. The Allies would have to recapture the Philippines and oust the Japanese from their island fortresses in Micronesia—the Gilberts, Marshalls, Carolines, and Marianas.

Of the 16,353,659 Americans who fought in World War II, only 431 were winners of the Medal of Honor, the nation's highest award. Kenneth A. Walsh, USMC, was one of them.

Walsh is proud that he himself climbed through every rank from private to lieutenant colonel. "When the war came along, I was offered a commission in reserve status. I told them I did not enlist in the Marine Corps to be in the reserves!" Meanwhile, he honed his flying skills, everything from scout planes to dive bombers to Wildcat fighters. Then came the Vought F4U Corsairs.

Ken Walsh's first kill was in the Russell Islands. "It was on April 1st, 1943, and I was on combat air patrol with seven Corsairs. Going on to close to two hours, we were relieved by six P-38s. I turned course to return to Guadalcanal when, suddenly, there was some commotion over the radio. I looked back over my left shoulder and the 38s had got pounced. They were badly outnumbered by a number of Zeros.

"Well, I alerted my flight to prepare to intercept. I turned to climb, and there was a wild mêlée going on. I decided to climb into it at high speed, and as I progressed, a Zero came right down in front of me, off my bow, and for a split second I couldn't but marvel at the beautiful configuration. It was the first time I ever saw a Zero that close up.

"But this was kill. I lined up and used a full-deflection charge, but couldn't get quite enough deflection on it. But my wingman, Lieutenant Raymond on that particular mission, was on the inside of the turn and he fired when I did.

He had the right deflection and shot down the plane. Shot him down, in flames.

"Raymond stuck with me after that. At twelve o'clock, right above me, I approached a Zero, below-rear, and shot him down. It was Raymond's first kill, and it was my first air victory." Twenty more would follow, until Ray Walsh emerged as the Marine Corps' fourth-ranking ace and a recipient of the Medal of Honor.

The capture of New Georgia was expected to take one month and involve one division. Instead, the 10,000 Japanese defenders held off four U.S. divisions for two months, primarily because the Japanese succeeded in slipping ashore thousands of fresh troops. Attempts to break up the convoys were repeatedly foiled, mainly because of a new Japanese weapon: an oxygen-fueled "Long Lance" torpedo, capable of taking a half-ton warhead 20 miles without a telltale track on the surface.

Army P-38 pilot George Chandler, from Holly, Colorado, was one of the pilots thrown into the desperate campaign to block the Japanese reinforcements. "They called it the Battle of Kula Gulf. Early the next morning after the battle they called us from the navy dugout and said, 'There's a Japanese destroyer that is crippled. And it's out in the slot. B-25s were assigned for a daylight takeoff to go up there and skip-bomb it and sink it, and eight P-38s were assigned to cover those bombers. And they said, 'We don't know what else is up there after this night battle—we don't know what other crippled ships may be up there.' They told us we had no friendly shipping in that slot at all.

"So we go up there on the deck and we know they've got a lot of Zero fighters, so we're nervous. The B-25s did a perfect job—they went in and they skip-bombed that destroyer and it exploded and just blew up. We were just all happy and bloodthirsty as we could be, and said, 'Let's go get some more of them.'

"The B-25s went on up around Vella Lavella, and as we came around, heading down towards our landing at Rendova, we saw all our ships there and three Japanese motor torpedo boats going along at a very rapid clip and, above them, about eight Zeros circling. We don't have any communications channel with the bombers—we can only talk to ourselves and our own controllers. So the bombers get set for a bomb-run attack on these motor torpedo boats, and we get set to keep the Zeros off the B-25s.

"And about that time, our squadron leader calls us and says, 'Hold it! Those aren't Zeros. Those are navy Wildcats!—F4F fighters. So those have got to be our own PT boats. So you P-38s, hold your fire.' The Wildcats recognized the P-38s, of course—so distinctive in its shape. But nobody's talking to anybody; we can't talk to the bombers, and we can't talk to the navy pilots. We can see what's happening, but there's nothing we can do about it.

"So we watched the B-25s go in and we watched them just blow one PT boat all to hell. And the other two PT boats shot down one of the B-25s. And there, the Wildcats and the P-38s just circled around, watching in horror. And then everybody sort of agreed, that's a hell of a way to run the war. And we all went home."

When Munda was finally captured on August 1, the Allies had advanced only 200 miles from Guadalcanal, and—except for Woodlark and Kiriwina—were still beyond fighter plane range of Rabaul. It appeared as if the Allies were going to have to slug it out all over again. Instead, Halsey's planners took a page from MacArthur's book: bypass Kolombangara and take lightly defended Vella Lavella beyond.

Ray Walsh was in the thick of the violent fighting over those steamy islands and shark-infested waters. He describes one mission, on August 12, 1943: "We were escorting a bunch of heavies—B-24 Liberators—from Guadalcanal clear to Bougainville. The Japs were waiting for us, and we had a running battle all the way from about 100 miles south of the target on into Bougainville and back down to Guadalcanal.

"During this battle, my wingman—Bill Johnson, a priceless wingman—really saved my life on that mission. We were protecting the bombers, making overhead gunnery runs, and on one of these passes, I had come on down when I got clobbered by a Zero who latched onto my tail. He put seven 20-millimeter cannon shells into my aircraft. Bill had to put my aircraft in his gunsight to get the lead. Now this was uncomfortable for Bill to do. But he did shoot the Zero off my tail. Another hit or two, and I never would have made it."

So far, Cartwheel's island fighting in the Solomons had cost the defenders 10,000 lives, the Americans 1,150 dead and 4,100 wounded, and the heaviest fighting was yet to come.

But, once again, the Tokyo Express was in operation, evacuating the marooned garrison from Kolombangara. Navy and marine fighter planes, destroyers, and PT boats hounded the nightly runs, sinking as many as 20 troop-barges in a single night.

It was during these operations that a skinny PT boat skipper named John F. Kennedy would make a name for himself as a hero. When his boat, PT 109, was rammed by the Japanese destroyer *Amagiri* in Blackett Strait, two of his 13 crew members were killed and one was badly burned. Despite his own back injury, Kennedy towed the man ashore by swimming with the man's tie between his teeth. Thanks to Lt. Arthur Reginald Evans, an alert Australian coastwatcher on nearby Kolombangara, Kennedy and his men were rescued after a six-day ordeal.

Meanwhile, Halsey maneuvered to move closer to his goal: he needed Bougainville. On November 1, men of the 3rd Marine and 37th Army Divisions swarmed ashore at Cape Torokina on Empress Augusta Bay, about halfway up Bougainville's west coast.

George Chandler was among those covering the Bougainville landings. He describes one particular mission, "the one I was most pleased with.

"On this day, November 8th, Captain—or Major?—Lawrence, our squadron commander, was leading eight of us, and I was leading number two flight. As I got off the ground, why I told Hank Lawrence, 'Okay, I'll meet you up there as fast as I can get there.' I got off the ground and my other three airplanes joined up and we were just high enough to get the radio transmissions from the destroyer off Bougainville that was our fighter controller.

"He called in and vectored Hank Lawrence in on many bogies. I quickly did a little mental calculation. When I tried to call my flight plan on my radio, I found I had a dead transmitter. I could listen, but I couldn't talk. So I motioned to the others that we're going to power—we had lots of fuel, the external tanks were full—so we went to almost full power.

"Hank Lawrence was already moving to meet this big flight of Japanese planes, and he didn't know we were coming, and I couldn't tell him. As we

The Grumman-built F6F Hellcat was faster and could outclimb the sleek, lightly armored Zero. Its ability to take punishment helped the manufacturer earn the name, "Grumman Iron Works."

got up there, I could see the enemy aircraft, about 150 of them, about 50 Zero fighters and about 100 bombers. So I slowed my flight up so we could drop the tanks and test-fire my guns.

"One of my wingmen says, 'God, I didn't know what was going on, but when I saw you fire those tracers, we knew we were into something.' So they all did the same. Well, I think the most exciting thing is that Hank Lawrence didn't know I was there—he didn't know anybody was coming to help him. But with just four airplanes, he didn't hesitate. He went right straight into the whole bunch of them.

"What he was doing was taking four P-38s and attacking the Zeros that were top cover and forcing them to turn and defend themselves against his attack. And Hank said afterwards, he said, 'I looked back to see what the Zeros were doing and all I could see was your four airplanes coming right in behind me.'

"Well, we harassed those Zeros—it was just eight of us making passes at them—to where the bombers got out ahead of them and the bombers got to Bougainville and there the marine fighters and our army P-40 fighters were all waiting for them, and here they were more or less unescorted, without fighters. And the P-40s and the marine fighters tore them all to pieces.

"The thing that made that mission turn out well for me was there were two Zeros going down in a steep dive, and I think they had bombs on instead of belly tanks 'cause they hadn't dropped them yet. And I had a lot of overtaking speed [and] I thought, 'Now, you don't dare go past an enemy fighter or you are the target. Instead of the hunter, you're the hunted. How can I get those guys and be sure of it? The surest way is the pilot himself. I won't shoot the airplane. I'll come up to where I can shoot at the pilot in the cockpit.'

"And when I came up to the first one I let fly and I could see the canopy just go all to pieces. And when the canopy goes all to pieces, so does that guy's head inside. So I went past him to the second one and did the same thing and pulled out."

The years go by: around 1950, Chandler attends a country club stag in his little town of Pratt, Kansas, and is introduced to a man named Rudy Fisher. "And," Chandler relates, "war stories came up, so I asked him where he was during the war. 'Well,' he said, 'I was down in the Solomons.' I said, 'That's interesting. What were you doing?' 'Well,' he said, 'I was on a troop ship and I was one of the infantry going ashore at Empress Augusta Bay.' And I said, 'When was that?' And he said, 'That was November the 8th. I remember it well.' And I said, 'What did you see there?' 'Oh,' he said, 'we had a big Japanese raid that day. And I was on the boat, and I looked up and I saw two'—he thought they were dive bombers—'coming right straight at us and I knew they had me. And then from someplace I never saw, here came a P-38, and *ka-wham*! He shot them both into the water.' I said, 'Rudy, I was the guy flying that airplane!'"

Within days of the Bougainville landings, 97 planes from the U.S. carriers *Saratoga* and *Princeton* badly damaged seven Japanese warships in Rabaul's harbor; General Kenney sent 27 B-24 Liberators and 58 P-38s to blast Rabaul's docks; and Halsey ordered pilots from five aircraft carriers to join MacArthur's planes pounding Rabaul. The next morning, reconnaissance photos showed Rabaul's Simpson Harbor entirely cleared of ships; the Japanese had pulled their navy back 800 miles to Truk.

But three Japanese aircraft carriers had managed to slip in and out of Rabaul undetected. They brought not only more planes and pilots, but crack pilots, Takeo Tanimizu among them.

"We received information," Tanimizu remembers, "that the Americans had landed on Bougainville, and we were assigned to Rabaul. When we got there we attacked, but it was not effective. We returned to our base and were preparing for another attack with 250 kilogram bombs.

"When we were transferred to Rabaul, all of us felt that we would never come back alive. Rabaul was a graveyard. We exchanged parting cups of water. [According to Japanese tradition, to meet in the world of the dead again, warriors exchanged cups of water on the eve of battle.] So many times a day, we woke up around three or four o'clock in the morning and flew for scouting. After we came back from scouting, we were not able to eat.

"Then there came the first enemy raids of the day. We flew up again. As for meals we ate riceballs. And we were tired because fighter pilots flew three or four times a day. Gradually we were losing weight. We received an injection of dextrose for our nutrition, but our appetite became less and less. Pilots had the most severe diarrhea. Pilots went up to an altitude where air became thinner. That was the hardest thing.

"In Rabaul, a pilot was ordered to fight until he died. Malaria. Fever. We could not rest. If a pilot would take a rest, he might have been called a traitor. So no one took rests. We became weaker and weaker. There was no one left in the end."

Sadamu Komachi—whose service took him all the way from Hawaii to the Indian Ocean—was among the Japanese pilots attempting to stave off the attacks on Rabaul. He won a commendation for his success in "bombing" B-24's using the Japanese Type-3 aerial bomb.

And Herbert "Trigger" Long, who joined the marines out of the University of Florida in 1941, was among the American pilots trying to make sure men

Grumman Hellcats often resorted to "Thach weave" maneuvers to protect each other's 6-o'clock positions from preying Japanese fighters.

like Komachi didn't get near the bombers. He recalls his biggest air battle: "We were flying off Guadalcanal, and the Japanese threw up 70-some Zeros from the field on Ballale [a tiny islet at the southeastern tip of Bougainville]. We had a 200-plane raid, and that was a pretty exciting thing. A lot of airplanes, a lot of parachutes, a lot of flames, a lot of crashes. It's a real show, if you could put a camera up in the middle of a dogfight of that type—it would be one of a kind."

Not until April 1944 was Bougainville neutralized: the Japanese lost 7,000 dead (some Japanese continued to fight until war's end), the Americans 1,000. But long before the island was secured, Allied planes were flying sorties over Rabaul and the rest of New Britain from three airfields at Torokina constructed by Seabees and U.S. army engineers.

The Japanese, meanwhile, were learning from the Americans. "Since the Battle of Bougainville," Tanimizu recalls, "our unit started four-plane formation attacks. Two-and-two formation flight was adopted, following the Americans' example, but the war was over before the Japanese got used to that new fighting strategy."

American pilots were busy refining their tactics, too, switching to stepped-down rather than stepped-up flights of four, so as to achieve better visibility. When attacked, they also resorted frequently to the "Thach-weave" maneuver—subdividing into pairs and then weaving in and out in a continuous series of turns thus closing off any opening for attack. Alex Vraciu comments: "Sometimes things got so wild that your wingman just couldn't stick with you. When you got separated like that, then the section leader and his wingman had to use the Thach-weave for protection."

The noose tightened. On December 26, 1943, MacArthur moved against New Britain, a huge jungle-wreathed island. He struck at Arawe, 270 miles from Rabaul on the island's south coast, and at Cape Gloucester, on the western tip. Both actions provoked heavy Japanese air response. By the end of 1943, Japanese air activity over Cape Gloucester had virtually ended. But not over Rabaul.

Like so many other combat pilots in this holocaust of a war, George Chandler went from boy to man with little space in between for growing up.

Now, decades later, he chokes up and weeps as he recounts yet another raid on Rabaul.

"I was leading the squadron that day. The bombers were at around 15,000 feet, and we were up above them, around 18,000-20,000 feet. I did it right, tactically, that day. They didn't get a Zero into the bombers.

"We had a couple of brushes with them, fired some guns, and kept 'em off the bombers. Heading home, I thought, 'Well, that turned out all right.' Now, Intelligence had warned us that the 5th Air Force had had some trouble with one particular Zero, not painted, but all silver in color. There was an extremely skillful pilot flyin' it. And to be aware that that guy was unusually aggressive—a real threat!

"We had joked about it, the usual braggadocio, you know, 'Let me have that SOB. I'll show him what this world's really like!'

"So, we're coming home, the fight was over. I was at about 12,000 feet, so I unbuttoned my oxygen mask and lit up that first cigarette. Old George let himself relax—the flight leader should *never* do that!.

"Then one of my guys says, 'Bogey at 12:00 high!' And my God! There was that silver Zero coming around out of those puffy clouds. And here he comes, and now I'm trying to get this thing out of automatic lean mixture, get the props back up, get the throttles back up, get the gun switches on, get the gunsight on—get this big machine, just a cruising airplane, to be a fighting airplane all over again.

"But I'm too slow, and I didn't get to that Zero in time. He went right through that bomber formation, and the lead bomber was lost. The whole crew was lost. And I'm the guy. . . . it still haunts me." (Forty-seven years have gone by; George Chandler's eyes fill with tears.)

In the end, the Allies decided to hold the New Britain territory they had and leave the 135,000 Japanese entrenched around Rabaul to sit out the rest of the war right there. Rabaul—the center of the gigantic spider web of atolls and islands sprawled across the Pacific, each studded with defensive armament—had been reduced to impotence. To make sure it stayed that way, MacArthur personally commanded an assault a few weeks later on the Admiralty Islands, some 300 miles northwest of New Britain.

They called them "the Black Sheep Squadron." Hard-living, hard-drinking, hard-fighting, they captured the world's imagination. Their leader fittingly cut his combat teeth in the flamboyant Flying Tigers. Gregory "Pappy" Boyington walked on the wild side even before joining the Tigers. Now once again in the uniform of the U.S. Marine Corps, Major Boyington racked up 28 kills—the highest score of any marine pilot in the war. On January 3, 1944, on a routine sweep over Rabaul, time ran out for the 30-year-old Boyington. His Corsair was shot down and he was forced to parachute into St. George Channel.

Takeo Tanimizu picks up the story: "When Boyington was shot down, because I had shot one Corsair down, a pilot wrote in his book that I shot down Boyington. I did not do that. How could I know who was inside a plane? Of course, if I had proved it earlier, it might be better. But there is no way to check it. Boyington was captured by a Japanese submarine. And until the war was over, he was at a prison camp, then he returned to America. As you know, he became a hero. I was requested to go to America to meet him, but I refused, saying that I was not particularly interested in seeing him. He died soon after. Black Sheep, wasn't it? Ba-Ba-Black Sheep?"

In the skies over Southeast Asia, the growing American air forces were becoming more and more aggressive.

Yohei Hinoki—assigned to the army's Aviation Unit 60, which scored 427 kills during the war—had already fought in Malaysia and Singapore. "Then," he reports, "I received an order that one unit, only my unit, should go to Rangoon for defense. The British air force, if it came to attack one day, it would not return for three or four days. But the American air force, they came without interval. Sometimes they came three times a night. They did not let us sleep at all.

"On November 25 [1943], we received a warning. So I was waiting for the enemy in the air; then I planned to land, when I looked up and saw airplanes with pointed heads. Seven of them. I wondered what they were, where they came from. I thought very hard, but I could not reach a conclusion. I had believed that Hayabusa [the Nakajima Ki43 fighter, or "Oscar"] and Zeros were the only fighters which could fly more than 1,000 kilometers."

Hinoki is reporting on the first appearance of land-based Allied fighter planes over Rangoon since the outset of the war: "I flew closer, because I did not understand why friendly planes were coming towards me. Then I saw the American markings, and in this instant, I thought, 'Oh, no!' In this instant, I was attacked. I was too close. There was a hole this big [he gestures to indicate a gaping hole] in the back of the plane."

Hinoki had just come face-to-face with the hottest piston fighter plane to see action in the war, the one which was transforming the air war in Europe: the P-51 Mustang.

The Americans, Hinoki reports, did not let up. "The American air force was full of energy. When I planned to sleep Captain Konoe hurriedly came to me and said, 'The enemy is coming.' So I prepared myself and went up in the air. Well, they were altogether 88 planes. They came from the north and bombed our air base. Then the B-24s made a 'T' formation and began to return. I tried to break inside the formation, but I could not manage it. Then the bombers were gone. All our bases were burned. I was confused again. I thought we were completely destroyed."

Hinoki was right to worry. Until earlier that year, the Liberators—with their ten .50 caliber machine guns—were considered invincible. But that changed on January 26, 1943. The man who changed it—Satoshi Anabuki—tells how he did it.

"Our Hayabusa had two .50 caliber machine guns. B-24s were not only well armored, but well armed. So I could not gun them down by two successive rounds of .50 caliber shells in one attack. To finish them off, I needed to position myself right above them and then shoot from the front. My attacks were deeply angled. When I flew away, I took about 80 degrees.

"If I didn't succeed in the first attack, and if the enemy was not shot down in the next attack, I came under and in front of the formation and shot upwards. In most cases, I was able to shoot them down by these two successive attacks." Altogether, between June 1942 and October 1943, Anabuki shot down 28 British and 13 U.S. aircraft, including that first B-24. On October 8, 1943, over Rangoon, he claimed three B-24s and two P-38 Lightnings in a single combat, ramming the tail of the third bomber before crashlanding.

Although the Lightnings were no longer considered invincible, the Japanese still held them in wary respect. Hinoki resumes his tale: "Even as I came closer to them, they did not notice me at all. So I flew closer, then shot, aiming

at the root of their wings. Then I lowered my altitude. Other planes were coming. I attacked seven and shot down two of them.

"The engines of some of the five left stopped. They looked like they were shaking. Then I was careless. When I looked far, far away, there were planes the size of adzuki beans. They were composing a formation, then coming back.

"I thought, 'The American air force is surely tough. They are something. Look what they were doing.' Then I was shot in my right leg. I found that about 10 centimeters [four inches] below the knee, my leg was blown off. I tied my scarf around the knee and returned to the base."

Amazingly, Yohei Hinoki, fitted with an artificial leg, flew and fought again. Reflecting on the events of that dramatic day, he says that what he "admired about the Americans was they composed a formation again and came back to rescue their own men, dropping medicine and life-saving equipment.

"Well, I think this—how can I say?—American spirit of settlers in frontier. I admired it."

Such a man was Rex Barber. Back in the States in June of 1943, Barber could have coasted for a while—he had already flown 110 combat missions from Guadalcanal. But he volunteered to join the Chinese American Wing and was assigned to fly P-38s with the 23rd Fighter Group, 449th Fighter Squadron. On April 29, 1944, Barber was escorting a flight of B-25s strafing Japanese supply sampans on the Yangtse River.

"In China," he relates, "we had a very limited supply of fuel. So we would wait to run missions until we had plenty of fuel. Well, we got three young pilots in there just out of flying school. And, of course, with that fuel limitation, we had no way to train them.

"Then Colonel Branch decided to send those B-25s down the Yangtse, and we were going to send eight P-38s to escort him. I figured this was going to be pretty much of a milk run, so I assigned one of the new pilots to my wing and one to the leader of the second section.

Japanese pilots, used to American aircraft such as the P-40 during the early part of the war, were unpleasantly surprised by the introduction of more advanced American fighter aircraft such as the powerful and fast North American Aviation-built P-51D Mustang. These P-51Ds are on patrol over the Marianas.

"We were flying at about 3,000 feet. Suddenly I looked up and saw several Japanese Zeros circling ahead of us. So I called Branch and told him to break right and that we would cover him—we were about to be attacked by Zeros. I banked up very sharply with my formation to cover him, probably a little more than I should have with the new wingman, because he dropped out of formation. This often happens with an inexperienced pilot.

"He was a sitting duck back there, so here come two Zeros down on him. I hollered at him, 'Hit the deck, and we'll swing around and cover you on the way out.' But he stayed straight and level—never changed his direction or anything. I hollered at him again. Nothing happened.

"Well, they were about to make the second pass, and I was sure that they would shoot him down at that point. And I was furious. So I just wheeled my airplane up out of formation and told the rest of the boys to cover the B-25s and I went back and flew over the top of him as they were coming down.

"The Zeros saw me coming and they broke up. Well, I should have swung around and gone back over him, but I was mad. And that's something you

The Lockheed P-38 Lightning.

never want to get in combat—mad—cause you lose your judgment. I started right up after these Zeros—they were going almost straight up, and they can go straight up faster and farther than our airplane can. So I stalled—I don't know how high it was, but they went higher. As I rolled around, they hit my right engine and set it afire. Then I saw my right engine lurch slightly and figured that the main spars were probably burning through. So I just set my feet in the seat and jumped.

"That is not a decent way to get out of a P-38. But it was about all I could do. On the way out, I hit my right arm—broke it badly. And my right ankle. I must have had a hole in my parachute; I never remember pulling the ripcord, but I had it in my hand, so evidently when I hit my arm, it jerked the cord. I swung once and hit the ground on a little hillside.

"I was picked up almost immediately by two little Chinese kids. They got me out of my parachute and put my arms over their shoulders and hobbled along. They took me over to a little ravine and buried me under a brushpile there. Pretty smart little guys.

"We could hear the Japanese hollering and yelling back and forth as they were forming their line—we were pretty close to their camp. Probably 10-15 minutes later, I heard the brush cracking and here came this Japanese soldier, passing within a few feet of the brushpile. Immediately after that, when the soldiers got down the hill a little ways, Chiang Kai-shek's guerrillas—he had guerrillas stationed all over China to help rescue us if we did go down—ran up and threw me on a door they had taken off a hut and carried me back to their village. They went right back towards the Japanese army camp to the village, more or less on the edge of the camp. I was two weeks in the camp before I could travel.''

Barber's combat career was over—he would miss it. Of combat he says: ''If you start to get afraid, then you'd better get out of that cockpit.''

John W. Mitchell, one of the American ''top guns'' of the Pacific Theater, knows exactly what Barber is talking about.

''There's nothing greater than combat in an aircraft with another aircraft. It's the greatest thing. You are pitting yourself against another man, a man probably just as smart as you are. And he's trying to kill you, and you're trying to kill him. As a rule, one guy gets the advantage pretty quickly and hopefully you go in and hit him, right off the bat, shoot him down, and that's the end of it. You pull off and go find another one.''

On the immense New Guinea battleground—the island is the size of Alaska—MacArthur uncorked the kind of offensive that he would use again years later in Korea: leap-frogging over an entrenched enemy to strike far behind his lines. He did just that on April 21, 1944, in what was up to then the largest amphibious operation of the Pacific war: 217 ships carrying 50,000 combat troops and 30,000 support personnel, sailed from the newly acquired bases on the Admiralty Islands and landed at three points on New Guinea.

MacArthur now faced the problem of the remaining 600 miles of coastline along northern New Guinea. Fighting, some of the bitterest in the war, would continue until the end of August. But by mid-1944, MacArthur had succeeded in removing New Guinea as an obstacle to his main—and cherished—goal, the Philippines.

But even as he launched those decisive campaigns in New Guinea, Mac-Arthur complained that despite the progress paid with so much blood he was still 1,600 miles from the Philippines and 2,100 miles from Manila. In the Solomons, the advance from Guadalcanal to Bougainville had covered only 280 miles. And when the last gun had gone silent, Tokyo was still nearly 3,000 miles away.

In the vast central Pacific—Nimitz' assigned area of operations—it was a vastly different story. In the first six months of the war, the Japanese had done what five previous imperial powers—the Spaniards, Dutch, British, French, and Russians—had failed to do: made themselves masters of all the lands surrounding the seas of Japan, some six million square miles.

To prepare for the coming battles, U.S. industry provided Chester Nimitz' Pacific Fleet with a veritable embarrassment of riches: a new ship slid down the ways at the rate of one a day, a new airplane, every five minutes.

Among the new planes was one in search of a base of operations: The Boeing B-29 Superfortress. The heaviest aircraft of World War II (53½ tons at takeoff), the Superforts had a range of 3,250 miles and could fly as fast as most fighter planes (357 mph at 25,065 feet). Assigned to a special force, the 20th Air Force under Maj. Gen. Nathan F. Twining, the Superfort was designed with one overriding purpose: to bomb and blast the Japanese into submission on their own home ground. Seizing the bases to do just that was what the next phase of the Pacific war was all about.

Butch Voris was aboard the *Enterprise* assigned to Fighting Squadron 2. He reminisces: ''Back when we started carrier landings—landing on a moving target that's like a postage stamp—we made a very flat approach. The carrier deck being about 60 feet above the water line, we flew downwind, and then

Kenneth Walsh stands before two unit signs marking the number of Japanese aircraft downed.

you made a 180-degree turn up to—as we say—the back end of the boat. You have a landing signal officer [LSO] with a set of paddles. If he holds them straight out, you're on a 'roger,' or a good pass. If he holds them high, you're high, you have to let yourself down a little bit.

''So you come on around in a turn, and you're only running maybe five to six knots above stall and spin. So you're right on the edge, because you have to fly as slow as you can to reduce the impact speed of hitting the arresting gear. Then you have to line up with the center of the flight deck. At the last minute, you level your wings, look ahead, and hopefully, it's there, the LSO gives you your cut, and down you go. If you miss the wires, there were barricades up ahead that you flew into and would trap the airplane, but you had a barrier crash.''

A remarkable man aboard the *Enterprise* tapped Voris, among others, for special training. Voris explains:

''The Japanese were more highly trained than our pilots at night flying. We did not have night fighters at that time, specifically engineered with radar and the ability to detect an aircraft by radar at night.

''So it really goes back to Butch O'Hare—the man O'Hare Field at Chicago is named for. Butch was our group commander and he came up with an

''The Japanese Bettys [twin-engined naval bombers] were making night runs down past the task force, hitting the landing forces at night. We had no way of defending them from the air.

''So Butch came up with the idea that we would just take the aircraft we had—the F6s—and we would have them fly wing on the TBF [Grumman TBF Avengers, carrier-based, three-seater torpedo planes] because they had a very simple radar. It looked like a bedspring out on the wing.

''Admiral [Arthur W.] Radford was working with Butch on this. So Butch picked a team made up of himself and myself, my skipper Bill Dean, Andy Scann, one other. And the skipper of the torpedo squadron and their 'exec' [executive officer]. So we formed two teams and we called them Bat Teams.

''The principle was using this team when the ship's radar detected the Bettys coming down at night. It would launch the torpedo planes and then

launch the fighters. The fighters would join up on the torpedo planes. Now, we're a unit of three: a mother, the torpedo plane, and two fighters.

"The ship would vector us out to within maybe five or six miles using its own radar. Then the torpedo planes with this Aps 26 radar would lock in on the target. We're still, the fighters, flying on the wing of the torpedo plane. He would take us directly astern of the target until we could see the exhaust stacks. Then the torpedo plane would break away and we would go in and fire visually on the exhaust and whatever night silhouette we could get at night—and hopefully shoot them down.

"We had some success that way. But I tell you, it was a hard way of getting there. But it was the beginning of night fighters. Shortly after that, we got F6Fs designed with radars on the wing and nightfighter gear."

The real target was Kwajalein Atoll in the Marshalls, enclosing a lagoon measuring 60 by 30 miles, the largest atoll in the world. The Japanese had operated a major air and naval base there. But first, to protect their rear, American strategists targeted the Gilberts, British islands seized by the Japanese shortly after Pearl Harbor.

Few had ever heard the names of the two atolls Vice Admiral Raymond A. Spruance's three task forces now converged on. Few then alive would ever forget the name of one: Tarawa.

Altogether, the task force numbered more than 200 American ships, including three dozen transports bearing the 2nd Marine Division and elements of the 27th and 105th Army Divisions. Screening them were 17 aircraft carriers, 12 battleships, 12 cruisers, and 66 carriers. Altogether, 108,000 soldiers, sailors, and airmen were aboard those 5th Fleet ships.

One armada headed for Makin Atoll, 100 miles north of Tarawa. The second for Tarawa. The fast carrier force under Rear Adm. Marc Mitscher was assigned the job of protecting the other two against enemy air attacks from Kwajalein, as well as from ships of the Imperial Combined Fleet.

Makin should have been easy, but its defenders—300 troops and 400 civilian laborers—were fanatical, and they held 6,500 American invaders at bay for four days.

Tarawa was a different story from the start; Rear Adm. Keiji Shibasaki, commanding the 2,600 defenders, had boasted that Betio—the largest of the atoll's 47 islands—couldn't be taken by a million men in a hundred years. Rear Adm. Howard F. Kingman, preparing to bombard the island on that November morning in 1943, threatened to wipe it out. The boast seemed reasonable: the fighting would take place over an area less than half New York's Central Park.

Shibasaki's braggadocio was part bluff. Still, the defenders had turned Tarawa's 291 acres into one of the most heavily fortified bastions of its size in the world. In preparation for the landing, B-24 Liberators had been bombing the island for days; and on the day itself, dive bombers and fighters raked the island for half an hour before dawn. Three battleships, five cruisers, and nine destroyers bombarded the island with 3,000 tons of shells—10 tons of high explosive per acre.

Yet the fighting was so fierce that at the end of the first day the beachhead was only 20 feet deep. At D-Day plus three, November 23, Tarawa was declared secured. In 76 hours, this tiny island claimed more than 5,500 lives; only 17 Japanese and 129 Korean laborers surrendered. Of 16,798 U.S. marines who fought at Tarawa, 1,027 died, 2,292 more were wounded.

The Japanese lost 200 aircraft in two days and one night of intense fighting near Truk Island while the American landing at Eniwetok began.

Butch O'Hare was among the casualties of Tarawa. Roy Voris remembers: "As we said, Butch developed this first approach to night fighters. It also killed him. He was lost on about the fourth night of operations. I wasn't up. We alternated sending up the two teams that we had. Butch had gone out and made contact, and he shot down a Betty. He was returning to join up on his mother torpedo plane, and the rear gunner in that torpedo plane thought he was an enemy airplane and unknowingly shot Butch down. We searched for Butch for two days. But to no avail. We lost a great guy."

Alex Vraciu adds detail: "It was on a night operation. It was kind of an ambitious deal and it was kind of raw, but it was the best we had at the time 'cause the Japanese night planes would come in, the Bettys would drop a bunch of flares all around our fleet, then they'd come in and make their attacks—it was like the Fourth of July every night.

"It wasn't until we got back to Pearl Harbor that we heard what happened. Somewhere between the gunner on the Betsy and the gunner on the torpedo plane, they opened fire. The last they saw was Butch disappearing towards the water. They looked, but he was just lost."

Vraciu's ship, the *Independence*, was torpedoed by a Japanese submarine and he landed his Hellcat at Hawkins Field on still-smoldering Tarawa before being taken aboard the carrier *Intrepid*.

From there, Vraciu and other volunteers were sent to Maui in the Hawaiian Islands for six weeks to continue the Bat Team training O'Hare had begun. Back aboard ship, the Bat Teams were ready for action when radar-equipped night fighters reached the fleet. "Maybe it's a good thing," Vraciu reflects, "because of the two torpedo pilots and the four of us in fighters, three of them were lost in the first Truk raid."

During a brief leave back in the States in the late winter of 1943, Vraciu performs a tough duty: "Explaining to Butch's family what I had learned. 'Cause they knew I had been his wingman for four-five months. That was probably the hardest thing for a boot lieutenant, junior grade, to have to do." The Fighting Six's tour was over, but Vraciu had far from finished his fighting, so he arranged a transfer to VF-16, this time aboard the brand new fleet carrier *Lexington*.

During the intervening months, Mitscher, heading the newly designated Fast Carrier Task Forces, all but wiped out Japanese air and naval forces around the Marshall and Gilbert Islands. On February 1, 1944, the rearmed and reequipped forces under Admiral Nimitz hit Kwajalein—hard. The new naval, air, and assault tactics paid off: casualties this time were 334 Americans during four days of fighting, while virtually all 8,500 Japanese defenders preferred death to surrender. (The 4th Marine Division, blooded there, would see only 61 days of action in the war, yet suffer 75 percent casualties—an intimation of the horrors ahead.) The huge lagoon at Kwajalein now became an advance base for Mitscher's fast carriers.

On February 17, a naval armada under Admiral Spruance reached the key Japanese air and naval base at Truk. The main purpose was to shield the landings at Eniwetok Atoll; the main result was to wreak havoc on Japanese defenses. In two days and one night of raids—during which planes from the nine carriers flew 1,250 sorties—the Japanese lost 200 planes as well as 41 ships. American losses were 35 planes shot down and torpedo damage to *Intrepid*. In the aftermath, Adm. Mineichi Koga, now commanding the Japanese navy, ordered his remaining planes from Rabaul to Truk.

It was during that first Truk raid that Alex Vraciu became a celebrity. Let him tell it: "I remember Admiral Mitscher saying the only thing we knew about Truk was what we read in the National Geographic.

"The plan was to have a 72-plane fighter sweep to begin with, to get control of the air. I was fortunate to be part of that. We stayed down low on the water, at a thousand feet, until barely in sight of Truk, when we pulled up to 13,000. Got in there, antiaircraft fire all over the place, varying colors.

"I had learned a lot of things from my skipper, Butch [O'Hare], and one of them was to have a swivel neck. We hadn't seen any planes yet, but we had seen planes taking off from down below, taking off from one of the fields over Truk Atoll. Our leader waggled his wings, started on down, and just before turning my section down to follow after them, I took a look back over my shoulder and good thing I did, because there were four-six Zeros already starting to come in our direction. I could even see the fire from their guns.

"I tallyhoed quickly, but the rest of the planes kept on going down—either they didn't hear or it was too late for them to do anything. The Japanese had a habit, they'd like to catch you as you were coming out of a dive if you were strafing.

"My wingman and I turned into them. The one firing directly at us broke off and headed down, but we couldn't do anything except just dodge in between all this air action. Another plane or two of ours—I don't know where they came from—were there and we kind of weaved with them and generally just kept turning into these guys to bring them down to our level. From then on, the fight became more of a fair one.

"Once I got on their tail, I just followed the first three down and burned them before they got to their altitude, as they were trying to get away."

Vraciu now has three kills in a few dramatic moments. But he's not ready to

An F6F Hellcat gets a takeoff flag from Lt. John M. Clarke during the battle for the Marshall Islands, November 23, 1943.

call it quits. "The fourth one, I played a cat-and-mouse game with him. He was ducking in and out of a cloud—cumulus clouds were all over. I'd make a run on him, and he'd duck back into a cloud. I thought, 'Well, okay, I'll get up on the sun side of him,' and he never knew what hit him."

Over the next few weeks, U.S. forces took Eniwetok and about 30 other small Marshall atolls and islands—losing only 594 men in the campaign. U.S. commanders had learned the lessons of Tarawa well. But there was another factor none could reckon with— Japanese desperation bred an even greater fanaticism.

Officially, that smattering of ships the navy begrudgingly released to Mac-Arthur's control was the 7th Fleet. The irreverent called it "MacArthur's Navy." The general himself was said to refer to it as "my navy." In early 1944, MacArthur was perhaps the most popular American military commander and his name cropped up more and more as a potential presidential candidate.

Against that backdrop, Alex Vraciu tells a tale of how he earned his reputation as "Grumman's Best Customer" (and how, still a lowly lieutenant, he managed to meet a three-star admiral). "Best Customer," because he was not only forced to ditch two Hellcats in the water, but had a third shot out from under him. But first let's hear about the second ditching, what he calls the "operational one," when he was told either to land in the water or parachute over the fleet

The scene was the second Truk raid, April 29, during which Vraciu had flamed two more Zeros, raising his tally to 11. The Allied goal was to maul Japanese air strength, key to "Operation A" drawn up by Admiral Koga to counter the expected attack on the Marianas which were within B-29 range (1,500 miles) of Tokyo.

On the way back from one of the Truk raid missions, Vraciu was hit by antiaircraft fire. "My wingman escorted me back to the carrier. My wheels were dangling, the hydraulic system was all messed up. When I got back to the fleet, that's when they gave me my choice. Well, the wind was pretty strong, and I figured if I landed in the water with a parachute I wouldn't be able to get out of my harness. Some of the guys had been drowned—they'd find them later on. So I figured, I'll ditch.

"I picked a destroyer on the screen [guarding the carriers] and landed alongside. They got me aboard, and the captain gave me his sea cabin. In the middle of the night, my eyes started bothering me—some of the shots had kicked up stuff in my face right in the cockpit—so they scraped my eyeball and got some of that Plexiglas out of my eye. No problem, it worked out all right.

"But the seas were rough, and the destroyer was bobbin' up and down, and I said to myself, 'Oh God, I've got to wait three-four days 'til we get back to Ulithi. Surely, I can think of some way of getting off this destroyer.'

"So I asked the skipper of the destroyer if I could send a message to Gus Woodhelm [operations officer aboard the *Lexington*]. I figured maybe he can get me off.

"In the message, I said, 'Get me off this danged rollercoaster—or I'll vote for MacArthur.' Now, MacArthur talking about 'my navy,' that rubbed the sensibilities of some of the navy people.

"Anyway, 45 minutes later, a message comes over addressed to the skipper of the destroyer. It says, 'Captain, in order to conserve aircraft, please retain my birdman until we reach Ulithi, at which time we will transport him back via rubber boat.' Well, I thought I was dead!

"But, sure enough, not too many minutes after that, they wigwagged a signal over and asked the destroyer to pull up alongside the *Lexington*. And there's old Gus, just grinning from ear to ear on the hangar deck. They highlined me over, and he says, 'Come with me.' And then he takes me up to Admiral Mitscher and says, 'Admiral, here's the character who sent that message.'"

The American attack in the Marianas began on June 15, 1944, spearheaded by Mitscher's Task Force 58. The entire 5th Fleet force numbered 535 ships; aboard were 127,571 marines and soldiers.

Butch Voris remembers: "Our task force was so big that if you were up at 10-12,000 feet over the force, it stretched from horizon to horizon—aircraft carriers, battleships, cruisers, destroyers. It was a spectacle you will never see again."

A well-developed tropical island, Saipan was the first Marianas objective. Army commander Lt. Gen. Yoshitsugu Saito had 25,469 soldiers; Vice Admiral Chuichi Nagumo added 6,100 naval troops.

Butch Voris sortied from the USS *Hornet*: "The landings were not going well. Do you remember the movies of the Saipan operation—where wave after wave of landing craft hit the shore and met with terrible resistance? The group I was in—58.1—was ordered to hit the enemy airfields at Guam to keep them neutralized.

"We went in on a Sunday afternoon, but they were waiting for us at about 20,000 feet and came down on our backs. We fought our way through it all; it was the kind of fight when we were scraping aircraft on the ground. We had both air-to-ground from the Zeros coming down on us, and air-to-air, and ground-to-air. I believe I got a few on that mission. We lost a few, but we're on the offensive. That was really the beginning of where we felt that we're on the move now, all the way to Tokyo."

The fighting for Saipan raged until July 9 and included the most devastating banzai attack of the war. When finally it ended, 4,311 Japanese bodies—some on crutches—were on the beaches. Even more gruesome: the day after the island was declared secure, thousands of the 22,000 civilians joined surviving soldiers in committing suicide, many hurling their children and themselves to their deaths from Marpi Point.

When news of Saipan's fall reached Tokyo, Emperor Hirohito declared in anguish, "Hell is on us." Ten days later, Prime Minister Tojo, the man most responsible for the war, resigned, along with his entire cabinet. The new government, headed by Prime Minister Kuniaki Koiso, thought the unthinkable: Should the war be ended?

The attack on Guam was scheduled for June 18. On the night of June 15-16, the U.S. submarine Flying Fish spotted Japan's First Mobile Fleet emerging from the San Bernardino Strait and flashed word to Admiral Spruance. Task Force 58 was dispatched to waters 180 miles west of Saipan to await the Japanese fleet.

Ozawa's 55-ship force consisted of virtually every remaining fighting ship in the Japanese navy. At 8:30 A.M., June 18, Ozawa launched his first raid. At 10:36 A.M., 11 Hellcats zoomed down in the first attack on the enemy ships.

Alex Vraciu was aboard Mitscher's flagship, the *Lexington*, and he "began to realize that there was a lot of extra activity. We found out later that the Japanese code had been broken and a lot of people on the staff knew what was going on. We figured the Japanese fleet would show at Saipan. They had to, to prevent our landing from taking hold, because we were going to hit Saipan, Tinian, and Guam. If we got Saipan, it would shut off a lot of their staging area bases. And, of course, Tinian was later used for the atomic bomb staging.''

Of the 69 planes in Ozawa's first strike, 42 were shot down. Ozawa's second strike flew into another maelstrom of Hellcats and antiaircraft fire. Alex Vraciu, lagging behind his group with supercharger trouble, was a deadly part of that maelstrom. He reports: ''Twelve of us were on the flight deck, our wings spread. Just standing there, waiting word. All of a sudden, they said, 'Pilots, man your planes!'

''I had a division, and mine was the second four-plane division to take off. We were told once airborne to go to full military power, head up to 25,000 feet.

''We got up to 20,000 feet, and I suddenly realized I couldn't go into high blower, so I couldn't make it to 25,000 feet. I reported this to the fighter director, and he told me to come back and orbit. Apparently, the first wave that had come in from the Japanese fleet had already been shot down, so we probably wouldn't have run into any action.

''I barely made a couple of orbits and, all of a sudden, the tone of the fighter director's voice changed and he vectored us out to another wave of enemy planes.

''I have pretty fair eyesight, and I spotted three planes out on the horizon. All of a sudden, I could see a swarm, a huge rambling mass of planes heading in that direction, and I tally-ho'd them. And we were in perfect position for 'em—you know, two-three thousand feet, opposite direction.

''We got into position and I waggled my wings—we weren't talking on the radio unless we absolutely had to—and we all went at these guys. There just wasn't time to go into divisional integrity, we broke up as much as we could. There were just too many of them to work over.

''I went after my first kill, came in on him, and he caught fire pretty quickly; he did a little mild maneuvering and the tail gunner was shooting at me with a 7.7. I pulled back up to altitude, then saw two more planes in a kind of a loose formation. I came in on the rear of one of the two, and he caught fire and headed on downward. I dipped a wing and slid over on the tail of the one beside him. After he caught fire, I almost felt sorry for him—but not for long. That tail gunner, after he caught fire and was heading down—as they do in the movies, you know, into a long, deep spiral, getting deeper and deeper— that tail gunner was still peppering away at me.

''I looked up ahead, and a little bit to the side, and I could see pieces of airplane, smoke, even tracers from other planes shooting at other planes. I went after a fourth one and he caught fire right away, sort of torching on and off.

''The first plane was already starting to go down when I went after the sixth one and caught him just as he was starting to head on down. I must have hit his bomb, because he exploded in a violent flash. I flew right through the pieces of that one. I took a look at a seventh one and thought, well, I gotta go get him, but before I could get in position to fire, somebody blew him out of the air. You know, it could have been a destroyer, it could have been a battleship, Lord knows who it was. All of a sudden, I looked around—there were no more planes in the air—nothing but Hellcats! When I looked back over the area we had fought I could see flaming oil slicks on the water, traces of smoke, and burning debris. It was time to return to the barn!''

In eight dizzying minutes, Vraciu had shot down six Japanese planes; for four months or so, he was the leading ace in the U.S. navy. All told, seventy planes in that second wave went down in flames. When the "Great Marianas Turkey Shoot" was over, Ozawa had lost 243 of the 373 planes he put in the air—three-quarters of Japan's remaining naval air arm.

With Spruance's blessing, Mitscher took off after the crippled Japanese fleet, finding them late on the afternoon of June 20 at an estimated distance of 225 miles (actually over 300 miles). Although his planes almost certainly could not make it back to their carriers before dark, Mitscher knew he must strike. He launched 77 dive bombers, 54 torpedo bombers, and 85 fighters.

Butch Voris was squadron operations officer aboard the Hornet: "I was in my bunk, and all of a sudden emergency flight quarters was sounded and I knew what had happened: we'd located the Japanese forces. So we manned the ready room and manned our airplanes and we knew that this was going to be a long one. It was already close to 1600 (4 P.M.).

"We were on emergency launch, and just as we came up to what we call 'Fly One,' the one who dispatched you down the flight deck, they hold up a big placard, new enemy range and bearing. The bearing was the same, but the distance was 325 miles. Right there you knew that probably half the planes could not return to the carrier, but we went ahead.

"So we went out, and as we're climbing and heading west, the sun is gradually going down and it's getting darker and darker—and we're not there yet.

"As I said, we're not great experts in night operations. Finally, at about 275, 280 miles, we saw the Japanese force. All you could see was white water, the wakes of each ship. They had gone to flank speed to defend against us. The sun had gone down, and we came up on them, and we made our attacks. The fighters dropped bombs, torpedo planes went in, low to the water, against all the surface guns from the Japanese carriers and battleships and cruisers and destroyers.

"We sank one carrier and set fire to another, and other ships were sinking—destroyers and cruisers.

"Now we had to get home, and it's dark, and we know we haven't got

The Mitsubishi J2M "Jake" was fielded by the Japanese later in the war partly in response to the American production upgunned and powerful fighters and bombers.

enough fuel. The torpedo planes are the first to call out, 'I'm out of fuel, I'm going in the water.' It was like that, all the way back.

"The fighters were better off—we weren't carrying big, heavy torpedoes, so we had better range. So we got back. But the ships in the task force stretched horizon to horizon—how to find your ship? Well, we got back, but it became a mêlée. So our admiral, he turned on our lights—something you never do, because of the fear of submarine or air attack—and I got down on the *Hornet*. My wingman crashed into the barriers, right behind me.

"From then on, we were pushing wrecked planes over the side. They were landing in the water, parachuting out. They just announced over the air, 'I'm bailing out,' or, 'I'm ditching.' And this went on until there were no more airplanes, they were all gone."

Of the 216 U.S. planes, 80 either ran out of fuel and crashed into the sea or crashed on carrier decks. But because of the lights, and because Mitscher had left part of his destroyer screen to straggle behind, 59 crewmen were saved that night, 101 the following day.

The Battle of the Philippine Sea had devastated Japan's once-vaunted naval air arm; the Japanese would never again mount a carrier battle on a significant scale.

Tinian, a smaller island not two miles off Saipan, was taken in a week. Guam, the first American territory to be recaptured, was a different story. Cloaked in parts with nearly impenetrable jungle, it took two weeks to subdue the main forces entrenched there. Scattered elements continued to fight from hideouts in the hills, in some cases for years.

Komachi was among the survivors. He reflects on the changed fortunes of war.

"When the war started, experience, one's own skill, were most important. However, because of victory in the Battle of Midway, American pilots became more confident. Their attacks were almost impudent.

"The reason was, unfortunately, Japanese communication technology was not very efficient. The enemy could tell our next movement beforehand. Despite a pilot's skill or experience, the enemy was in a better position. Like sports, when one is on a losing streak, one cannot win easily. The war was quite similar. Very good pilots, very experienced pilots, lost their lives one after another. From the middle of the war on. We were no match against the enemy any more at that time."

Alex Vraciu adds a thought or two of his own on the subject: "Fighter pilots love air action. We never worried about our enemy opposition. The longer we were out there, the more experienced we became, the more we figured we could handle the Japanese. We were more concerned about the ground fire. That's where the troubles came in. Most of the people killed in the war were killed by ground fire."

For Iyozo Fujita, the learning curves were going in the wrong directions: American pilots were getting better, Japanese pilots worse. Plus, the Americans had better tools to work with. "The Americans found a Zero fighter at Dutch Harbor and studied it. Then they realized that the Japanese defense [armor-plating to protect the pilots] was very weak. So, very often, they shot from the front. Also, the American fighters had strong power, so they shot from beneath us. Their weapons were excellent, too. And the skills of our pilots became worse. Also, we had no defense. It was fatal."

Gerald Johnson, who racked up 22 victories in P-38s, commanded the 49th Fighter Group in the U.S. 5th Air Force. As did other American pilots, he

Speaking of the growth of American resolve as the war raged on, Sadamu Komachi said many years later, "We were no match against the enemy . . ."

observed that, by and large, the quality of Japanese fighter pilots deteriorated. Generally, enemy pilots were what he called "stick-and-rudder" men—their maneuvers could be anticipated.

In all, the Marianas cost the U.S. 4,750 dead and 20,000 wounded; the Japanese lost 46,000 dead. Now, Japan itself was no longer safe. On November 24, 1944, 21 Bomber Command sent 111 B-29s to raid the Musaki aircraft engine plant outside Tokyo. It was the first of many, many blows against the Japanese homeland.

On July 26, with the battle of Guam still raging, President Franklin Roosevelt disembarked from the cruiser *Baltimore* at Pearl Harbor where he was joined by his top commanders in the Pacific: MacArthur and Nimitz. MacArthur was adamant that the next strike should be the Philippines; Nimitz wanted Formosa (Taiwan).

Roosevelt agreed with MacArthur. But first, Nimitz insisted, the Palau Islands had to be neutralized. In the days leading up to the Peleliu landings, however, Halsey's Task Force 38 encountered so little air opposition that he flashed Nimitz a stunning message: Cancel Peleliu and Mindinao and strike immediately against Leyte. MacArthur quickly assented.

As is the way in war, there was always just one more piece of business to take care of first: the communications facility on Chichi Jima, a spit of land in the Bonins, not quite 500 miles southeast of Tokyo. Chichi Jima was the Japanese link to the Palaus.

Planes from Mitscher's task force hit the island, but the flak was so heavy they left the target standing. The order came to go again. Among the pilots manning the big Grumman TBM Avengers selected for the job was a boyish-looking navy lieutenant just past his 20th birthday, one year past winning his wings as the youngest flyer in the navy. His name was George Herbert Walker Bush.

Just as the planes were about to take off, an old friend of pilot Bush's—Ted White, a ship's gunnery officer—wangled permission to fly with Bush, bumping the enlisted gunner, Leo Nadeau. Bush warned his friend it would be rough, and rough it was. Skies were clear as they came in at 10,000 feet, Bush third in behind Squadron Commandr D.J. Melvin and Doug West. As they neared the target, black smoke filled the sky, the worst flak he'd ever seen. At 6,000 feet it happened—the shock, the lurch, smoke and flames. The young pilot struggled to get rid of his bombs, then he struggled to reach water—if they bailed out over land, the Japs would kill them. He shouted the order to bail out.

On the way down, Bush searched the sky frantically for signs of other parachutes. There were none. He clambered aboard the raft, bleeding from the blow to his head when he hit the tail stabilizer. When the U.S. submarine *Finback* picked him up, he asked tearfully for his crew. But Ted White, who simply *had* to know what aerial combat was like, was lost. The future president returned to do battle over the Philippines until war ended; he went home with two Gold Stars, the Air Medal, and the Distinguished Flying Cross.

Paving the way for the Philippine invasion, U.S. airmen pounded Japanese air bases throughout the region. In two days over the Philippines in September, David McCampbell continued his fast pace, shooting down seven more Japanese planes. Then, on October 20, 1944, the largest and most powerful amphibious force ever assembled—more than 700 ships, 200,000 men—converged on Leyte Gulf, exactly where Ferdinand Magellan's ships had sailed 423 years before. The Japanese, expecting an assault on Mindinao, were caught completely flat-footed by the strike at Leyte. That afternoon, MacArthur and Philippine President Sergio Osmena went ashore, MacArthur declaring, "People of the Philippines, I have returned."

Those landings were the signal for the Japanese to activate yet another desperate gamble: Operation VICTORY. It resulted in the biggest sea fight in history—the Battle of Leyte Gulf. In the skies over the three battle zones, U.S. and Japanese pilots dueled relentlessly.

Commander McCampbell and one other pilot found themselves engaging an estimated 40 enemy fighters. In that running battle, they shot down 15 of them—McCampbell scoring nine, a record for an American pilot. And he wasn't even supposed to be there. But this native of Bessemer, Alabama, who had graduated from the Naval Academy in 1933 but had been denied pilot training until 1943, had waited far too long before the navy finally put him in the cockpit of a combat plane to let a little thing like an order get in the way when there was so much fighting to be done. He tells the story:

"I was actually flying against orders. Well, when the loudspeaker passed the word, 'All fighter pilots, man your planes,' I figured I was a fighter pilot, so I told my plane captain, 'Get the plane on the hangar deck and gas it. I'm flying today.' But when I manned the plane, they had not finished gassing it. Usually they kept my plane down on the hangar deck by the elevator. So they passed the word on the bullhorn, 'Group commander's plane is not ready to go; send it below.' With that, I waved the gasoline detail off the gassing—my main tanks were half full and my belly tank full at that point.

"I ordered the second division to go down on the bombers, and I told 'em

Commander David McCampbell shot down a record nine Japanese aircraft in a single engagement, helping the lopsided battle earn the moniker, the great "Marianas Turkey Shoot." The Japanese fielded pilots with poorer experience as the war continued.

I'd take my division up and take care of the fighters. But we had't formed yet, so when he jumped down on the bombers, he took five of 'em, and when I looked around, I saw it was just my wingman and I up there.

"Then I called the ship and told them that we had about 40 fighters up there, would they please send some help? Word came back from the fighter director; he says, 'We don't have anybody else to send yet.' 'Well, it's just my wingman and I. What do you suggest?' 'Use your own best judgment,' says the fighter director. It happens that the fighter director was John Connally [who, as governor of Texas, rode in the same car with President John F. Kennedy when he was fatally shot in Dallas in November 1963]. I knew then that he would be a damned good politician when he said that.

"Anyway, Roy [Rushing] and I climbed up and we went to work on 'em. I knew they were gonna' have to break out of that Lufbery one of these days, so I told Roy, I says, 'We'll just sit up here and wait for 'em to come out of that Lufbery, and then we'll go get 'em.'

"We circled above 'em for—I don't know—ten, fifteen minutes. I know I had a cigarette and found out later Roy did, too. Anyway, we went down and started working 'em over for as long as we could keep 'em in formation. And we whittled 'em down just by getting the ones that tried to climb up to our altitude, or the ones that would pull out away from the formation. We'd go down and knock those off first. And then we'd go back to work on the mass of 'em.

"This went on until Roy ran out of ammunition and he called and told me. I says, 'Well, Roy, I've got ammunition left, and we'll make a couple more attacks. You wanna' go down with me or wait up here and watch the show?' He says, 'Oh, I'll go down with you.' He didn't want to get caught up there without any David McCampbell. So we made a couple more runs and I knocked off a couple more planes. And I'm out of ammunition and I'm low on gas, so we head back to the ship.

"As soon as I landed, I gave it the gun to taxi out of the landing gear and park the plane, and the engine went dead—it quit on me. I was completely out of gas."

As a result of that action, McCampbell—the man who wouldn't take the navy's no for an answer—was awarded the Medal of Honor, added to the Navy Cross, Silver Star, Legion of Merit, Distinguished Flying Cross, two Gold Stars, and Air Medal.

Kurita's counterpart, Vice Adm. Teiji Nishimura, didn't even make it to the Leyte beachhead. The U.S. 7th Fleet intercepted him as he came through Surigao Strait and practically annihilated his Force C. Victory at Surigao Strait was sweet revenge: five of the six ancient U.S. battleships engaged that night had been sunk or grounded at Pearl Harbor.

Meanwhile, off Cape Engano, the "divine wind" which had been counted on to save the Japanese carriers did not blow; the only blows struck that day were by the U.S. navy.

Despite their heavy losses, the Japanese succeeded in reinforcing their Leyte forces—with men as well as planes. McCampbell downed a Zeke and a Val dive-bomber on November 5, followed by a third plane four days later, raising his tally in just five phenomenal months to 34, the highest score by an American pilot during just one tour. Air Group 15—the "Fabled Fifteen"— headed home, having shot down a record 318 enemy aircraft during its tour, plus 348 on the ground.

The fight to liberate Leyte continued until Christmas Day 1944. The U.S.

Japanese navy Warrant Officer Hiroyoshi Nishizawa was Japan's number two ace with 202 claimed kills. Some historians argue that his record is more accurate at half the figure.

lost 15,500 dead and wounded; the Japanese 80,577 dead, 878 prisoners.

On October 21, 1944, a lone Japanese plane dove into the bridge of the cruiser *Australia*, killing 20 men, including the captain. The kamikaze, as they came to be known, had made their grisly entrance on the war's stage—a mass suicide attack in which the pilot would deliberately dive his plane into an enemy target, usually with an extra load of bombs or torpedoes. They were born of desperation, sired by tradition. Japanese naval power had now ceased to exist.

Top ace Saburo Sakai betrays some of the ambivalence Japan's airmen felt about kamikazes. "Kamikaze is a surprise attack, according to our ancient war tactics. Surprise attacks will be successful the first time, maybe two or three times. But what fool would continue the same attacks for ten months? Emperor Hirohito must have realized it. He should have said 'Stop.'

"As for kamikaze attacks, those who ordered and encouraged them, those in commanding positions, lied. Every pilot volunteered for a kamikaze unit? 'I go! I go! I go!—did everyone say that? That's a lie!'

Forty years have passed. Sakai pauses. "Even now, many faces of my students come up when I close my eyes. So many students are gone. Why did headquarters continue such silly attacks for ten months! Fools! Genda, who went to America—all those men lied that all men volunteered for kamikaze units. They lied.

"That's why Americans think we are strange. Where are the people who will volunteer to die? No one wants to die. But if a pilot was ordered, we were all military men. We would go. I went, too. The Japanese army lost 2,500 men. The Japanese navy lost 2,500 men. They all died, while being disappointed."

Kazu-o Tsunoda's combat ribbons include China, New Guinea, Guadalcanal, Iwo Jima, Formosa, and the Philippines. He provides a rather different insight on the suicide missions.

"Japan seemed to want Leyte to be the last battle and wanted to have a peace treaty. But before Japan finished the war, in the last battle, the Japanese wanted to chase the Americans away from Leyte, and this would then bind a peace treatment.

"To achieve such a big victory, a small number of pilots was not enough. Japan sent out three squadrons. I thought if all the members in the air forces' squadrons sent to the Philippines died, the emperor would put an end to the war. Therefore, when I escorted a kamikaze unit, I thought this would be the end.

"Some of the commanding officers might have shared my opinion, but there were various different opinions among the officers. That's why the kamikaze mission continued for a long time."

When the shooting ended for Kuniyoshi Tanaka, he had shot down 17 enemy aircraft. Now he reflects: "At the Battle of Midway, we lost aircraft carriers, but there were still experienced pilots left. During the South Pacific war, many skillful pilots died. I think around that time, Japan started becoming inferior. Japanese became less capable of doing damage to the Americans."

Tanaka knew what so many other Japanese knew, from Tokyo to Rangoon: suicide weapons notwithstanding, Japan's Rising Sun was definitely setting under the weight of far mightier adversaries. As 1944 ended, it was no longer a question of how the war would end; it was now only a question of how bloody the end would be.

12 THE WAR'S LAST DEADLY DUELS

Germany lay in ruins. Allied armies were massed along the Reich's borders, while vast fleets of bombers blasted Germany's cities and what remained of its war machine.

Still, the shattered remnants of the Luftwaffe fought on.

Adolf Galland, commanding the tattered fighters, explains: "Everyone knew perfectly well the war was lost. We kept fighting because it's unimaginable that a responsible German soldier would stop fighting when the Fatherland continues to fight, when the Fatherland bleeds."

Friedrich Oblesser, an Austrian who had first seen action in far-off Russia, now fought with his back to the wall. By December of 1944, he concludes, "it became clear that whatever we had done up until that point, our only duty now was to defend our homeland."

Walter C. Beckham—for a time the top American scorer in the European Theater with 18 victories—believed all fighter pilots had something in common: nervous exhaustion. At the beginning, when crossing the Channel on a mission, "I expect most of us were gung-ho, let's go, and where are those little black specks, and let's find 'em, and shoot'em, and go! go! go!" Later: "'I hope I don't see any more Germans today. I don't feel like it. If I do see one, I'll try to shoot him. But, my heart's not in it.'"

At the end of those later missions, Beckham remembers, "I'd get back home, dead tired, and park the airplane, and I'd feel like just lying down on the concrete."

Yet for Walter Beckham, as for most American pilots, it was a short war: a couple of years, a couple of hundred hours in combat. For men such as the German ace Martin Becker, the war had been going on for over five years— five years with precious few days when he wasn't in the cockpit of his fighter plane. "Between missions," he says, "or even after a mission, you were often depressed. It was really exhausting, because at the end we were constantly on duty."

Hans Marquardt, among the thinning ranks of Luftwaffe pilots trying to stem the inexorable Red tide, speaks of "the constant pressure, the constant duty, practically no leave. We coped between sorties playing cards, smok-

Friedrich Oblesser, Erich Hartmann, and Gratz stand together laughing, a show of emotion increasingly hard to come by as the air war over Europe intensified.

ing cigarettes, drinking a lot of coffee. We lived in a tent normally, we didn't have showers over there in Russia. But we were young, we were healthy. We could relax quickly and digest all we had to deal with. We spoke briefly about our sorties in the evening, and then we slept. There wasn't time for more than that."

As 1944 became 1945, no serious doubt remained about the outcome. But much fighting, and much dying, was yet to come. For the war was now in its frenzied finale.

The poet-pilot Arsenii Vorozheikin returns to spin yet another tale born of those epic times.

"Our fighter division had only about 200 men and 40 girls who worked as gun specialists and putting together the parachutes. On May 2nd, 1944, almost all of our 2nd Air Army was supposed to strike the German airfield in the region of Lvov, but the attack was not successful. As soon as we flew over the front lines, the territory turned out to be covered by fog. So we landed and had breakfast, and as soon as we started having breakfast, the alarm sounded.

"Before that, we always had two 406 fighters above the airport, like sentries that protected us. On that day, there were no fighter planes on duty. Instead, we had radar, because radar at long range could detect the enemy coming. But I didn't trust radar. It was very easy to outwit it. You could simply approach at a low altitude and the radar wouldn't notice it.

"That was why I went towards my fighter—at the front, you always feel better when you have your weapons right there—and I saw an unusual picture there. There were three young girls sitting behind my plane. This was at Ternopol [in southwestern Ukraine], and around the aircraft there were lots of flowers: dandelions, lilly of the valley. So they had made wreaths out of the white flowers, and had wreaths on their heads—as though admiring themselves in the mirror.

"I also admired those young daughters, their childlike naivete really appealed to me. I said, 'Girls, how beautiful you are!' They said, 'Oh, Commander, sorry, we didn't notice you come up here.' And then they put a wreath of flowers on my head.

"I said, 'In whose honor are you putting those flowers in your hair? Why?' And this very modest little girl, Nadia, who was from Ivanovo, she said, 'Why in honor of the goddess of spring, Oster.' She was a very well-read young girl.

"And I said, 'Rather than any goddesses, you're not mythical goddesses— you're genuine Russian Madonnas and beauties. But you have one little sin.' And they said, 'Well, don't hide them—what are those little sins?' And I said, 'Not sins, but one little sin. Spring, everything is in bloom, and you've bloomed, too. Some of you are in love. And one of you wants to leave to get married.'

"I said, 'Well, at the front, even beauties are not supposed to do that.' Nadia said, 'Well, Havel and I have changed our minds, we'll get married after the war. Right now, I am writing an application. I want to leave the army. I want to continue working in the institute.'

"I said, 'Well, what you're doing is like what was described by Fonvizin, except the other way around, that you don't want to get married, you want to study!'" (The reference is to a play by Russian playwright Fonvizin in which the hero reiterates, "I don't want to study, I want to get married.")

"Right at that moment, my ear heard a suspicious noise from the east, from the rear of our army. I looked up and saw two fascist fighters. Experience said to me, these are not hunters—hunters would have immediately attacked the airport. These must be reconnaissance planes, which is a bad omen. I wanted to go to the phone right away to report this in order to get the duty squadron up into the air.

"But right behind the reconnaissance planes I saw about 50 fascist fighters coming toward the airfield with bombs. I immediately jumped into the dug-out, and as I looked up, I saw over my head those black crosses of the fascist fighters. And then, over my head at about 150-200 meters altitude, four of the German fighters dropped two cannisters each with about a hundred small bombs in each cannister.

"At that moment, over our heads, there was simply a huge cloud of death. There was nowhere to go, nowhere to run. I pressed myself into the earth, trying to look for protection, but the ground somehow treacherously kept pushing me back up. The earth was a mound, and I couldn't press myself against it. It seemed to be pushing me up into that cloud of death.

"Then something covered me up, pushed me down. There were explosions all around, the smell of exploding materials, and then silence.

"'Where is the silence coming from?' I asked myself. I was ready to die, and the dead are not supposed to hear silence. Or, is it the opposite—the dead hear only silence? I moved my hands, my feet. I was alive. I got up and looked around. I saw the tails of those fighter planes leaving, going back over Ternopol.

"I looked down and there were three wreaths. I rememberd very well that the wreaths of the girls were white and yellow flowers. Now there were red ones, and the three girls were lying there. Their eyes had already become glassy. Only then did I understand that the red petals were from the life flowing out of those girls.

"They were lying together in the trench with us. They'd also seen that death was there. But no, what they did was simply, at the cost of their own lives, to leap and cover us with their own bodies—I and the mechanic of the plane. Two of those huge bombs had exploded on their backs.

"That was really a heroic deed. How many such heroic deeds there were during the Great Patriotic War! There is no higher and greater deed than saving a life through your own life."

As 1944 wound down, the Eastern front was stabilized on the northern and central sectors, running roughly from the East Prussian border down along the Narew and Vistula rivers to the Carpathian Mountains straddling eastern Czechoslovakia and Poland. Although through 1944 the USSR was losing five to six men for every German, Soviet strength *vis-à-vis* the Germans was far greater going into 1945. Frequently, Luftwaffe airmen who found their bases suddenly surrounded by the rapidly advancing Soviet forces could only escape by flying out.

Friedrich Oblesser, who fought his entire war on the Eastern front, paints a vivid picture: "My memories of that time are overshadowed by the fact that it was impossible to even come close to fulfilling our orders. We were so low on fuel that we positioned our planes for takeoff by having them pulled by oxen in order to save on fuel."

As for pilots, Goering's hubris and stubborness cost the Luftwaffe dearly. Believing his forces all but invincible after the stunning triumphs in Poland and France, Goering's Luftwaffe fielded only 28,000 fighter pilots. By contrast, Stalin's beginning goal of 100,000 trained Soviet pilots remained level

throughout the war. (The U.S., by 1945, had a pool of some 160,000 pilots.)

Vasily Kubarev—later colonel general—trained about 200 pilots before the war after finishing his own training on the stubby Polikarpov I-16s, the backbone of the Red air force's fighter arm going into the war. He had already flown about 100 combat missions when, in May 1942, with the Germans advancing on all fronts, "those of us who managed to survive were sent to a three-month retraining class to learn how to use Yak-1 planes."

Kubarev's moment of truth came during the decisive battle of Kursk, in July 1943. "Here, we really had to fight. Our main assignment was to cover the battlefield, to protect the crossing of our troops across the rivers." In one battle there, leading a formation of six fighters, he tangled with 50 German planes—27 Ju-87s and 20 FW.190 and Me.109 fighters. He shot down five dive- bombers and two fighters.

"We had to constantly deal with the enemy fighters," he recalls, "and they were very tough, very good pilots. The only thing that saved me, I think, was the training which I had in school, very, very good training."

As the war ground on, the Luftwaffe's ability to provide quality training to its pilots declined steadily. Heinz Marquardt, who was assigned to the Russian front in August 1943, says, "The pilots who were trained later, the younger ones, had a tough time. They had few flight hours in training, they had little experience, and they had little time in which they could accustom themselves to combat on the front. That's why there were so many losses among those younger pilots."

The Russians brought not only well-trained pilots, but better weapons. By the end of 1943, the MiG-3 appeared, the only Soviet aircraft superior to the Messerschmitt at altitudes above 16,000 feet. But it was viewed by the

The number of Russian fighter pilots reached 100,000 near the middle of the war and stayed there throughout.

The La-7 was said to have been the best low-level fighter of the Second World War. Russian military equipment continued to improve.

Russians as a transitional fighter plane and relegated to secondary roles. That was consistent with the Soviet air doctrine of using fighter planes primarily in ground-support, low-altitude roles.

Fritz Losigkeit underscores the point. The Russian air force, he says, was "not a strategic weapon. They were an operational weapon, usually operating directly on the front. They attacked targets behind the lines, but they never went farther than 50-60 kilometers, or at most, 70-80 kilometers, behind our front."

Not that the Germans didn't fly ground-support missions as well. Of all the many variations of the Ju.87 Stuka one, in particular, made a powerful impact on the Eastern front—the Ju.87G, which mounted two 37 mm cannon and a machine gun for the crewman in the back seat. It was in a Ju.87G that Hans Ulrich Rudel, flying 2,530 combat missions, destroyed no fewer than 519 Soviet tanks.

Inevitably, the Stukas became a prime target for the ever-bolder and stronger Russian pilots. Arsenii V. Vorozheiken relates: "I must say, we really liked those planes. We liked them because they burned very well. You approached them, you get closer, and . . . ! They have practically no ability to fire from the back."

He describes one air combat during the fighting around Kiev the year before, when he blasted several Stukas, causing them to drop bombs on their own tanks. "And they did that," he gloats, "very successfully—they hit them." Later, when he found that reports of the battle by the German press were distorted, he wasn't surprised, "because we knew that lies and deceptions were what fueled fascism."

Fedor F. Archipenko flew 467 missions and engaged in 102 dogfights, one of which he describes. He decided to ram a Stuka, and "when I was approaching the plane from behind to ram it with my propeller, it made a turn and opened the hatches. The bombs started falling. I barely got away without having the bombs falling on me and exploding. After that, I got the idea never again to make that mistake!''

Stukas were less common over England. New Zealander Robert Spurdle tells of intercepting the last Stuka raid there: ''The Ju.87 had a reputation far in excess of its actual ability as a plane,'' he asserts. The Stukas, on that raid, got temporarily separated from their fighter escorts by a cloud bank, allowing RAF pilots to ''slaughter'' them. ''It was,'' Spurdle adds, ''a marvelous thing for once to catch them and really give it to them!''

Fighter pilot chief Adolf Galland calls reliance on the Stuka—instead of developing a long-range, four-engine bomber—one of Germany's blunders in the air war. Galland also heaps scorn on the development of twin-engine fighters—the Me. 110, 210, and 410—without adequate prior testing. ''They would have seen that the two-engine fighter was useless. But they didn't look for the truth, just confirmation of their preconceived ideas. The consequences were very great indeed!''

As Russian air superiority mounted, so too did its offensive posture, sending bombers deeper into enemy territory. In aid thereof, the Russians unveiled the Yakolev Yak-9, a more powerful and better-armed successor to the Yak-7. The year 1944 saw two other outstanding fighter planes enter the Soviet inventory: the Yak-3 and the Lavochkin La-7. The Yak-3 was not only faster than its most serious rival, the Me. 109G, but outclassed both the Gustavs and the Focke Wulf 190s below 6,000 meters (19,736 feet). The La-7, which replaced a Stalingrad veteran, the La-5, was one of the best low-level fighters of the war.

Joining these two was a new version of the two-seater Ilyushin Sturmovik, the Il-10, powered by a 2,000-hp Mikulin AmM-42 engine and boasting even thicker and more extensive armor than its ''flying tank'' predecessor, Il-2.

Vasily Kubarev flew Yaks during the war and speaks of the view from the cockpit: ''The first period of the war, when the Germans killed on the ground a great number of our planes, we suffered great losses. There were a lot of pilots who died. The shift to new equipment, to new planes, all of this made us carry on a very difficult battle with the enemy, who was always superior to us in numbers.''

Ivan Lakyev is even more pointed: ''The Yak, the MiGs—they had not really been completed. But after that, we had very good planes with really good pilots. We weren't afraid of the Focke Wulfs. We were not only not afraid of them, we sought them out ourselves.''

Arsenii Vorozheiken, two times Hero of the Soviet Union, agrees. Besides, he adds, because the new Yaks were so maneuverable, ''with good piloting techniques, you could always get out of battle if you had to—always.''

The Soviets were not alone in praising their new planes. Top German ace Friedrich Oblesser—who, like Kubarev, went on to become a lieutenant general—spent his three years of combat on the Eastern front. German planes, he says, were better than anything the Soviets had, including the American P-39 Airacobras and P-63 Kingcobras, ''until we encountered the Yak-9s, which were, in many respects, superior to the German aircraft.''

Despite Oblesser, the P-39s received warm praise from most Soviet pilots who flew them. Among them is Mikhail S. Komelkov, who flew his first combat mission on the first day of the war and his last on the last day of the war. Komelkov, the Soviet's second-ranking ace with 32 confirmed victories and seven shared, flew his P-39 on 321 missions.

''At that time,'' Komelkov recalls, ''the Cobra was an outstanding plane in

Ivan Lakyev said Russian aircraft improved towards war's end.

terms of its technical and tactical specifications," and he points out its ability to land and take off from highways when "our airports were already left far behind."

Anatoly L. Kozhevnikov, another top ace, flew P-39s from 1943 onward. "By that time, after the Battle of Kursk, America had delivered to us a sufficient number of Aircobras. Our entire division, commanded by the well-known Commander Pokryshkin, was armed with Cobras. I liked the plane. I liked the weapons system—in war, you need a strong weapons system. A cannon, two large caliber machine guns, four smaller machine guns. [The Soviets apparently substituted four small wing-mounted weapons for the two heavy .50 caliber machine guns on the wings.] Later on, I removed those four smaller machine guns because the two large caliber ones and the cannon were enough for me. Then, when I took away the smaller guns, the plane became lighter, easier to control—and I had sufficient weapons."

As, for example, when once, over the Dnieper River, "I encountered several bombers, and right away, I shot down three bombers, Ju-88s." He added only one to his own tally, however. "We had a system, then. It was accepted that part of the planes I shot down I could hand over to my wingman. After all, he was there with me, too. That was a kind of combat friendship."

Komelkov flew with the legendary Soviet ace, leader, and teacher, Alexander Ivanovich Pokryshkin. "As a pilot," he says, "he was number one. He was a first-class pilot, superb, the best kind." Because of his rank, Pokryshkin "was forbidden to fly, but he desperately wanted to, and there were some days where he managed to." In fact, "I guess you would say he violated the ban. He flew and he shot down planes."

On one of those surreptitious missions, Pokryshkin is believed to have tangled with a man worthy of his talents—Gerhard Barkhorn, at that point the Luftwaffe's highest-scoring ace and, in the opinion of another great ace, Walter Krupinski, the very best fighter pilot he knew.

Barkhorn began his military flying career in 1938. During the early stages of the Battle of Britain, he was shot down twice within a few days. The second time around, he bailed out over the Channel. A fellow flyer saw him splash down and directed a nearby German patrol boat to pick him up—minutes before a British vessel reached the scene. Barkhorn resolved never again to bail out—a resolve that led him to crash-land eight crippled planes in the years ahead.

Returning from his sixth mission of the day in the summer of 1944, Barkhorn got careless and failed to look behind after engaging a large formation of Russian bombers. Suddenly, cannon shells and machine gun bullets fired from a P-39 Airacobra blasted his Me.109 and wounded Barkhorn. Pokryshkin is believed to be the man who flamed Barkhorn.

The cream of the Luftwaffe's fighter force—JG.52, commanded since November 1, 1942, by Col. (later Maj. Gen.) Dietrich Hrabak— sought vainly to protect the encircled German forces in the "Courland pocket" in northern Latvia and Estonia. Hrabak had finished molding the fighters of JG.52 into the highest-scoring aces in combat aviation history. He drilled his men on two basic rules: "Fly with your head and not with your muscles," and, "If you return from a mission with a victory but without your wingman, you have lost your battle."

Hrabak preferred flying the Me.109 himself, but beginning in October

Pokryshkin reportedly tangled with and shot down one of the Luftwaffe's ace of aces: Major Barkhorn.

1944, he was in the cockpit of a different plane, the FW.190. "The 190 had the advantage of a much greater firepower. It helped considerably in scoring a kill." It did just that on Hrabak's last mission, his 820th of the war.

"My group was covering the unloading of ships in Courland at the harbor at Labiu, carrying the supplies necessary for the survival of the German troops. We were attacked by a formation of Pe-2s [dubbed "the Russian Mosquito" for the many qualities resembling its RAF cousin]. They were heavily escorted. I shot down a fighter in a dogfight due to the incredible firepower of my aircraft. He flew right at me and I was able to destroy the entire rear half of his aircraft."

The first of the two great Soviet offensives opened on January 12, 1945. Commanded by Marshal Ivan Konev, the first offensive drove across southern Poland to Breslau (Wroclaw). Two days later, Marshal G. K. Zhukov's forces moved out on the Warsaw-Berlin axis, seizing Warsaw on January 17.

Senior Lt. Anna A. Timopheeva Egorova was in action over Warsaw. She began her fighting career flying reconnaissance missions and transporting the wounded with the all-female Night Witches squadron in rickety Po-2 plywood planes which, she ruefully relates, could be shot down by just about anything, including a rifle. That, she said, didn't inhibit the Messerschmitts from "chasing us. It was very easy for the fascist planes to shoot us down during the day—and they got the same awards as if they had shot down any other combat aircraft!"

Anatoly Kozhevnikov said American-supplied P-39s made excellent gun platforms. While still little match for Germans flying Me.109s and Focke-Wolfe-190s, the P-39s' quality and level of technology boosted the confidence of Russian pilots used to inferior equipment.

The transition to combat did not come easily to Egorova. Flying a reconnaissance mission near Grodno, she found herself "being chased by Messerschmitts, firing from all sides. While I was maneuvering, the plane hit a tree and fell down. Well, I felt my arms and legs to see if I was in one piece. I was, but the aircraft was completely in pieces. When I managed to get back to my airfield, Aul Shali, near Grodno, I decided to say that I myself had smashed up the airplane. The commander of the squadron, Bulkin, really bawled me out. But the deputy commander for political affairs came up and said, 'Commander, let's send Egorova to the reserve regiment.' So I was sent to the reserve regiment in Sal'yany, beyond Baku, in Azerbaidjan.

"I very much wanted to fly Sturmoviks, but when I got there, there were no Sturmoviks at all. All they had were very old, obsolete airplanes—the [Sukhoi] Su-2 [a two-seat, low-wing monoplane fighter bomber]. The Su-2—the only plane in which the motor was fueled by castor oil. We all laughed at it. The pilots said that the airfield smelled of pancakes.

"I started flying on those very old planes. And then a comrade came from the front and started choosing pilots for his division. I asked him to take me. He was, at first, I would say, not exactly nice. But then I said to him, 'I'm not going to leave until you enroll me in your division.' He said, 'Well, I see there's no way I can get rid of you.' When I went to say goodbye to the commander of the reserve regiment, he said, 'Why are you doing this? Stay here as an instructor. We'll give you a room. Nobody's going to fire you here. You'll have a great time here.'

"I thanked him, but said, 'No, thank you, I want to go to the front!' Well, we were stupid then. We were stupid."

Anna Egorova got her wish—she flew Sturmoviks. On August 20, 1944, going into combat at a bridgehead over a river south of Warsaw, "I was leading 15 Sturmoviks, covered by ten fighters, and I was shot. I must say that the antiaircraft people, both ours and the Hitlerite ones, they usually shot at the lead plane because once you shot down the leading one, you would ruin the entire formation. Then the bombs would not be thrown accurately, shots would not be fired accurately.

"I should have turned back to our lines. But these 40-odd years have passed, and I still don't understand why I tried to go out on the second attack. They kept yelling at me over the radio, Get away! Get away!' They saw that the plane had been hit, the nose of the plane was pitching upward. With great effort, I managed to squeeze the controls, go into a dive, and to open fire. It was, of course, very foolish. Maybe I continued to lead the group because I was the only woman. We always did several attacks on the target, until we had used up all our ammunition, until everything was destroyed.

"I had become a flying target. The engine was on fire. The cockpit was on fire. Everything was jammed. The gunner was killed. The controls were shot up. The instruments failed and didn't work. And I was on fire, too.

"The cockpit was jammed and I couldn't open it. I came to when I was already falling, without the plane, and without my parachute. I had jumped before that with a parachute and pulled the ring. When I came to, I saw standing in front of me a fascist. For some reason, he had his foot on my breast and was tugging at my broken hand. I again lost consciousness. I had apparently hit my head very hard. I had fractured my spine, but without damage to the spinal fluid, as the doctors told me later. I had fractures of the arms and legs. I was all burned. You can't see it now, but then my legs and hands were burned. It was really bad luck. I had been flying, not in my overalls flight uniform, but in a skirt. I had tied the parachute straps so my knees were bare. And then the skirt was on fire, too."

Egorova pauses to explain the skirt. That day, Soviet Air Force Day, was being celebrated. "The commander of the battalion had said that he was going to organize a dance on the estate of Count Zheltovsky in Poland. But there was no dance in the afternoon, because we'd been given a mission and flew off on it."

Egorova continues:

"When I came to lying there with those Germans, they tried to pull me up, but I fell. I thought as soon as I came to, 'They'd better kill me off as soon as possible, because the moral, spiritual pain is stronger than the physical pain.

"Then they sent me to the Radomsky concentration camp. There, they scattered some kind of powder on my burns. I remember I was making some sounds, screaming or something, and then the Poles—this was during the Warsaw Uprising, there were a lot of Poles there in that camp—they started breaking the windows and doors shouting, and saying, 'Stop torturing and making fun of the Russian pilot.' They put me in a freight car, and for five days, they took me into that great Germany, into Berlin. We turned at the Oder river to the Kussel camp. I didn't know where I was or what was going on.

"There, I was saved by a Russian doctor, Georgi Fyodorovich Sinyakov, and a professor from Belgrade University, a Yugoslav, Pavlik Arkinads. They did that for all the prisoners. There were Americans, there, French, British, but the biggest section was the Russian section.

"And the Russians were kept in the worst conditions because Stalin had said that we have no prisoners of war, we only have traitors. But, after all, pilots were fighting over the enemy's territory. It was very simple. You were shot down, and that was that. I was there for five months in the camp, then our troops liberated me, on the 1st of January 1945. But I could no longer fly, because I was too badly crippled."

To her earlier medals—including two awards of the Order of the Red Banner—Anna Egorova earned yet another: Hero of the Soviet Union. But, because of Stalin's political machinatons, she did not receive it until the 1960s.

General Lakyev, the fiercely loyal Party member who fought for his country from Spain to Mongolia, speaks also of Stalin, and how his purges hurt the war effort. "What impeded our progress?" he asks. "The purges." He says he worked with people who disappeared, who were taken to prison or killed. "It affected the course of the war very much. And if that hadn't happened, we would have been better off during the war."

By January 31, 1945, Marshal Zhukov was at Kustrin (Kostrzyn), only 40 miles from Berlin. There, against stiff German resistance, his drive stalled. Marshal Konev, sweeping up from the southeast, drove to within 80 miles of Berlin by February 13. That same day Budapest fell.

James Goodson, the ex-Eagle Squadron pilot, recalls some of the pilots he flew with, including one who became a casualty of the fighting for Budapest. They were "very outstanding, unique and wonderful people," and, "of course, many of them didn't survive the war. There was the volunteer Pole in our outfit. There was the playboy who'd been a great man with the ladies. There was our boss, Colonel [Don] Blakeslee, who survived—a great leader. He led by inspiration, by example. Led every mission almost. We revered him very much. We had some great characters—the young kid who was always off on his own, a real maverick" who, Goodson says, "was probably shot down by Erich Hartmann over Budapest."

Walter Krupinski, who flew 1,100 combat missions, witnessed the changes along the Eastern front. Because of the terrible beating the Soviets had taken in the early days of the war, he reports, the Russians switched their tactics and "flew in packs of 20 to 30 aircraft," while Germans continued flying two-plane *rotten*. "As a typical example of our feeling of superiority and of our morale," he continues, "we were the ones that attacked those packs of 30." But by early 1944, the Soviets "had a considerable numerical superiority and we had to become much more cautious about attacking a pack. We had to make sure there wasn't a second pack waiting to shoot us in the back."

By mid-November 1944, all six Allied armies in the west were on the offensive, and both the French 1st and U.S. 7th Armies had reached the Rhine in Alsace.

Jack Ilfrey, back in action after training pilots in the U.S., describes a mission he flew at that time: leading a flight of five P-51s to escort two P-38 Lightnings on a photo reconnaissance mission over Berlin ("Photo-Joe's, we called 'em"). Having completed their mission, and finding cloud cover over the target area, the Lightnings decided to head home. But Ilfrey thought it would be wrong to waste all that gas and ammunition, so he pulled his flight down for a strafing run or two. Reaching Maastricht, Holland—hard by the Belgian border and still in German hands—"those hands started firing at us." His wingman was hit. Ilfrey told him he had spotted what looked like an emergency strip nearby, with some wrecked aircraft and wrecked buildings on it, and urged him to set down there. "And if he thought I could come in, wheels down, to give me the thumbs-up signal. When I circled around and saw him on the ground with his thumbs up and a big grin on his face, I thought to myself, 'My God, am I out of my ever-loving mind!'"

Hundreds of German fighters would often defend against more than a thousand Allied bombers, mostly four-engined heavies, and Allied fighter escorts during the daily and nightly raids on the German heartland.

Putting down, Ilfrey headed for the cover of trees, and as his wingman came sprinting toward the plane, Ilfrey jumped out on the wing and threw off his parachute and dingy. Then he lowered the seat as low as it could go, making a kind of bucket seat.

"He jumped in and I sat down on top of him. We realized, almost immediately, that four legs right down in this tight little area of working your rudders, we're not going to fit. So I stood up, and he got up and put his legs underneath him and I sat down on top of that—which put me pretty high up in the air. Fortunately, this was a P-51D, with the bubble canopy, meaning they were rather large inside, so I was able to get the canopy closed. I started to take off, but as I was pulling back on the stick, I didn't have enough margin for the stick to come back far enough to get us off the ground. So I pulled and pulled 'til I almost hurt myself and threw down the little flaps, which made the thing kinda' want to bounce up in the air, and off we flew to Brussels, only about twenty minutes away.

"I was pretty drunk that night in Brussels—but at least I've been there!"

Merle Coons' next-to-last mission was flying escort in his P-51 for a raid on Berlin, December 5, 1944. He describes it:

"It wasn't difficult to join up with the bombers because there was a solid contrail all the way from England to Berlin—must've been a thousand of them. Things started to get pretty active when we looked up over our shoulders and saw about a hundred FW.190s—not a formation, the Germans never flew formation, but what we called a gaggle—at least 4,000-5,000 feet above us. As they approached the area where the bombers were releasing their bombs over Berlin, the flak suddenly stopped. It was unbelievable to us how well coordinated it was, because until then, the sky was black over Berlin with all the flak.

"Those fighters made passes down through the bombers, and we lost an awful lot of them on that one pass. In one group of about 32 B-17s, at least 17 of them fell out of the sky.

"We finally got ourselves in position to try to catch the straggling fighters, and there were a few of them that came back to make second passes at the bombers. It was on one of those passes where I found myself in position not to sight on him so much as just hose him. I just started shooting as he flew through my path and saw strikes from one end of the fuselage to the other. I think I probably hit the pilot through the cockpit as he flew through my hail of bullets. He never came out of it, but just went straight down into the ground from about 16,000-17,000 feet.

"I never saw so many airplanes in my life in one place. There must have been a thousand bombers, and at least a thousand U.S. fighters, and I don't know how many German fighters in the area. Whatever way you looked, there were airplanes."

Finally, the battle cleared. Coons joined six others heading for a Luftwaffe base 20-30 miles north of Berlin. "We saw about nine 109s descending through the clouds, trying to evade us. I'm sure they were a little low on fuel or they would have been willing to come back and take us on. However, there was only one who came back and made a head-on pass at us. Apparently he didn't see me, or didn't understand the correct maneuver to make because he gave me a perfect opportunity just to fly in behind like I was joining formation.

"I found myself with a tail shot, an airplane absolutely impossible to miss. Didn't have to be a gunnery instructor to get him. I shot him down.

"Without exception, in the five victories I got, the other pilot did something stupid or I wouldn't have been in a position to get him. It wasn't that I was that much more skillful; it was just a question of being in the right place at the right time."

Neither of the German pilots Coons shot down that day managed to escape their damaged planes. Other times, it was not so clear. New Zealander Patric Jameson, asked whether he knew the pilots he shot down managed to get out, says: "It wasn't a scenic tour you know. That could be just the time when somebody would jump you and shoot you down. So you didn't spend too much time looking around. You tried to spend enough time to confirm that he was destroyed. And yes, you usually looked to see if he got out. But I didn't have many get out."

By mid-January, 1945, the last remnants of the German units that had thrust into Belgium during the Battle of the Bulge were back in Germany.

"With each month," Adolf Galland recalls, "the chances that this war could be reasonably concluded became less and less. Of course, the morale of the fighting troops diminished." But they fought on, in part at least, he says, because of the Allied demand for unconditional surrender, "a terrible condition, the worst condition. I think a lot of the destruction would have been prevented if we didn't have this word, 'unconditional' surrender."

Galland resolved to use to the utmost a superior weapon the Germans possessed: the Messerschmitt 262 Schwalbe (Swallow) jet fighter. Late in November 1944, Galland created a new jet fighter squadron. "This," he says, "was a voluntary squadron. These were selected pilots—and they fought to the last day, until we blew up our planes in front of the American tanks. We didn't create this squadron to win the war or to gain better conditions for peace or negotiating positions. No, we fought because we did have a superior weapon. We were faced with greater numbers, but we could still hold our own. And we could not capitulate before the German people being in possession of those possibilities which we still had. This is the reason why this unit perished in flames.''

Galland indignantly recalls Hitler's insistence on using the new jet as a vengeance-type bomber rather than as a bomber-destroying fighter plane. Had Hitler's delay not occurred, Galland has no doubt it ''would have resulted in a complete disaster for the American bombers—the big formations would have been broken. For me, there is no question that 200 or 300 Me. 262s would have stopped the American offensive in one week. Nobody could have tolerated losses like this.''

On New Year's Day, 1945, Galland launched his last great attack, though with a very small jet force. With his Me.262s, Ar.234 jet bombers, and Ju.88s leading the way, all remaining fighters—about 750—joined in a low-level surprise attack on Allied airfields in the Netherlands, Belgium, and Luxembourg. The raid succeeded in destroying or severely damaging about 800 British and American aircraft, many on the ground; the Luftwaffe lost somewhere between 150 and 300 planes (accounts vary), and, even more disas-

This P-47 was forced to crash-land at its base in Belgium. The pilot escaped injury before the aircraft burst into flames.

trously, some 230 airmen, including such outstanding leaders as Oberst Gunther Specht (32 kills), commander of JG.11.

Wolfgang Späte, who participated in that attack, could almost have flown it blindfolded, so vast was his experience—although his flying career got off to a shaky start: "When I was a little boy, I jumped off a steep cliff, holding a huge umbrella. But I made an aerodynamic error and jumped off with the wind— and my jump ended rather tragically." In the years ahead, he flew everything from trainers to big, trimotor Junkers Ju.52 transports, and a number of fighter planes in between, seeing action over Poland, France, and Britain. He was among the first Luftwaffe pilots to fly the rocket-powered Me.163 Komet as well as the 262. Test-flying and evaluating those revolutionary new planes, he says, was "the highlight of my flying career, more important than my victories in the air."

Späte discusses the two jet fighters, beginning with the 262, which was "different from all of its predecessors due to its new propulsion system and the attendant high speed. But because it didn't have any speed brakes—today, aircraft of this kind have air brakes but neither the 262 nor the 163 had any form of air brakes—you couldn't reduce speed easily. And one could reach speeds in those aircraft which would have seemed impossible in earlier fighter aircraft.

"But, for example, if in combat you needed to land urgently, to be able to escape the enemy aircraft harassing you, you first had to circle the field 'dead stick,' then you reduced your velocity sufficiently to be able to lower your landing gear and flaps safely.

"So the high speed had advantages and disadvantages in air combat. It had the advantage of allowing you to close on the enemy more quickly. When you tried to close on a bomber formation in a propellor-driven aircraft, it took too long to come within range, and by the time you were within range, the enemy's defensive firepower had already caused such damage that you often had to break off. So the high rate of closure was an advantage.

"But it was also disadvantageous, because you closed on the formation so quickly that you only had a couple of seconds in which you were able to fire. With the Me.163, you could accelerate to 950-960 kilometers per hour and your opponent was only flying at 350 kilometers per hour—600 kilometers slower—so you only had three-four seconds in which to fire and then you sped past the formation."

Galland, who also was among the first to fly an Me.262 prototype, recalls that, once airborne, "it was a wonderful experience: the aircraft was fine, wonderful, smooth, no torque, no vibration, and fast. It was an unbelievable feeling, like an angel is pushing you through the air."

Späte survived that last great offensive; Galland, in a sense, did not. He angered Goering by continuing to press for the deployment of the Me.262 jet exclusively, or at least mainly, as a fighter plane, and, as a result, was fired and put in charge of a jet fighter squadron.

Johannes "Macki" Steinhoff was among the key men Galland recruited for JV. 44. Steinhoff describes the advent of the jet as the end of "the classical battle where you would see the whites of the eyes of your opponent." That era in aerial warfare "was gone forever."

Steinhoff saw his mission clearly: "We had to do everything in our power to prevent the last German city from being pulverized. The 262 was superbly armed for that mission: by the end of the war, we had 12 rockets on each wing, so we had 24 rockets which could be released simultaneously at a bomber. You had to fly close to the bomber so that, at a distance of a thousand meters, the 24 rockets covered the entire breadth of the bomber. And then, when the rockets were released, the bomber would be destroyed. This was a forerunner of modern jet fighter tactics.''

By now it was widely accepted that the skies belonged to the Allies, but there were some who still contested it. Among them was Walter Krupinski. He describes the Me.109G he was then flying: ''After '44, we called the new models the Bumps because after '44, every new model had another bump or hump on the fuselage, which naturally was bad for the flight characteristics of the aircraft.''

Krupinski, back in the west after more than two years on the Russian front, was assigned to a high-altitude Me.109 escort group protecting the FW.190s that attacked the huge American daylight bomber formations. ''As a result,'' he says, ''new engines were installed in the 109 with a special carburation, the methanol fuel injection. So at altitudes above 10,000 meters [33,000 feet] this aircraft was not so bad in level flight—even in comparison with the Mustang and the Thunderbolt, which were our primary opponents.''

No matter how black the skies may have been with enemy planes, Krupinski kept his eye on a more finite target: ''As a high-altitude fighter pilot, my job was to protect the attack-and-destroy aircraft and to repel the enemy fighter aircraft, such as the Mustang and Thunderbolt. One doesn't fly against a huge formation; rather, as a fighter pilot, you seek to gain the best position in reaction to the other aircraft in the sky and you try to attack them.'' Experienced pilots, he adds, knew how to maneuver for such one-on-one positions in a dogfight. Younger pilots did not, ''and,'' he adds, ''they were unable to survive in a dogfight.''

Following Yalta, the Western Allies, to demonstrate to Stalin that they were doing all they could to support his offensive, pulverized one of the most beautiful cities in Europe. On the night of February 13-14, 1945, 800 RAF Lancasters drenched Dresden with 2,659 tons of incendiary and high-explosive bombs. The next day, 400 aircraft of the U.S. 8th Air Force followed, finishing off the job with 572 more on April 17.

Walter Hoffmann was among the handful of Luftwaffe night fighter pilots challenging the raiders. He recounts: ''As the bombs exploded below, and the sky over Dresden was illuminated for short periods of time, for seconds, I saw masses of English fighter aircraft. But I was unable to engage them because it would suddenly be dark again, and we were being jammed by the English. Then one felt a hideous sense of inferiority and desperation.''

Jim Goodson, an American with a long combat record stretching back to his RAF days at the outset of the war, narrates an incident after the war. ''I was asked a few years ago, when Sir Arthur Harris was still head of RAF Bomber Command, to give a speech at the annual Bomber Command dinner. Before the dinner, I was talking to Sir Arthur when Gus Walker came in and said, 'I'm sorry, Sir Arthur, but the press are here and they're insisting on an interview, but they say if you give them five minutes, they'll leave.' So, Harris said, 'Certainly, if it's any help.'

''The press came in and Harris asked me to stay. And they went into a tirade about how could Harris justify losing 45,000 air crew, and did it really do any good destroying the beautiful cities of Germany, particularly the Dresden

Flying Forts throwing off contrails which, during large raids, seemed to blanket the sky.

thing; the war was nearly over, why did he drop bombs on Dresden and kill a lot of innocent citizens? Was the air war really worth it?

"Sir Arthur listened to all this, and when they'd finished, he said, 'Well, gentlemen, we did not start the war—but we were asked to win it, and I am reliably informed that that is what we did!' And then we went in to dinner."

As Allied forces swarmed across the Rhine, Hitler committed his last reserves—the 11th and 12th Armies—in a futile attempt to drive them back. Hitler, increasingly a prisoner of his own hallucinations, lived out his final 105 days in an 18-room bunker 55-feet below the Chancellery gardens.

Hans-Joachim Jabs scored his two final kills of the war on February 21, 1945, shooting down two Lancasters. He relates: "At that time in the war, there were no more German fighter aircraft stationed on the Western front. They had been pulled back to Berlin due to the American daylight bombing raids to protect against enemy entrance and enemy escape." Jabs echoes the familiar plaint: the quality of the pilots "suffered because of the considerable losses and the growing need for replacement pilots. The nightfighters, especially the group leaders, were not as well trained as I had been."

But he also has high praise for those young pilots: "They were trained to fight for their Fatherland. I mean, that's how they were raised, and that's how they flew. The people who shot down many aircraft are praised, but the nameless cadet, the nameless junior officer who was flying late in 1944 and 1945, they were the ones who achieved an unbelievable amount."

Erich Hartmann looks over a map with Major Barkhorn.

"Macki" Steinhoff describes what it was like, for young and old alike, to face massed formations of Allied bombers, day after day. "Of course, none of this had anything to do with the elegant, one-on-one fights between fighter pilots." Attacking a B-17, he says, was "like flying through a snowstorm of projectiles. You would close your eyes. Young pilots, by the end of the war, our young pilots on the average could survive only two such attacks and they were dead."

It was a vicious cycle. As Friedrich Oblesser points out, "by the end of the war, we had problems getting fuel. This meant that each mission had to be successful. Only the most experienced pilots were used for difficult missions. But then the experienced pilots also suffered greater casualties. As a result, the younger pilots who had even less training—many of them had no training in shooting, for example—they were even more exposed by the time they went up for their first flight."

Among the top aces lost in those last days of the war: Otto Kittel, 267 victories, shot down by an Il-2; Erich Leie, 118, flamed by a Yak; Franz Schall, 137, killed in a crash landing.

Another top pilot narrowly escaped death. Taking off from a hastily repaired runway at 125 mph, one of the wheels of Steinhoff's jet dug into a half-filled crater. The plane veered out of control, losing its landing gear. Momentum carried it up an incline and into the air at the end of the runway, crashing 50 yards away. The plane burst into flames. Though horribly burned, Steinhoff fought his way out of the wreckage amid explosions of the plane's rockets. His face was badly seared about the cheeks and ears. With his eyelids burned off, he was unable to close his eyes from that day in 1945 until 1969 when an RAF surgeon made new eyelids for him. General Steinhoff became the commanding general of the West German Air Force in the 1970s.

Walter Hoffmann describes the kind of desperate measures taken during those desperate days, in this case, defending against a Berlin raid. Because the weather was so bad, it was agreed that only the best pilots would be sent up. But after the experienced pilots were in the air, inexperienced pilots were also sortied. ''Those crews,'' he says, ''didn't reach the opposing force because they had taken off much too late, and as a result of the weather, we lost a lot of those crews. This mission was politically motivated, and in terms of flying safety, it was thoroughly irresponsbible.''

Heinz Marquardt agrees. Towards the end of the war, he says, the high command began ''issuing orders apparently given by non-flyers.'' Many, he said, were impossible to carry out. Missions beyond the round-trip range of the German planes were ''luckily refused by squadron commanders.''

Vasily Kubarev, recovered from the wounds suffered at Kursk, was back in action flying cover for the Soviet bombers now joining their British and American allies in blasting Berlin. ''It was toward the end of March, the beginning of April. We were transferred to the Byelorussian front near Berlin, because that marked the beginning of the Berlin operation.'' Soviet bombers, he said, ''were trying to destroy the main points of resistance, the main hotbeds of resistance in the city, where there was firing.''

On April 6, Zhukov seized Vienna. On the 16th, Zhukov and Konev launched their final drive on Berlin. On the 18th, the Western Allies completed their encirclement of German armies defending the Ruhr industrial region, taking 325,000 prisoners. This operation was the largest envelopment operation in the history of American warfare.

''The word 'duty' was very important to us,'' remarks Friedrich Oblesser. ''We were suffering setbacks, but nevertheless, the idea that a fighter pilot could be successful personally, on his level, was a great motivating force. This made it possible for us to live through those nagging questions of—'Why are we doing this? Does this make sense anymore?''' And, he adds, there was the example of the fighter pilot he most admired: Gunther Rall.

Rall, Germany's third-ranking ace (275 kills), lived by his own code of behavior: ''The motivation for a fighter pilot is his ethos, his duty. If you're a leader in the air, you have a great deal of responsibility which you cannot shirk in front of your men.'' Rall did not.

As Oblesser notes, Rall had a fanatical desire to fly sorties. ''He didn't leave us any choice other than to emulate him. It was out of the question not to emulate such a person who played such an important role in setting a role model for pilots. It never occurred to me.'' Rall, shot down five times in the course of 621 missions, fought to the end of the war.

Heinz Marquardt: ''At the end of the war, the sorties became tougher from week to week due to the superiority of the enemy at that time. The pressure on us increased because our numbers decreased steadily, and we received neither replacement aircraft nor replacement pilots. And we saw the refugees fleeing the cities and the destruction of the cities. I can't tell you how we dealt with it at that time. We felt that we had to do our duty, to help those on the ground, and did our best to do so. We were like hunted rabbits and tried to attack and tried to save that which we could, but we'd known for some time that we couldn't win the war.''

On April 25, the Russians completed their encirclement of Berlin. That same day at Torgau, 75 miles south of Berlin, patrols of the U.S. 69th Infantry Division linked up with forward units of the Russian 58th Guards Division. The Reich was cut in two.

American and Soviet aircraft were also meeting frequently in the air—sometimes too closely. Anatoly Kozhenikov tells of one such occasion.

As the Americans and Russians fought inside Germany, the two Allied air forces brushed against one another. Russian pilots were initially startled at the size and numbers of the heavily armed, four-engined bombers such as this Liberator.

Flying alone not far from his front lines, he spied two Messerschmitts flying cover for "an enormous, four-engine airplane. I had never seen such a big plane before. I thought that it must be some kind of big German boss flying on that airplane. But in order to attack that airplane, first I had to get rid of the fighters. So I gained altitude and engaged in a sudden attack from above on the Messerschmitts. But they refused to fight. They simply turned and got away.

"I transmitted to the ground that I see a large plane. I got orders: force that plane to land. Well, to force a big plane like that to land, you've got to get very close to it. He's armed, after all, and he's shooting. The only thing I could do was show him the international signal of waggle wings in front of his nose and turn around indicating, 'follow me.'

"I gained altitude and went down waggling my wings. But they opened fire at me and also didn't know that the Messerschmitts were chasing them. I reported over the radio that they were firing.

"'No matter what the cost, shoot them down,' they said. Once again, I gained altitude, made a turn, and was on top of them. Did a dive, a burst of fire. Then, as I was going by, I saw the American insignia.

"The Americans also had seen the star on my plane. They immediately fired a red and green flare, showing that I'm one of your guys! That was the signal for a friendly aircraft, and they followed me.

"Frankly speaking, at that moment, I really didn't feel very good. Well, at least—thank God!—I missed. The only thing that made me feel better was that I also had hits on my wings from their firing at me. So we were quits.

"We went back and landed at our base. The pilot emerged from the plane. I could see he was smiling, seemed very pleased. We found an engineer who was a very good interpreter. It turned out that they had only three minutes of fuel left in their plane. They would have been forced to land on German territory and they would have been made prisoners.

"My wife was the senior engineer of the regiment. She organized repairs for the plane, and it was ready by morning. But that evening, we all sat down at the table. The Soviet pilots for the first time saw American pilots. The Americans saw Soviet pilots for the first time. What was interesting was that we really had something in common. We couldn't really speak in one language, but our relations were so close as if we'd known each other for a very long time."

Before they parted, they exchanged souvenirs. The American pilot—a Captain Forrest—"ripped off his belt and from inside he took out a map, printed on silk. It was intended so that if they were shot down on enemy territory they could get out using that map. That's why it was called a life-preserver map. He said to me, 'You saved me once, I don't think I'm going to need this again.'" The Russian reciprocated, writing on the tablecloth: "Your road will be as smooth as this tablecloth." He affixed his signature, Maj. Anatoly Kozhevnikov, and that of his wife, Captain Kozhevnikov."

The story has a postwar sequel: Forrest attempted to make contact after the war with his rescuers. Kozhevnikov explains, "He searched for me, but each time he was told there are no such people. Finally, the Cold War ended—thank God!—and now, 43 years later, I opened the newspaper, and there in the newspaper is a photograph of my tablecloth. And there was a letter from Forrest, he wrote me from Texas. So right away we got on the phone. And last year, in April, the crew came here to Moscow." A year later, they were back again—this time with all the surviving members of Captain Forrest's "enormous airplane," the Flying Fortress. A final footnote: Forrest bought and paid for the Fortress when the war was over, to exhibit it "parked somewhere on some field."

Fedor Archipenko relates yet another tale. He was based at Liegnitz, Germany (today Legnica, Poland), resting after a mission over Dresden, when "everybody on the airfield started shouting, 'The Fortress is burning!' It was a four-engined Flying Fortress.

"I saw the parachutes starting to come down. Everybody used whatever vehicles we had to go and pick them up. By that time, the Fortress had crashed in the forest, and I saw the explosion. I was very sorry that apparently the commander of the airplane had been killed.

"When the crew was brought in—we brought in ten people—none of us could speak English, but they were all very happy. They kept saying, 'Roosevelt, Stalin, Roosevelt, Stalin.' They were very pleased they had landed on territory where our troops were.

"We fed them, we welcomed them according to the Russian tradition, and then we sent them off to the higher command, to the headquarters of our air division. In the evening, our ground forces brought in to us the commander who, at a distance of about 200 meters, had jumped from his plane with his parachute.

"Since it was late, he spent the night with us. There was even a movie, a film about air forces in aviation. I think he was a senior [first] lieutenant, like ours. All of us were very happy to see him, but there was one thing that really surprised us. At the movie, he was a bit noisy and loud; of course, he had been through a lot of stress. We were surprised that he put his feet up on the seat, on the chair, in the movie. That made a big impression on us. I remember it as if it were yesterday."

Archipenko adds that he also met some American pilots at Poltava, the Ukranian airfield where U.S. bombers landed after their ill-fated shuttle raid on Ploesti from England. "I must say," he goes on, "that they were outstanding people. They were young, very far from their home country. Very honestly, in good consciences they carried out their sacred duty of fighting against fascism."

On April 30, Hitler put a bullet in his head. Hitler had ruled 12 years and a day as chancellor of the Third Reich. The Thousand Year Reich had a week to live.

On May 1, Heinz Marquardt flew his last combat mission escorting fighter bombers flying towards Berlin. On the return leg, the formation was jumped by Spitfires. Sending four planes to defend the airplane, Marquardt and his wingman took on the Spitfires. His plane badly shot up, Marquardt managed to bail out. "That day," he says, "I celebrate as my birthday."

Adds Marquardt: "The best fighter pilots were those who flew to the end of the war, who had the courage to continue despite the great superiority of the enemy, and had the courage to continue to help his comrades on the ground and in the air."

Berlin fell on May 2; the 70,000 surviving German forces surrendered to Soviet Gen. Vasili Chuikov. An estimated 125,000 Berliners died in the siege, a significant number by suicide.

General Vorozheiken relates: "On the first of May, the flag of victory was raised over the Reichstag. We, the fighter pilots, decided also to drop our own flag of victory over the Reichstag." He went on to describe the dense grey-pink smoke covering the ruined city, and the view the fighter pilots had of the city in flames and the artillery battle raging below them.

"Our ground forces later told us that both the Germans and the Russians had seen those flags coming down, those two red pieces of cloth. They were a symbol of the victory of our weapons and a harbinger of that peace and victory which was soon to come."

On May 4, northwestern German forces surrendered to Field Marshal Montgomery. The next day, over Hamburg, the RAF shot down its last German plane of the war, a Siebel 204 light transport plane. It was shot down by two pilots flying Spitfire 14s—Flight Lieutenant Gibbons and Warrant Officer Seymour of 130 Squadron.

For Walter Hoffmann, his nine-year career with the Luftwaffe ended with a curious bang.

"We capitulated at the airbase in Husum near Hanover before the official surrender. An English sergeant appeared at the airbase with a driver to organize the takeover of the base. At this point, an officer—who thought he had to win the war on the last day—tried to damage the English car with a pistol. We found that rather odd—he had had four years in which to fight."

For Gunther Rall, "the most frustrating experience was when we blew up our machines. We had to bid farewell to a lifestyle and our comrades. And, of course, we didn't know what the results would be—historically, or otherwise."

Lt. Col. Hans-Joachim Jabs speaks of the patriotism German soldiers felt at war's end. "Many were ashamed of themselves for not being able to continue to fight. We believed one must defend our Fatherland."

In the camps of the victors, the end of the long nightmare aroused powerful emotions as well. Sergei F. Dolgushin, who went to war the day the Germans

invaded his native land, flew an uneventful mission on May 6, then returned to base to learn they had been ordered to stop all flights.

"I looked at them and I said, 'OK, kids, it's the end of the war.' As to what I felt, I can tell you, I simply couldn't move. I couldn't move my arms or my legs. I was a 24 year-old kid. I was used to combat. I wasn't particularly weak. Here, I just couldn't do anything. I simply lay down flat under the wing."

Late on the morning of the last official day of the war—May 8—Capt. Erich Hartmann was leading his squadron over Czechoslovakia. He saw a Soviet fighter performing aerobatics over the town of Brunn, apparently celebrating the imminent final victory. Hartmann shot him down.

The war exacted its horrible price in millions of lives—both military and civilian—lost and maimed; in devastated cities and uprooted populations; in broken promises and blasted futures.

Pilots too were part of the carnage. In Germany, of the 28,000 men trained as fighter pilots, only 1,400 survived the war. Many *Jadgeschwader*—normally numbering about 120 pilots—saw their numbers turn over six and-a-half times during the war. The Luftwaffe lost 97,000 killed, wounded, or missing. The Luftwaffe destroyed a total of 120,000 aircraft during the war, about 70,000 of them shot down by fighter pilots. The rest fell to flak—antiaircraft units were part of the Luftwaffe—or were destroyed on the ground. About 15,000 German fighter planes were destroyed in action, another 7,500 under noncombat conditions.

Hartmann saw a Soviet fighter performing acrobatics over a Czechoslovakian city on the last official day of the war and shot him down.

The U.S. Army Air Corps lost 11,000 pilots killed and 4,000 wounded in the European and Mediterranean Theaters. Combined RAF and USAAC aircraft losses, 1941-1945, were 42,000—about 25,000 lost to Luftwaffe fighter pilots.

France's *Armée de l'Air* reported 201 killed and 231 wounded during the Battle of France.

The Soviet Union is believed to have lost about 40,000 pilots and a total of 77,000 aircraft.

Lying on the ground beneath the wing of his plane on the day the war ended for him, Sergei F. Dolgushin thinks back on the battles, on the comrades he'll never see again. But the melancholy gives way to rejoicing, "a feeling of exultation, of triumph—finally, the victory we had been waiting for for nearly four years, and for which we paid much too heavy a price."

13 VICTORY IN THE PACIFIC

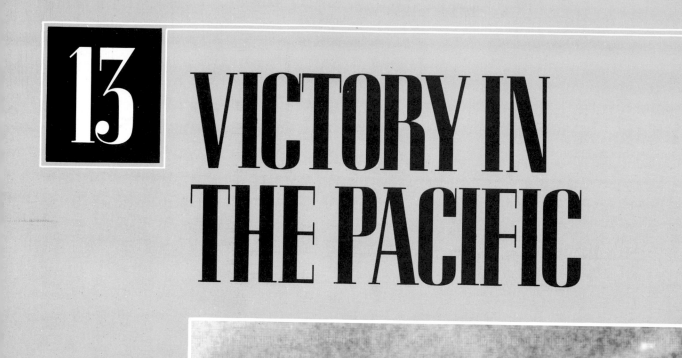

Warrant Officer Takeo Tanimizu recalls:
As our losses became bigger, the enemy's
confidence grew. In the beginning, the Japanese
pilots were called 'Messengers from Hell.' As
the war proceeded, we began to be nicknamed
'Paper Fighters.' The morale of younger pilots
steadily deteriorated.

The war drags on. USS *Ticonderoga* crewmen preparing for the first air strike against Manila, November 5, 1944.

Tanimizu was far from alone in that gloomy judgment as the war in the Pacific entered its final months. But, however dark his cast of mind, however inevitable the outcome, Tanimizu and most of the five million and more men Japan had under arms fought to the finish.

Robert Aschenbrener cut his combat teeth in the ferocious fights over New Guinea, flying 270 missions in a P-40. Rotated back to the States, he instructed new pilots on P-51 Mustangs before returning to his old outfit, the 49th Group of George Kenney's "Gang of Gangsters," the 5th Air Force. His outfit, meanwhile, had shifted to P-38 Lightnings for the fierce fighting for Biak Island.

"When I rejoined them on Leyte," Aschenbrener reports, "it was a pretty hot war then—a lot of combat, a lot of flying, and rather close quarters. I hadn't flown the 38 before, but I was given a ship and told, 'This is it.' I got a few pointers—no instruction, no piggy-back stuff, nothing to do but to get in the 38 and fly it."

Iyozo Fujita—who fought his first air battle against Americans over Pearl Harbor—met his first P-38 in the Philippines. Fujita recalls: "I fought many kinds of American fighters. But the one that surprised me the most was the P-38 I encountered in the Philippines. It was fast—too fast for me. It kept its distance, turning, turning, then it attacked again."

John E. "Jack" Purdy, after a hectic combat tour—184 combat missions in 18 months—with the 475th Fighter Group in New Guinea, was shifted to the Philippines for the invasion of Leyte.

The call was heard: "Pilot down!" The deputy commander of Purdy's group, a top ace, was missing. From his base at Dulag, Purdy and three other Lightning pilots rose to cover the Catalina flying boat searching for the downed flyer on the shores of Ormoc Bay on the opposite side of the island.

"In order to do that," Purdy explains, "you have to do an S back and forth because the Catalina is not only going a lot slower than the P-38, but is right down on the deck, and we're 1,500-2,000 feet above them.

"Well, I glanced down, and there was a convoy over in Ormoc Bay, heading towards Leyte. I assumed the convoy was friendly because the Catalina was heading right towards it." That's when the call came, "Bogies, at three o'clock high," followed by, "Bogies at ten o'clock high."

"Then it dawned on me that this is a Japanese convoy! I was so doggone mad that the Catalina would lead us straight into this thing that I told him to make a 180-degree turn and get into cloud cover as fast as he could, because we were climbing for altitude to get out from under these Japanese fighters. I stayed with him 'til he got into the clouds and continued on climbing with the four-ship flight until we got up to about 20-25,000 feet. I looked back and the Japanese planes are circling this convoy. We estimated there were between 25 and 30 of 'em."

Purdy decided to make one pass through them, then head for home. "We made the pass, and, as we would approach the planes, they would do what in fighter terms we called 'a split S.' In other words, they would turn over on their back and roll down to a lower altitude.

"The main thing we wanted to make sure of is that we stayed above them. So, when they all dove and were still below us, I thought, we'll make another pass. As things turned out, we made a number of passes—and never a shot being fired back at us. Between the four of us, we got five and two probables. Now that's ideal combat—when you don't get shot back at!"

A PBY-5A Catalina patrol bomber was the navy's amphibian equivalent of the army's "deuce-and-a-half" general purpose truck.

On the way home, Purdy discovered he was in trouble. Having jettisoned the belly tanks when the shooting started, he used up the reserve in the outer wing tanks without realizing it. "And that is not normal. Usually, the flight leader uses less fuel than the other members of the flight, because they're jacking their throttles and the flight leader has a constant throttle—whether it's all the way to the floor boards, or just cruising."

Purdy set his Lightning down on a sandbar on a little island about 15 miles from Doolag. Filipinos took him ashore and looked after him until a Catalina came for him. "We had been briefed that if you went down, don't worry, we'll find some way to find you. But you're kind of skeptical as a fighter pilot, thinking that this is part of their propaganda to make you feel good and help your morale. But when it actually happens, it's a great feeling."

Sometimes, as Purdy discovered, humor could leaven the danger. Now Captain Purdy and operations officer of the 433rd Squadron, he began to lead flights, this one a 16-plane sortie covering the landings at Mindoro. "So we get over the area and we've only been there a few minutes when one of the wingmen calls in, 'Bogies at three o'clock high!' Sure enough, here's four airplanes flying about 10,000-feet higher than we are."

Orders were to attack any single-engine aircraft. Since the P-38s were twin-engine, the brass, to avoid confusion, tried to assign only P-38s to one area at a time. "That way," Purdy continues, "we didn't have to worry about airplane identification.

"I gave the order, 'Drop belly tanks.' They're practically full—we had just arrived on the mission. We started climbing like mad, keeping those bogies out on the corner of our eyes at all times, just waiting—feeling that they're going to start their move, attack, at any time."

The bogies were flying parallel-sideways to Purdy's flight. "Just as we get to their altitude, I turn in towards them, they turn towards me, and—they're four marine Corsairs! As I made the turn, they said, 'Let's go fellows—the odds are just about even.' Those four marines and the 16 of us. They'd heard me order everybody to drop belly tanks and they let us climb—they were on our same doggone wave band! And they didn't say a word until we turned into them. I was so doggone furious, because here I am, first time ever leading the doggone squadron . . ."

Like Purdy, Aschenbrener was now an operations officer, in his case for Squadron 8, still based on Leyte. He assigned a mission over Clark Field, north of Manila, to intercept a flight of Japanese airplanes suspected of hunting Allied shipping. Some ten minutes after his men took off, the flight leader returned with engine trouble. Aschenbrener grabbed his parachute and took off. Catching up with his flight, he spotted a lone Zero over northern Luzon.

"I ordered the squadron to stay at that altitude and cover while myself and a wingman went down to try to get this boy. And he was good! Every time I would line up for a shot at him, he'd flip over on his back and do a quick split-S and was gone. He did that several times, and all I could do was move out, turn, and come back in on him. Before I knew what was going on, he had me right over Clark Field, right down on the runway. I couldn't have been 50 feet off the concrete runway, right past the 20-millimeter gun emplacements. They put my left engine out of commission. My wingman followed, and they got him on the other side of the field. I pushed down to ground level to escape as much fire as I could and made it about three miles from Clark before my damaged right engine also quit."

Aschenbrener belly-landed in a rice paddy. Hukbalahap guerrillas

Robert W. Aschenbrener was shot down by ground fire over the Philippines and was returned to his unit with the aid of Philippino guerrillas.

("Huks") operating in the area pulled him out of the smashed-up P-38 and carried him to a hideout where he lay wounded while Japanese patrols probed the area, searching for him.

Since the Huk guerrillas were Communists and rivals of the U.S.-backed regular guerrilla force (USAFFE) "they had no means of returning pilots, air crewmen, to their units," Aschenbrener explains. "Still, wanting to help us, they arranged to turn us over to the USAFFEs. By that time—I had spent most of it on my back, unable to walk—I had been joined by two navy crewmen shot down in a TBF and a Hellcat pilot who had also been shot down."

To get across the Lingayen Valley while evading the many Japanese patrols, the Huks sent runners from village to village. "On the first day, we couldn't stop. The runners would approach the patrols in the next village, alert us, and then we'd have to move."

The next problem was crossing the highway knifing through the valley to Manila. The entire party numbered about 150 guerrillas and the four Americans. The leader decided the best time to cross was noon, when the tropical sun was hottest and traffic lightest. They had no sooner hunkered down in the high kunai grass in a ditch at the side of the road than a Japanese truck clattered to a stop: it had a flat tire.

That night, the Huks made contact with the regulars—"it was almost like crossing enemy lines." The guerrillas loaded the four Americans on carabao (water buffalo)—"with their loose skin, it was hard to hang on." When a sentry cried out "Halt!" in the darkness, the carabao bolted, dumping all four men—"we walked the rest of the way that night."

There were moments when it seemed as though those hills were alive with Americans. Vraciu, after being fished out of the Pacific earlier that year, was strafing a Japanese airfield on Luzon when he was brought down by anti-aircraft fire. Bailing out, he, too, was rescued by Filipino guerrillas. Now, at a mountaintop hiding place, Aschenbrener and company cross paths with Vraciu and recognized him as the celebrity navy ace.

"Alex and his group only stayed a day or two," Aschenbrener reports. Vraciu's group moved out to the north while Aschenbrener's group rested and dodged Japanese patrols until deliverance suddenly arrived from the sea, part of the force landing at Lingayen Gulf.

The campaign to liberate the Philippines was moving towards its dramatic conclusion. Manila was the scene of some of the bloodiest fighting of the Pacific war. Jack Purdy led his squadron on January 9, 1945, on a bombing raid on the Meycauayan bridge, just north of Manila.

"They put a 2,000-pound bomb in the P-38, and one belly-tank, and gave us the option of whether to dive-bomb or skip-bomb. The idea was to knock

Marine aircrew catch a little rest and relaxation (R&R) on their gull-winged F4U Corsair on Bougainville, April, 1944.

out all the bridges that day between Manila and Lingayen. When I looked down at our target, it didn't look like there's an enemy within miles of this bridge. It just looked very peaceful down there.

"But just as I started down on the target I could see they were firing straight up. I released my bomb—it had an 11-second delay—then pulled straight up, and got up to better than 5,000 feet when I looked out and saw I had about a five-inch hole through one of the wings. One of my engines started running rough." Purdy's rescue experience a few weeks before filled him with confidence. "And not just the Catalina. We had a submarine operating down there, and we'd been briefed where the friendly guerrilla territories were."

Realizing he couldn't make it back to the coast, he searched anxiously for a place to put down. "If I had to go down, I wanted it to be in friendly territory."

Landing hard, the plane flipped sideways and Purdy was knocked out cold. Flames started licking up from the right side of the aircraft. Purdy, groggy, stumbled onto the left wing. Overhead, his buddies circled. In his semiconscious stupor, he reached into the burning plane, retrieved his parachute, hefted it over his left shoulder, stepped down from the airplane, and stood about 10 or 15 feet from it—"like I would do after a normal mission. We'd stand by the airplane, like waiting for a jeep to come and pick me up."

"The first thing I remember is that I'm running through the jungle with some Filipinos. From then on, it was just like a movie, clear in my mind that I was seeing somebody else.

"I can't say enough for the care the Filipinos gave me. They had sent ahead for a nurse to doctor my head. They absolutely treated me like a king. Their custom there, when they come to visit somebody, they would bring a gift, and I had everything from raw eggs, which is a delicacy, to wine that they had been saving for the victory celebration, to I don't-know-what-all. I have the greatest respect for the Filipinos, and I have great respect for our Intelligence because they told us this is what would happen with the Filipinos—that they were 100 percent for the Americans."

While the struggle for Manila raged, American troops quickly cleared the small Japanese garrison holding the Bataan Peninsula. Corregidor, now as three years earlier, proved a tougher nut, but by March 2, no living Japanese remained on the island.

On February 28, MacArthur reestablished the Philippine Commonwealth Government in Manila, saying, "My country has kept the faith." But it was July 5 before MacArthur could proclaim, "All the Philippines are now liberated."

In the aftermath, before being evacuated back to his Japanese homeland, Iyozo Fujita reflects: "I flew a Zero to 30,000 feet. The sea looked so beautiful, I asked myself, 'What is a human being? What am I?' Human beings are like worms fighting each other down on the earth. The Japanese fighting the Americans. It seemed ridiculous. The value of my life seemed small. I started to feel that I did not mind dying."

After his rescue, Jack Purdy was given a choice: rotate back to the U.S., or take a leave in Australia and then back to his unit. Purdy chose the latter. "We were too young and stupid to know the meaning of the word fear. It was a challenge, a job you had to do. We tried to make it a fun job. We didn't dwell on any victory, we did not judge other fighter pilots by the number of victories. We were a bunch of young kids, havin' a good time while we were doin' it." Besides, "I just wasn't ready to go home."

But fear stalked even the young—particularly after they had flown nearly 200 combat missions.

Back with his unit, Purdy flew a route Japanese Zeros had pioneered—except in reverse: hitting Formosa (Taiwan) from the Philippines. Flying with three other pilots out of Clark Field, Purdy found he was almost bored. "We didn't find anything. It was a gravy mission, because all you're doing, you're looking for stray enemy airplanes, maybe get an easy victory without really getting into a fight." His luck changed on the way back: bad weather, getting worse.

"The more I tried to get back, the madder I got. Because here I was: I had a chance to go home and turned it down. Fortunately, we made it back. But by the time we hit the ground, I knew that I was finished flying. I just wanted no part of it. I never did fly again. I knew I had just had it." Purdy stayed in the Pacific Theater, but on the ground. His air war was over.

No fighter plane on earth could escort a B-29 Superfortress on a 2,800-mile round-trip raid on Japan from air bases in the Marianas. But Iwo Jima lay only 660 miles from Tokyo—easy fighter-plane range—and it possessed two airfields, one of which could take B-29s immediately. Iwo Jima was a tempting target for two other reasons: its capture would protect the newly acquired Marianas and, as traditionally a part of the Japanese homeland, its loss would deal a harsh blow to Japanese morale.

Carrier planes began bombing and strafing the island on June 15, 1944. Now a group leader, Lt. Comdr. Iyozo Fujita was among the pilots assigned to defend Iwo Jima. Fujita believes the defense was "passive" and describes one incident:

"In the beginning, we had radar at Iwo Jima. One day, we received a warning, 'The enemy is coming.' So we took off. But the enemy was not coming at all. In fact, the enemy pretended a big formation would be coming—they tried to confuse us. So we landed. Then a lookout saw the enemy's planes coming in at low altitude. We went up in the air after his warning and were told to meet in the air above northern Iwo Jima. We were flying in one line at a low altitude. Our straight line of formation was cut off by bombing. Our loss was very severe. In just two days, we were completely destroyed."

Late in 1944, Maj. Gen. Curtis E. LeMay took over 21st Bomber Command. The first B-29 raid on the Japanese mainland had flown out of China on June 15. The first Marianas-based raid on Japan went out on November 24, 1944; 111 B-29s of the 73rd Wing were led by Brig. Gen. Emmett O'Donnell. But these raids, like those from China, produced mounting losses and negligible results. Ice, high winds, poor visibility, and air turbulence made navigation and accurate bombing difficult. The Japanese, moreover, were finally reacting to the menace to their homeland.

The best Japanese fighter overall in the last two years of the war was the Nakajima Ki-84 Hayate ("Storm," code-named "Frank" by the Americans). Marginally faster than the best American fighter, the P-51, significantly faster than the P-47 Thunderbolt, the Storm could fly 426 mph at 20,050 feet; the Ki-841b version packed four 20 mm cannons, the lc two 20 mm and two 30 mm cannons.

Another new plane, the Kawanishi N1K1-J Shiden ("Violent Lightning," or "George"), proved to be too difficult for inexperienced pilots, and several died trying. Designed to combat the carrier-based U.S. Hellcat, the George was well armed (four 20 mm cannon), armor-plated, and maneuverable despite its weight. Yet another new plane was the Mitsubishi J2M Raiden ("Lightning," or "Jack"). But plagued by engine problems, only 476 were produced and they were used exclusively by Imperial Navy pilots in the campaign against the bombers.

The real problem, however, was not equipment, but trained pilots. When Kuniyoshi Tanaka first tasted combat—in 1937, in China—the problem was too many pilots, too few aircraft. But as the war progressed, fighter pilots got a maximum of three months' training. "In three months," he says, "a pilot only learned how to fly. Formation flying training, shooting training, and air fighting training—there wasn't time. Before the war, young pilots had a year or two for training. But after war broke out they flew to attack soon after they finished flying school. So there weren't many pilots with good skills."

Hyoe Yonaga adds: "We had to mass-produce pilots around the final stage of the war. So the quality of the pilots gradually declined."

Iwo Jima—the costliest battle in the history of the U.S. Marine Corps—was finally taken. Before it was over, the marines counted 5,931 dead and 17,372 wounded. Offshore, hundreds more fell to kamikaze raids from the Tokyo-based 3rd Air Fleet. Of the 21,000 Japanese defenders, only 216 were taken prisoner.

America's military planners now faced the frightening question: If the Japanese fought so hard for an eight-square mile that had been theirs only since 1891, what would they do to defend their homeland? For General LeMay, the answer was to bomb Japan into submission. With the island in American hands and P-51 fighters able to escort his bombers, he could do just that. Over the months ahead, 24,716 American pilots and air crew were saved by making emergency landings on Iwo Jima.

Satoshi Anabuki was in the cockpit of a brand new Kawasaki Ki-100 when Osaka was bombed. Anabuki first gained fame over Burma when he shot down an "invincible" B-24 Liberator in January 1943. Back in Japan, he had added six F6F Hellcats to his tally while ferrying Nakajima "Frank" fighters to the Philippines.

"B-29s," Anabuki explains, "could fly at a very high altitude. But if we waited at the anticipated altitude beforehand, it was all right, because their flying performance was superior to ours. It was in the sky over Osaka that I encountered B-29s. I downed one of them. I didn't confirm whether the plane had actually crashed to the ground, but it did catch fire. I saw it catching fire and flying away, emitting smoke."

Yohei Hinoki met a Mustang for the first time in November 1943 when a flight of B-24s, flying home from a raid, made "a mistake." Overconfident, they broke formation over the Indian Ocean and Hinoki moved in. When the Mustangs jumped him, he was wounded and subsequently lost his leg below the knee.

One year later, Hinoki, fitted with an artificial leg, was at the Akeno Aviation School training on Ki-100s. "The brake," he reports, "looked like a stirrup. With this artificial leg, I could not step on it—unless I cut it in half and made it round." His CO okayed the modification.

One day, word flashed that a formation of B-29s, which had bombed the Hanshin area, was heading their way. "I commanded my battalion members to fly up. However, the American army made a mistake. They were coming

Yohei Hinoki was jumped by a P-51D Mustang because he was concentrating too much on the B-24 Liberator he was trying to bring down.

back without formation, at an altitude of about 10,000-13,000 feet. We attacked them and we shot down about 13 airplanes and captured 23 prisoners of war. Because they were careless, we attacked. I achieved glories because the enemy was careless.'' Meanwhile, the Japanese remained entrenched in the entire area of China south of the Yangtse as well as up the coast and into Manchuria and Korea.

Air supply to these far parts had its vagaries. Ask David (George Samuel Richardson) Cox. Now a wing commander flying Spitfire 14s, he was posted to Burma in 1945, having racked up eight-and-a-third victories in the Battle of Britain and later during the Tunisian campaign.

''Living conditions,'' he reports, ''were—I won't say much worse than our early days in Tunisia—but the great difference, of course, was supplies. It all had to be dropped by air, by Dakotas, every day—unless, of course, the weather was really down. And those Dakota pilots used to fly in some absolutely atrocious weather. Sometimes there was a slightly lighter side to air drops because obviously somebody back at headquarters got things wrong because we were supposed to have a mixed bag of rations. I remember one week we nearly lived on Kellogg's cereal and tinned pears. To this day, I will still not eat tinned pears! Another time, all we got was tinned sardines. Another time, we got cigarettes and toilet paper—but no food.''

With Japanese air power in the area all but gone, there were slow days. Cox relates what happened on one of them. ''Being rather bored, myself and the armored officer went for a walk around the airfield and went off into some bush. Suddenly, I found this great stack of bombs which, it appeared, had been left there by the Americans in, I suppose, '42, when the Japs were coming through Burma at a high rate of knots and they'd had to evacuate, leaving these.

''I must say my eyes lighted up because we'd been attacking the Japanese army positions with 20-millimeter cannon shells which, in the jungle and scrub and all that, were only partially effective—I mean we got good reports, but no devastating casualties or anything. So I said to this ordnance officer, who was a real old sweat from prewar, 'Come on, do you think you could get these fitted onto our Spits? Just think of it!' And he went out and rigged up an outfit of a few things underneath the Spitfire, a bit of wire up to the cockpit and another thing with a red light and a green light to show you whether it was armed or not and a button on the throttle and said, 'Away you go!'

"A couple of days later, we got a position for a village where the Japs were concentrated and told to go and strafe. And, of course, we went in with our bombs and dropped them. Not long after that, a report came from Air Command, which obviously had heard from the army about Spitfires dropping bombs—what authorization, etcetera, etcetera. Wing Commander Cox, please report to Air Headquarters!

"But not long after that, the brigadier commanding the army there sent full congratulations—instead of the usual 50-60 Japanese dead, there are about 400. So the visit to Air Command was cancelled forthwith and we used these bombs for a long time after—well, to the end of the war. In fact, we learned a new thing. The bombs had a four-second delay to give us time to get away. One day, I dropped one by accident at rather a low level, and instead of diving as I was pulling out, it skipped and then burst, and I suddenly realized it had a much more devastating effect—traveling, as it was, horizontal with the ground and just digging itself in. So we began what now is called skip-bombing, which had been done before us—we'd just never thought about it."

The invasion of Japan—Operation OLYMPIC—was now set for November 1, 1945, to begin at Kyushu, southernmost of the main home islands. Two of the stepping stones were now in place: Luzon and Iwo Jima. The next stone: Okinawa.

Iwo Jima was a bloody foretaste of what the Japanese troops could expect on the ground. A raid by Adm. Marc Mitscher's Task Force 58 on the Inland Sea, March 18-19, provided a foretaste of what the fleet could expect from the air.

Those raids presented Takeo Tanimizu with a personal as well as a professional challenge. Badly burned when his plane was flamed off Amoy the previous November, Tanimizu was back on duty with Air Group 203 based on Kyushu, assigned primarily to its air defense. While convalescing, his mother had suggested a marriage. "My marriage arrangement," he relates, "was at a final stage when Kyushu was raided by the Americans. I thought that Japan would not be able to win anymore, so I requested to cancel my engagement.

"However, my wife was in Oita [in Kyushu]; her neighborhood was attacked by an air raid, too. She convinced me of accomplishing my promise. Then we got married.

"After I was married, it became harder to fight. But once I flew up in the air, I never returned during my mission. Never. But since a plant of Nakajima that manufactured airplane engines was attacked, we did not have any good engines. Troublesome engines were repaired once again. Most of the planes' engines were in bad shape, so many unreliable engines.

"But if I returned, I would be scolded, 'He became a coward because he got married.' After I was married, I did not want to be scolded like that. So even if an engine was not perfect, I forced myself to fly."

* * *

Vice Admiral Marc Mitscher presents Lt. Roy Voris with a D.F.C. air medal, 2nd air medal, 3rd air medal, 4th air medal. Captain Arleigh Burke, center.

Having inflicted heavy damage on the air arm, Mitscher's attacks switched to the Japanese naval bases at Kobe, Kure, and Hiroshima, and to shipping in the Inland Sea itself.

Maj. Herbert H. "Trigger" Long, who understudied the legendary Greg "Pappy" Boyington back at Guadalcanal, was aboard Mitscher's flagship, the *Bunker Hill*, on this raid. At the controls of an F4U Corsair, Long led fighter elements of Air Group 84 and VMF-451 against the Kure naval base and scored three rocket hits.

"We were probably a hundred planes or more, and we were assigned to protect the bombers, going after the shore installations. Well, the fleet was there, so we attacked it. I started my dive on the biggest ship in the harbor, but there was so much antiaircraft artillery coming up at us that I released my rockets early.

"But I became so fascinated with the path, the smoke trails heading for this big ship, that I stayed in the dive and unconsciously was squeezing the trigger. And I took pictures of the whole thing, not knowingly, really—I didn't know I was taking pictures. And I just barely pulled out. As a result, I did record some pictures of the rocket hits on the biggest carrier they still had afloat. I didn't know that 'til I got back to the ship and they developed the pictures. But that was an air-to-ground type attack on naval shipping."

More than 550,000 men—on land and sea—were committed to the invasion of Okinawa, code-named Operation ICEBERG. At 4:06 A.M. on Easter Sunday, April 1, the order was given: "Land the landing force." On April 6, with casualties mounting, about 900 aircraft—a third of them kamikazes—attacked the amphibious fleet.

Robert Wade saw his first combat in those hellish skies.

"We were all lined up ready to go into the beach at Okinawa— three LFSs in line, and a kamikaze came through and hit the center LFS, which was 322, and sunk it. That was our first experience with the kamikaze—and it was rather frightening!"

The next day, kamikazes struck again. The unrelenting attacks rubbed nerves raw aboard those "tin cans." Those in the air were less vulnerable, in a way. Wade recounts: "My heroes used to be guys like Joe Foss, Greg Boyington, Kenny Walsh, Don Sapp, Marion Carl—all those guys who were out there at Guadalcanal. We didn't have it like they had. They had tough customers up there to fight with. The Japanese fighter pilots were outstanding people at the beginning of the war. We didn't have that problem at Okinawa." Still, as Dave McCampbell points out: "They, the best of them, sure weren't all gone, or people like Saburo Sakai wouldn't be surviving today!"

Wade then makes his point: "But we did have our own antiaircraft fire to be concerned with, because if you're on the tail of one of those things, pretty soon those poor guys down on that destroyer are kind of trigger-happy and they've got to fire, 'cause they took a horrible lacing. Those poor destroyers out there on the picket patrols with all the radar gear on them, warning us on the island about the enemy coming in—we used to fly picket patrols around them to protect them. There was a point at which you must break off and get out of there and let them shoot if you hadn't got the guy yet. In other words, if you're close enough to think you're going to nail him in time to keep him from hitting the destroyer or whatever, you stay in there and shoot him.

"But when the AA gets pretty heavy, then you get the hell out of there! Some of our people flew right through their AA and were rewarded for it with Navy Crosses and things like that."

Herb Long didn't get the Navy Cross, but he did get shot down by friendly fire. "It was the USS *Beale*, trying to fire at a Japanese airplane. They hit the

Below:
Fire fighters of the USS *Intrepid* tend to the aftermath of a kamikaze hit during the Battle of Leyte Gulf, November 25, 1944.

Herb Long, apprentice to Pappy Boyington, fixated on the exhaust of the rockets he fired at a Japanese ship, just managed to pull out of his dive before crashing.

wrong airplane. I had to bail out and floated around on a raft for a while."

Robert Wade had his own secret weapon as he went into action over Okinawa: his long-time pal, Johnny "Radar Eyes" Ruhsam. The leader of their four-plane division, Wade relates, had a rule: first man to spot the enemy leads the flight, and that, he adds, usually meant Ruhsam. First time off the captured Japanese airfield at Kadena, Ruhsam dropped a Zero not far from the end of the runway. Wade wasn't so lucky—a hydraulic problem sent him back to base. Next time out, Johnny spotted them again, this time four or five Tonys, off the end of Okinawa. "We split up into two sections, and there was a typical hassle. I don't think those people were kamikazes—they weren't acting like kamikazes. It was funny because John sets up on a section and is firing on one, and I'm on this side of him firing on another one, and they almost simultaneously dropped together."

In late April, Gen. Mitsuru Ushijima attempted to smash the center of the 10th Army and drive the remnants into the sea. Wade was among the marine pilots flying close support.

"At Shuri Castle, they had a hell of a fight going on there on the ground. With our Corsairs, we could hit the slopes with napalm and things like that— rockets and bombs and whatnot. We did a lot of that, 'cause they got into a lot of trouble down there."

The American commander, Lt. Gen. Simon Bolivar Buckner, was killed when a Japanese shell sent pieces of coral piercing through his body. His adversary, General Ushijima, along with senior members of his staff, committed *hara-kiri*.

Hyoe Yonaga had worked hard for months patching together his fighter group in the 100th Wing, 6th Air Force. Shortly before the onset of the Okinawa campaign, the chief-of-staff proposed breaking up the 100th Wing and assigning its pilots to kamikaze missions. Yonaga explains:

"I objected. Kamikaze pilots were trained mainly at the Akeno Flying School. Those pilots who actually flew kamikaze missions, they were innocent and pure. They were brave. Particularly those who were trained in the Akeno center and had an adequate training period. Their case was different from those who were suddenly ordered to fly kamikaze missions like a day before the attack.

"But as for my own group, I couldn't accept such an order from the center to deliver fighters for kamikaze missions only because there were not enough left in the center.

"If I had let that happen, the 100th Wing would have lost its military capability immediately. Our wing would be useless. If this wing was broken down bit by bit for kamikaze missions, what would be the point of having trained this wing, organized the wing, and taken the pain of transporting the wing? Why waste our efforts?"

As a result of his stand, Yonaga and his wing commander were sacked. His successor selected 53 pilots for kamikaze missions.

"The 101st and 102nd wings followed," Yonaga reports. "But the 103rd wing—I think it was Tojo who was the wing commander—didn't give any of his pilots. After the war, I asked him why he didn't. He said, 'Because I made a promise to you, Mr. Yonaga.' So the 103rd Wing did not deliver fighters to kamikaze missions."

Sadamu Komachi, the pilot who though badly burned when shot down by a Grumman F6F Hellcat over Guam the year before had managed to return to the homeland, reflects on the ambivalence of many Japanese pilots toward kamikaze missions.

"From the middle of the war on, compared to the number of planes which made kamikaze attacks, the results were not very satisfactory. The losses were greater than the glories.

"I felt so sorry for those pilots who died. Towards the end, the level of pilots—experienced pilots who had been flying more than 1,000 hours—decreased greatly. Inexperienced pilots who had just finished training made up 80 percent of the total pilots at the end of the war. And these inexperienced pilots were assigned to a kamikaze unit. Their skills and experience were not enough.

"They received an order to attack an enemy's carrier but they did not know how to react, they had never experienced battles against the Americans. But they had to fly through so many bullets coming from a carrier which they had never seen before. Victories were not achieved as expected.

"I feel deeply for the dead. There was no strategy other than making suicidal attacks, carrying bombs. The Commanding Officer had no other strategy. It was a dying struggle. But, in fact, there was no other way to go other than kamikaze attacks. The Japanese chiefs of staff and commanding officers were struggling very hard— the strategy was 'Must is Master.'"

Satoshi Anabuki: "When we lost Okinawa, I realized that we had lost the war. America's enormous war potential defeated us."

Defeated, perhaps, but not finished. Hyoe Yonaga underscores the point: "If headquarters had ordered me to fly kamikaze missions when the U.S. forces attacked Japan, I, as a group commander, would have fought as a kamikaze pilot. That was my attitude."

Komachi claims an even more sweeping order actually was given, at least for Japanese naval forces defending the homeland. "In the mainland, all the planes—including transport planes, everything that could fly—were supposed to carry bombs along the coastline from Kyushu to Hokkaido. If the enemy's fleet was seen coming closer to the coastline, no enemy ships were to be allowed to reach the mainland. That was an order. All the pilots were ordered to make sacrifice attacks. To carry out the order, all the planes, including the ones that looked like scrap, were hidden in airplane sheds, and all the planes were repaired, repaired, repaired. The planes which could fly were hidden in the shade, covered by leaves. All the planes were hidden. That was the strategy for winning battles for the mainland. After Okinawa's fall, only the mainland was left.

"Also, all the ships at sea—torpedo boats, destroyers, cruisers—all the ships which could move, were ordered to carry torpedoes on both sides and attempt suicidal attacks. All the navy men were expected to die at sea—that was an order. But even though we had tried to stop them, the Americans could have landed on the mainland. After that, the fate of Japan would have been in the hands of the Japanese army. But all the navy men were ordered to die at sea. This was all-out kamikaze attack.

"At the decisive battle for the mainland, the order for the navy was to fight until the last minute and die. On the coast. Our tension was immense."

Emotions darkened and curdled as the end neared.

Alex Vraciu: "When some of your pilots have their eyes gouged out, and their ears cut off—when they find their bodies later like they did at Saipan—you know it doesn't leave you any feeling of camaraderie. I thought I was over it, that maybe all these years would blank out some of this feeling."

**A marine gunner aboard the USS
Lexington tracks a Japanese "Kate"
torpedo bomber as it heads in,
December 1944.**

Joe Foss: "When you're in battle with those birds, it's off the end of the plank and into the deep."

John W. Mitchell, who earlier described machine-gunning Japanese soldiers in the water off Guadalcanal after bombing their troop transport, adds: "A guy's coming down in a parachute, I'd shoot him if I had the time. Chances are you're not going to have the time to do that because you're in a dogfight. You shot the guy down. But it certainly wouldn't be anything I would consider has anything to do with ethics. War is not an ethical thing. It's a horrible thing."

Saburo Sakai: "Every battle was important—not only shooting down a plane, but a pilot in the plane will die, too."

Butch Voris: "I remember reading paperback novels about World War I aviators, the Germans, the French, the Americans. How they would wave to each other when they ran out of ammunition, almost a salute, 'I'll come back and see you tomorrow.' It was an unspoken bond between people of this calling. That may not have been carried on in that same tradition into World War II because the character of the opponent was different. We got into shooting people out of their parachutes after they had bailed out. It became bitter."

Increasingly, the Allied commanders looked to the air to break Japan's will to resist. LeMay now had 600 Superfortresses available for the job. Between May and August, 158,000 tons of bombs were dropped on Japan's 58 largest cities.

The "Manhattan" project—the development of the atom bomb—was born in 1941 and given a two billion dollar budget. At 5:30 A.M. on July 16, 1945, from a tower at a place called Jornada del Muerto (A Day's Journey into Death), a deafening roar was followed by a giant mushroom cloud rising to 41,000 feet. It was the birth of the atomic age.

On July 24, President Truman decided to drop the bomb. It was entrusted to the men of the 509th Composite Group of the 313th Wing of the 21st Bombing Command of the 20th Air Force at their base on Tinian. At 1:45 A.M. on Monday, August 6, three Superforts took off from Tinian headed for what the B-29 pilots referred to as "The Empire": Japan. Their target was Hiroshima.

Saburo Sakai had sensed Japan's defeat way back at Guadalcanal. That did not deter him from fighting on, even after the loss of one eye, even after the excruciating wounds he suffered when shot up by the rear gunner of a Douglas SBD Dauntless. "When the bomb was dropped on Hiroshima, that's when I really thought Japan would be destroyed. Still, Japan said 'no' to put an end to the war. The Japanese headquarters was really stupid. Crazy!" Yet dutiful to the end, Lieutenant Sakai shot down his 64th plane on the very last day of the war.

On August 8, Russia declared war on Japan and sent 76 divisions thundering into Manchuria. Ivan Lakyev (12 kills) had fought against the Japanese there at the beginning of the war. For him, they were a tougher foe than the ones he had dueled against in the skies over Spain, tougher even than the Luftwaffe pilots he had fought. He illustrates with an anecdote:

"At the command post where I was stationed, they had surrounded a Japanese pilot and were shooting him down. They shot the plane down. He ejected with a parachute. I was able to get a car, drive the kilometer to where he was landing, and he was standing there, bold and very aggressive."

But now, six years later, the Japanese no longer had air superiority. In just 12 days, the Soviet troops crushed Japanese opposition in North Korea and Sakhalin and linked up with Mao Tse-tung's Chinese Communist forces.

On August 9, the second plutonium-type bomb was dropped on Nagasaki. On August 14, Japan prepared to surrender.

Yohei Hinoki, the one-legged ace who refused personally to give up, expresses the reaction of many of Japan's fighting men: "Our planes were completely equipped. We had plenty of soldiers in our homeland. We were training for a decisive battle. Important cities were all bombed—there were no more places the enemy could burn. Planes had their life span, and after several attacks, they became less useful. And the supply period would become longer. So, because of defense on the mainland, strategy on land would become important.

"Americans would have a difficult time. Right before the end of the war, we had created Air Unit 20, under Lt. Gen. Buzo Aoki. Our unit 111 together with unit 112, we had about 240 Ki-100 fighters. We moved to Komaki Air Base and did training. They were ready for loading rocket bombs. Then we went to another air base.

"Then came the emperor's speech about ending the war. When I heard the emperor announce that, I was very frustrated. I was really frustrated. Some of us might have felt that we might lose the war. However, for me, I did not think about losing the war until the last minute. When we were suffering, the enemy was also suffering, I thought. I felt that way. Also, I was always lucky with planes. I flew only good planes. I had never been completely defeated . . . "

Sadamu Komachi (18 victories) differs: "If a decisive battle actually happened, Japan would be disaster. But the atomic bombs were dropped. Because of that, our lives were saved. If we really would have had a decisive battle for the mainland, we—all the navy men—would have died along the coastline."

The formal surrender ceremony took place on September 2. With Mac-Arthur presiding, representatives of Great Britain, China, Russia, Australia, Canada, New Zealand, the Netherlands, and France signed the documents on the main deck of the *Missouri*. Mamoru Shigemitsu, the foreign minister, signed for Japan. That done, a flight of hundreds of aircraft overflew the ship. At 9:25 A.M., MacArthur directed a radio broadcast to the peoples of the United States—and the world:

"Today the guns are silent. A great tragedy has ended. A great victory has been won . . . "

Opposite page:
The men of the USS *Lexington* attending to the burial of their comrades at sea, November 1943.

For the Japanese fighting men who had fought honorably, war's end brought new wounds. Fighter ace Sgt. Satoshi Anabuki tells what it was like: "When the war ended, psychologically, there was a big gap between those who had been commanding officers and us. When we returned to Japan right after the war, due to Japan's defeat, the Japanese military forces had been abolished. So the country, the society—even I myself—felt the same way. Everyone gave me a cold shoulder, as if I were useless."

Other honorable fighting men for a time could not face the reality of defeat. Takeo Tanimizu had been fighting for his country since 1937. "When the war ended, I gave my wife a pistol and told her if she suffered a shameful thing at the hands of the enemy, kill yourself. I was afraid to be captured because I fought until August 20 and was sure the Americans would kill me. I changed my victory score from 36 enemy planes shot down to half that number in case that might help. I hid out for a month. I am truly grateful. I did not think I would come home alive."

For the world at large, the cost of the war was ghastly: between 35 million and 60 million dead. Whole civilizations were shattered, thriving nations reduced to ruin and rubble.

But this was not the doing of the brave men who risked all, and often lost.

Roy M. Voris, captain, United States Navy, three Distinguished Flying Crosses, 11 Air Medals, and the Purple Heart, speaks for many aces:

"If I leave one thought, it is the self-respect you have for yourself for what you accomplished over so many years as part of naval aviation. And I sleep easily with that thought."

The great nineteenth-century political philosopher, John Stuart Mill, wrote: "There is something worse than war, and that is having nothing worth fighting for."

Kenneth A. Walsh, lieutenant colonel, United States Marines, winner of the Medal of Honor, his nation's highest award for gallantry, believed he had something worth fighting for—freedom. Now, half a century later, he likes to believe others would be willing to pay the same price should those values which give life meaning ever be at risk:

"I just hope that as time goes by, we'll always be prepared to defend this country. Teddy Roosevelt summed it up: 'Walk softly and carry a big stick.' That's how I feel. With just as strong a conviction today as I had then."

Kenneth Walsh with his wife at his Medal of Honor ceremony.

PHOTO CREDITS

128-Right-Elly Beintema; 130-Imperial War Museum; 133-Top-Herbert Molloy Mason, Jr.; 133-Bottom-Imperial War Museum

Chapter 7: 135-Smithsonian Institution; 136-Christopher Shores; 137-Smithsonian Institution; 138-Elly Beintema; 139-Christopher Shores; 141-Top-American Fighter Aces Association; 141-Bottom-Smithsonian Institution; 144-Smithsonian Institution; 145-Imperial War Museum; 146-German Archives (Koblenz); 147-Top-German Archives (Koblenz); 147-Bottom- German Archives (Koblenz); 148-Raymond F. Toliver; 149-Left-Smithsonian Institution; 149-Right-Herbert Molloy Mason, Jr.; 150-Top-Sir Harry Broadhurst; 150-Bottom-Herbert Molloy Mason, Jr.; 151-Christopher Shores; 152-Top-German Archives (Koblenz); 152-Bottom-Elly Beintema; 153-Michael Russo; 154-Christopher Shores; 156-Top-Herbert Molloy Mason, Jr.; 156-Bottom-Herbert Molloy Mason, Jr.; 158-Imperial War Museum

Chapter 8: 159-Smithsonian Institution; 160-Top-Smithsonian Institution; 160-Bottom-Herbert Molloy Mason, Jr.; 161-Raymond F. Toliver; 163-Left-Herbert Molloy Mason, Jr.; 163-Right-Smithsonian Institution; 164-Smithsonian Institution; 165-Top Left-Raymond F. Toliver; 165-Top Right-Herbert Molloy Mason, Jr.; 165-Bottom-Raymond F. Toliver; 166-Top-Herbert Molloy Mason, Jr.; 166-Bottom-Herbert Molloy Mason, Jr.; 167-Top-Raymond F. Toliver; 167-Bottom-Raymond F. Toliver; 168-German Archives (Koblenz); 169-Top-Smithsonian Institution; 169-Bottom-Herbert Molloy Mason, Jr.; 170-Herbert Molloy Mason, Jr.; 171-Top-Smithsonian Institution; 171-Bottom-American Fighter Aces Association; 172-Raymond F. Toliver; 173-Smithsonian Institution; 174-Top-Smithsonian Institution; 174-Bottom-Smithsonian Institution;

175-Top-Raymond F. Toliver; 175-Bottom-Herbert Molloy Mason, Jr.; 176-Imperial War Museum; 177-Raymond F. Toliver; 178-Herbert Molloy Mason, Jr.; 179-Smithsonian Institution; 180-German Archives (Koblenz)

Chapter 9: 181-Smithsonian Institution; 182-Herbert Molloy Mason, Jr.; 183-Raymond F. Toliver; 185-Smithsonian Institution; 186-German Archives (Koblenz); 187-Raymond F. Toliver; 188-Herbert Molloy Mason, Jr.; 189-Top-American Fighter Aces Association; 189-Bottom-Herbert Molloy Mason, Jr.; 190-Smithsonian Institution; 191-Herbert Molloy Mason, Jr.; 192-Top-Herbert Molloy Mason, Jr.; 192-Bottom-Herbert Molloy Mason, Jr.; 194-Raymond F. Toliver; 195-Raymond F. Toliver; 196-Top-Imperial War Museum; 196-Bottom-Herbert Molloy Mason, Jr.; 197-Imperial War Museum; 198-Imperial War Museum; 200-Imperial War Museum; 201-Left-Imperial War Museum; 201-Right-Imperial War Museum; 202-Imperial War Museum; 203-Herbert Molloy Mason, Jr.; 204-Smithsonian Institution; 205-Roland P. Beamont; 206-Herbert Molloy Mason, Jr.; 207-Top-Herbert Molloy Mason, Jr.; 207-Bottom-Smithsonian Institution; 210-Christopher Shores

Chapter 10: 211-Herbert Molloy Mason, Jr.; 213-Imperial War Museum; 214-Herbert Molloy Mason, Jr.; 215-Top-Herbert Molloy Mason, Jr.; 215-Bottom-Christopher Shores; 217-Herbert Molloy Mason, Jr.; 220-Top-Herbert Molloy Mason, Jr.; 220-Bottom-Herbert Molloy Mason, Jr.; 222-Herbert Molloy Mason, Jr.; 223-Herbert Molloy Mason, Jr.; 224-Left-Herbert Molloy Mason, Jr.; 224-Right-Herbert Molloy Mason, Jr.; 226-Herbert Molloy Mason, Jr.; 228-Left-Smithsonian Institution; 228-Right-Raymond F. Toliver; 229-Christopher Shores; 231-Smithsonian

Institution; 232-Top Left-Smithsonian Institution; 232-Top Right-Herbert Molloy Mason, Jr.; 232-Bottom-Herbert Molloy Mason, Jr.; 234-Herbert Molloy Mason, Jr.; 235-Herbert Molloy Mason, Jr.

Chapter 11: 237-Smithsonian Institution; 240-Top-Saburo Sakai; 240-Bottom-Raymond F. Toliver; 244-Smithsonian Institution; 246-Herbert Molloy Mason, Jr.; 249-Smithsonian Institution; 250-Smithsonian Institution; 252-Raymond F. Toliver; 253-Smithsonian Institution; 255-Herbert Molloy Mason, Jr.; 259-Herbert Molloy Mason, Jr.; 260-Raymond F. Toliver; 262-Herbert Molloy Mason, Jr.; 263-Raymond F. Toliver

Chapter 12: 265-Herbert Molloy Mason, Jr.; 266-German Archives (Koblenz); 269-Elly Beintema; 270-Smithsonian Institution; 271-Moscow Central House of Aviation and Cosmonautics; 272-Raymond F. Toliver; 273-Moscow Central House of Aviation and Cosmonautics; 276-Herbert Molloy Mason, Jr.; 278-Herbert Molloy Mason, Jr.; 281-Smithsonian Institution; 282-German Archives (Koblenz); 284-Herbert Molloy Mason, Jr.; 287-German Archives (Koblenz)

Chapter 13: 289-Left-Raymond F. Toliver; 289-Right-Dwight Long; 290-Wayne Miller; 291-Horace Bristol; 293-Raymond F. Toliver; 294-Fenno Jacobs; 298-Dwight Long; 300-National Archives; 301-Top-Raymond F. Toliver; 301-Bottom-Barrett Gallagher; 304-Edward Steichen; 306-Raymond F. Toliver; 307-Victor Jorgensen

Back Jacket:
Clockwise from Top-Moscow Central House of Aviation and Cosmonautics; Raymond F. Toliver; Elly Beintema; Raymond F. Toliver; Raymond F. Toliver; Christopher Shores; Background-Smithsonian Institution.

INDEX